The Politics of Economic Despair :

Shopkeepers and German Politics 1890 - 1914

The Politics of Economic Despair:

Shopkeepers and German Politics 1890 - 1914

Robert Gellately

SAGE Studies in 20th Century History *Volume I*

SAGE Publications   London · Beverly Hills

For information address: 330.943

SAGE Publications Ltd.   G 31 p
44 Hatton Garden
London EC1N 8ER

SAGE Publications Inc.
275 South Beverly Drive
Beverly Hills, California 90212

International Standard Book Number 0-8039-9917-8

Library of Congress Catalog Card Number 74-81024

FIRST PRINTING

Printed and Bound in Great Britain by
Burgess & Son (Abingdon) Ltd.

CONTENTS

Robert Gellately was born in 1943 in St. John's, Newfoundland. He received his B.A., M.A. and B.Ed. from Memorial University of Newfoundland, and in January 1974 he was awarded his Ph.D. from the London School of Economics. Dr. Gellately was a Fellow of the Canada Council from September 1970 to December 1973, and has been a Fellow of the Alexander von Humboldt-Stiftung since March 1974. He is at present at work on another book, *The History of Conservatism in Germany from 1866 to 1918.*

PREFACE

This study examines the economic position and the political
activity of independent retailers in Germany in the period
from 1890 to 1914. It outlines the economic position of retailers within the context of a rapidly expanding retail market
and delineates the nature of those aspects of the social and
economic developments of pre-war Germany which retailers
came to consider to be the threats to their economic existence. Retailers responded to these economic threats by developing a whole series of organizations at the local, state, and
national levels which were designed to secure their economic
independence. While retailers organized initially at the local
level, they became gradually aware that local organization
(even in cities, such as Hamburg where retailers were well
organized) was insufficient in itself to achieve their objectives.
The frustration or non-fulfilment of the interests articulated
by retailers' organizations at the local level led them to seek
affiliations at the state, regional, and national levels. Each of
these steps marked an extension of the political mobilization
of retailers. Particularly after the turn of the century, these
organizational activities merged and became an integral part
of what contemporaries referred to as the *Mittelstandsbewegung*.

Retail trade and, more particularly, retail traders are nar-
rowly defined to include only the non-producer, the independent shop-owning, final seller to the consumer. There is no
attempt to look at the economic, then the political, behaviour
of all those people involved, at one stage or another, with re-

tail trade or with that aspect of the distribution system technically termed "channelling outputs to the consumers". This study, therefore, largely excludes all those involved in retailing outside shops, such as those engaged in fairs, markets or itinerancy. These activities and those engaged in them receive attention only in so far as they exercised an impact upon the independent shop-owning retailer. Consumer co-operatives, mail-order houses, and the larger chain stores receive similar consideration. The department store owners receive some attention, primarily because, in the minds of the small retailers, they developed into the great enemy. Finally, the narrow definition of retail trader as non-producer excludes the artisan, who, if a master, might be an independent selling directly to the consumer.

The approach to a social-historical study of almost any aspect of Germany's past is complicated by several quite difficult problems. These may be summarized as problems concerning the extent to which either a geographical area, a particular social group, or even a religious body (to mention but a few examples) may be said to be "representative". The geographical question is complicated enough in a Germany where variation often appears so striking. This problem is further exacerbated by economic conditions which seem so unamenable to systematization and generalization, and by innumerable other factors, from difference of religion to variation in traditional enmities, local patriotism, and even foreign ties. If the establishment of close connections were to be drawn between such local peculiarities and the political activity of the retailers, including their numerous local squabbles and alliances, any single area might well suffice to occupy a student for several years. A local study, or any case-study, makes sense only when it can be set within the context of wider developments. Local studies of the Nazi Party, for example, can be linked up with the great deal that is already known about national developments and thereby further the overall understanding of how the Nazis came to power. As yet, there is no national or regional (or local) study of sufficient reliability and scope of the retailers in pre-1914 Germany. A local study would have remained narrow because it could not have been related to the political activities of retailers at the regional or national level. I decided therefore to attempt a national rather than a local study.

The present work is based heavily upon the reports of the political police and other material, including contemporary surveys and analyses located in archives throughout Germany. There has been extensive use of the newspapers of retailers' organizations of all types, as well as the more prominent newspapers of the period, from the SPD *Vorwärts* to the conservative *Kreuz-Zeitung*. While sources published by individuals and groups outside retailers' circles have not been overlooked, more attention has been given to retailers' accounts of their own activities which appeared in their newspapers and in their published reports of their meetings. Throughout the study, my aim is to evaluate how retailers themselves viewed their own position and how far their view corresponded to the social, economic, and political realities of the period.

I should like to thank the staffs of the many libraries and archives in which I conducted my research for their kind cooperation. A list of the archives in Germany will be found in the bibliography. I was also kindly received at the British Museum and its newspaper library at Colindale, the Wiener Library, the British Library of Political and Economic Science, the Library of the University of London, the Institute of Historical Research, and the Public Record Office. I should like to extend my gratitude to the staffs of the following libraries in Germany: the *Commerzbibliothek* (Hamburg), the *Weltwirtschaftsarchiv* (Hamburg), the university and city libraries of Hamburg, Bremen, Tübingen, and Munich. I am indebted both to Dr. Henning Timpke of the *Forschungsstelle für die Geschichte des Nationalsozialismus* in Hamburg and to Dr. Ernst Manfred Wermter of the *Stadtbibliothek* in Mönchengladbach. The library in Mönchengladbach, which contains the old library of the *Volksverein für das katholische Deutschland,* provided me with rare and otherwise unobtainable material. Unfortunately, I did not obtain permission to work either in the Central Archives or in the libraries of the German Democratic Republic. Several scholars in the Federal Republic very generously placed their own microfilmed copies of the most important files of the Central Archives at my disposal. It was possible to compensate for the limited use of material from the Central Archives by visiting the archive in Berlin-Dahlem and other archives throughout the Federal Republic.

I should like to thank the following individuals who came to my aid at various stages of my research: Dr. G. Bassler, Ms. M. Fleming, Dr. L. Kettenacker, Dr. J. Kocka, Dr. K. Krohn, Dr. W. Lenz, Dr. T. Mason, Dr. J. Noakes, Dr. P. Pulzer, Dr. C. Saul, Dr. H. A. Winkler, and Prof. B. Yamey. I am grateful for the helpful advice which I received from Prof. W. Laqueur and Mr. E. Hearst of the Institute of Contemporary History. Special thanks are due to Prof. F. Fischer and, in particular, to Dr. D. Stegmann, both of whom devoted considerable time to my problems when they were already burdened with the pressures of their own work. Finally, I should like to thank Prof. J. Joll who supervised an earlier version of this study as a Ph.D. thesis at the London School of Economics and Political Science. His concern and encouragement, as well as his prompt attention to my problems, helped to make my work both rewarding and enjoyable.

The preparation of this study has been made possible by the financial assistance of the Canada Council, the Central Research Fund of the University of London, and the Alexander von Humboldt-Stiftung.

Robert Gellately
Münster May 1974

ABBREVIATIONS

Abt.	*Abteilung*
Aufl.	*Auflage*
Bay. Haupt. St. Ar.	*Bayerisches Hauptstaatsarchiv München*
Bd., Bde.	*Band, Bände*
B. Dahlem	*Geheimes Staatsarchiv Berlin-Dahlem*
BdL	*Bund der Landwirte*
B. N. Nach.	*Berliner Neueste Nachrichten*
B. Tagebl.	*Berliner Tageblatt*
Bundesarchiv	*Bundesarchiv Koblenz*
CDI	*Centralverband Deutscher Industrieller*
DDP	*Deutsche demokratische Partei*
DHV	*Deutschnationaler Handlungsgehilfen-Verband*
DMV	*Deutsche Mittelstandsvereinigung*
DNVP	*Deutschnationale Volkspartei*
Dortmund WWAr.	*Westfälisches Wirtschaftsarchiv, Dortmund*
DZA, 1	*Deutsches Zentralarchiv, Abt. 1: Potsdam*
Echo	*Hamburger Echo*
Frank. Ztg.	*Frankfurter Zeitung*
G. A.	*General Anzeiger (Hamburg)*
G.d.S.	*Grundriss der Sozialökonomik*
H.	*Heft*
HB.	*Bremen*
HB. HK.	*Archiv der Handelskammer Bremen*
HB. St. Ar.	*Staatsarchiv Bremen*
HH.	*Hamburg*
HH. C.	*Hamburgischer Correspondent*
HH. F.	*Hamburger Fremdenblatt*
HH. HK. Ar.	*Archiv der Handelskammer Hamburg*
HH. Neueste Nachrichten	*Hamburger Neueste Nachrichten*
HH. St. Ar.	*Staatsarchiv Hamburg*
HK.	*Handelskammer*

hrsg.	*herausgegeben*
H.V.S.F.R.K.	*Hefte für Volkswirtschaft,*
	Sozialpolitik, Frauenfrage,
	Rechtspflege und Kulturinteressen
IRSH	*International Review of Social*
	History
Jahrbuch für G.V.V.	*Jahrbuch für Gesetzgebung,*
	Verwaltung und Volkswirtschaft
	im Deutschen Reich
JCH	*Journal of Contemporary History*
Köln. Ztg.	*Kölnische Zeitung*
M.N.N.	*Münchener Neueste Nachrichten*
Neue HH. Ztg.	*Neue Hamburger Zeitung*
NL	*Nationalliberal*
Norddeut. A. Ztg.	*Norddeutsche Allgemeine Zeitung*
NPD	*Nationaldemokratische Partei*
	Deutschlands
NSDAP	*Nationalsozialistische deutsche*
	Arbeiterpartei (Nazi Party)
Nr.	*Nummer*
NS. St. Ar.	*Niedersächsisches Staatsarchiv*
	Hannover
P.A.	*Parliamentary Affairs*
PP.	*Polizeibehörde — Politische Polizei*
PVS	*Politische Vierteljahrsschrift*
RDMV	*Reichsdeutscher Mittelstandsverband*
SPD	*Sozialdemokratische Partei*
	Deutschlands
St. Ar. München	*Staatsarchiv München*
St. Ar. Münster	*Staatsarchiv Münster*
T.	*Teil*
VDH	*Verband Deutscher Handlungsgehil-*
	fen zu Leipzig
VfH von 1858	*Verein für Handlungskommis*
	von 1858
V.f.Z.	*Vierteljahrsheft für*
	Zeitgeschichte
ZHGD	*Zentralverband der Handlungsgehil-*
	fen und -gehilfinnen Deutschlands
Ztg.	*Zeitung*

INTRODUCTION

Academic interest has focused upon the polarization of German society after 1890. There has been intensive research on the impact of the rapid social, economic, and political changes on the working class, who came to be represented as the most serious threat to the established order. The "social question" was essentially the discussion concerning how this threat in its many forms could be checked. In the 1890s, the SPD, which claimed to speak for the workers, emerged from its period as Germany's "outlawed party" anxious to re-form its organizations and to equip itself with a suitable program. The conservative powers, who were at the other pole, have frequently been the subject of research. This elite, which included the much maligned Junker, the officer corps, and the bureaucracy, was supported in its position "above" the masses by the powerful interest groups of the industrialists, as well as those of the agrarians. The political activities of those "in the middle", however, have been largely ignored. As has been maintained, "it is usually not the style of the *'Kleinbürger'* to appear independently upon the political battlefield, in open antithesis not only to capitalism but also to the proletariat".[1] One of the chief consequences of this political timidity in Germany was the late emergence of re-tailers as an independent political force. Although retailers came to play a decisive part in the so-called *Mittelstands-bewegung* which occupied an important position within the power constellation of pre-1914 Germany, their political activities and particular ideology have received little atten-tion.[2]

The ideology inspiring and nourishing the political activities of the small independent retailer in all countries is the element which gives these activities their particular significance. Lack of detailed research notwithstanding, there exists a general consensus concerning not only the ideology of shopkeepers, but also their probable or likely political behaviour. According to conventional wisdom, the small retailer is likely to be "right-wing", fascist, and almost certainly anti-Semitic.[3] The present study questions such clichés. Were retailers in pre-1914 Germany rabid nationalists, Pan-Germans, Naval League supporters? How far were they interested in imperialistic adventures and the construction of the fleet? Were they really "colonial enthusiasts"?[4] Was there even such a thing as a unitary ideology to which all retailers subscribed (the *Mittelstandsideologie)*, to what extent were retailers captivated by it, and, most important, what meaning did they attach to that ideology? Did they really suffer from some form of false consciousness (or untrue calculation of interest)? Were retailers used as pawns in a power game designed to keep Social Democracy at bay? Did retailers, at the same time, help to stabilize the established order in which they actually had no stake?

There is little doubt that retailers in countries other than Germany and at other times have expressed social discontent remarkably similar to that voiced by German retailers prior to World War I. However, an examination of France, the United States, Great Britain, and Germany reveals important variations in the response of established authorities and elites to retailers' problems and activities.

The Poujadist movement in France of the Fourth Republic had historical roots which can be traced back to the pre-1914 era. Organizations such as the *Ligue syndicale pour la Défense des Intérêts du Travail, de l'Industrie et du Commerce* (membership in 1890, *circa* 33,000), and the national *Fédération des commerçants détaillants de France* (membership in 1908, *circa* 350,000), exerted considerable pressure on government to pass special laws taxing the department stores (and other large retail distribution outlets).[5] These discriminatory taxation laws, which were enacted as early as 1844, were progressively tightened in 1890, 1893, 1905, 1912, and 1917.[6]

The hopes and fears of *"la petite bourgeoisie"*, as pointed out by André Siegfried[7] in 1913, were not unlike those which are said to have inspired the Poujadist movement in the mid-1950s. The element which more than anything else binds the Poujadist movement to earlier movements among retailers in France may also be counted as the primary unifying theme which runs through the political activities of retailers in most countries. As Peter Campbell has stated

> *The Poujadists have preferred the motto of the Republic to the various trinities of the extreme Right (such as Marshal Pétain's "Work, Family, and Fatherland") but they have stressed their own special interpretation of "Liberty, Equality, and Fraternity". Les petits gens already enjoy (although precariously) the essential liberty of conducting their own affairs instead of working for others; they want this freedom to be enjoyed by others also and oppose the economic developments that menace it. Les petits gens defend equality: it exists between self-employed persons and in little firms but not in big ones, where some people have too much authority, prestige, and pay, but most have too little. Fraternity is to be restored by the union of all ordinary folk: the original Poujadist movement was for shopkeepers and artisans, but further organizations have been formed for peasants (rather unsuccessful) and other social groups (very unsuccessful); together the various groups will purge the State and tame big business.[8]*

The oft-cited criticism of the Poujadist movement, that it contained "as much intellectual content as a scream" is a comment on the lack of understanding by outside observers of the meaning which supporters attached to the movement. Poujadism was an expression of very real hopes and fears of *les petits gens.* The movement was charged with the duty of protecting the threatened interests of *les petits gens* just as much as a trade union, for example, working through a socialist party, is designed to further the interests of workers. The avowed aims appear "irrational" to the outsider either because he has failed to understand how supporters of the movement have defined their own situation or because he is convinced that the objectives of the movement cannot be realized. In his view, realization of these objectives is predicated on a complete reversal of economic trends, such as the process of concentration, a process considered "inevitable" by both Marxists and the large capitalists. The chief aim of the small independent retailers has been to resist the process of concentration which poses a direct threat to what they conceive of as their economic independence—to keep the clock still, if not to turn it back. Retailers' movements, like the Poujadist movement, have, therefore, been branded as "irrational", doomed for attempting to resist the inevitable.

While retailers in the United States appear to have been no less active than those in France and Germany, little research appears to have been concentrated upon the small independent retailer. There is some evidence that in the Populist-Progressive era, small retailers experienced fear of precisely the same kinds of economic developments which had swept across pre-war Germany. In the United States, the post-Civil War period in particular witnessed the development of department stores, mail-order houses, and similar concentrated forms of retail distribution.[9] There has been some difficulty in characterizing the protest of the 1890s and early 1900s in the United States because this protest occurred during an era of general prosperity. If the small retailers are isolated for closer study, however, a good deal of the confusion may be overcome without having to resort to Hofstadter's controversial and largely ill-substantiated thesis on protest movements in eras of prosperity.

Hofstadter (briefly stated) contends that the Progressive movement was occasioned by "status anxiety" and that the "Progressive revolt" was a "status revolution".[10] In another essay, he attempts to apply a slightly expanded version of this thesis to post-1945 "right-wing extremism" in the United States. He suggests that there are always two types of political processes going on in inextricable connection with each other: "interest politics, the clash of material aims and needs among various groups and blocs; and status politics, the clash of various projective rationalizations arising from status aspirations and other personal motives".[11] "Interest politics" occur during periods of depression and economic discontent and "status politics" occur during periods of prosperity.

According to this thesis, which remains to be tested by a study of urban social groups in the United States, the small independent retailer would, prior to the First World War (an era of "prosperity" in the United States, as well as in most European countries, particularly in Germany), have been worried more about his "status" than about his "interests". The extent of the participation of retailers in the Progressive movement, and in movements since 1945 in the United States (also a period of prosperity) which have been branded as "right-wing extremist", has been established only in a very general fashion.

One of the most important questions a more detailed study of retailers' politics in the United States may answer concerns the use of the term "prosperity". While this term contains suggestions of universal (economic) well-being, in fact the term refers only to general economic trends which by their very success imply that the larger and more economically rational economic activities are moving forward unhindered. The small independent, if politically mobilized, will seek to resist continuing "prosperity", or, at the very least, those aspects of "prosperity" which spell his doom. In 1897 for example, there was an anti-department store campaign in Chicago. The objective circumstance of economic "prosperity" may be interpreted by various social groups in a widely different fashion. It may well be that in periods of "prosperity", retailers become conscious of their "relative deprivation" and hence are mobilized by what they consider the inconsistency between their stationary, declining, or even threatened status and the upwardly mobile status of a reference group (the working classes, for example). It was in the prosperous 1960s that the neo-Nazi NPD, in which the retailers were "over-represented", came into existence in Germany.[12]

A comparison of the small independent retailers of Great Britain with those of Germany, France, the United States, and Belgium shows a variation not so much in the expressions of discontent and the nature of that discontent as in the reception accorded to these expressions. It may be said that in Great Britain the retailers have been very nearly "officially" ignored. Small independent retailers in Great Britain can count few legislative "successes". The reasons for the relative impotence of retailers' movements and organizations in Britain are many. Perhaps the most fundamental reason for the lack of success of the British small retailers is that their political activities have been neither considered a threat to established authority nor required as part of a "third force" to be used as allies against other movements (especially those of the workers) which posed threats to established authority. Although the "shopocracy" was thrust into a position of relative political importance following the 1832 Reform Bill, retailers were all too soon ignored by the Whigs (whom they helped into power) after the latter's electoral victory. While the "shopocracy" may well have continued to represent a "latent strength", the rise of the working class into the ranks of the electorate and, to a large extent, into the ranks of the Whigs as the century wore on gradually nullified that "latent strength".[13] In view of their lack of significant political importance in Great Britain, therefore, small independent retailers remained largely outside the realm of party politics and concentrated their attention upon self-help measures. The most pronounced tendency among British retailers has concerned self-regulation in matters of competition. From the mid-nineteenth century onwards, grocers were particularly active in this area and, by 1891, formed the Federation of Grocers' Associations of the United Kingdom out of the Traders' Defence Association.[14] These organizations had as their chief method of protecting the small independent a technique that is referred to today as resale price maintenance (RPM).

In 1896 the first successful RPM association was founded in Great Britain. This association and other such organizations, having apparently given up on direct government intervention in their competitive struggle for survival, attempted to force manufacturers to price branded goods in order that the small independent retailers could compete with larger retail distribution outlets which sold the same branded goods. When the price was fixed by the manufacturer, the small retailers had what was then called "price protection"; they could not be undercut by larger firms. Manufacturers were more or less cajoled into fixing prices on branded goods under the threat that retailers' associations would advise members to order from other, more sympathetic manufacturers.[15] While it is difficult to generalize on the significance of the early adoption of the technique of RPM by retailers in Great Britain, retailers were left with few alternatives in their competitive struggles with the larger retailing firms. In the absence of state-help, self-help in forms other than RPM, such as various co-operative ventures among retailers, was exploited. In France, where RPM was widely practised, the decision to make it illegal to fix prices in any form was taken only in August 1953, or at the moment when the Poujadist movement was in its infancy.[16] A similar attempt to ban RPM in Great Britain through the Resale Prices Act of 1964 not only saw small retailers bombard the Conservative party with thousands of letters, but was the cause of a minor revolt in the Tory back bench when 21 Conservatives voted against the government and 17 others abstained. In other words, retailers in Great Britain were satisfied to restrict their activities to self-help endeavours and to remain outside party politics so long as the "tradition" of handling RPM questions was left substantially intact.

The present study originally began as an attempt to research the social bases of the politically organized anti-Semitism that appeared in Germany in the last third of the nineteenth century, to reveal the extent to which it could be accounted for as a movement of social protest of a very particular kind. For some time it has been suggested, even when the essential research has been lacking, that there was an interrelationship between this anti-Semitism and the social protests of those "in the middle". Hans-Ulrich Wehler not only claims to have seen these interrelationships, but suggests a comparison with contemporary American Populism.[17] In another essay, Wehler identifies the social bases of "organized anti-Semitism" in pre-war Germany with *kleinbürgerlich-mittelständische Gruppen* and characterizes the movement as a variety of "early fascism".[18] Another writer has made the interesting observation that in pre-war Germany "anti-Semitic resentments were strongest among the independent retailers" *(beim mittelständischen Einzelhandel)*. [19]

In the course of the original research into the social bases of political anti-Semitism in Germany, it became gradually clear that anti-Semitism could frequently be but one of the elements (and not necessarily the most important) in the "politics" of a particular social group or interest group. The same conclusion emerges from the numerous fine works now beginning to appear on Germany's *Verbandsgeschichte*. To abstract the anti-Semitism out of the context of the other beliefs, prejudices, problems, and fears of either particular interest groups or social groups would be to distort the role of anti-Semitism. Simply collecting the innumerable expressions of an anti-Semitic nature and linking them together in a coherent fashion would not conceal a most pertinent and often forgotten fact: that the anti-Semitism of the peasant, the small shopkeeper, the Junker, the student, and the professor, was often motivated by very different drives.[20] It is almost the inevitable tendency of intellectual history in particular, as well as that of many works which seek to investigate the ideological antecedents of National Socialism, that little account is taken of differentiation in the response to the appeals of this pre-war anti-Semitism.

It is not the association of the small retailers with this pre-war anti-Semitism, or with anti-Semitism in general, which distinguishes Germany's retailers from the retailers of other countries. Poujadism in France, for example, was heavily tinged with anti-Semitism. There is evidence that in the inter-war period there was some anti-Semitism among small retailers in Great Britain and in Belgium.[21] What distinguished the small retailer in Germany from his counterpart in other countries was that peculiar component of his ideology which expressed his desire to remain part of (or to become part of) the *Mittelstand*. In order to evaluate the significance of retailers' political activities in pre-war Germany, it is essential to bear in mind the special significance which this concept came to assume.

The concept of the *Mittelstand* has no equivalent in the English language and should not be equated with such social-economic categories employed in English as "lower middle class" or simply "middle class". The term harked back to the Romantic past and the semi-mythical *ständische Gesellschaft*.[22] In this idyllic society, everybody "knew his place" within a fixed social hierarchy. Advocacy of the necessity to keep the

Mittelstand in existence may be located within the main-
stream of "corporatist" thought. The hierarchic, deferential
society was "natural" rather than "mechanical": it alone
offered the possibility of the realization of man's true nature.
It guaranteed equilibrium and stability instead of the social
chaos which resulted from the acceptance of liberalism and
the class warfare propagated by Socialism. The importance of
these attitudes within the "conservative revolution", the
"ideological attack on modernity", has been emphasized by
several writers.[23] George Mosse has identified the *völkisch*
element in this way of thinking.

> *Volkish thought could at times support a conservatism
> which, though revolutionary, nevertheless stressed the
> importance of social hierarchy, the family, and personal
> property. It believed in a pluralistic society, but ex-
> pressed this belief not by advocating parliamentary
> government but by emphasizing the corporate nature of
> society and politics. This corporatism stressed the har-
> mony necessary for the unity of Volk and society. It
> sought to reorganize politics by grouping men by pro-
> fession: the owner and the labourer within one industry
> or profession would be united in one organization. There
> would be no class struggle; instead a consensus would
> emerge. Such a reorganization of politics would produce
> a true group rather than an artificial one, without des-
> troying social and economic hierarchies.[24]*

Mosse goes on to admit that his own work, concerned primarily with intellectuals, had only permitted him to formulate
an hypothesis on how far this "attitude of mind" had actually
penetrated German society.

The "ideology of resentment", which was, at the same
time, an ideology of self-defence, found its mass base among
members of the *Mittelstand*.[25] It was the *Mittelstand,* certainly the small retailers and artisans, which was threatened
by certain advances of large scale capitalism. Moreover, the
Mittelstand feared that the society, pronounced as inevitable
by Social Democracy, represented an immediate threat. In
terms of day to day living, it was the *Mittelstand* which was
faced with the practical consequences of what intellectuals

could bemoan as undesirable. Intellectuals could afford the luxury of mistaking change for decline.[26] For members of the *Mittelstand*—or at least for the small retailers and artisans—"change" frequently was "decline".

Werner Sombart, writing at the turn of the century, claimed that it had merely "become fashionable" for people such as the artisans and retailers to refer to themselves as members of the *Mittelstand*.[27] In attempting to dismiss the problem so simply, however, Sombart effectively failed to understand these people and the importance they had begun to attach to their membership in the *Mittelstand*. His contention was that it was only well after the middle of the nineteenth century that those occupational groups which in the latter part of the century liked to view themselves as having always constituted "the" *Mittelstand* came to be popularly accepted as constituting part of the *Mittelstand*. (This attitude was true of the master artisan, the independent retailers, the "house owners", and, to a lesser extent, the independent peasants.) The relatively late expression of a desire to belong to this *Mittelstand* by the retailers, for example, suggests that it was only in this period that retailers were becoming conscious of their precarious economic position. Their status aspirations inclined them to seek government assistance not in the name of mere economic self-interest, but in that of the preservation of the state to which a "healthy" *Mittelstand* was essential. It is an indication of the importance placed on the subjective self-evaluation (consciousness) of the various groups claiming membership in the *Mittelstand* (whatever it was!) that there never developed a fixed and universally accepted definition of *Mittelstand*. It has been suggested that, because so many retailers could be classified as "proletarian" on the basis of income, they psychologically compensated for the objective economic realities, not only by insisting that they were part of the *Mittelstand,* but that they were "the heart of the *Mittelstand*".[28] The primacy accorded to consciousness was most marked among white-collar workers whose claim to *Mittelstand* status emerged only late in the century. White-collar workers came to be recognized as members of the *Mittelstand,* even though the social-economic differences dividing them from the rest of the *Mittelstand* were so great that they are usually referred to (and were referred to at the time) as the "new" *Mittelstand* in opposition to the "old". The ability of the "new" *Mittelstand* to achieve economic independence—upon which the "old" *Mittelstand* prided itself—was clearly missing. The claim was primarily, although not exclusively, one for special status recognition.[29]

The term *"Mittelstand"*, both in pre-war and inter-war Germany, conveyed a "status valuation".[30] It represented to its members an entitlement to "certain privileges", and, in a sense, it "bespoke real sources of comfort for Germany's 'little men' ".[31] It is, however, in pre-war Germany that one finds the initial organizational forms of a social movement which embraced, albeit in a highly differentiated fashion, an anti-Semitic *Mittelstandsideologie*. It is a far more difficult exercise to study this anti-Semitism or, more broadly, the *Mittelstandsideologie*, in terms of those actually captivated by it than in terms of the leaders or intellectual proponents. This study sets out—while admittedly only on a modest scale—to confront the ideology as well as the politics of one of the specific social groups "in the middle", within the existing social, economic, and political realities of the period.

The development of the organizational representation of retailers' interests presupposed the existence of a degree of political consciousness. Political mobilization involves two essential processes. The first is attitudinal, the process whereby one becomes committed to action; the second is concerned with the development of a means of translating this commitment into action. The political mobilization of the *Mittelstand* in general and the retailers in particular not only brought these social groups into greater participation in the political life of Imperial Germany. Their mobilization was to have profound ramifications beyond the direct influence their movements inspired in pre-war Germany. Retailers became sensitive to issues and ideas about which they had been formerly apathetic or ignorant, and they became open to influences which might otherwise have passed them by. In so far as institutionalized means of solving their problems proved insufficient, they became more prepared to accept non-institutionalized solutions to these problems. Their politics became the politics of economic despair.

1

The Economic Development
of the Retail Market in Germany 1871-1914

Distribution systems, like the economic and social systems of which they are a part, vary almost infinitely.[1] The variations in distribution systems may be accounted for in terms of the level of development of the economy with its transportation and communication systems, the size and distribution of the population it must serve, the standard of living of the population, and a host of other factors, from the degree of self-sufficiency to usage imposed by custom, law, or even religion. From the point-of-view of the entrepreneur—in this case the retail trader—all or any of these factors must not make it impossible for him to make a living in pursuit of his trade. There exists, therefore, an ever-changing relationship between the retailer and his market. In Germany the retail market became rapidly transformed in the period from 1871 to 1914. This change had a direct impact upon the retailers.

Industrialization

Industrialization is considered one of the most remarkable developments to have taken place in the German Empire from its founding in 1871 down to the war in 1914. The process of industrialization very largely determined the nature and extent of the retail market. Although there is always considerable controversy over the problem of precise dating of the process of industrialization,[2] there is general agreement on the remarkable expansion of the German economy in the late nineteenth and early twentieth centuries. Aggregate industrial production (1913 = 100), which stood at but 20.6 in 1871,

increased from 39.9 in 1890 to 100 in 1913.[3] Steel production
(1913 = 100), which was but 6.0 in 1870, increased by a
factor of 3 to 18.0 in 1890 and further, in the next twenty
years, to 100.[4] Production of producers' goods in the period
from 1871 to 1914 increased by a factor of 6.25, consumers'
goods, by a factor of 2.86.[5] The great aggregate gains, therefore, came after the founding of the Empire in 1871; the
increases after 1890 were even more dramatic.[6] It was only
in the 1840s and 1850s that the transformation of retail
trade even began to take place in Germany, that is, the transformation from a primarily itinerant trade to trade from fixed
stores. (The dates would be earlier for the large centres and
later for the small centres.) Most scholars agree with Sombart,[7]
who claimed that the really significant and widespread changes
in retailing took place in the last quarter of the century. There
are some who suggest that the great changes took place after
1895.[8] In either case, there appears a correlation between
industrialization and expansion of retailing.

Implicit within the process of mass production or production for a distant, non-specified, even non-solicited customer
was the development of a division of the functions of production and distribution. Roscher called the factory "the ally of
retail trade".[9] He realized that in a division of labour, the
factory needed a go-between to sell its wares while it concentrated all its energies upon production. Industrialization, or
the changeover to industrial production, provided the possibility for a corresponding expansion of retailing. It may be
said that industrialization may have even necessitated such an
expansion. Retailing expanded, for example, because of the
manufacture of electrical appliances when retail establishments to sell such appliances were opened for the first time.
The artisan had never produced and sold these appliances.
The retail establishments owed their existence directly to
advances in industrialization and in manufacture. It is, therefore, misleading to suggest that retailing was a "pre-industrial"
occupation and that retailers shared a common aversion with
the artisans, for example, to industrialization.[10] Although independent retailers shared certain economic interests with
the artisans, opposition to industrialization was not one of
them.

Population Growth and Urbanization

The expansion of the retail market of pre-war Germany was related to the meteoric growth of the population and its concentration in urban centres after 1870. Between 1870 and 1913 the population of Germany increased from 40,805,000 to 66,978,000. The yearly growth rate rarely fell below one per cent per annum.[11] In 1817 the population had been 25,009,000. In less than 100 years (from 1817 to 1913) the population had increased by a factor of approximately 2.7. This increase in population implied considerable expansion of the distribution system in order to meet the increase in gross demand upon it. These demands upon the distribution system were further increased because of the changing distribution of the population. Table 1 graphically illustrates the radical population redistribution which took place in Germany between 1871 and 1910.

Table 1: Urbanization in Germany 1871 - 1910

Of each 100 persons resident in:	1871	1910
Communities with over 100,000 inhabitants	4.8	21.3
Communities with 10,000-100,000 inhabitants	7.7	13.4
Communities with 5,000-10,000 inhabitants	11.2	14.1
Communities with over 5,000 inhabitants; total	23.7	48.8
Communities with 2,000-5,000 inhabitants	12.4	11.3
"City"* dwellers; total	36.1	60.1
"Country"* dwellers: total	63.9	39.9

Source: Köllmann, *Bevölkerung und Raum in Neuerer und Neuester Zeit*, 1965 : 92.
*"City" = communities with 2,000 or more inhabitants.
"Country" = communities with fewer than 2,000 inhabitants.

The most dramatic expression of this population redistribution was the growth of the large urban centre. At mid-century only four cities had had populations in excess of 100,000; in 1910 sixteen exceeded 250,000, and seven, 500,000.[12] This rapid urbanization, particularly when coupled with the great "inner migrations"[13] which were so prominent a feature of this period in Germany, implied considerable expansion of the retail market.

There is always a far greater percentage of the population engaged in distribution activities in urban areas, and the larger the urban centre, the greater the percentage required to serve it. Schmoller has suggested that the numbers engaged in distribution activities correspond to the size of population, the degree of urbanization, and economic development. Although Schmoller's figures are open to some question, they indicate the pattern of increasing numbers engaged in distribution activities. He estimated that there were 68 retailers per 10,000 inhabitants in East Prussia in 1895, 138 retailers per 10,000 in Prussia as a whole, 141 in Baden, 160 "on the Rhine", and 384 in Hamburg.[14] The reasons for the greater percentages of retailers to the total population in the more urbanized areas were many. To begin with, the degree of self-sufficiency tended to be much smaller in urban areas. In the rural, and even in the less fully industrialized areas, incomes could be supplemented through self-production and especially by providing home-grown food. The rural area was more self-sufficient and tended to produce non-agricultural products solely to meet local needs. Itinerants could be counted upon to provide incidental supplies not available locally. Periodic markets and fairs supplemented these activities. Although most small cities and even many villages had a petty retailer from the end of the eighteenth century, it was usual for exchange to take place directly between the producing artisan and the final consumer. The growth of the large urban centre, together with the rise of industrialization (the development of a mass demand and supply) provided the economic impulse behind the growth of retailing in the modern sense of the word.[15]

The direct relation of changes in the distribution system with population growth and urbanization may be illustrated by a brief review of steps taken by certain administrations of the larger cities in Germany to deal with problems of provisioning food. In smaller or less developed localities, food distribution continued, as of old, to involve direct commerce between the producer and the consumer. This older style exchange activity persists in most areas of Germany even today. The populations of the rapidly expanding urban centres of the late nineteenth century were often considerably removed from place of birth and no longer always able to provide their own food. The urban centres, therefore, required supplies of food which had to be drawn from farther and farther afield. The final consumer could not always expect to deal with the producer, and some evidence of a decline in quality appeared. The older markets were proving increasingly inadequate. City government came to sponsor the idea (first in Frankfurt a.M. in 1879) of the periodic (weekly) market to be carried on in covered halls erected at public expense. These halls had existed in warmer climates, notably in France, much earlier. The market halls, which still exist in many of Germany's large cities, were more sanitary and more conducive to commerce and, ultimately, provided a better and cheaper service. In Berlin alone, eight such halls were opened between 3 May 1886 and 1 May 1888 at a construction cost (inclusive of stock) of 16,595,628 Mk. By 1914, 42 market halls *(Markthallen)* had been constructed. With the exception of Berlin, the great majority of the market halls were established after 1890.[16]

The market halls were used by producers (especially small farmers living on the outskirts of the larger cities), non-producing retailers, and wholesalers. Retailers' stalls were quite often run by women whose husbands either pursued another occupation or collected wares from wholesalers or from more distant farms. Stalls were frequently set up by large firms who used employees to operate them. Fees were paid for a stall in the market halls according to the value of the wares handled, the space occupied, and the cost of any necessary equipment. Although there were obvious practical advantages in the market halls for stall owners (such as protection from the weather), the market halls eliminated the profitable stalls which the retailers had previously operated at the weekly market. The market halls provided ideal storage and distribution centres for wholesalers and were, therefore, more economically advantageous to wholesalers than to retailers. That development was completely contrary to the original intentions of the founders of the market halls. Food trade in the public streets and plazas of Germany was not eliminated, but it never became as common a practice as in the streets and plazas of England, for example, largely because of the successes of the German market halls.[17]

Standard of Living

The retail market in Germany between 1871 and 1914 underwent considerable expansion partly because of the massive population growth. Urbanization and subsequent decline in self-sufficiency imply that per capita demand as well as gross demand on the distribution system also increased. It is not necessary to determine whether the standard of living rose in the period under consideration in order to establish the extent to which the retail market expanded. As the standard of living controversy in English economic history has shown, there are at least two sides to the question, the first having to do with material conditions and the other with the much less tangible "quality of life".[18] The relevant factor in the determination of the extent or size of the retail market was the increase in consumption, when consumption is measured in terms of retailed goods (as opposed to bartered or self-produced goods, for example). Indices for the "consumption" of planted foods, meats, and "luxuries", such as wine, beer, cognac, and tobacco, reveal great increases during the period.[19] The total value (1913 = 100) of exchange activities *(Produktion des Handels)* increased from 17.8 in 1850 to 28.5 in 1870, 49.0 in 1890 and 67.9 in 1900.[20] Real national income per capita (1913 = 100) stood at only 46 in 1871. For the period from 1871 to 1913, population increased by a factor of 1.63, while exchange activities *(Produktion des Handels)* increased by a factor of 3.14. Production of consumer goods increased by a factor of some 2.86.[21] Part of the reason for not automatically concluding that the standard of living rose is that rises registered on consumption indices may indicate little more than a transformation from, to point to just one example, growing one's own vegetables to buying them at the corner store. Illustrative of the transformation of Germany's retail market into something of a "consumer" society were increases in the value of goods sold through restaurants *(Gaststätten)* which (1913 = 100) increased from 20.0 in 1870 to 41.6 in 1890 and 64.0 in 1900.[22]

The inference that disposable incomes must have been rising seems justified. There is, not unexpectedly, much controversy surrounding the precise movement of real wages in Germany. It has been frequently suggested that after the setbacks of the 1870s, real wages rose sharply in the 1880s and continued to rise until 1914, although at a slower rate in the 1890s.[23] The real wage increases appear to have slowed down in large measure because of an accelerated rate of growth of employment,* as well as because of sharp rises in the cost of living.[24] The slowing down of increases in real wages does not appear to have had adverse effects on the retail market. Although individual purchasing power may have declined slightly, aggregate demand (or, at least, aggregate disposable income) increased with the accelerated rate of growth of employment. In other words, aggregate purchasing power increased even though the individual may have suffered a decrease in real wages.

Transportation and Communication

The retail market was extended by the rapidly expanding transportation and communication systems which helped to further break down local, regional, and even national self-sufficiency. The main function of the transportation and communication system is to close the gap between producer and consumer, either by moving goods to consumers or, particularly at the local level, by carrying consumers to goods. The revolution in German transportation, represented most spectacularly by the railroad, made its critical gains in the late 1840s. By 1850 goods and passengers could move by rail

---

*Desai, *Real Wages in Germany*, 1968 : 105 comments:
   "If there is a shortage of consumer goods, faster increase in real wages can be achieved only by lowering the rate of growth of employment. The growth of employment was rapid in the nineties and the following decade: the high rate of investment created employment opportunities, and there was a large increase in the population of working age owing to a rise in birth rates fifteen years earlier. As much of the increase in the supply of consumer goods went to the newly employed, less of it was available for a rise in real wages."

from Aachen to Breslau and from Kiel to Munich, albeit with many changes. The importance of the development of the railroad to the rise of industry is well known. Such a major technological change affected supply no less than demand.[25] Efficient and cheap transportation helped maintain and even lower certain food prices. The wholesale prices of such agricultural products as wheat, rye, barley, and oats all declined steadily after 1870, in spite of the fact that, from 1875 onward, there was not a single year when grain exports exceeded imports.[26] The railway system was supplemented by an extensive canal and river system for which Germany was famous. Between 1875 and 1895, the canal system increased by one per cent (from 21 up to 22 per cent) its share of the total traffic of Germany, measured in ton-kilometers.[27] Such a greatly expanded transportation system also helped reduce costs of manufactured goods, thereby making them accessible to a wider public.

Changes in the transportation and communication systems made the importation of foreign goods cheaper and more readily available. In this respect, it is hardly an exaggeration to state that the seed from which retailing later developed depended for its early nourishment on dealing in foreign wares. From the middle ages, municipal law had attempted to discourage retailing. The law had rested on two main principles: that "as far as possible, sale must be public and at first hand, and that everything which can be produced within the town itself shall be produced there".[28] No intermediary trade was permitted with products of local manufacture; even imports could be dealt with only after they had been vainly offered on the open markets and were subject to innumerable restrictions. There did exist some petty retailing. The poor, who lived from hand to mouth, relied for their daily fare upon the small retail trader *(Kleinhändler)*. Local economic relations were heavily regulated and both master artisans and merchants shared a common desire to preserve a local monopoly.[29] The desire to retain this self-sufficiency was gradually eroded with the importation of wares which would otherwise have remained unavailable. By the beginning of the nineteenth century, the retailers, where they existed at all, might deal in tea from Russia, tobacco and sugar from America and the

West Indies, wine from France, Portugal and Spain, spices from the Orient, and citrus fruits, olive oil, and silk from Italy.[30] In the course of the century, the per capita consumption of many such wares increased considerably[31]—and it will be seen that grocers increased more rapidly than any of the other types of retailers. The availability of greater quantities of such goods, their declining prices, can be related to changes in the transportation system of Germany and, indeed, of the whole world.

The virtual revolution in transportation helped to reduce costs of food and manufactures, made available foreign wares, and contrived to develop a national market. It also provided an incentive to increasing consumer wants at the local level by showing "country cousins" what the city had to offer. That there was a great "demonstration effect" appears quite certain. Contemporary foreign observers noted with some amazement that the efforts of government to force agricultural labour back to the land were having little success. As one put it, the workers felt it "better to starve in idleness in the town than return to the dreariness of the land".[32] Within the larger towns, expanded transportation systems made it possible for consumers to broaden the area of competition to which retailers were to be subjected. As a result, local monopoly or oligopoly situations were broken down. City transportation developed from the late 1880s. It grew from some 1.8 billion passenger-kilometers in 1889 to 11.8 billion by 1913.[33] With the development of the department store, the chain-store, and other types of large scale undertakings in central urban areas of the same period in Germany, developments in transportation were to have some important implications for the independent retailer.

Trade Cycles

Assertions have often been made about the importance of the "Great Depression" (1873-1896) to the economic problems of the retailers and their subsequent political activity.[34] However, no systematic attempt has been made to relate the economic problems of the retailers to the trade cycles of the period from 1871 to 1914 in Germany. Many of the assumptions about the relation of the political activities of the *Mittelstand* (including the retailers) to the trade cycles of this period have been based on the theory put forward by Hans Rosenberg.

Rosenberg's ideas—which he presents with many more reservations than some who have come to accept his theory— have been heavily criticized, perhaps most successfully by David Landes. Briefly stated, Landes contends that this so-called depression was actually an "optical illusion". In fact, he maintains, "the nineteenth century was marked by a pro-tracted and sharp deflation, stretching from 1817 to 1896 with only one short interruption", the period immediately prior to the "crash" of 1873. "The price decline of the nine-teenth century", he adds, "is the consequence and barometer of European industrialization."[35]

Close examination of what Rosenberg describes as the "economic character" of the "depression" reveals that his own thesis is not entirely incompatible with that of Landes. Rosenberg emphasizes the decline of wholesale prices of agri-cultural products, the decline indeed of prices in general, including interest rates. The "negative" effects were felt, he admits, far less in the industrial sector. He characterizes the effect of the "depression" on the industrial sector as a "slow-ing down of economic growth".[36] He admits to the great increases in nominal and real wages from 1880 and points out that, in this deflationary period, those on fixed incomes and salaries benefited greatly.[37] When all is said and done, Rosen-berg admits, the "depression" was really more a "social-psychological" phenomenon affecting certain investors and industrialists and especially those in particular branches of agriculture more than anyone else.[38] He even concedes that the feeling of malaise, that the years from 1873 to 1896 (which were considered by some to have been "lean years" and "bad times") "often had only little or nothing at all to do with economic reality and its actual social conse-quences".[39] Therefore, only with a great deal of caution should Rosenberg's theory be used to demonstrate the adverse effects of the "depression" upon both the artisans and re-tailers.[40] Nowhere does he attempt to discuss what sort of effects this "depression" had upon the latter two social groups.

If a consciousness of the existence of a depression can be shown to have existed within the ranks of the *Mittelstand* in general, Rosenberg and those who claim to have accepted his thesis have failed to illustrate it. Quotations from contemporary publicists are usually the only "proofs" put forward. Although these upon examination reveal no particular consciousness of a depression, they perhaps reflect vague dissatisfactions with the era in general.[41]

It would be most confusing and misleading to assume that the effects of this "depression" were anything comparable with those in post-1929 America. The period from 1873 to 1896 did not have a unitary "depression" character but had its "upswings" in the years from 1879 to 1882, from 1886 to 1889, and after the end of 1894.[42] To argue that the psychological impact of the downswings (after 1882 and 1889) was all the greater because of the experience of the period from 1873 to 1879[43] seems to imply that 1882 and 1889 appeared to contemporaries very much as 1873 and the "great crash". While the contention may have a certain validity for limited groups, the period from 1871 to 1914 may be viewed quite differently. "Once the setbacks of the mid 1870s were behind her, Germany resumed her high rate of growth. And she had not exhausted this momentum when the new opportunities at the end of the century gave her economy another push. As a result, one has the impression of an uninterrupted rise."[44] The specific problems confronting the retailers appear in no way to have been related to the so-called "great depression". Factors of moment to the economic existence of the retailers, namely the aggregate expansion of the retail market, were of far greater importance than, say, falling agricultural prices, declining wholesale prices, and interest rates.

Artisan and Retailer: The Changing Pattern of Consumption

A positive correlation can be established between the rise of industrialization, the emergence of retailing as an important element in the rapidly changing distribution system, and the decline of the independent artisan. It was not infrequently the case that a problem that posed a threat to the existence of the artisans had positive implications for the economic existence of the retailers.* What threatened one offered sustenance to the other. The economic decline of the independent artisan was already apparent well before 1871 and continued more or less down to the war.[45]

The economic problems of the artisans in pre-1914 Germany may be summarized under five main headings.[46] The first, and most fundamental economic problem of the artisan stemmed from changes in demand. The vast new concentrations of demand represented by the large urban centre could not be satisfied by individual craftsmen, but only by factories with mass production and more sophisticated distribution outlets. Second, the demand had changed qualitatively as well as quantitatively. There was a widely recognized tendency toward uniformity in consumption. Fashions, for example, whether in clothing or household furniture could be made available to all only if they were mass produced. The artisan was too expensive and his goods were not always in step with current fashions. Third, patterns of purchasing had also changed. Few customers were prepared to commission a piece of furniture, for example, perhaps pay for it in advance or supply the materials, wait many months for delivery, and even add the finishing touches to the product at home. The new city dweller wanted to buy his wares "ready made", to inspect a wide variety of finished products before making his purchase, and to have the use of his purchase immediately. Custom work, on which the artisan prided himself, had to give way to factory-like production. If the artisan were to survive, he, like the factory, had to work up a stock of goods and sell through retail outlets. Furthermore, in the city the independent artisan might become relegated to repair work or give up his trade altogether to become a retailer of factory-produced goods. Not infrequently, he might hire on at a factory as a skilled worker. Finally, certain technical advances simply made the artisan redundant. The retailer could be found in the period after 1871 selling goods which had been previously produced by artisans and passed directly to the customer. For

*The most recent work to touch on the pre-war *Mittelstand* in Germany (Winkler, *Mittelstand*, 1972) does not delineate clearly the precise differences between the economic problems of the artisans and those of the independent retailers.

example, clock and gun makers, weavers, pin, button, hat, and card makers, shoe and rope makers, nailsmiths and coopers, had all virtually disappeared as independent artisans. By the end of the century, the artisan determined to carry on his trade was to be found more and more in rural areas where the pattern of demand, and economic life as a whole, had changed less. In the developing urban centres, the retail-trading outlet, supplied by the factory (if, in certain circumstances, by the artisan as well) pointed the way to the future.

The economic problems of the retailers were largely of a different nature. The retailers suffered, for example, from what was generally felt to be a too rapid increase in numbers. This view came to be something of a contemporary axiom.[47] The complex economic problems of the artisans, on the other hand, were reflected in the decreasing, rather than increasing numbers.[48] The artisans enjoyed a completely different tradition of organization and activity from that of the retailers, most specifically represented by the artisans' guilds. The retailers had hardly any tradition of organization at all and only began to organize significantly in the latter part of the nineteenth century. They had to fight at that time, and even into the present century, for representation in the already existing Chambers of Commerce.[49] From 1897, the artisans had their own Chamber, the *Handwerks* or *Gewerbekammer* from which the retailers were deliberately excluded.

Many master artisans were convinced that the 1869 legislation[50] usually summarized as the laws on "freedom of trade" (*Gewerbefreiheit*) lay at the root of their problems.[51] Opposition of the artisans to demands of freedom of trade can be traced back to an earlier period, particularly to 1848.[52] The legislation passed by the North German Confederation in 1869 was incorporated into the laws of the Empire in 1871. The artisans sought repeal of this liberal economic legislation, generally saw their salvation in raising the qualifications necessary to practise a trade, and, with rare exceptions, even sought re-introduction of compulsory guilds.[53] Many of the activities of the artisans, therefore, took on a very technical nature and had little relevance or interest for the retailers. The latter had their own reservations about full freedom of trade, but advocacy of a guild system as envisioned by the artisans would have made little sense to them. Historically, guilds had favoured direct dealing between producer and consumer, instead of contact with the non-producing middlemen.[54]

The artisans had suffered economic problems earlier than the retailers, or, at least, had had organizational structures through which they could voice their grievances. The artisans appear, therefore, to have turned to political activity much earlier.[55] The development of specific retail trader interest groups may be taken as one of the indications of the awakening political consciousness of the retailers. It was really only after 1890 (despite some attempts to date political activity earlier) that the retailers were driven into independent political activity.[56]

While such differences between artisans and retailers were too substantial to be ignored, some master artisans and retail traders could unite, as independents, to fight what they considered to be common enemies, such as the department store, the consumer co-operatives, even false advertising or too-generous granting of discounts or credit. Nevertheless, the retailers remained conscious of the divide that separated them from the artisans, especially because the latter tended to make a great deal of their superior qualifications—and therefore social status—won in long years of apprenticeship. The connection between status claims and such emphasis on qualification differentiation is well known.

A virtual "panic over status" may result when economic conditions threaten to obliterate the (then subjectively over-asserted) qualification differentiations and economic independence (where, as in this instance, "independents" are involved) and lead ultimately to forced proletarianization.[57] The small independent retailers responded in various ways to their own sense of panic over status in the period before 1914. They attempted, for example, to raise qualifications through creation of an elaborate system of technical schools. Again, in distinction to the artisans, the retailers rarely had the authority to compel; their organizations could only recommend and advise that further education, of a general, as well as of a more vocational kind, was one of the weapons retailers had to use in their fight for economic survival. The development of the retailers' schools lagged behind those of the artisans.[58] It appeared necessary to raise qualifications for a number of reasons. It was being suggested, for example, that more and more women were turning to retailing because so many other occupations were closed to them. This development was testimony in itself that retailing was declining as a status activity.[59] The joint activity of the retailers with the artisans and other "independents" (as well as with the white-collar workers) was not infrequently justified in the name of their common membership in the *Mittelstand.* Nevertheless, the *Mittelstandsbewegung* was eventually split over the question of which social groups were entitled to refer to themselves as members of the *Mittelstand* The so-called Düsseldorf section had broken away from the *Mittelstandsvereinigung* by early 1909 because the latter organization wanted to include in its membership social groups usually referred to as the "new" *Mittelstand.* The Düsseldorf section was determined to restrict membership of its organization to artisans and retailers only.[60]

Conclusion

The rise of the function of retailing was directly related to expanding industrialization and the processes which accompanied it. The economic problems of the independent retailer were not caused by factors such as population growth, urbanization, growth or shifts in demand, as these factors worked to expand the retail market and the economic function of retailing. Unlike the artisan, the retailer was not in competition with the factory. Retailing was rather a logical extension of the factory. There were certain developments, particularly after 1890, which came to threaten the existence of the independent retailer and which he, in association with other retailers (and, from time to time, in association with artisans and white-collar workers), was determined to fight.

The pronounced differences between the more fundamental economic problems of the artisan and those of the retailer were reflected in different political attitudes. Emil Lederer, writing in 1910, summarized these differences very succinctly:

The most superficial observation immediately reveals the different politics of the various groups within the Mittelstand, *particularly the basic difference between retail trade and artisanship. Artisanship has long since ceased to fight industry. It is now trying to win ground by working out specific measures which can support it in its competitive struggle. (The content of the positive demands of the artisans is predicated on this orientation.) The policy of the* Mittelstand, *in so far as it deals with the affairs of artisans, rests in large measure on the solution of technical problems. The policy of the* Mittelstand *for retail trade is, however, still in the primary phase of* Mittelstand *policy for independents. The objective of retail trade is to fight the large undertaking, particularly in the form of the department store and the consumer co-operative.*[61]

Lederer also observed the political implications of the under-lying economic differences between the artisans and the retailers, "that this difference in character of the individual groups of the *Mittelstand* and of their orientations is extremely significant. Moreover, the creation of a unified *Mittelstand* organization is, thereby, made more difficult."[62]

2

The Development of Economic Problems Which Threatened the Existence of Independent Retailers 1890 - 1914

As the nineteenth century drew to a close, German retailers received greater attention than ever before. They were studied either in an attempt to understand what was happening to the retailers specifically or the *Mittelstand* in general. The reasons for this attention (and for the previous neglect) are many. The attention was, however, in many instances directly related to the growing interest of retailers as a group in politics at a time when politics was becoming more and more invaded by interest groups and when the spectre of a victory of Social Democracy at the polls loomed more and more in view.[1] Most studies of the retailers which appeared at this time began with an analysis of the economic problems of the retailers, pronounced (according to the political convictions of the writer) what the "tendencies" in retail trade were, how these tendencies were to affect the independent retailer, and, often, whether state-help or self-help was necessary, possible or worthwhile. There was much agreement on what the actual problems of the retailers were. These problems have not been systematically investigated however, for, unlike the artisans, the retailers have largely escaped the notice of such interested bodies as the *Verein für Sozialpolitik*.

Representatives of federal, state, and local government were called together on 9 June 1914, with the leading representatives of the retailers, for the purpose of drawing up plans for an officially sponsored survey of the conditions of retailing in Germany on a national scale. Because of the war, this enquiry was never carried out. In the preliminary discussions of 9 June, however, many of the economic problems generally held to threaten the independence of the retailers were raised.[2] These discussions were conducted among the "decisive powers" of both government and the retailers at the end of the period upon which this study concentrates. They may be assumed to reflect what the "decisive powers" considered to be the most significant problems of the retailers.

In his long and detailed analysis of the economic problems of the retailers in Germany, the representative of the Federal Ministry of the Interior, Dr. Schwarzkopf, emphasized first, the general concern over increases in the numbers of retail establishments.[3] The concern was widespread and had existed well before 1914. There was anxiety not only about the actual increases in the numbers of retailers, but also about the type of retailer who was being recruited and, in particular, about his training and general qualifications. It was generally held that, to some extent, the economic problems of the independent retailer could be traced to the retailer himself. Leaders of the retail traders' interest groups were aware that most independent retailers knew little bookkeeping, that their stocks were often too large in relation to turnover, that too much credit was granted to customers for too long, that discounts and bargains were sometimes given in the face of competition, and of a general lack of community spirit *(Standesbewusstsein).*[4] The discussion of 9 June 1914 reflected an awareness of these aspects of the retailers' problems.[5]

Increases in the Numbers of Retail Establishments

The question of numbers in retailing had two fundamental aspects. The first concerned what is usually referred to as "cost to the economy". This concept refers to the share or proportion of total resources available in the economy which had to be allocated to the distribution system and which, therefore, could not be released into other sectors of the economy. There was a direct relationship between the share of total resources allocated to the distribution system and the level of services provided. This side of the economic problem of retailing, which has important social implications beyond providing something of a barometer of the extent to which an economy is "developed", is not discussed in the present

study.* The other aspect of the "numbers question" in retailing concerned whether the independent retailers could
manage to survive on what was considered to be a steadily
declining number of customers per retailer. Both aspects of
the question could and did merge when, for example, the
discussions turned to the influence of retailing on increasing
prices and rises in the cost of living. Although the assessment
of these influences lies beyond the scope of this study, it is
important to note that much concern was expressed by retailers in pre-war Germany that they ought not to be blamed
for rising prices.

It was indicated above that it is extremely difficult to fix
the precise numbers of those engaged in retailing in pre-war
Germany. Although there is no agreement on specific, absolute numbers, there is some agreement about the general
trends. Schmoller's estimates for the "old Prussian Provinces",
although questionable on several grounds, are illustrative of
the increases in the numbers of retail outlets (*Laden* and
Einzelverkaufsgeschäfte) over the course of the nineteenth
century. He estimated that in 1837 there were 47,000 such
undertakings, in 1861 some 82,000 and in 1895, 200,000 or,
respectively, 33, 44, and 77 businesses per 10,000 inhabitants.[6]
Sombart estimated that, in the "more developed" Saxony of
the 1860s, there were some 256 "traders"*(Händlerschaft)* per
10,000 inhabitants and in 1895, 637 per 10,000.[7] Although
"traders" was, he admiteed, a necessarily vague term (as retailers and wholesalers were not differentiated in the national
statistics), Sombart expressed his conviction that "for the
most part, it is a question of an increase in the number of
retailers".[8] Sombart and Karl Rathgen made similar rough
calculations for Germany as a whole. They claimed that, in
the census years 1861, 1875, 1882, 1895, and 1907, there

---

*A recent study of retailing in England has demonstrated that, in an
economy going through the early phase of industrialization, it is very
nearly impossible to say whether or not the social function of a distribution system (employing more people than necessary, but thereby providing some form of employment to those who would otherwise go without) compensates for possible technical inefficiency. In other words, the
assessment .of the so-called "cost to the economy" of the distribution
system ought not to rest on the assumption that economic efficiency
and technical efficiency are the same thing. See Alexander, *Retailing in
England,* 1970 *passim.* .

was one "trader" for every 83, 65, 54, 38.8, and 30 inhabitants respectively.[9]

A more detailed analysis of the census returns, as Dr. Schwarzkopf pointed out, offers little hope of introducing more certainty into the calculations not only because retailers and wholesalers are not differentiated, but because the statistics are not comparable. For example, the statistical returns on retailing in the national census of 1882 were divided into 13 groups, those of 1895 into 15, and those of 1907 into 48. Dr. Schwarzkopf demonstrated that a number of more reliable conclusions might be drawn from the census returns. However, as his own discussion makes evident, such a study would entail a long and painful analysis which would ultimately only confirm the more general statements of Schmoller, Sombart, and Rathgen.

The most striking feature of the statistics on undertakings in trade in the census years 1882, 1895, and 1907 was the great increases both in absolute figures and in percentages in comparison with the increases of undertakings in all other branches of the economy. It is assumed that the percentage of retail to wholesale undertakings remained constant, even though non-statistical evidence is unanimous in claiming that the relative share of wholesaling in the figures actually diminished considerably. This assumption is made because it is not possible to stipulate the precise relative percentages.

The number of undertakings listed under the census category *Warenhandel* (where, it was accepted, retail undertakings predominated over wholesale undertakings) increased in the period from 1882 to 1895 by 29.1 per cent, and the number of persons employed rose by 61.9 per cent; for the economy as a whole, the figures were but a 1.3 per cent increase in undertakings and a 39.9 per cent in employed persons. For the period from 1895 to 1907 undertakings in *Warenhandel* rose by 41.7 per cent, the employed persons by 55.0 per cent. The figures for the economy as a whole for the period showed a 10.0 per cent increase in total undertakings, 39.7 per cent in employed persons. Of those sub-categories under *Warenhandel* which had been counted in either of the two previous censuses and which were, therefore, comparable, increases in certain instances were even more striking. There were several examples where retail undertakings are known to have predominated over wholesale undertakings. The number of businesses dealing in tobacco, cigars, and cigarettes, for example, increased in the period from 1882 to 1895 by 53.7 per cent (the numbers employed by 50.4 per cent); between 1895 and 1907, the increases were 136.4 per cent and 113.7 per cent, respectively. Firms trading in "machines and apparatuses" of various types, from bicycles to sewing machines (counted as a separate category under *Warenhandel* first in 1895), increased in the period from 1895 to 1907 by 386.7 per cent and in numbers employed, by 308.0 per cent. The increase for firms trading in "wines and spirits" between 1895 and 1907 was 45.6 per cent, in persons employed, 35.3 per cent.[10]

These national trends were reflected in local statistics as well. In 1866 there were 577 residents per retail firm dealing in manufactures in the town of Celle; by 1896 there were 486 per firm.[11] In 1865 there were two embroidery shops and a population of 27,000 in Rostock, or 13,500 inhabitants per business. By 1895 there were six such undertakings and only 8,295 inhabitants per firm.[12] In the same city, there were three chemists, or one chemist per 11,396 inhabitants in 1875; by 1897, there were 17 chemist shops or one chemist per 3,059 inhabitants.[13] In the city Hanover-Linden, there were some 9,059 inhabitants for each retail firm dealing in iron wares in 1860; by 1896, the number had been reduced to 4,678 inhabitants per firm.[14] A survey of 14 small cities in the Baden Black Forest area (the Chamber of Commerce area of the Villingen) revealed that in 1866, some 142 independent retail outlets of all branches shared 25,660 inhabitants or 180.6 inhabitants per firm. By 1897 there were 384 firms, a population of 35,221 or but 91.7 inhabitants per firm.[15] A survey of 26 towns of the same area showed a similar trend; in 1866 there were 357 inhabitants per firm, but in 1897, only 182 per firm.[16]

The trends did not always develop in the same way, particularly in the smaller and more rural areas in the east. In these areas, other factors often operated, especially improvements in communication links, to increase the number of inhabitants per retail firm. A survey of a small city in East Prussia showed that for the decade 1866/1876, there were

190 inhabitants per firm dealing in groceries and household goods *(Kolonial - und Materialwarenhandel)*; in the period up to 1898, the number of retail outlets declined (from 25 to 24) while the population increased, so that there were in 1898, 225 inhabitants per firm.[17] In some areas in the east, increases in the number of firms in the dominant retail branches kept abreast with increases in the population. The governmental area *(Regierungsbezirk)* of Posen, for example, showed that population in its five main cities was equal to 1,105 inhabitants per firm in 1872 and 1,061 per firm in 1895.[18] Much more in line with national trends was a city like Brunswick, the population of which rose in the period from 1887 to 1901 by approximately 60 per cent, while its firms dealing in groceries increased in the same period by approximately 90 per cent.[19]

Official statistics, scholarly estimates, and the testimony of the retailers themselves appear to confirm that the increases in the numbers both of undertakings and of persons employed in retailing represented individuals entering the trade for the first time. According to Schmoller's estimates, the massive increases in the number of firms represented firms employing five or fewer persons. Although firms *(Haupthandelsbetriebe)* employing fifty or more persons increased by a factor of 4 between 1882 and 1907, there were still only a thousand such firms in 1907. On the other hand, in that year 791,178 firms out of a total of 842,140 employed five or fewer persons. In 1882 firms worked by the owner alone *(Alleinbetriebe)* had represented more than double the number of firms which employed from one to five persons (293,339 and 141,386 respectively). By 1907 firms employing from one to five persons stood at 472,878 while firms worked by the owner alone had increased to 318,300. The growth rate of firms worked by the owner alone had, therefore, fallen behind that of firms employing from one to five persons.[20] The increases in the numbers of undertakings, at least of undertakings in retailing with "open selling outlets", indicate that the increases were due not to the development of multi-outlet firms, but to the creation of new, individual, single-outlet firms. In 1907 firms with "open selling outlets" were first counted in the national census. Of a total of 481,294 such firms in retailing some 450,568 had but one selling outlet, 12,166 represented a single firm with two outlets, and only 1,452 firms had three outlets or more.[21]

These great increases in the numbers of retailing establishments were, in very great measure, a response to the ever expanding retail market. The magnitude of the increases appeared so great at the time, however, that the increases in numbers came to be widely regarded as a threat, perhaps even the most important threat, to the continued existence of the independent retailer.[22] This conviction was reflected in the discussions carried out at the highest level in June 1914. The fears over the increases in the numbers of establishments in retailing were not based simply either on a belief that the retail market could support a certain number of retailers before prices had to be driven so high that the public and the government would tolerate the situation no longer, or on a fear that consequently, increasing numbers of retailers would be driven to bankruptcy. In fact, much of the apprehension, both of government and retailers, may be said to have been due to the kind of retailer entering the field.[23]

Recruitment and Training

Much of the evidence which exists concerning the new recruits in retail trade prior to 1914 in Germany is extremely diverse. However, the two broad categories of recruits suggested by Hirsch[24] for the early post-war period indicate the types of persons who were attracted to retail trade in the pre-1914 period. Hirsch believed that those who opened up the new smaller firms dealing in goods, such as cigarettes, food or groceries, came from the ranks of the proletariat. Often, however, in the pre-war period, such retailers were new arrivals in the urban centres, fresh from having sold out their farms— and with them their independence—and anxious not to join the ranks of the proletariat. The latter group of recruits would likely have been even more anxious to maintain their independence than recruits from the proletariat. Another group, retired persons, also opened small shops. There is also evidence to suggest that wives of workers opened small shops to supplement the husband's wage. Generally speaking, these

groups, at the bottom of the scale among independent retailers, possessed very little specific training and had minimum
capital.[25]

The second major category of recruits to independent retailing suggested by Hirsch covered those who had previously
been artisans. In the pre-war period, such an artisan might
open a retail outlet broadly associated with his previous trade
and for which he possessed some training. The most obvious
example was that of the shoemakers who gave up producing
their own shoes and sold the factory-produced variety. Others
might open retail firms which sold goods associated with their
previous craft. The iron or nail smith might open an iron-
ware and kitchen appliance shop, for example. Still others
are known to have broken all ties with their previous trade, in
order to open up small food stores. At the turn of the century,
for example, of 28 grocers in Gifhorn, 11 had been artisans of
various types, from two shoe makers, one carpenter, one
plumber, to a wool spinner.[26] It seems clear, therefore, that
some ex-artisans were hardly better qualified to carry on a retail business than those who had previously been farmers or
workers. However, the degree of qualification necessary in
order to carry on a successful retail business was related not
only to the particular goods in which the retail firm dealt, but
to the size of the firm as well, and, perhaps even more important, to the size and location of the village or city. It was
pointed out, for example, that while the retailers in a small
East Prussian town were not very highly educated, their education was sufficient for their needs, given the size of the
firms and the size of the town.[27]

In surveys of retailing carried out by the retailers themselves, the direct relationship between lack of training (and
the innumerable consequences resulting directly from it) and
the propensity to bankruptcy was made clear.[28] It is no easy
task to establish the rates and types of bankruptcy in retailing in Germany, either at the local or national level. Statistical
evidence, where available at all, does not differentiate between the types of undertakings forced into bankruptcy.[29]
Moreover, the hearings of the bankruptcy courts appear not
to have survived. Even with such official evidence, it would be
impossible to trace with any degree of accuracy the rates at

which firms changed hands (and the reasons for the changes). It was well known that many firms went into a state of insolvency and sold out, but did not go through the official bankruptcy proceedings in order to avoid paying the high court costs. In Leipzig, there were small retail cigarette firms which frequently went insolvent without declaring bankruptcy. These firms were small with minimum capital and their proprietors appear to have been less than well trained. Although they may not have been representative of retailing as a whole, figures indicate an extremely high rate of firms changing hands without declaring bankruptcy.[30]

The information available on incomes in retailing tends to support the observations of scholars both before and after World War I about the growing impoverishment of the independent retailer. There were, again, extreme fluctuations among the various branches and localities. At the turn of the century, the incomes of ironmongers in Hanover were greater than the incomes of cigarette dealers in Leipzig.[31] A detailed review of surveys carried out by the retailers leads to the conclusion, variations aside, that newer firms in retailing (obviously with the exception of the "new" large concerns) had lower turnovers and incomes, had less capital, grew up in the lower-rent areas away from the main market areas, and displayed a greater propensity to bankruptcy than the older firms. Sombart, writing in 1903, spoke of the growth of "proletarian-like" existences in retailing.[32] Geiger, writing in 1932 (after the war and inflation) estimated that, on the basis of income, 44.4 per cent of those engaged in retailing, compared even to the chronically beset artisans, were "proletarian".[33] The lowly existences of the retailers, such as those in the working class areas of Berlin or Munich, impressed the British commission sent out to study the cost (and condition) of living in Germany prior to the war.[34]

For political reasons the retailers' surveys reflected their desire to underestimate the importance of lack of proper training among retailers. As the results of their surveys made clear, many retailers were unwilling to answer detailed questions. In Kiel, only 23 of 111 grocers and 21 of 64 dry-goods dealers answered the survey at all. Those that did answer were determined to make clear that their problems could be traced to the "new" competition of the consumer co-operatives and the department stores.[35] For the most part, retailers were loath to admit that they were responsible for their own problems and anxious, therefore, to avoid revealing to governments the general lack of training of retailers. To suggest that retailers were responsible for their own problems might be to suggest that state help, particularly in the form of taxes on the department stores and the consumer co-operatives, was not necessary. The smaller independents were prepared even to question the entire spirit of the capitalist system*, much to the horror of the larger firms, represented, for example, in the *Verein Berliner Kaufleute und Industrieller.*[36] Many retailers were not opposed to "guild-like" economic relations when these promised to work in favour of their survival.

The larger firms on the other hand tended to appeal to biases which the "little people" digested only with difficulty. It was fine to say that advocacy of special taxes on the larger firms was tantamount to asserting that hard work by the entrepreneur was not capable of overcoming all obstacles. Department store owners, in campaigns carried on in newspapers all across Germany at the turn of the century frequently claimed that special taxes on the department stores were taxing hard work, that, at best, the idea behind the taxes (which they derided) could be summarized by the "wishful thought", "the weak are strengthened if the strong are weakened".[37] The small retailer, faced with developments in retailing over which he could exercise no control whatever, could hardly be expected simply to go on accepting uncritically economic axioms (which under "normal" circumstances he might be said to embody) which were driving him out of business.

Development of Consumer Co-operatives

The discussions of 9 June 1914 in the Ministry of the Interior reflected the opinion that new developments in retailing,

*Wernicke, *Wandlungen und neue Interessen-Organisationen im Detailhandel,* 1908 : 15 ff. attempted to demonstrate how few those people were even in the *"Mittelstand"* who had anything to gain by special taxes on department stores. He also claimed (p.12) that the competition in retail trade was a good thing and that only the "overcrowding" made it ruinous for some.

such as the consumer co-operative and the department store, had "brought with them disadvantages and difficulties".[38] if not for the consumer, certainly for independent retailers. The crystallization of the political conflict concerning tye very existence of independent retailing, as opposed to the newer forms of retailing, presented itself most vividly in the case of the consumer co-operative.

Although the development of the consumer co-operative has a long pre-history in Germany, it was only from the 1890s that the consumer co-operative, invigorated with fresh ideas, underwent its great expansion.[39] The pioneer societies—although they resemble the later consumer co-operatives in few respects—are usually considered to have been the *Ermunterung* Society, founded in 1845 in Chemnitz (others founded in 1848 in Berlin), and the *Gesellschaft zur Verteilung von Lebensbedürfnissen* founded in 1852 in Hamburg. The names of people such as Victor A. Huber, Eduard Pfeiffer and, particularly, Hermann Schulze-Delitzsch, are usually associated with the intellectual inspiration which led to the beginnings of the movement in Germany. After the founding of a durable central organizations in 1864 (there had been predecessors), the *Allgemeiner Verband der auf Selbsthilfe beruhenden deutschen Erwerbs- und Wirtschaftsgenossenschaften,* the co-operative movement (which continued to be extraordinarily varied in its co-operative endeavours) established itself on a firm basis. Schulze, who exerted the greatest influence at this formative period, considered consumer co-operatives to be no more important than (and perhaps èven less important than) other forms of co-operation, such as co-operative credit societies *(Vorschlussvereine)* and co-operative purchasing societies of artisans *(Rohstoffvereine).*[40] In 1865 the *Allgemeiner Verband* counted 45 consumer co-operatives, 43 *Rohstoffvereine,* but 447 *Vorschlussvereine.*[41] By 1900 there were 870 co-operative credit societies and 568 consumer co-operatives.[42]

Statistics on the development of consumer co-operatives in Germany[43] confirm the contention that consumer co-operatives really only established themselves in large numbers in the period after 1888.* The first years' statistics of the *Allgemeiner Verband* in 1864 listed only 38 consumer co-operatives, having a total membership of 7,700 and a turnover of 802,767 Mk.[44] It is widely known, however, that some 97 consumer co-operatives existed at that time.[45] In the twenty-fifth year of its existence (1888), the *Allgemeiner Verband* received reports from 198 consumer co-operatives with a membership of 172,931 and a turnover of 46,814,416 Mk. The increase in the next decade is remarkable. A peak (for the *Allgemeiner Verband*) was reached in 1901 when 638 consumer co-operatives reported a membership of 630,785 and a turnover of 155,684,048 Mk.[46]

A struggle over policy developed within the *Allgemeiner Verband* in the 1890s. In 1902 the problem was exacerbated by pressure exerted by newer members (largely working class) in favour of far greater emphasis on consumer co-operation, instead of credit co-operation. The disagreement led to a split in the movement. The immediate impact of the split was a sharp decline in the numbers of consumer co-operatives associated with the *Allgemeiner Verband* and the beginning of a new central organization specifically dedicated to the propagation of consumer co-operation. In the first year of its existence (1903), this new organization, the *Zentralverband deutscher Konsumvereine,* had some 639 local associations report a membership of 575,449 and a turnover of 176,456,549 Mk.[47] In 1913 the figures were 1,169 associations, 1,633,644 members and 673,579,979 Mk. turnover.[48] In 1913 there were still 282 consumer co-operatives associated with the old *Allgemeiner Verband,* with a membership of 323,228 and a turnover of 83,510,109 Mk.[49] In 1913 therefore, there was a total ("reporting associations") of 1,451 consumer co-operatives with a membership of 1,956,872 and a turnover (exclusive of their own production) of 757,090,488 Mk.

The working class was slow to accept consumer co-operation and turned to the co-operative movement only in the

*Completely accurate statistics on the development of the consumer co-operatives are lacking, primarily because of the reluctance of the individual local undertakings to submit reports to the central organization. Many of the well known works on the subject restrict their statistics to associations which reported their activities. The picture that emerges may therefore be quite misleading.

1870s in the Kingdom of Saxony and in Rhineland-Westphalia. It has been maintained that following the anti-Socialist laws, "many ardent socialists found in co-operation a field for the energies which were denied an outlet in politics".[50] This suggestion ignores the not unimportant fact that the great expansion in the co-operative movement came after the anti-Socialist laws had ceased to exist. By 1886 there were eight regional branches of the *Allgemeiner Verband* in existence. The *"Vorwärts"* consumer co-operative, founded in 1894 in Saxony, was, however, to prove a more significant organization and it played an important role in the split (in 1902) in the movement. The formation of this organization is considered to have risen spontaneously in Saxony as the fruit of the endeavours of the workers who received the help of some Social Democrats, in spite of the lack of any "red theory of consumer co-operatives". Their first public statement already spoke of the *Allgemeiner Verband* representing "an out-of-date policy current".[51]

The changing attitude of the SPD in Saxony toward the consumer co-operatives was, at least partially, a tactical response to the charges of Saxony's *"Mittelständler"* that the consumer co-operative movement possessed a "social democratic character". From the 1890s onward, the SPD began reviewing its (hitherto) negative attitude to the consumer co-operatives. The policy statement by Kautsky in 1897 indicated that though the consumer co-operatives were aimed at the *'Mittelstand'* instead of the "capitalists", they could play "a not unimportant role" in the struggle to emancipate the workers.[52] The founding in Hamburg two years later (1899) of the consumer co-operative *Produktion* proved to be the real turning point in the development of co-operatives in Germany. The importance of *Produktion* to the German movement has been compared with that of Rochdale to the English.[53] "The Hamburg policy", as the very name of the organization implied, was expressive of an interest in production as well as distribution. The creation of co-operatives on the pattern of *Produktion* had momentous political consequences because it opened up possibilities for closer collaboration with both the trade union movement and the SPD and led to the subsequent great expansion of the consumer co-opera-

tives throughout Germany.[54]
As in most other countries, the consumer co-operatives in
Germany were largely confined to the cities. In general, there
was a direct relationship between the level of industrialization
of an area and the development of the consumer co-operatives.
Growth of consumer co-operatives began when this industrialization began to be mirrored in developments in the retail
market. For example, some 16 consumer co-operatives were
founded in industrialized Saxony in the period before 1869;
in Bavaria, only one was founded. By 1889 there had still been
only 11 consumer co-operatives established in all of Bavaria;
13 were founded between 1890 and 1899, and 18 between
1900 and 1904.[55]
The economic impact of the consumer co-operatives presented itself to the independent retailer as increased competition, competition which was quantitatively and qualitatively
so different as to appear to him "unfair". The concept of
"unfair competition" *(unlauterer Wettbewerb)* became one of
the independent retailers' most important political slogans. It
is extremely difficult to establish the precise economic influence of the consumer co-operatives upon the independent
retailer because it includes dissecting retail price determinants.
Other "new appearances" in retail trade, especially the department store, the chain store, and the mail-order house may be
said to have exerted a similar economic impact on the independent retailer.

Development of Large Concerns in Retailing

Schmoller's figures, which are of questionable validity, suggest an increase in concerns in trade *(Haupthandelsbetriebe)*
employing over 50 persons (the usual statistical definition of a
Grossbetrieb) from 250 firms in all of Germany in 1882 to
1,000 such firms in 1907.[56] Such figures would embrace all
types of large retailing firms of greatly differing character,
from the large specialized firms *(grosse Spezialgeschäfte),* to
the mail-order houses *(Versandgeschäfte),* to the hire-purchase
firms *(Abzahlungsgeschäfte),* and the department stores
(Waren- und Kaufhäuser). While each type of enterprise presented the independent retailer with different forms of com-

petition, much of the political activity of retailers was directed against the department stores.

The definition of "department store" varied according to the statistics of each of the German states. In most states, the concept of "department store" (along with the concepts of other large concerns) was defined only in the legislation which imposed various types of special taxes on such concerns. This legislation came into existence first in Bavaria (from 9 June 1899), then in Prussia (from 18 July 1900). Most states passed some form of tax on large concerns prior to 1914 and each state gave its own definition of "department store".[57] An important part of the political struggle of the retailers consisted in attempts to persuade the various state governments to accept the broadest possible definition of the large concerns.[58]

A detailed survey of the department stores in Germany suggests that in 1906/1907 there were approximately 200 department stores in existence.[59] Some 90 department stores were subject to the special tax in Prussia *(warenhaussteuerpflichtig)*, for example, and 41 in Bavaria. Although only 38 firms answered the survey's questions on the age of their firm, the statistical evidence corresponds to the generally held view that the very "oldest department stores in Germany" could be traced back no further than 1885.[60] There appears to have been no example of a founding of a department store before 1890, apart from *"der deutsche Offizierverein"* (in 1884) and *"das Warenhaus für deutsche Beamten"* (in 1889).[61] The only department stores tracing their beginnings to the period prior to 1890 were firms which had begun as specialty shops *(Spezialgeschäfte)* and subsequently transformed themselves into department stores. This was the background of the most famous department store owning family in pre-war Germany, the Tietz family.

Leonhard Tietz had begun in Stralsund in 1879 as the owner of a small haberdashery business. (He handled both the wholesale and retail sides of the business.)[62] A relative, Oskar Tietz, had opened a small retail business in Stralsund in 1882. (Incidentally, another well-known department store chain, A. Wertheim, also began in Stralsund in this period.)[63] By 1906 the Tietz name could be seen on department stores in 27 different cities all over Germany. At this point, it may be mentioned that all forms of branch stores (Filialgeschäfte), and not just the branches of the large department store chains, came to be included by retailers in their demands for special legislation.

Oskar Tietz claimed that his success was due simply to two factors. There was, first, the determination to order direct from the factory, thereby avoiding the cost of the middle man. The second factor was his adoption of the principle of a small mark-up and emphasis on increasing turnover. Even when he applied this principle in his original small haberdashery shop, he found that he could undercut his competitors by almost 100 per cent. Moreover, he could happily fix his prices and display these fixed prices (in marked contrast to most other retailers, who .tended to vary prices and discounts with different customers) as a form of advertisement which other retailers, dealing with the expensive wholesalers, could not match. Tietz took advantage not only of buying directly from the factory, but of making common purchases of greater and greater quantities of stock in association with his relatives. His competitive position was still further improved when he developed his trade both by expanding the size of his firm and by increasing the number of articles which were handled. With the expansion of the firm, the "economies of scale" came into effect.

Retailers reacted strongly to this kind of new competition, claimed that it was "unfair", and demanded protective legislation. The reaction of department store owners and their supporters was to maintain that "in the entire civilized world and in every aspect of life, the future belongs to the large concern (Grossbetrieb). No law will prevent that development."[64] The Prussian taxes on the department store, although their imposition coincided with a decline both in the number and in the turnover of department stores, appear to have failed to check the further development of such firms. In 1901, 109 firms had to pay the department store tax in Prussia; the firms subject to the tax declined to 73 in 1903. Thereafter, however, the number of firms increased steadily, to some

126 firms in 1913.*

The geographical distribution of the department stores in Germany coincided, like that of the consumer co-operatives, with the areas of higher population density and the more industrialized areas. In 1909 only 13 firms out of 101 department stores in Prussia were located in cities with populations below 50,000 and none existed in cities with fewer than 10,000 inhabitants.[65] A detailed survey of the 90 firms in 1906 in Prussia showed that almost one-third (27) were located within Berlin (13) or the immediate area (14). Most of the remaining firms were to be found in areas of heavy industry, such as the Rhineland (19), Silesia (9), Westphalia (8), and Saxony (6). There were only two in all of East Prussia and only one in Posen. Developments of the department stores in other German states appear to have conformed to the pattern in Prussia.[66]

The development of an efficient railway system, the introduction of the 50-*Pfennig* tariff on a 5 kilogram package on 1 January 1874, and the introduction of postal C.O.D. in 1878 are usually regarded as having been among the most important pre-requisites for the later expansion of the mail-order houses.[67] The great expansion in the mail-order houses appears to have occurred in the latter part of the nineteenth century and in the early twentieth century. Sombart maintained that C.O.D. deliveries ("which for the most part probably owe their existence to the mail-order house")[68] increased from 3.9 million deliveries in 1880 to 13.4 million in 1900 alone (with a value of 57.1 million Mk. in 1880 and 540.3 million Mk. in 1900), Hirsch[69] suggested that the number of C.O.D. deliveries for 1910 had increased dramatically to 61.8 million, with a value of 1184.4 million Mk.

*In the period from 1905 to 1911 alone, the turnover in department stores in Prussia grew from 176 million Mk. to 296 million Mk., or increased by 68 per cent in 6 years. Department stores with a turnover of under 400,000 Mk. were not subject to the special tax. In the period from 1905 to 1911, these latter stores increased from 22 stores (with a total turnover of 7 million Mk.) to 65 stores (with a turnover of 22 million Mk.). The number of these stores increased therefore, by 195 per cent and their total turnover by 214 per cent.
See *B.Dahlem. Pr. Justizministerium. Rep. 84a, 5.Finanzen. Nr.9022,* for the meeting of 16.3.1914 on new tax proposals designed to fill the "holes" in the old law.

The mail-order house operated not only by extensive newspaper advertising (and this was the period when newspaper reading became a widespread activity in Germany), but by the distribution of attractive catalogues. Mail-order houses often employed travelling salesmen whose job it was to encourage local customers far removed from the larger trading centres to purchase the most up-to-date consumer goods. In this way, the mail-order houses came into more direct competition with the local retailers.[70] Retailers were as opposed to the new type of travelling salesmen as they were to the more traditional and smaller travelling traders or hawkers.[71]

Another form of large concern, the hire-purchase firm, was given much attention by the retailers. It was the lower classes, particularly those in the larger cities, which tended to provide the bulk of the customers of the hire-purchase firm.[72] The number of such firms increased steadily in the period from 1890 to 1914.[73]

The retailers fought against all forms of large concerns. They enjoyed some "successes" against the department stores. Various types of legislation were enacted against the travelling salesmen employed by the mail-order houses, as well as against the old hawkers. The opponents of such legislation argued that it would lead only to the destruction of the petty hawkers and that the way would be open for the larger mail-order houses to move in. Against the latter competition, the small local retailer would have no hope.[74] In the retailers' demands for legislation, the hire-purchase firms were almost always grouped with mail-order houses and travelling salesmen. In February 1891, for example, some 972 petitions from all types of organizations representing the interests of the retailers were forwarded to the petitions commission of the *Reichstag*. These petitions demanded action against all such institutions.[75]

The Independent Retailer and the "New" Competition

The immediate economic impact of consumer co-operatives and the larger undertakings in retailing (such as the department and chain stores) presented itself to the independent retailer as greatly increased competition. The extent to which this increased competition led to lower retail prices, however, became very much a political question of some importance. In a political struggle for special taxes (for example) on department stores, the independent retailers' interest groups had to contend with charges that such taxes would be inflationary. Advocates of the consumer co-operatives confidently claimed that it was the growth of consumer co-operatives that was responsible for keeping down retail prices at a time when rapid increases in the numbers of retail establishments would otherwise have driven prices higher.[76] This argument was vehemently denied by the independent retailers' interest groups.[77] It is shown below, in the discussion of the political activities of the retailers, that they reinforced their denials with certain moral arguments about the necessity and importance of keeping independents in existence.* It was necessary for retailers to employ such moral (and political) arguments, in part because the economic arguments in favour of consumer co-operatives had only formed part of the appeal which, it was alleged, co-operatives possessed. In their proposals to establish co-operatives, the prophets with faith in co-operation saw social and even ethical dimensions which were considered no less important than the economic advantages.[78]

Economists, in particular, came to consider the process of concentration in retailing, like the process of concentration in all branches of the economy, to be inevitable. The sheer economic rationality of one large firm, such as a department store, replacing many tiny independent (and, in their terms, inefficient) retailers usually proved a compelling argument in itself in favour of concentration.[79] Accordingly, the demands of the "little people" for protection could be easily dismissed as, at best, romanticism and wishful thinking (since the process could not be resisted) or, at worst, selfishness. With very rare exceptions, the academic economists of pre-war Germany agreed that there were certain economic tendencies in train which would lead inevitably to a greater concentration in retailing (whether represented by the co-operative, department or chain store) with a corresponding natural and logical decline of the independent small retailer. Because this basic argument

*It was also argued by proponents of the consumer co-operatives that the non-independent ought not to be held to ransom in order to save the remaining independents. See Wilbrant, *Die Bedeutung der Konsumgenossenschaften*, 1914 : 26-29.

was so widely accepted (although, today, its political bias is obvious), enquiries which were carried out in attempts to outline retail price determinants largely accepted the thesis that instances of declining or stationary retail prices were due to concentration and that the causes of increasing prices could be traced to the over-supply of small independent retailers.

The independent retailers produced what they considered to be sufficient data to establish that the creation of consumer co-operatives and the larger undertakings in retail trade were exerting considerable competitive pressure. The surveys of the retailers, because they were intended ultimately to support certain claims for protective legislation from the various governments,[80] almost invariably emphasized the detrimental effects of the "new" competition and simultaneously suggested that the consumer was not actually reaping any benefits from the competition at all.[81] It is extremely difficult to establish a direct link between the creation of a new consumer co-operative or department store, for example, and subsequent lowering of retail prices. One survey of some thirty-five co-operatives from all parts of Germany suggested quite convincingly that the establishment of consumer co-operatives exercised three main influences on the retailers.[82] First, their prices declined in comparison with earlier prices and with the prices for similar goods in neighbouring areas where no co-operatives existed. Second, the profit margins of the independents were forced down. Finally, the retailers were either forced out of business, forced to grant dividends and discounts of their own to off-set those granted by the co-operatives, or driven into supplementary work to augment their declining incomes.[83] Another independent survey of Breslau reached similar conclusions.[84] It suggested that while it was economically "irrational" for the consumer to buy from (in their opinion) the persistently more expensive independent, the propensity could be viewed as a luxury. Some people, it was said, could afford to pay higher prices at the independent retailers' shops and preferred to frequent these shops either because of the more personalized service and the more attractive surroundings in retailers' shops or simply because of social prejudice.

It was not mentioned in these surveys that the consumer

dealing with the co-operatives (and, to a great extent, with the department and chain stores) had to pay for his purchases in cash. If the consumer wished to deal with the co-operatives, he had to have enough money to buy into the society as well. Customers who could neither afford the cost of these initial shares nor pay in cash were, in effect, condemned to buy their goods at the traditional retailers' shops. From the point-of-view of the retailer, the co-operatives and the large undertakings were robbing him of his best customers while he was forced to rely on the patronage of credit customers. The smart specialty shops might retain the patronage of those who could afford luxury shopping, but the small grocer was left with only the poorest customers. Of all the retailers, the grocers were said to have been most adversely affected by the consumer co-operatives.[85] Because of the risks of granting credit and the need to elicit payment of interest on money due, it was necessary for the dealer who granted credit to charge more than his cash-only competitors* who could parade the obvious differences in prices with shrewd advertising. Consequently, a very important aspect of the retailers' self-help activities was the attempt to discourage credit sales by offering special discount stamps in return for cash sales. These stamps were, at the same time, one of the retailers' chief economic weapons to be used against the consumer co-operatives' attractive dividend schemes.

Contemporary observers saw that the development of chain stores and, particularly, mail-order houses meant the destruction of local isolation. The retailers in the smaller cities and villages felt the competitive impact of the mail-order house, as the retailers in the larger urban centres felt the competition of the department stores and the consumer co-operatives.

The purchasing habits of the rural dwellers of Germany

*Crüger, "Einfluss der Konsumvereine auf die Preisbildung des Kleinhandels" *Schriften des Vereins für Sozialpolitik*, Bd.87, 1900 : 158 claimed that the major surveys of the influence of retailing on prices were seriously underestimating the (inflationary) effects of the independent retailers because these enquiries tended to restrict themselves to cash dealing, not to credit sales. Cf. Bayerdörffer, "Einfluss des Detailhandels auf die Preise" *Schriften des Vereins für Sozialpolitik*, Bd.37, 1888 : 1-139; van der Borght, *Einfluss des Zwischenhandels. Schriften des Vereins für Sozialpolitik*, Bd.36, 1888 *passim*.

changed dramatically towards the end of the nineteenth century. Local supplies of all sorts had been previously purchased by the local small merchant on his annual or semi-annual excursions to the relatively inaccessible and distant urban centre, market, or fair. His customers had had to be satisfied with the styles in clothing which he had selected. Because of the development of the mail-order house, with colourful catalogues full of the very latest fashions, there was a dramatic change. The advantages of such new developments for the consumer were as obvious as were the disadvantages of the developments for the local retailer. The surveys of the retailers were full of examples of complaints about the competition of the mail-order houses.[86]

There is no documentation on the effect of concentration, as represented by the department and chain stores, on retail prices. It appears likely, however, that such enterprises exercised an impact upon the independent retailer similar to that of the co-operative.[87] Partially because of the dearth of solid statistical data, it is very difficult to disentangle the political elements surrounding the impact of concentration on retail prices. At the time, the theory was widely circulated, both by independent economists and by the interest groups of the large concerns, that because the larger concerns bought in great bulk, they could offer lower prices. The validity of the economics behind such truisms may hardly be questioned.[88] Few would question the so-called "economies of scale" thesis. It is also easy to see that the operating principle of the large firm is "large turnover and small mark-up". Unfortunately, however, none of these theories provided a convincing rebuttal to the charges of the small retailer of the time that concentration (in the form of the department store) led only to greater profits and that certain articles were marked down and publicized to attract the unwitting customer who subsequently paid higher prices for other purchases. Whether the consumer benefited from increasing competition in the form of lower prices more than he might have in the absence of concentrated competition remains an unanswerable question.[89] Even the surveys of the retailers reveal remarkable and irreconcilable differences.[90] It was widely held that the consumer was reaping the benefits. The independent retailers had to suffer, therefore, under the pressure of public opinion which accused them of responsibility for inflationary pressures. The destructive capacity of the theory that concentration in retailing led to lower prices for the consumer extended beyond the level of local competitive activities. To a remarkable degree, that theory coloured the political struggle of the independent retailers for protective legislation.[91]

The militancy exhibited by the independent retailers in their demands for special taxation on the consumer co-operatives and the department stores, as well as their demands for stricter laws on "unfair competition", suggests that the competitive position of the independent retailers was being undermined very seriously. The primary motive behind the special taxes was, after all, to force prices up in the establishments of competitors, in order to decrease obvious price disparities and to curtail misleading advertising, behind which (according to the independent retailers) the large firms charged higher prices and made greater profits, while they paraded as the consumers' friend.

The Retailer and his Employees: Between Economic Conflict and Political Alliance

Of all the economic problems which came to threaten the existence of independent retailers in Germany between 1890 and 1914, the problem presented by the pressure of the salaried or white-collar worker is the most often overlooked. Even the early surveys of the retailers themselves tended to ignore the problems presented to the independent retailer both because of the growing militancy of his employees and because of the economic burden involved in shouldering the new social legislation which came to be passed for the protection of the salaried employee. It was the independent as employer who came to be faced with the economic implications of the very first "domestic political success of the 'new course' ", a law (proposed initially on 12 April 1890 by Prussia to the *Bundesrat)* which mentioned the need, for example, to restrict Sunday work in retail trade to five hours.[92] In the course of the next 24 years, many additional laws were to be passed in the interest of employee welfare.

This new legislation, together with the organization and activity of white-collar interest groups, carried important implications for the relationship between employer and employee. Between 1890 and 1914, this relationship became subject to considerable pressure. Real economic conflicts developed and were reinforced on both sides by the development of interest groups.

The great majority of the white-collar organizations developed after 1890. Of the three largest such organizations which existed at the end of 1910, with a total membership between them of 315,233 (out of a grand total of 534,109 in 16 different such organizations), the largest had not even existed until 1893, while the other two shared but 56,067 members in 1890.[93] Although these organizations varied greatly in aims, methods, and outlook, they expressly sought, with one relatively minor exception,* to retain the confidence of the employers. These white-collar organizations sought to satisfy their members' demands for reform while, at the same time, attempting to narrow the gap between employer and employee by holding out the possibility of political alliance to the employer organizations. The white-collar organizations sought to avoid a complete break with the employers, primarily because such a break was anathema to the employees' estimation of themselves as members of the "new" *Mittelstand*. Even if it were true that the expectations of the "new" *Mittelstand* were not being borne out, an open break with the employers would too clearly conform to the Social Democrat's contention that the salaried employees were becoming proletarianized. The little success enjoyed by the Social Democratic-oriented employees' organization (the ZHGD)[94] reflected the general desire of white-collar workers to distinguish themselves from the working class. When the claims of

*The exception was the ZHGD (which had 12,380 members in late 1910). This organization was linked with the *Generalkommission der freien Gewerkschaften*. The ZHGD attracted the lower paid personnel and women. It considered that "in the present social order, employees in retail establishments belong to the class of wage-earners . . . and can achieve better working conditions only by way of a trade-union-like struggle against the interests of the owners". See Lange, *Handlungsgehilfenbewegung und Sozialpolitik*, 1908 : 11. Cf. the lead article in *Handlungsgehilfen Blatt*. 5.9.1897.

the white-collar workers were not borne out, the expectations were not lowered or reduced, but emphasized. One writer has maintained that the more the social-economic differences between the white-collar workers and manual workers diminished, the more emphatically did the white-collar workers stress the ideological differences.[95]

It was easier for some employee organizations than others to form alliances with, or at least to gain the co-operation of other similar employee organizations. The employee organization *Verband katholischer kaufmännischer Vereinigungen* (Essen) reported that in early 1908, 43.8 per cent of the membership (or 4,223 members) were independents.[96] The high percentage of independents, they claimed, formed part of the difficulty in uniting with other white-collar organizations. But even the much larger white-collar organizations* were always conscious of the special relationship which they wished to preserve between employer and employee.[97] This factor alone did not form a sufficient basis for national unity of white-collar organizations. There were repeated efforts, particularly by the DHV, not only to broaden the area of agreement between the various competing organizations, but also to achieve nationwide unification. From early 1908 (although there were earlier attempts as well), meetings were held with other unions. No basis for unification could be found, however, apart from general social-political *desiderata*, because there was a general feeling that each organization had a greatly different character.[98]

The political activities of the various white-collar organizations reflected their desire to work as closely as possible with the interest groups of the independent retailers. For example, the white-collar organizations frequently phrased their own petitions to the *Reichstag* in such a manner as to appear to be working in alliance with the employers. The thirteenth annual meeting of the VDH on 19 August 1894 linked one of their own pet demands in a petition to the *Reichstag* with one of the employers, in order to appear to be working, as they said, "in co-operation *(Gemeinschaft)* with the employers".[99] In

*In 1910, the three largest white-collar organizations were the DHV with 120,289 members, the VfH von 1858 with 102,633 members, and the VDH with 92,301 members.

the same brochure in which it rejected the charges of the retailers that eight o'clock closing would lead to the destruction
of many retailing firms, the DHV spoke of the "department
stores and mail-order houses" as the "natural enemies" of the
employees.[100] The *Verband deutscher kaufmännischer Vereine*
claimed at its meeting at the end of 1904 that it did not hold
employers responsible for the (at times) long working hours
and bad conditions. They expressed the belief that there was
much employer-employee solidarity still to be found in retailing, and they claimed that that was because "retailing has
remained free from the class struggle".[101]

The development of the large and powerful white-collar
organizations was of great importance to employers. Their
creation was certainly as important to the eventual creation
of the retail trader interest groups as the creation of the
department store, consumer co-operative, or travelling salesmen's interest groups.* The reaction of the various retail
trader interest groups to the political activities of the white-
collar organizations is investigated below. In general, it may
be said that the employers were anxious to maintain co-operation with their employees as long, at least, as the measures
required to placate the employees did not cost too much.**
If the creation of the white-collar organizations was not a
result of the spread of the "class struggle", the creation of
these organizations most certainly signified a great change in
the consciousness of the white-collar workers. These organizations were, in part, responsible for the pressure behind the
enactment of various welfare measures passed for the protection of the white-collar workers between 1890 and 1914.[102]
These measures exerted a considerable economic pressure
upon the retailer as employer.

*Wein, *Verbandsbildung*, 1968 : 104 ff. suggests the importance of the
interest groups of the department store owners and of those of other
large concerns *(Grossbetriebe)* to the politics of the independent retailers.
He completely neglects the role of the white-collar organizations.

**It is generally accepted (especially in the works of Kocka) that the
larger industrial concerns, such as Siemens, were prepared to accept the
demands of the employees in return for assurance of the latter's loyalty.
Kocka contends that only the smaller firms opposed the special
insurance schemes of 1911.

The surveys of the *Reichskommission*[103] which was set up in 1892 to investigate the hours and conditions of work in trading firms with open selling outlets reported its findings in the autumn of that year. Of the 8,235 completed forms returned by both employers and employees from all sizes of cities all over Germany, some 61.4 per cent of the "personnel" were still being provided with full room and board by the employer. Some 32.5 per cent of the employees were provided with neither room nor board. The hours tended to be longer in those establishments where room and board was provided as part of the wage than in those where none was provided. The hours of work for all employees were long. Some 81.3 per cent of the full employees *(Gehilfen)* and 85.22 per cent of the apprentices *(Lehrlinge)* worked more than 12 hours per day. Almost half (44.6 per cent of the *Gehilfen* and 49.72 per cent of the *Lehrlinge)* worked more than 14 hours a day. All employees might expect to work Sundays and most holidays.[104]

It may be said that a patriarchal relationship persisted between employer and employee. This patriarchal, even authoritarian, relationship existed even in the more modern retail establishments, such as Wertheim's department store in Berlin where many hundreds of employees were engaged.[105] The employer benefited from the employees' conception of the tasks of the full employee *(Gehilfe)*; the latter did not see himself as an employee, but as a helper, essentially involved in the task of learning his trade. This service was seen as a necessary first step, but a definite step *(Durchgangsstadium)* toward the establishment of the "helper's" own independent business. The entire relationship to the employer, both of apprentices and of full employees, was centred around this future possibility. As long as the possibility and the likelihood of achieving independence continued to exist, the intolerable remained tolerable. The individual and collective demands of employees remained unspoken. It has been recognized that the authoritarian position of the employer was easy to reinforce. Because so many employees were living on the premises for very long periods each day, the employer had simply "to hang the house key a little higher" in order to keep his employees in line.[106] The position of the employer and his relationship to his employees was assured only so long as his employees continued to believe that independence was really attainable or that the social compensations outweighed the risk of upsetting the employer. By the turn of the century, both beliefs began to be questioned. Lederer recognized the importance of this development when he wrote in 1912:

> Whether the employees will be able to exist as members of the Mittelstand in the future depends upon the relationship of the employee to the employer, upon the possibility of raising salaries accordingly. The resistance which employees have shown against the tendencies towards proletarianization are most pronounced in the transformation in the relationship of employee to employer. The position of employee within a firm no longer represents a temporary stage in the process of establishing his own business. The changing employee employer relationship has, therefore, become the central concern of all employee politics.[107]

As independence became a vanishing dream, the employees came to view everyday hardships in a new light. The development of employee organizations represented their determination to mitigate as many of these hardships as possible without embarking upon a proletarian-like struggle against their employers. The majority (32 out of 53) of all the white-collar organizations, even as late as 1913, remained open to the self-employed and did not, therefore, fall into the same category as the manual workers' trade unions.[108] Protests began to be heard against the various kinds of abuses. The apprentices and women were becoming widely used to keep wages down and to reduce the number of full employees required. The survey of 1892 had shown that the training period of male apprentices had lasted two years or less in only 3.9 per cent of the businesses; in 55.6 per cent of the businesses, it had lasted between two and three years, and in 40 per cent, more than three years. In spite of this long training period, barely a third of the firms had afforded their trainees the opportunity of attending technical or further educational institutions.[109]

By 1910 the determination of the white-collar organizations had led to a whole series of legislative enactments in support of their welfare. A summary by Lederer of some twelve demands still outstanding among the various organizations in 1910 indicates the extent to which these organizations were in the process of transformation from organizations of "new" *Mittelstand* to trade-union-like organizations. The following list represents primarily the demands upon which most of the white-collar organizations could agree and does not represent the optimal demands of either the right-wing oriented DHV or the left-wing oriented ZHGD. Lederer lists the following demands:

1. Extension of Sunday rest.
2. National legislative regulation of eight o'clock closing.
3. Regulation of the hours of work and its extension to clerks in wholesaling.
4. Introduction of a trade inspectorate.
5. Incorporation of the courts pertaining to trade *(Kaufmannsgerichte)* with the industrial courts *(Gewerbegerichte)*.
6. Legally regulated, paid vacation. Legally recognized duty of the employer to pay the salary of the employee up to six weeks during military exercises.
7. Restriction and eventual abandonment of the competition clause (the *Konkurrenzklausal* which dictated the period which an employee had to wait after he left a firm before he might set up his own establishment).
8. Introduction of a Chamber for employees alone (and not simply the creation of employee committees within Chambers of Commerce).
9. Extension of instruction at technical schools, particularly compulsory training schools with state-supervised teaching.
10. Introduction of a time-scale for apprentices with a minimum period of training (three years).
11. Extension of group sickness and accident insurance to employees in trade establishments.
12. Legal regulation of pensions and life insurance for employees in private concerns.[110]

In October 1909 a retailers' newspaper, *Der Detaillist,* had drawn up an even longer list, based on the various demands emerging from meetings of the more important white-collar organizations during the previous summer. There was very much an alarmist tone to the long article, for the writer seemed to consider it outrageous that white-collar workers should be demanding such things as the abolition of all Sunday work, obligatory eight o'clock closing, minimum hours of rest, paid vacations, minimum wages, pensions, and even the right to form unions. The article, representative in so many ways of the views of the retailers towards these new developments, concluded that "for a long time to come, the social-political questions will be the most important subject for independent retailers".[111]

Conclusion

Changes in the retail market exercised profound pressure on the retailer. However, the kinds of changes in the retail market, almost by definition, were far beyond the control of the retailer. There was precious little scope for political activity to achieve much against developing industrialization, population growth, or trade cycle fluctuations. It may be said that—at any rate prior to 1914—these factors rarely posed a direct threat to the continued existence of the independent retailer. When the threat to the existence of the independent retailer was far more direct, when it was linked with the development of consumer co-operatives and large concerns in general, there existed the possibility that political activity might well win concessions from government. The government was in a position to help the retailers and, thereby, to make a bid for their support by opposing the new appearances in retailing which were directly threatening the independent retailer. The political activities of the retailers were not, therefore, condemned from the outset to a search for the narrow, almost vocational, reform to which the political activities of the artisans were directed. To help the artisan would be to oppose industry.[112] The relationship of retail trade to the process of industrialization was very different from that of artisanship.

3

The Political Reaction of Retail Traders to their Social and Economic Problems 1890-1914

The role of interest groups in politics in Bismarckian and post-Bismarckian Germany has been reviewed in some detail by a number of historians. A wide variety of these interest groups have been studied within the context of other elements of the political system. Their significance has been evaluated in terms not only of their own activities, but also of the reaction which these activities have produced on men in power. Almost without exception, however, these interest groups have been viewed either as the wielders of power or, more frequently, as the objects of influence. Only rarely have interest groups and their activities been studied with the view of discovering what they reveal about the social, economic, and political views of their members. It has been partly because of these failures that few attempts have been made to relate the creation of interest groups to the impact of the rapid social, economic, and political changes which characterized pre-war Germany.[1] Some suggestions have been made about the concrete economic interests represented by the agrarians' BdL or the industrialists' CDI. However, even the studies of these organizations have tended to concentrate upon the political pre-conditions necessary for the creation of these well-known interest groups, rather than to assess the social-economic pre-conditions.[2] The very prominence of an organization such as the BdL stems from its involvement in party politics in general and in specific tariff issues in particular.[3] Such interest groups have been studied, therefore, not because of what they may reveal about the society and economy, but because of the light which they may throw upon political decision-making. The study of interest groups, therefore, has become an important aspect of political history.[4]

The interest groups of the retailers, while aimed directly or indirectly at influencing the decision-making process, were, at the same time, articulating the kinds of problems besetting the retailers. These organizations were themselves products of discontent and were designed to overcome that discontent in various ways. Although the interest groups of the retailers neither always worked in concert (in fact, they were frequently in conflict with one another) nor propagated a closely defined, explicit ideology, these organizations spoke the language of adaptation to the existing society. The demands of the retailers for state-help, no less than their own self-help endeavours, whether or not they were consciously designed with a view to adaptation to the existing society, worked in the direction of adaptation rather than that of revolution. An examination of the interest groups of the retailers, with the aim of revealing the extent to which these interest groups related to the social-economic change of the period, may, therefore, add another dimension to the understanding of the interrelation of politics, political mobilization, and rapid social-economic change.

Political Organization and Activity:
The Typology in Retail Trade

The political reactions of retailers represented by their interest groups were extraordinarily varied. At certain points, these political reactions overlapped and, not infrequently, even conflicted. For the purposes of analysis, these political activities are divided into two broad categories.

(1) Category One is limited to organizations in which activity extended to something less than direct involvement in party politics. In so far as there was any attempt to influence government decision-making, the political activity of organizations in this category was almost entirely restricted to the direct appeal approach. Within this category, there are three main sub-categories. First, there were the technical

(Fach)* organizations. These organizations tended to confine themselves to specific types of self-help. Retailer-purchasing co-operatives *(Einkaufsgenossenschaften)*, for example, belong to this sub-category. These co-operatives were established by retailers to buy in bulk and to distribute wares to members. They were designed both to minimize the need for retailers to rely upon wholesalers and to improve the competitive position of retailers in relation to large concerns which followed the principle of bulk-buying. Within the technical organizations, the relation of members to the organization, while initially voluntary, tended to be very close. There was a tendency toward formalized relationships because so many of these co-operative ventures among employers (like those among consumers) had a "business" character about them. Commitments, once made, had to be upheld. A second sub-category includes organizations which were both self-help organizations and protective organizations (or *Schutzverbände)*. The discount savings unions (or *Rabattsparvereine)* are examples of such organizations. These organizations were characterized by voluntary membership. Within them, the relationship of member to organization was not nearly so formally regulated as that within *Einkaufsgenossenschaften*. The individual member was committed to following the statutes of the organizations. Moral suasion, rather than the threat of legal action, provided the incentive for close adherence to the statutes. In the present chapter, these two sub-categories of the first major category of organizations in retail trade are examined. The third sub-category, the *Schutzverbände* proper, because of their multiplicity and heterogeneity, require a separate chapter.

Schutzverbände included such organizations as the legally constituted *(öffentlich-rechtlich) Detaillistenkammer* and the specific committees demanded by retailers in the already existing Chambers of Commerce *(Kleinhandelsausschüsse)*, as well as the more radical *Schutzgemeinschaften für Handel und Gewerbe* and *Vereine gegen Unwesen im Handel und*

---

*Schweitzer, *Big Business in the Thrid Reich*, 1964 : 138 translates *Fachverbände* from German into English as "occupational corporatives". This translation should be understood within the context of "corporativism" (or *berufsständische Wirtschaftsordnung)*.

Gewerbe. These latter organizations, as their names imply, had, as their chief aim, the protection of their members. Membership in these organizations was almost entirely voluntary. The relation of member to organization was, therefore, more flexible than that within the organizations of the other two sub-categories already mentioned. At the same time, the *Schutzverbände* were by far the most politically active of all the organizations included within the first major category. In a very real sense, these *Schutzverbände* were among the most active organizations in the political endeavours of the retailers. They, almost more than any of the other organizations of the retailers, represented the response of the retailers to the imperative "organize or perish".[5]

(2) Category Two is limited to those organizations which were determined to go beyond strict party-political neutrality. This category is divided into two sub-categories. The first sub-category includes organizations within the traditional party-political context. Attempts by various political parties to win the support of retailers and the relation of retailers to the political parties is examined. The political parties sought to win the support not only of the individual retailers, but of their organizations, particularly the *Schutzverbände.* The avowed party-political and religious neutrality of the latter organizations notwithstanding, they frequently played an active part in party-political struggles at all levels. (This activity was most consistent in its anti-Socialist orientation.) The relationship of member to organization within the organizations of this category was also voluntary and far more subject to local variation and colouring than that within the organizations of the first major category.

The second sub-category includes retailers' activities within what is usually termed the *Mittelstandsbewegung.* Within the *Mittelstandsbewegung,* the activities of the retailers extended beyond party-political neutrality to a more radical extent. Some of these activities were designed to create retailers' own party-political forces. Although voluntary participation was the rule, an element of greater commitment and militancy was involved. Within this group, there were efforts by some retailers not only to create party-political influence, but also to go beyond the party-political sphere. There were, for example, attempts to circumvent the increasingly powerless political parties in order to appeal for legislation from governments who were in search of support in the fight against rising Social Democracy. At times, these latter activities were deliberately restricted to retailers. At other times, the program of these organizations was broadened so that alliances might be formed with other groups within what the retailers considered the *Mittelstand*.[6]

Both major categories of organizations and activities existed simultaneously and interacted not only with other elements in the political system, but with each other. The particular typology which has been presented has the advantage of providing an organized guide to the extremely heterogeneous nature of the political organizations and activities of the retailers. Other attempts which have been made to construct such a typology tend to ignore the political element involved in the creation of all forms of interest groups, whether these organizations participated in party politics or not. Josef Wein, for example, designs his typology of interest groups in retail trade according to whether they were (1) *ständisch-traditional,* or (2) *sachlich-rational.*[7] This typology is unsatisfactory for the purposes of the present study because it largely omits any "political" element. The political orientation of the interest group activities of department store owners was no different from that of the retailers when either sought government policies in their interest. Yet Wein's typology places the retailers' *Schutzverbände* in his (1) and the department store owners' interest groups in his (2).[8]

Once the political element is introduced, a scale of growing radicalization or militancy may be introduced into the typology. The organizations and activities placed in Category (2) in the present study did represent something of a progression or, at least, an extension of the political mobilization of the retailers. Organizations in the second category not only sought more radical measures than those in the first category, but, by definition, were more aggressive in pursuit of such measures. In so far as possible, the typology does take into account the factor of time, but some organizations in the first subsection of the first category (such as the *Einkaufsgenossenschaften)* came into prominence later than the *Mittelstands-*

bewegung. The typology may be regarded, therefore, as a spectrum. When the various elements of the spectrum come into prominence and when they fade into the background is made apparent in the course of the discussion.

Technical Organizations (Fachverbände) in Retail Trade

The technical organizations in retail trade were characterized by their avowal of party-political neutrality and their reliance upon self-help, as opposed to state-help, in the battle for the economic survival of the retailers. These organizations embraced virtually all branches of retailing in Germany prior to 1914. They existed in all parts of the country and were active at the local, state, and national levels. Although they had existed in certain forms from the early nineteenth century, they came into greater prominence as the century progressed. The peak of their organizational activity was reached during the war and in the immediate post-war period. In spite of their avowed intention to avoid even any discussion of party-political or religious matters, it would be a mistake to assume that they remained completely faithful to their well-publicized statutes. It was consistent with the alleged "technical" character of these organizations that much lip-service was paid to their non-political nature. There were at least two fundamental reasons underlying the desires of these organizations to declare their non-political character. First of all, they did not want to alienate fellow retailers whose "technical" (economic) problems they shared. Second, they wished to offer their support to any party or public authority willing to give assistance. These organizations sought to achieve their aims in at least three quite distinct ways.

Technical Organizations: Methods

The first method used by the technical organizations was that of self-help. This method was also the predominant and most characteristic approach of these organizations to the economic problems of the retailers. Although all branches of retail trade had developed some form of technical organizations, the grocers *(Kolonialwarenhändler)* were, with traders in various branches of textiles, among the most highly organized. It was also the grocers who were most directly affected by the rise of the consumer co-operatives, and the textile traders by the department and chain stores.[9] It would, how-ever, be an over-simplification to suggest that all grocers or all dealers in textiles shared similar political views, or even similar views on their economic problems. Nevertheless, a leading article in the Hamburg press in 1901[10] was certainly repre-sentative of a good deal of the thinking within the technical organizations. To the question "How are our retailers to be helped?", the article postulated that the state could not be relied upon for such help. *Einkaufsgenossenschaften,* credit societies, insurance societies, schools for further education, and all other forms of working together could provide real help for the retailers. There was even the suggestion that some of the techniques of the hated department store might be worth emulating. Similar resolutions were passed at the gen-eral meeting of the *Verband deutscher Eisenwaren-Händler,* held earlier in the same year.[11] The implication was that retailers were their own worst enemies and, as such, were at war with each other. The real problems at the day-to-day level could be solved only in coming together in a spirit of co-operation.[12] The whole range of self-help activities which were suggested by the technical organizations were designed to solve or at least to alleviate these day-to-day problems. Many of these suggestions were in no way unique to the tech-nical organizations in retail trade.[13]

Although there are a few examples of *Einkaufsgenossen-schaften* which were formed in the late 1880s, the vast major-ity of them were established well after 1890. The first *Einkaufsgenossenschaft* in textiles began in Bamburg in 1886. However, in textiles, as in most other branches of retail trade, *Einkaufsgenossenschaften* developed mainly after 1900.[14] An *Einkaufsgenossenschaft* first appeared in the grocery trade in Frankfurt a.d.O. in 1888. By 1893 there were some 30 *Einkaufsgenossenschaften* spread throughout the country and in 1906, as many as 208.[15] These societies were located pri-marily in Saxony (also a centre of consumer co-operatives). They existed in Rhineland-Westphalia and in North Germany. There were only three in all of Bavaria.[16] In the groceries branch, there appears to have been a direct correlation be-tween the existence of consumer co-operatives and the sub-sequent establishment of *Einkaufsgenossenschaften.* It may be concluded that retailers in areas most adversely affected by consumer co-operatives displayed the greater propensity to develop their own form of self-help as a means of economic survival.[17]

Similar developments occurred in other branches of retailling. On 14 April 1904 the *Nord und Süd Einkaufsgenossenschaften für Luxuswaren, Porzellen, Steingut, Glas, Beleuchtungsartikel und Küchengeräte e.G.m.b.H.* (headquarters, Eisenach) was formed in the face of much opposition within the parent organization. It sought openly to win concessions from factory owners who had previously also belonged to one of the common organizations (the *Verband deutscher Porzellen-, Steingut- und Glaswarenhändler, Grossisten und Detaillisten e.V.,* founded in Berlin in 1900).[18] The *Einkaufsvereinigung Deutscher Schuwarenhändler e.G.m.b.H.* (founded in Erfurt, 1903) was also created in the face of similar opposition, but was the result of the conscious effort to combat the competition offered to independent retailers by producers' retail stores, such as those of Salamander, Mercedes, and Bata.[19]

The theme running through all the activities of technical organizations, and of the *Einkaufsgenossenschaften* in particular (to which these technical organizations had given birth), was, as one writer put it, "Only by coming together can anything be achieved."[20] The idea of joining together for protection, rather than engaging in competitive battles which were costly to all parties, was an idea that developed in retail trade in Germany only after 1890, and even then only to a limited extent. The success of the technical organizations, like the success of all the other organizations in retailing, was circumscribed by the degree to which that idea found fertile soil.

Some idea of what was achieved by the *Einkaufsgenossenschaften* may be gained from Dr. August Engel's account of the social and economic problems of the retailers which was written under the auspices of the *Volksverein für das katholische Deutschland.* In 1906, he claimed (in a report published in 1907) that *Einkaufsgenossenschaften* represented "one of the most significant weapons of a co-operative nature in the struggle for existence of retail trade".[21] He cited a number of examples, primarily from the groceries branch of retailing where progress in this direction was most evident. The *Einkaufsverein der Kolonialwarenhändler zu Hannover* (founded, 1900) had, in 1903, a capital of 17,268 Mk. but a yearly turnover of 700,000 Mk. Even more impressive results were reported from similar organizations in Bremen, Oldenburg, and Berlin. On 20 January 1904, the *Zentraleinkaufsgesellschaft deutscher Kolonialwarenhändler G.m.b.H.* was founded in Hamburg. The establishment of this organization was an obvious attempt by the retailers to set up large central organizations for buying similar to those which had been set up by the consumer co-operatives. It remained for the future for numerous local *Einkaufsgenossenschaften* to be founded by retailers, dealing in turn with the national or regional organizations. From 1 January 1905 an additional *Grosseinkaufsvereinigung* was founded in Mannheim. In 1906 two others were founded, one in Munich and the other in Stuttgart. In 1907 a further attempt was made to found a national organization. On 21 October the *Verband deutscher kaufmännischer Genossenschaften . e. V.* (later shortened to the now famous *Edeka*) came into being in Leipzig. By 1913 this organization embraced some 6,400 grocers in 122 member organizations.[22]

The chief problem faced by the retailers' organization in Hamburg was the attempt by various retailers to purchase from the *Zentral* as individuals. As the *Zentral* became flooded with small orders, the over-head costs per purchase were driven too high. In the textile branch, the problem of keeping overhead costs within reason in their *Einkaufsgenossenschaften* appears to have been dealt with more effectively. The *Verband deutscher Kurzwaren- und Posamentengeschäfte G.m.b.H.,* founded in 1893 (headquarters Berlin) established an *Einkaufsgenossenschaft* almost immediately. The turnover increased from 152,000 Mk. in 1893 to some 1,300,000 Mk. in 1898.

In all these organizations, membership appears to have remained rather small. The *Verband deutscher Kurzwaren- und Posamentengeschäfte,* for example, had a membership of 67 in 1893. The membership had increased to only 170 by 1903. The impression which emerges from Dr. Engel's report is that the idea of co-operative purchasing among retailers did not achieve widespread support in Germany in the period prior to the war. Even the largest organizations, such as *Edeka,* acquired only a small following.[23] Dr. Engel complained that this aspect of self-help in retailing, although capable of accomplishing so much, was advancing (in 1906) far too slowly. He was sure that all organizations in retailing had a duty to their fellows to develop the *Einkaufsgenossenschaften* further.[24] Yet only five years earlier another Catholic organization had included *Einkaufsgenossenschaften* with all other forms of co-operation (such as consumer co-operation) under the same heading. From the annual meeting of the *Verband katholischer kaufmännischer Vereinigungen Deutschlands* of 1901 came the view that it was wrong to help one class *(Stand)* at the expense of another. An *Einkaufsgenossenschaft* would hurt wholesalers (who, it was alleged, performed an invaluable economic function) without even guaranteeing that it would help the retailers.[25] The available evidence indicates that retailers in general viewed the *Einkaufsgenossenschaften* with some skepticism.

The second method used by the technical organizations was based on the belief that once retailers were solidly organized, even in a wholly "non-political" or technical organization, they could present a bargaining force with which factory-owners, if not governments and political parties, would have to contend. The *Verband deutscher Eisenwarenhändler* (in 1912, membership 3,200) suggested in April 1898 a system of boycotts against factories which sold to consumer co-operatives and department stores. The factories were to be sent forms in which they were to agree to stop further deliveries to such outlets or suffer the penalty of a collective boycott by all the remaining retailers.[26] The suggestion of boycott was by no means unique to the ironmongers.[27] It is clear that a great deal of group solidarity among retailers would have to be present in order for a boycott to be really effective. Group solidarity would prevent one retailer from taking advantage of a competitor involved in a struggle with a factory. However, boycotts themselves were high on the list of aversions of the *Mittelstand* in Germany. At various times and places, the retailers united with artisans specifically to fight boycotts organized by the SPD or trade unions.[28] The very aversion to boycotts among retailers and the association of boycott with the working classes and the "powers of Revolution", made the widespread acceptance of the weapon of the boycott by retailers unlikely.[29]

Far more congenial to the retailers were attempts to deal with factory owners not as enemies, but as allies. The *Verband deutscher Detailgeschäfte der Textilindustrie* made repeated attempts to reach agreement with factory owners, agreements, as one newspaper report put it, "favourable to both parties"[30] in late 1907 and early 1908.[31] These attempts as well as similar endeavours by other organizations, had only limited success. The potential threat of an agreement between independent retailers and factory owners, however, was sufficient to induce both wholesalers in general and the *Verband deutscher Waren- und Kaufhäuser* in particular to come to more amicable arrangements with independent retailers. It has been suggested that any meetings which took place between the department store owners' interest group and the *Verband deutscher Detailgeschäfte der Textilindustrie* might be explained by the representation in the latter organization of larger and more powerful specialty shops.[32] Nevertheless, the very general agreements reached between the two organizations at the end of 1908 were broken before the end of 1909.[33]

The third and final method that characterized the activities of the technical organizations was participation in the political sphere either indirectly or, in extremely unusual cases, even directly. Direct participation was so unusual, in fact, as to be unique. The *Verein der Kolonialwarenhändler von 1872* in Hamburg (which had "more than" 1,200 members in 1912) was strong enough to put candidates forward in elections to the local *Bürgerschaft.*[34] This political activity should be understood within the context of the highly privileged position of the house owners in the *Bürgerschaft.* It was not a reflection of radical tendencies within a technical organization of noted conservatism.[35]

It was more usual for the technical organizations to seek to achieve their aims outside the party-political arena. There existed a whole range of possibilities. They could work with the numerous and more politically active *Schutzverbände,* for example. The relationship between these two types of organizations was often very close, although in general the

Schutzverbände regarded the technical organizations as their more conservative allies, even their foster children.[36] In a very real sense, the technical organizations had developed out of the *Schutzverbände.* A most obvious example was the *Verein Berliner Kaufleute der Kolonialwarenbranche* which had grown out of the more general *Schutzverband* (the *Verband Berliner Kaufleute)* in 1883.[37] Most technical organizations in retail trade belonged to the leading *Schutzverbände.* In 1903 the *Zentralverband deutscher Kaufleute und Gewerbetreibender* (with 17,000 members) counted fifty different associations among its members, in addition to 10 different regional branches. Although *Schutzverbände* made up the majority of the membership of the *Zentralverband,* many technical organizations were also members. This tendency was also reflected in the regional organizations.[38] Acting alone, or in conjunction with others who dealt in the same goods, the technical organizations exerted considerable pressure not only upon the *Schutzverbände,* to which they might still belong, but also upon factory owners and various political institutions. The larger the technical organizations were, the more pressure they could exert. However, the technical organizations were by no means always in conflict with the *Schutzverbände.* National, as well as regional and local technical organizations, often supplemented the pressure applied to public bodies (such as the Chambers of Commerce) by the *Schutzverbände.*[39]

The political activities of the technical organizations consisted largely of efforts to enforce already existing legislation. Their *raison d'être* was itself at least a partial assertion that little was to be expected from the political activities in the party-political sphere. On the other hand, the activities of the technical organizations (particularly setting up *Einkaufsgenossenschaften),* although far more mundane than taking a direct hand in party-political activity, offered real hope to the retailer in his struggle for economic survival. The demands for legislation came from organizations which were convinced of the necessity of state-help. State-help, they believed, would create an environment in which self-help activities could have some hope of success. Organizations in the other two subcategories of retailers' organizations (such as the *Rabattsparvereine* and the *Schutzverbände)* justified their more state-help oriented policies as necessary complements to their own self-help endeavours.

Rabattsparvereine

The *Rabattsparvereine,* or discount saving unions, formed a further, quite distinct, series of retail trader organizations which developed in Germany at the very end of the nineteenth century. It was only after the "great depression" from 1873 to 1896 that *Rabattsparvereine* began in Germany. Those writers who are determined to link the political mobilization of retailers to this "depression" find difficulty in accounting for the *Rabattsparvereine.*[40] Retailers belonging to or associated with the *Rabattsparvereine* granted a fixed discount to customers on cash purchases. Although the percentage of discount granted by the organization was subject to variation, it was usually about five per cent. All member firms agreed on the percentage of discount to be granted. This agreement, in particular, was designed to avoid cut-throat competition between retailers in the form of offering greater and greater discounts to customers when the practice was ruinous to all the retailers concerned. The discount was granted in the form of stamps of similar type and value; books of these stamps could be later exchanged by the customer for cash or, much more usually, for goods. To some extent such organizations belong with self-help organizations in retail trade, such as *Einkaufsgenossenschaften.*

However, from its founding in Leipzig, on 3 August 1902, the national organization, *Verband der Rabattsparvereine Deutschlands,* under its extremely active general secretary, Heinrich Beythien, moved in the direction of direct and open participation in party-political struggles.* At the eighth annual meeting, held in Freiburg from 24 to 27 July 1910, he claimed that it had not always been his intention that the organization should take up conventional politics. His own faith in self-help however, had not been entirely sustained. As he then admitted,

---

*In 1917/1918, Beythien became one of the most important *"Mittelstand* functionaries of the *Deutsche Vaterlandspartei".* See Stegmann, *Erben Bismarcks,* 1970 : 44. Beythien was by no means the only leading member of the *Verband der Rabattsparvereine Deutschlands* to take a leading part in party-politics, either prior to 1914 or later.

*besides self-help, however, the state must intervene. I
admit that in the beginning of our movement I believed
it was perhaps possible to succeed through self-help alone.
But the more involved one is in the struggle for existence
of our class, the more one recognizes that the weapons
are unequal.*[41]

The development of *Rabattsparvereine* does not represent a
stage in a progression (or regression) by the retailers from advocacy of organizations in favour of state-help to those in favour of self-help. It does not represent a transitional stage in
retailer political activity. These organizations believed in self-
help in very specific terms, but they were no less specific on
the subject of party politics. Beythien, for example, who became the effective director of the *Rabattsparvereine Deutschlands,* was at the same time (from 1905) secretary of the
overtly political *Mittelstand* organization, the *Deutsche
Mittelstandsvereinigung.*

Although some of the leading *Schutzverbände* were very
much opposed to the *Rabattsparvereine,* there is no evidence
that the leading national *Schutzverband* of the retailers, the
Zentralverband deutscher Kaufleute und Gewerbetreibender—
which in early 1914 had approximately 30,000 members, 13
branches, and 250 associated organizations[42]—was opposed to
the *Rabattsparvereine.*[43] The *Rabattsparvereine Deutschlands*
had after all been founded under the auspices of the *Zentralverband.* Moreover, the *Zentralverband* remained the leading
retail organization in favour of the *Rabattsparvereine.*[44] Beythien, writing in 1913, listed numerous examples of *Rabattsparvereine* which continued to work with both the *Zentralverband* and the party-political *Reichsdeutscher Mittelstandsverband.*[45] C.A. Nicolaus, member of the executive of the
Rabattsparvereine Deutschlands from the beginning, took a
leading part in the founding of the *Reichsdeutscher Mittelstandsverband.* Although conflicts developed between
Rabattsparvereine and individual *Schutzverbände,* in general,
the activities of both types of organizations complemented
one another. Although the *Verband katholischer kaufmännischer Vereinigungen Deutschlands,* at least in 1901,[46] opposed
the creation of *Rabattsparvereine,* other Catholic spokesmen,
such as Dr. August Engel, praised the *Rabattsparvereine*

*Deutschlands.** He was not the only noteworthy publicist in favour of the further establishment of *Rabattsparvereine.*[47]

Progress in the development of the *Rabattsparvereine* among retailers in Germany was rapid. At the beginning of 1914, Beythien wrote that there were some 503 local organizations associated with the *Rabattsparvereine Deutschlands,* with a total membership of 73,495.[48] At the discussions of 9 June 1914 at the Federal Ministry of the Interior, the *Rabattsparvereine Deutschlands* was by far the largest retailer organization present.[49] This achievement was remarkable, particularly in view of the widespread resistance inspired by the original ideas at the turn of the century.

The First Retailer Rabattsparvereine

The idea of granting discounts in the form of stamps or various kinds of coupons in return for cash purchasing had circulated in Germany in the 1870s and early 1880s. Although this idea accompanied the consumer co-operative movement, it was by no means the exclusive idea of the consumers' movements.[50] Among traders, some such ideas had been briefly introduced in the 1870s and 1880s because such schemes had offered the attractive prospect of cash dealing over credit dealing. At that time, so-called "wild" discount unions, sometimes even organized by private limited liability companies, enjoyed some success in Germany. Even specific retailer *Rabattsparvereine* appeared briefly at the end of the 1870s. However these had largely disappeared by the mid-1880s.

The chief reason for the initial failures of the retail traders' organizations was the inability of retailers to achieve unity. Granting a discount in any form had remained a factor in improving the competitive position of one firm and worsening that of another. Rather than leading to a gradual replacement of the old competitive spirit by one of co-operation based on granting discounts of the same percentage, the old spirit of

*Engel, *Detaillisten-Fragen,* 1907 : 86 ff. Although he favoured the *Verband der Rabattsparvereine Deutschlands,* he was quick to point out that "it appears rather doubtful whether, in the long run, the discount unions are a suitable means to forcefully combat the competition of the consumer co-operatives and other large businesses".

regarding competitors as virtual enemies persisted. Another reason for the failure of these initial organizations also stemmed directly from the persistence, in the retailers' minds at least, of the old spirit of *Händlerstolz*. This pride was summarized by a contemporary: "the consumer came to the trader, not the trader to the consumer and so it ought to remain."[51] Granting a discount, viewed from this perspective, was lowering the dignity of the trader. Because of the great changes which were affecting the retail market and the development of newer forms of retailing, however, it was useless to discuss whether the old conditions "ought" to remain unchanged. Retailers were forced to accept the reality of a transformation in their own relationship to consumers. If facing the economic realities implied living with self-esteem uncomfortably in conflict with the old *Händlerstolz,* economic survival dictated the course to be taken.

The initial stirrings of what was in reality a new movement of the *Rabattsparvereine* began with the founding on 22 November 1898 in Hanover of an organization specifically designed to fight one of the remaining "wild" discount unions. The aims of the organization, as given in its statutes, were to work toward more unity between retailers and to attempt to encourage the public to deal more in cash instead of credit. The statistics of the first business year (1899) reported a membership of 157 and a turnover in their firms of approximately 712,000 Mk. By 1908 there were 1,328 members and a turnover of 12,311,000 Mk.[52] This new organization did not succeed in driving the "wild" discount unions in Hanover out of business. The continued existence of these "wild" unions implied considerable disunity among retailers in an area noted for the political awareness of its retailers. In 1901 there were at least three different types of discount unions in Hanover.[53]

On 15 May 1899 the discount union *Brema* was founded in Bremen. From mid-1895 the *Verein Bremer Ladeninhaber und Gewerbetreibender* had come out very strongly against the encroaching consumer co-operative movement. The various attempts of the *Verein* to diminish cut-throat competition between retailers, the advocacy of greater attempts to win the public to cash dealings, and the suggestion that retailers give a common discount as a means of counteracting the discounts of the consumer co-operatives, all failed. The arrival of a "wild" discount union in Bremen in April 1899 proved to be the necessary "last straw". By 15 May *Brema* was launched. *Brema* proved an immediate success; even after driving the "wild" discount union out of business in Bremen, *Brema* continued to grow from 862 members in 1900 (with a turnover in their firms of 6,068,200 Mk.) to 1,597 members in 1910 (with a turnover of 18,701,400 Mk.).[54] Once the "wild" discount union had been driven out of town, the aim of fighting the consumer co-operative movement, among other aims, reasserted itself and came to characterize the activities of *Brema* much more than those of the Hanover organization. ·*Brema* in turn was to exert considerable influence upon the further development of discount unions throughout Germany. The development of discount unions following the initial successes of the unions in Bremen and Hanover was very rapid.

National and Regional Organizations of the Rabattsparvereine

C.A. Nicolaus, one of the original founders of the Bremen organization suggested the creation of some form of national co-ordinating body or some type of alliance with an already existing organization to unify the activities of local unions. This idea was a logical extension of the unification of retailers at the local level. The meeting of the *Zentralverband deutscher Kaufleute und Gewerbetreibender* on 3 August 1903 in Leipzig provided the opportunity for discussion of such views. This *Zentralverband,* far from being in "direct competition"[55] with the *Rabattsparvereine,* was, as a contemporary wrote, "the single largest retailer organization which was sympathetically disposed towards the idea of organized retail discounts and which itself advocated the founding of retail *Rabattsparvereine. "*[56]

As Beythien later wrote, the original suggestion put forward by Nicolaus hardly envisaged a specific national organization.[57] The intention was simply to work within the already existing *Zentralverband* and to use the annual meetings of that organization as a forum for the exchange of information. There was, in fact, a motion put to the general meeting of the *Zentral-*

verband to come out in open support of the further establishment of *Rabattsparvereine.* Chiefly because of the opposition
of delegates from Hamburg, however, the motion was not
passed. The meeting did declare its support for those individual
groups which favoured the establishment of these unions. It
considered that "granting discounts in the defence against
consumer co-operatives and department stores is unavoidable
in view of the present economic circumstances". It was suggested that individual member organizations adopt this weapon
(Kampfmittel) in their struggle.[58] Eleven of the fourteen associations represented at a separate meeting called by Nicolaus
favoured setting up an independent organization. However,
there was no suggestion of a break with the *Zentralverband.*
These eleven organizations were of the opinion that their interests were sufficiently specific to require a separate organization.[59]

   Certain enemies of the *Verband der Rabattsparvereine
Deutschlands* (who were, at the same time, bitter opponents
of the very idea of granting discounts in any form) later suggested that the leading figures behind the establishment and
administration of the *Rabattsparvereine Deutschlands* were
merely careerists, interested more in perpetuating lofty positions for themselves as administrators than in solving the
economic problems of the retailers. For example, the *Schutzverband,* the *Verein gegen Unwesen im Handel und Gewerbe
e.V.* (Hamburg) claimed that the first category of those
favouring *Rabattsparvereine* were "professional speakers, employees, that is paid enthusiasts . . . supporters and promoters
of everything if there is anything in it for themselves, perhaps
an honorary office or some good position".[60] It has been
suggested that the reason behind the failure of the political
movements of the retailers to achieve unity (and, therefore,
their failure to exert any real influence) can be traced to the
kind of weakness pointed out by the Hamburg *Verein gegen
Unwesen im Handel und Gewerbe.* Max Weber has even maintained that such weaknesses are inherent in all forms of
organizational activity.[61]

   Regardless of the motives of the organizers, the temporary
headquarters of what was to become the new organization of
the *Rabattsparvereine Deutschlands* was established in Bremen.

The organization was formally constituted at its first general meeting held in Magdeburg on 12 July 1903. The national organization (with its permanent headquarters at Hanover) represented some 50 member-unions. By the end of the first business year (June 1904), the member-unions associated with the national organization had grown to 62 with a collective membership of 12,000. These figures increased every year until, at the beginning of 1914, the national organization counted 503 member-unions with a total membership of 73,495.[62]

The first regional organizations within the *Rabattsparvereine Deutschlands* appeared in Saxony in 1905. This first regional branch organization was formally constituted only in 1907. During the next few years others developed in Thuringia, Rhineland-Westphalia, Württemberg, and finally, in Bavaria (on 24 November 1912). According to the newspaper of the national organization, the late development of a regional organization in Bavaria reflected the continuing widespread opposition of retailers in Bavaria to the very idea of discount unions.[63] This opposition was most evident in Munich itself, although, as Beythien pointed out in 1913, much of the opposition of retailers to the establishment of *Rabattsparvereine* came from most of Germany's largest cities.[64] It may be argued that the development of regional organizations within the *Rabattsparvereine Deutschlands* was itself in part symptomatic of the persistence among retailers of an unwillingness to link their fate with that of fellow retailers at the national level. Opposition from within the ranks of the retailers was, however, not directed at the aims of the discount unions, but at their methods.

Rabattsparvereine: Aims and Methods

Very few retailers in pre-war Germany would have based their opposition to the discount unions on disagreement with the avowed aims of these unions. According to the original statutes, there were six main aims:

1)   To induce cash payment and to fight against the credit system *(Borgsystem)* in retailing.

2)   To unify the discount granted and, thereby, to fight

against all forms of misuses of the discount,
3)   To fight against all forms of "unfair competition" in retail trade,
4)   To fight against the competition of consumer co-operatives, civil servant co-operatives, and department stores,
5)   To recruit a definite group of steady customers.
6)   To raise the level of consciousness among retailers.[65]

Implicitly, these aims are statements of the concrete social and economic problems which confronted the retailers.

As the discussions in the Commission on Retailing of the *Deutscher Handelstag*[66] in September 1906 indicated, *Rabattsparvereine* offered to put an end to a real scourge of retailing, credit dealing. It had become common practice for customers to shop at consumer co-operatives when they had cash, thereby collecting the very attractive discount stamps, and to deal with the retailer only when shortage of funds made credit buying necessary. Offering credit, therefore, became one of the means employed by the retailers to attract customers. Many of the ills besetting the retailers could be traced to the necessity of granting credit. Apart from all the economic disadvantages involved, the relationship of the retailer to the customer became easily strained. It did not fit into the retailer's conception of his task to have to haggle with customers over unpaid bills. Being able to offer a reliable discount presented the retailer with a means of attracting the customers away from the consumer co-operatives without placing himself in either a socially or an economically disadvantageous position. Unification among retailers would provide the individual retailer with the collective support of his fellows. Unity among retailers would mean that the discounts which were granted in the form of stamps could be made uniform and, therefore, all the more attractive to the customer. It would be more convenient for the customer to collect similar types of stamps from all participating retail shops instead of the innumerable different stamps from all the various shops in town. Uniformity of the type and the denomination of the discount would encourage customers to frequent the same stores rather than to spread their money to department stores and consumer co-operatives, neither of the latter being acceptable members to the discount unions. The very influential *Handelstag*, the national central organization of the Chambers of Commerce, was very much in favour of the establishment of *Rabattsparvereine*. The Commission on retailing declared these latter organizations

> *a means of supporting the principle of cash dealing and through this, as well as through the co-operation of retailers, to strengthen retail trade and to make it more vital in relation to consumer co-operatives and department stores.* [67]

The *Rabattsparverein* was a form of self-help among retailers which was very much in accord with the generally liberal economic views of the *Handelstag*. The advocacy of formation of *Rabattsparvereine* by the *Handelstag* gave them an air of respectability which was important to their continued success.

Perhaps the most important aim of the *Rabattsparvereine Deutschlands*, at least as far as Beythien was concerned,[68] was to raise the level of consciousness among retailers. In terms of political mobilization, this aim consisted in developing among retailers an awareness of what they had in common and how they differed from other social groups. This all-important aim was, at the same time, very largely the most important pre-condition for the success of these organizations. Their success was dependent upon the development among retailers of a sense of togetherness *(Zusammengehörigkeitsgefühl)*. This new spirit was to replace the traditional competitive relationship of retailers to one another. Beythien visualized that, once the retailers were really united, more radical methods than distributing discount stamps would be employed. He considered, for example, the use of "yellow lists" against factories and wholesalers who sold their goods directly to the public. Similar lists were to be employed against both department stores and consumer co-operatives. However, as within the technical organizations, the idea of employing a boycott against the offending factory or wholesaler did not receive much support within the *Rabattsparvereine*.[69]

There seems to have been a desire among the organizers of

the *Rabattsparvereine* that the available customers should be divided among the retailers equally. This attitude toward economic and social problems was similar to that of the old guilds. There was at least one attempt reported (in Hanover) at the turn of the century to found a guild among retailers dealing in groceries; high on the list of its aims was spreading the sense of "community spirit".[70]

In order for an organization such as the *Rabattsparverein* to achieve its more specific goals, a new spirit would have to replace the traditional competitive spirit. It is noteworthy that, even at the founding meeting in Leipzig in 1902, a minority opposed the creation of a national organization and took the positive step of petitioning the national government to pass laws forbidding the granting of all or any discounts, particularly in the form envisaged at the meeting. This attitude indicated that at least a minority wanted to return to the days of "fair" competition between retailers when market forces, outside such extraneous inducements as discounts, would determine which entrepreneurs would survive. At the same meeting, the idea, mentioned briefly, of simultaneously founding an *Einkaufsgenossenschaft* did not elicit any support. Creation of *Einkaufsgenossenschaften* would have formed a natural supplement to the *Rabattsparvereine*.[71] The failure of the two to develop as part of one movement is difficult to explain. The expressed aversion of retailers who were willing to join *Rabattsparvereine* to co-operatives may provide part of the explanation. The *Rabattsparvereine* may be regarded as having represented the minimum program of self-help for retailers and the *Einkaufsgenossenschaften* as having represented the maximum program. According to this interpretation, the far greater success of the former indicates that retailers in pre-war Germany were reluctant to accept a new spirit of working together.

In the years immediately prior to war in 1914, more and more retailers within the *Rabattsparvereine Deutschlands* began to call for the founding of *Einkaufsgenossenschaften*. This demand was particularly in evidence within the discount unions of the grocers. Some 129 of their unions within the *Rabattsparvereine Deutschlands* made this request in 1913 and committees were busy working out the details. The growing demand for the establishment of *Einkaufsgenossenschaften* indicated a growing acceptance of the "maximum" program of self-help. That this acceptance was so gradual, however, indicated how slowly the "feeling of solidarity" spread among the retailers.[72] It has even been suggested that part of the reason behind the creation of regional organizations within the *Rabattsparvereine Deutschlands* can be traced to a failure of this new spirit to develop.[73]

Rabattsparvereine: An Evaluation from a Review of Hamburg

It would be incorrect to assume that because the *Verband der Rabattsparvereine Deutschlands* achieved some success when measured in increases in membership, the opposition among retailers was gradually diminished. It is true that there was some "demonstration effect". However, not all retailers were convinced by what the *Rabattsparvereine* regarded as the beneficial effects of the founding of local unions associated with the increasingly powerful national organization.[74] The nature of the successes (and failures) of the *Verband der Rabattsparvereine Deutschlands* may be evaluated (beyond listing membership statistics) by looking briefly at some reactions among retailers in Hamburg. More information on the political activities of the retailers appears to have survived in Hamburg than in most other areas of Germany.

In Hamburg the idea of discount unions, even in the face of the development of *Produktion* after the turn of the century, had been strenuously and continuously opposed. Although Hamburg was one of the centres of the consumer co-operative (and Socialist) movement, the idea of *Rabattsparvereine* won little support. The *Central-Ausschuss Hamburg-Altonaer Detaillisten—Vereine* began its campaign against the discount unions in the middle 1890s. This campaign was directed not only against the "wild" discount unions, but against organizations which granted any form of discount. The protest meetings and newspaper advertisements continued sporadically until 1901 when, as in 1902, virtually every meeting of the organization ended with a resolution specifically opposed to the idea of *Rabattsparvereine.*[75] The widespread opposition of retailers in Hamburg to these discount unions was reflected in the attitude of the *Detaillistenkammer* in Hamburg. This body, although otherwise in general agreement with the *Deutscher Handelstag,* was against the establishment in Hamburg of a branch of the *Rabattsparvereine Deutschlands.* [76] It is significant that a representative view of the opposition of retailers in Hamburg was issued just after the decision of the *Handelstag* to support in principle the foundation of *Rabattsparvereine.*

The view of retailers in Hamburg was that retailers had enough problems to face already without introducing yet another one in the form of the discount unions. It was argued, not without some justification, that those retailers who needed to grant special discounts to improve their competitive position were the very ones least able to afford to grant such discounts. On the other hand, those retailers whose competitive position was such that they were able to afford to grant a discount no longer needed to grant it.[77] According to this interpretation, the practice of granting discounts was not only superfluous, but positively harmful. The public, it was claimed, would very soon come to the view that paying in cash was something extraordinary when it was no more than their duty to the retailer to pay cash. The persistence of *Händlerstolz* in Hamburg was obvious. The great opposition to the *Rabattsparvereine* continued in Hamburg down to 1914.

In Munich, the *Freie Vereinigung selbständiger Kaufleute*— although it was claimed that it represented only some 40 or 50 members[78]—raised considerable opposition to the *Rabattsparvereine.* This opposition was carried to the point of petitioning the federal government to place those businesses using the discount system under the same category as department stores. *Rabattsparvereine* would have been, in that event, subject to the taxes placed on department stores. The Munich organization proposed other forms of taxation on the *Rabattsparvereine* to supplement the department store tax to which, it was hoped, *Rabattsparvereine* would become subject.[79] In January 1904 the *Allgemeiner Verein der Gewerbetreibenden Deutschlands* was created in Berlin, "primarily as a defence against *Rabattsparvereine*". The new *Verein* sought the "consolidation of all tradesmen *(Gewerbetreibenden)* in order to preserve the *Mittelstand*". The organization eventually broadened its sphere of activity to fight against other "evils" *(Unwesen)* such as the department stores and consumer co-operatives.[80]

The opposition in Hamburg flared up at times when proposals were being publicized to set up *Rabattsparvereine,* although the actions which were proposed in Hamburg were much less radical than those proposed in Munich.[81] In early 1914, reports that yet another attempt was to be made to establish a branch of the *Rabattsparvereine Deutschlands* in Hamburg led to a protest meeting of retailers determined to oppose it. Members of some 24 local retailer organizations of all branches gathered on 23 March 1914. It was with some irony that announcements of the meeting claimed that a discount union in Hamburg would bring "dissatisfaction and disunity into the circles of the Hamburg retailers". Members were strongly urged to attend the meeting. "Your attendance is absolutely necessary. You have become subject to new pressures. Help to avoid the danger to your existence.''[82] The failure of the discount unions was symptomatic of the failure among the retail trader organizations to achieve unity. In retrospect, this failure is difficult to explain, particularly because as the example of Hamburg indicates, the very organizations most actively opposed to the discount unions were among the most prominent organizations advocating goals which were almost exactly the same as those of the *Rabattsparvereine.*

4

Schutzverbände in Retail Trade 1890–1914 Local Organization

It was at the local level that the function of the *Schutzver-bände* was most apparent. The pattern of the establishment of the local *Schutzverbände* in retail trade only rarely corres-ponded to the organizational pattern of a national central organization creating local or regional branches. The retailers' *Schutzverbände* usually grew from the initial establishment of a local *Schutzverband*. The local organization would seek to affiliate itself to other local *Schutzverbände* and only then begin the search for additional allies at the regional and national levels. This pattern was illustrated by the *Verband der Rabattsparvereine Deutschlands*. The local activities of the *Schutzverbände* may be said to have been indicative of the general trend of the political mobilization of the retailers at the initial stage of their mobilization. That the local organ-izations played such a prominent role in the politics of the retailers was a measure of the spontaneous impulse behind their political activities. Nevertheless, the local activities of the *Schutzverbände* have received least attention in works dealing with the retailers. The little *Schutzverbände* at the local level, because they appear to have played an almost insignificant role in political decision-making, may seem hardly worthy of serious study. As has already been suggested however, the study of interest groups may be justified on other, no less important grounds than whether or not they had a direct impact upon the decision-making process at any level of governmental activity.

The present chapter is a study of the local activities of the

Schutzverbände, while the following chapter concentrates upon the activities of the *Schutzverbände* at the regional and national levels. Particular attention is paid to the local activities of the *Schutzverbände* in Hamburg because the economic pre-conditions as well as the political pre-conditions for the political mobilization of the retailers existed in Hamburg, especially after 1890. Fortunately, the study of the *Schützverbände* in Hamburg has been made possible by the availability of the vast quantity of relevant material that has survived the war.

The Retailers in Hamburg: Special Problems

The peculiarities of Hamburg's economic development, represented by a reliance upon her position as a port, diminished considerably after 1890. The retail market of Hamburg, Germany's second largest city, underwent the whole range of developments outlined above. The economic problems which threatened the existence of the independent retailers were also present. Through occupation in shipbuilding and manufacturing and processing industries, Hamburg's work force came to resemble the work forces of other large cities in Germany.[1]

Retailers in Hamburg were faced with an increasing burden after 15 October 1888, when Hamburg formally joined the German customs' union. This *Zollanschluss*[2] ended many of Hamburg's special customs' privileges. The voluntary termination of these privileges came about when it was realized within Hamburg that the great freedom to trade with the outside world was not worth cutting Hamburg off from fuller participation within the economic life of the rest of Germany.* Prior to 1888, retailers in Hamburg had had a near local monopoly of the retail market by virtue of the customs wall which had been erected around Hamburg. When this wall came down at the end of 1888, retailers' hopes for a flood of new customers from neighbouring Schleswig-Holstein and Mecklenburg did not materialize. Instead, local retailers found

*The greatly increased tempo of economic activity from 1890 onward in Hamburg provides some indication that sound consideration underlay the decision to join the *Zollanschluss.*

themselves confronted with the competition of new firms established by outside merchants. These merchants, mainly from Berlin, used the most up-to-date merchandizing techniques, much to the chagrin of the Hamburg merchants, who had grown accustomed to dealing with their customers on a more personal basis. The *Zollanschluss,* therefore, represented a considerable challenge to retailers in Hamburg[3] above and beyond the numerous other threats which retailers had to face throughout Germany. One of these threats, the consumer co-operative, presented itself in Hamburg in an especially blatant fashion. *Produktion* had reached a membership of 74,328 by 1914. It controlled at that time (as it continues to control today) a whole range of business activities in direct competition with the independent retailers.[4] As if to make matters more obviously disadvantageous to the retailers in Hamburg, the three deputies sent to the *Reichstag* from Hamburg were, from 1890 onward, without exception, members of the SPD.*

The pattern of establishing interest groups to represent economic interests was highly developed in Hamburg and could, therefore, provide precedents for the organization of retailers in local *Schutzverbände.* The larger industrial employers[5] and their workers[6] were well organized in pre-war Hamburg. Not only did Germany's two largest employee organizations have their headquarters in Hamburg, but the continuing drive and impulse behind the employee movement seemed to be generated from Hamburg. Within the social, economic, and political complex of Hamburg, retailers too organized in local *Schutzverbände.*

Schutzverbände at the Local Level

While there are examples of the creation of local *Schutzverbände* from the 1860s, retailers' organizations grew up

*It was far more difficult for the SPD to gain victory in local elections because of the peculiar three-class voting system used in local elections. An elector qualified by having paid taxes on (at least) 1,200 Mk. income over the previous five consecutive years. There was a further three-way division which, on the surface, made the infamous Prussian three-class voting system appear more democratic. For a full history, see Bolland, *Bürgerschaft,* 1959 *passim.* For the background, see Baasch, *Geschichte Hamburgs,* 1924 - 1925 *passim.*

primarily in the 1890s and in the early decades of the present century. The *Detaillistenverband für Rheinland und Westfalen,* created in 1894 by the work of local retailers' organizations in Barmen, Crefeld, Elberfeld, and Essen, counted but two organizations from its total of 21 organizations in 1903 (membership *circa* 900) which had existed before 1890.[7] While the Rhineland organization had been created only in 1894, the independent local organizations affiliated to (and not simply branches of) even the oldest state and regional *Schutzverbände* in retailing came into existence after 1890. The *Sächsisch-Thüringischer Verband der·Schutzgemeinschaften für Handel und Gewerbe* (in 1903, membership 4,000) which traced its origins back to 1867, counted two-thirds of the organizations associated with it in 1903 (or 14 out of 21 organizations) with foundation dates later than 1890. In fact, almost one-half of the organizations (10 out of the 21) had been founded after 1895, and six of these had been founded after 1900.[8] The *Verband selbständiger Kaufleute und Gewerbetreibender des Grossherzogtums Baden (e. V.),* founded in 1895, counted 13 independent affiliated organizations in 1903 (membership 800). Only two of these local organizations had been established before 1890.[9]

Some of the regional and national organizations did not seek affiliates at the local level, but established their own local branches. The *Detaillistenverband für Hessen und Waldeck (e. V.)* founded in 1895, counted 19 associated local branches in 1903 (total membership in 1903, 996); only two of the local organizations were not branches and these accounted for only 82 of the 996 members.[10] None of these local organizations had existed before 1895 however. According to the 1903 inventory of organizations compiled by the Federal Ministry of the Interior, the Hesse and Waldeck organization was unique in establishing branches in this manner. The inventory, which contains many thousands of organizations, lists only one other organization in retailing (with more than three member *Vereine* affiliated to it) that established any branches at all.[11] The large national organization, the *Deutscher Bund für Handel und Gewerbe* (which had a membership of 10,000 in 1903), had been founded in 1899. By 1903 there were 39 affiliated local organizations, only 10 of which were founded prior to 1890; four of these 10 were founded after 1885.[12]

Examination of the various archives in cities including Hamburg, Bremen, Hanover, Munich, Dortmund, Bochum, Bielefeld, and Münster shows that the local *Schutzverbände* in retailing established themselves primarily after 1890. There are some examples of political activity among retailers before 1890. It would appear misleading to suggest, as Winkler does, that these organizations were created primarily in the period from 1873 to 1896[13] or to maintain, as Wein appears to, that they were created more or less evenly over the entire period from the late 1860s down to the war.[14] The development was uneven, and it definitely accelerated after 1890.

Schutzverbände in Hamburg: Schutzverbände outside the Detaillistenkammer Hamburg

The chief function of the *Schutzverbände,* as their name implies, was the protection of their members. At the local level, where contact between the executive and membership was closest, the sphere of activities of the retailers' *Schutzverbände* was very much centred on local problems. As affiliated members or as branches of larger regional or national organizations, local *Schutzverbände* could exert some influence on matters of more general concern. During the period from 1890 to 1914 the specific causes behind the creation of the local organizations varied considerably, not just in Hamburg, but throughout Germany. The specific cause behind the establishment of a retailer organization might vary according to the need to fight the local establishment of further consumer co-operatives, department stores, or even *Rabattsparvereine.* There were many examples where retailers at the local level expressed very strong desires to organize in *Schutzverbände* because they suffered "so many shackles from all sides" and they, alone among other social groups, remained unorganized.[15] Whatever particular form the economic pressure assumed in any local area, mobilization of retailers was the response. The form of the response, or organization, varied according to the aims of the retailers involved. Certain organizations, which had been designed for specific purposes, only later broadened the scope of their activities. The aim of the *Schutzverein zur Bekämpfung der Warenhäuser,* which was founded in Hamburg in 1904, appears to have been fairly clear and specific.[16] The *Gewerbe Schutzverein Hamburg* was created in 1903 specifically to fight the creation of a department store in Barmbeck.* The aims of the local *Schutzverbände* were frequently much more general.

The *Verein gegen Unwesen im Handel und Gewerbe (Hamburg) e. V.,* which was an extremely active organization under the highly energetic leader, Amandus Werbeck,[17] deserves special attention. This organization, which was certainly among the most active of the local *Schutzverbände* in Hamburg, worked with many others. The organization, founded on 7 November 1893, reported a membership of 1,100 in some 50 associated local organizations in May 1913. In addition to working with retailers, the *Verein* had extensive dealings with various local artisan organizations and with the technical organizations of the retailers.[18] This Hamburg organization also formed the core of the *Verein gegen Unwesen im Handel und Gewerbe für Norddeutschland.* Other organizations *(gegen Unwesen)* with similar names existed at the turn of the century in Chemnitz, Cologne, and Dresden, among other cities.[19]

According to its original statutes, the Hamburg *Verein gegen Unwesen im Handel und Gewerbe* was designed to combat all forms of dishonesty and swindling in trade, including false or misleading advertising.[20] Although there was nothing specifically nationalistic or anti-Semitic in these statutes, both elements were very much in the foreground from the outset. From early January 1894 the *Antisemitischer Wahlverein von 1890* (the *Deutsch-soziale Reformpartei)* openly gave its support to the organization.[21] The initial press releases of the Hamburg *Verein gegen Unwesen* began with much talk about

---

HH.St.Ar.PP. V825 and *Kolonial- und Fettwaren-Handel Ztg.* 22.8. 1903. The original meeting was attended by 1,500 persons. All promised personal boycott of the department store as a first step in fighting its existence. There was a good deal of talk about the many empty stores to be found in Cologne, thanks, in large measure, to the creation there of a Tietz department store.

raising the level of morality in business dealings and in society as a whole, but ended in a manner later popularized by anti-Semites within the *Mittelstandsbewegung*.

> *He who still thinks and feels German, who wishes to know how to preserve German morality and honour of the business world, he supports the re-establishment of the German* Mittelstand.[22]
> . . . *We wish to enlighten the* Mittelstand, *as well as all other classes, about the dangers of modern economic development by word of mouth and through the press and to protect everyone from harm; we ask also, however, that we not be left alone in our difficult struggle.*[23]

From the outset of its activities the organization linked the "re-establishment" of the *Mittelstand* with fighting the "un-German", the dishonest.[24] Having identified, if initially only very generally, the causes of the difficulties of the *Mittelstand*, the methods of the organization at the local level were as good as fixed.

The local method most characteristic of the Hamburg *Verein gegen Unwesen* was the issuing of more or less continuous warning both to entrepreneurs and to the public of dishonest dealings which the organization managed to uncover. Throughout the period from its creation down to the war, the local newspapers were filled with such dire warnings.[25] The organization began issuing its own handbills, then separate series of bulletins which appeared regularly after 1894. Soon, its call having grown more shrill, the organization began issuing a newspaper, *Der Weckruf!*, and, from time to time, little pamphlets *(Mahnwörter)*. The very considerable files which the political police in Hamburg managed to collect on the organization and its leading figures testify to the great activity of the organization. The issuing of warnings in the press about supposedly dishonest dealings by various types of firms often led to prosecution of the *Verein* (usually in the person of Werbeck) before the courts. From the beginning of his activity in the early 1890s until 1914, Werbeck appears to have been involved in various court cases.[26] Toward the end of 1901 several (unsuccessful) attempts were made by members of the organization to unseat their controversial leader.[27]

The business ventures which initially bore the brunt of Werbeck's attacks were the auctions. Auctions were resented by owners of fixed stores *(die offenen, stehenden Gewerbe)* not only because auctions offered very stiff competition, but also because the men who ran the auctions avoided paying taxes to which local retailers were subject. The resentment of the urban *Mittelstand* against the auctions was comparable to the resentment of the rural *Mittelstand* against travelling salesmen and hawkers.[28] The Hamburg *Verein gegen Unwesen im Handel und Gewerbe* began in 1892 as the *Verein zur Beseitigung schwindelhaften Auktionen und zur Hebung des Gewerbestandes.*[29]

The struggle against this kind of "evil" *(Unwesen)* remained the chief aim of the organization, even after its name was changed and broadened. A survey of its monthly bulletins confirms that this aim was pursued vigorously. The bulletin for April 1903, for example, contained five main articles on various types of malpractices *(Unwesen).*[30] It has already been mentioned that the reports of the organization to the public were full of all kinds of specific charges against named firms. The impression which emerges is that the organization performed a kind of watch-dog service. Its "bite" consisted in making both members of the organization and the public aware of the allegedly fraudulent dealers that were lurking about. It is noteworthy that the organizations did not appear to prey upon Jewish firms and that its attacks were aimed at what it considered "unfair" or dishonest practice regardless of who the proprietor happened to be.[31] It was because the organization saw, or thought it saw, so much fraudulent dealing everywhere that it came to consider consumer co-operatives and department stores as basically fraudulent enterprises.

Prior to the turn of the century, the so-called civil servant consumer co-operatives were under attack.[32] The attack of the *Verein gegen Unwesen* (in so many ways representative of the views of retailers throughout Germany) was based on the view that tax-payers were paying the salaries of civil servants and that the latter should be at least grateful enough not to establish co-operatives which drove these tax-payers out of business.[33] A petition of May 1890 of the *Zentralvorstand kaufmännischer Verbände und Vereine Deutschlands* to the Prussian government claimed that the state had a duty to protect the "loyal classes" from becoming part of the "menacing proletariat". The specific demands of this organization did not go so far as to suggest that all civil servant consumer co-operatives should be dissolved. However, numerous organizations among retailers' *Schutzverbände* did make such a demand, especially from the late 1890s onward.[34]

The conception of the department store held by the *Verein gegen Unwesen im Handel und Gewerbe* in Hamburg appears to have been typical in many ways of the conception held by other retailer organizations. The department stores came in for attack primarily after the turn of the century. The operation of these stores appears to have mystified many retailers. Retailers tended to explain the workings of the department stores in semi-conspiratorial terms.[35] It was claimed that these stores used "more or less" unfair advertising to get the public to enter the store at all and that they employed the ever-present *Lockvölgeln*. The *Lockvölgeln* were articles ostentatiously reduced in price to win the consumers' attention, while (it was claimed) prices on other articles were marked up.[36] At the discussion-evening on the department stores sponsored by the *Verein gegen Unwesen* on 19 May 1903, there was a consensus that the department stores were "dangerous to society". An owner of such a store should (under certain circumstances) be considered "dangerous to society" in that he

1. forces his employees to witness unfair competition every day.
2. supplies his own goods through creation of his own factories.
3. can undermine the state through the destruction of many independent existences.[37]

As far as the retailers were concerned, the department stores represented *Grosskapital* in its crassest form and were determined to destroy the *Mittelstand*. The recurrent point was that the department stores existed, and could only exist, on an "unfair" basis.[38]

By July 1903 the *Verein gegen Unwesen* in Hamburg felt the need to rethink the policy established in its statutes on party-political and religious neutrality. In a long article of

July 1903, it explained that only by shedding this neutrality (or appearance of neutrality) could the organization even hope to achieve its most important aims. Moreover, as an affiliated member of the *Deutscher Bund für Handel und Gewerbe,* itself "with both feet in the political arena", party-political neutrality was already a thing of the past.[39] From 1903 there appeared in the publications of the Hamburg *Verein* many public statements in open opposition to the SPD, to Catholics, and especially to the Jews.

In May 1905 a clear statement of the political views of the *Verein* appeared in its bulletin. The Jews were attacked as the "aristocracy of wealth" who lived in the grand fashion at the expense of the nation as a whole. The Social Democrats were attacked because they sought to over-turn the existing order. Other "international powers", including the Catholic Church, were attacked in the name of nationalism. It was conceded that the "Break-with-Rome Movement", "anti-Semitism", "economic *Schutzverbände*", and the *"Mittelstandsbewegung"* had had all too few successes. It was no wonder that *"Deutschtum"* did not feel well". In the face of these failures, it was folly for "a minority of earnest men" to renounce political activity and to occupy themselves with petty matters. Much more direct involvement in the important affairs of Germany's retailers was demanded.[40]

An important aspect of the new concentration on those matters which were felt to be most important to the welfare of Germany's retailers was the open renunciation of Germany's imperialism, her efforts in international affairs. "The international interest is driving the national interest into the background; the domestic needs of our nation *(Volk)* are at least no longer in the foreground."[41] To understand that imperialism could and did serve the important social and political function of diverting attention from domestic problems to those of foreign affairs was to recognize the existence of what has recently been termed "social imperialism".[42] No further mention of anti-imperialism can be found in the publications of the *Verein gegen Unwesen* in Hamburg after the national elections of 1907, when the idea of *Weltpolitik* served to unite parties against the SPD. Werbeck, as a member of the executive of the *Verein der selbständigen Geschäftstreibenden von Hamburg, St. Pauli und den Vororten*[43] and the *Gewerbe Schutzverein* Hamburg (later Barmbeck)[44] made no further mention of the idea. The *Deutscher Bund für Handel und Gewerbe,* to which the *Verein gegen Unwesen im Handel und Gewerbe* (Hamburg) was affiliated, also did not take up the idea. Therefore it would be an exaggeration to suggest that retailers in Hamburg, or in Germany generally, were overtly opposed to the federal government's imperialistic policies.[45]

Among the retailers in Hamburg there continued to be expressions of opinion directly opposed to Germany's colonial policies, although these opinions were becoming increasingly rare. Moreover, there was almost no published support for these policies by retailers' organizations. As a recent study has pointed out, "because of its economic interests, the attention of the independent *Mittelstand* was directed above all to domestic politics. . .The urgent economic problems permitted the independents of the *Mittelstand* little time for fanciful dreams of conquest."[46] In late 1903 there was concern expressed by the less controversial *Central Ausschuss Hamburg-Altonaer Detaillisten-Vereine* that American trusts were beginning to pose a threat to Germany's "economic life and well-being". These fears were based, however, on American economic conquests within Germany.[47]

The anti-Semitism, which remained comparatively mild in the *Verein gegen Unwesen im Handel und Gewerbe,* generally appears to have enjoyed a no less mixed reception than imperialism among retailers' organizations in Hamburg. The mere association of the *Antisemitischer Wahlverein von 1890* with the *Verein gegen Unwesen im Handel und Gewerbe* provided a sufficient basis for a number of retailer organizations in Hamburg to dissociate themselves from the *Verein gegen Unwesen,* although several of these organizations did leave the way open for their members to join the *Verein gegen Unwesen* as individuals.[48] The *Hamburgischer Verband der Detaillisten und sonstiger Gewerbetreibenden* was very much opposed to a policy of anti-Semitism. At its meeting of 18 September 1909 it was pointed out how the *Mittelstand* had been and would remain "a bulwark against Social Democracy". It was expressed that the *Verband* wished to deny the apparently widely held belief that every retailer was an anti-

Semite.[49] The earlier comments of the local *Wirtschaftlicher Schutzverband* indicated that expressions of anti-Semitism, far from offering an additional attraction to prospective members, could repel them. In fact, this organization claimed that Socialist newspapers such as *Vorwärts* or the local *Echo* attempted (as a matter of policy) to brand all new *Mittelstand* organizations as anti-Semitic in order to discourage Jewish merchants from joining.[50] Because of the tenuous relation of the *Wirtschaftlicher Schutzverband* with the anti-Semitic newspaper, the *Deutsches Blatt,* there were perhaps some grounds for suspicion. By mid-1903 the *Israelitisches Familienblatt* (Hamburg) reported that the *Wirtschaftlicher Schutzverband* claimed to be "in no way" anti-Semitic.[51] In April 1904 the local branch of the national organization, the *Bund der Handwerker,* dropped the stipulation from its statutes that only "Christian-Germans" could join, in order to make it possible for Jews to become members.[52] Particularly after the turn of the century many retailer circles came to recognize that open avowal of anti-Semitism might have adverse effects on the popularity of a particular organization.[53]

Although anti-Semitism received a negative reception among various local Hamburg *Schutzverbände,* there were retailer organizations in Hamburg which did embrace anti-Semitism. Particularly prone to accept anti-Semitism were those organizations in which members of the executive of the employees' association, the *Deutschnationaler Handlungsgehilfen-Verband,* played prominent roles. The nationalism and anti-Semitism of the DHV are well known.[54] These aspects of the policy of the DHV were often condemned by other large employees' associations at the time. Leaders of the DHV, especially Friedrich Raab[55] and Johann Henningsen,[56] were, from time to time, not only members of the executive of the DHV, but members of the executives of a number of local retailer organizations and active members of the local anti-Semitic political parties. Moreover, Raab in particular acted as spokesman in the local *Bürgerschaft* (when elected) on matters usually identified as being in the interest of the retailers. It seems that their activities, as well as the condemnation of their activities in the *Echo,* created the impression that anti-Semitism was widespread among retailers.

The *Echo* had for example branded Werbeck as early as September 1894 the "anti-Semitic furniture dealer".[57] The Hamburg *Verein zur Hebung der christlichen Geschäfte und des Handwerkerstandes* which came into existence on 3 March 1894 (Raab was on the executive) restricted membership to Christians. The avowed methods of this *Verein* were similar to those of the *Verein gegen Unwesen im Handel und Gewerbe.*[58] The *Schutzverein zur Bekämpfung der Warenhäuser* (Hamburg),[59] created in late 1903 (with Henningsen on the executive), was also tinged with anti-Semitism and participated more directly, if primarily by way of propaganda, in party politics. This organization was most outspoken in its opposition to Social Democracy. The *Echo* responded by vigilantly branding all Henningsen's public statements as anti-Semitic.[60] In mid-1905 the *Echo* also labelled as anti-Semitic the *Gewerbe Schutzverein Hamburg* (with Werbeck on the executive).[61]

Opposition to the SPD was one of the few policies shared by the great majority of retailers' organizations in Hamburg. The *Central-Ausschuss Hamburg-Altonaer Detaillisten-Vereine* was noted for eliciting promises from candidates at election time on specific issues of importance to retailers. Candidates of various political parties would be sent a list of retailers' legislative demands and asked to state their policies concerning the demands. Questionnaires to candidates were to publicize the position of the candidates on tax on turnover for various large concerns, on the dissolution of civil servant consumer co-operatives, and on the need to strengthen the law of 27 May 1896 on unfair competition. The results of the survey would be published in order to inform retailers of candidates who were sympathetic to the retailers' "cause". The SPD was under no circumstances to be supported either in local or in federal elections. The SPD candidates were never even sent copies of the retailers' demands.[62] The anti-SPD feelings of retailers in Hamburg were especially stimulated when the Berlin organization, the *Liga zur Herbeiführung des Achtuhr-Schlusses in sämmtlichen kaufmännischen Betrieben,* set up a branch organization in Hamburg in early June 1896. The anti-Semitic newspaper, the *Deutsches Blatt,*[63] was not the only local newspaper to brand the organization as one inspired by the insidious SPD, and therefore one to be condemned out of hand.[64]

This brief and very selective view of local organizations in Hamburg has indicated the kinds of resentment among retailers upon which the anti-Semitic parties capitalized—even if initially this "capitalization" may be seen primarily in the form of dual memberships of executives in anti-Semitic parties and retailers' *Schutzverbände*. The local study has also indicated that a consciousness was developing among retailers and that this consciousness was extremely differentiated. On 13 February 1898 the *Echo* carried a very long poem illustrating what the newspaper regarded as the ambivalent attitude of retailers toward anti-Semitism.[65] The poem ends

> *D'rum wache auf, du Detaillistenstand:*
> *Geh' mit dem Arbeiterstande Hand in Hand,*
> *Heraus aus deiner geist'gen Säuglingswindel,*
> *Der Antisemitismus ist der reine—*
> > *SCHWINDEL!**

There was a growing consciousness among members of the *Mittelstand* in general that they were being ignored by government at all levels. Werbeck's anti-imperialism gave some indication that this consciousness existed. The *Schutzverbände* did perform the important function of mobilizing retailers, particularly at the local level. The endless newspaper campaigns·of the *Schutzverbände* may be considered, however, as little more ,than first steps taken in an effort to ameliorate the economic problems of retailers. Retailers themselves came to consider that the self-help activities of the *Schutzverbände,* as well as those of the other retailers organizations, were insufficient to overcome the economic problems with which the retailers were faced. The demand by government and the political parties that the *Mittelstand* engage in still further self-help activities came to be recognized by the *Mittelstand,*

---

*Therefore wake up, you retailers:
Go with the working class hand in hand,
Put aside your mental crutch,
Anti-Semitism is the complete—
> SWINDLE!

and especially by the retailers, as an excuse for governments to do nothing. When more powerful and influential social groups sought government support, however, matters might be seen in quite a different light.

> Our trade treaties protect large over-seas trade just as they protect large industry: however, as soon as the artisan, small industry and retailing complain of their plight, then the answer is: 'Help yourself' or 'retailing and small firms raise the cost of living without bringing any advantage'.[66]

Among retailers there developed the conviction that further pressure had to be exerted through the unified activity of Schutzverbände.[67] Unification at the regional and national levels offered greater prospects of success. Retailers became convinced that government circles at all levels had to be penetrated. One local aspect of the drive of retailers to win official recognition for their demands for protection was their attempt to establish legally constituted (öffentlich-rechtlich) Chambers, equivalent to the already established Chambers of Commerce (Handelskammern). Although retailers succeeded in establishing such Detaillistenkammern in Hamburg and Bremen, the attempts of retailers to achieve their own specific forms of representation were not entirely successful throughout Germany. The endeavours to establish various forms of such official representation marked a further step in the political mobilization of the retailers.

The Position of Retailers in the Movement for Official Representation of Economic Interests

In Hamburg the attempts by retailers to establish their own official representation (amtliche Vertretung) resulted in the establishment of their legally constituted Chamber, the Detaillistenkammer. In the present study the endeavours of the retailers to establish their own Chambers are viewed as additional aspects of the creation by retailers of local Schutzverbände and hence as further steps in the retailers' political mobilization.[68] A brief note on the position of the retailers in the more general movement in Germany which sought official representation of economic interests in specific Chambers (or in committees within Chambers) provides some understanding of the significance of these endeavours for the political mobilization of the retailers.

The oldest type of Chamber in Germany was the Chamber of Commerce. Members of these organizations, particularly of those in the *Hansa Städte,* took great pride in tracing the origins of their Chambers back many hundreds of years. Chambers of Commerce were founded in Prussia and Baden after 1820, in Bavaria after 1842, in Württemburg after 1855, and in Saxony after 1861.[69] Although the constitution of Bismarck's Empire attributed to the federal government the right to regulate trade legislation, including the right of the regulation and organization of interest representation in trade, the legislation on Chambers of Commerce as it existed prior to the foundation of the Empire remained *de facto* and *de jure* in effect. Therefore, there were nearly as many variations in the legislation pertaining to Chambers of Commerce as there were Chambers of Commerce. The *Hansa Städte,* Hamburg, Bremen, and Lübeck, for example, differed in this respect not only from all the *Bundesstaaten,* but even from each other. By 1906 there were 151 Chambers of Commerce established throughout Germany, with ninety in Prussia alone.[70] Developments in Prussian legislation on various types of Chambers are worth reviewing not only because of their intrinsic importance, but also because of the important implications of that legislation for the other individual federal states and for Germany's federal legislation. By setting forth these wider developments, it is easier to assess the efforts of retailers in both Hamburg and in the other areas of Germany to establish their own official representation.

Prussian legislation on Chambers of Commerce, which had been passed on 24 February 1870, remained in effect until 1897. According to this legislation, Chambers of Commerce were largely restricted to the function of advisory bodies to government at various levels. While Chambers of Commerce were to be representative of all trade *(Handel),* the application of the three-class voting system virtually excluded the retailers from all participation.[71] In the course of the early 1890s a number of events occurred which eventually opened the way both for the entry of retailers into Chambers of Commerce in Prussia and for the considerable broadening of the powers of these organizations.

When the Prussian Minister for Trade, Freiherr von Berlepsch, introduced new legislation on Chambers of Commerce in the Prussian House on 24 April 1896, he made the point quite clear that such legislation was demanded in order to grant "trade and industry" a measure of self-administration comparable to that enjoyed by agriculture.[72] (Since 30 June 1894 Prussia had established Chambers for Agriculture with considerable powers of self-administration.)[73] The granting to Chambers of Commerce of powers comparable to those granted to Chambers for Agriculture gave more official recognition to trade and industry. In retrospect, this policy seems to have been in part a reflection of the changing orientation of Prussia's (and Germany's) entire governmental policy and, specifically, its attitude toward the various social classes. Particularly since he had received the 31 July 1895 letter from Wilhelm II,[74] von Berlepsch had been forced away from a social policy more or less oriented toward the workers to one oriented to the *Sammlung,* or "to all the rest". The present study does not investigate the complex genesis of what came to be hailed as the *Sammlungspolitik,* inspired in part by the Prussian Finance Minister, Johannes Miquel.[75] It is noteworthy that von Berlepsch began the reorientation before leaving office in the summer of 1896.[76] It was perhaps merely coincidental that Miquel coined the expression of the *Sammlung* in a speech on the final consideration of the Chambers of Commerce reform bill on 23 July 1897.[77]

The increased powers of the Chambers of Commerce which came into effect in 1897, and the growing possibility for retailers to participate within them provided a stimulus for retailers to seek some form of official representation. The new Prussian law of 19 August 1897 had granted to Chambers of Commerce powers broadly similar to those granted to the Chambers for Agriculture. Although Chambers of Commerce remained "advisory bodies" they were granted considerably increased powers of local self-administration. Throughout the debate on the bill in the Prussian House, the spokesman for the government made only scant reference to the retailers. The most that was granted (that in any sense could be viewed as a concession to the retailers) was that individual local

Chambers of Commerce might decide whether they wished to retain the old three-class voting system or to broaden it in order for retailers to gain at least some opportunity to participate.[78] By 1906 37 of the 90 Chambers of Commerce in Prussia retained the old system, while the remainder had introduced a general and equal suffrage.[79] The introduction of this suffrage, however, did not convince the retailers that their interests would receive equitable representation. Prussia had not attempted to force its Chambers of Commerce legislation upon the other federal states. The latter states did, however, pass their own legislation on Chambers of Commerce either prior to the Prussian legislation or almost immediately following it.

The introduction of *Handwerkskammern* (Artisans' Chambers) after 26 July 1897, from which the retailers were deliberately excluded,[80] gave retailers a further incentive to attempt either to win equal representation in the Chambers of Commerce or to establish their own Chambers similar to those of the artisans. The new central organization of the *Handwerkskammern,* the *Deutscher Handwerks- und Gewerbekammertag,* restricted its activity to technical matters of concern to the artisans alone. From its first meeting in mid-November 1900 until 1914, the meetings of the *Handwerks- und Gewerbekammertag,* with two possible and not very significant exceptions, never discussed any subjects of concern to the retailers.[81]

In July 1897 the *Reichstag* passed a law on the artisans which had been proposed to the *Bundesrat* by Prussia. An important aspect of the legislation concerned the establishment of local *Handwerkskammern.* Where *Gewerbekammern* already existed (as in Bavaria from 25·October 1889, in Hamburg from 18 December 1872, and in Bremen from 25 October 1849), they were transformed to comply with the new federal law of July 1897.[82] Where, as in most areas of Germany, such Chambers did not exist at all, they were to be introduced. The function of the *Handwerkskammern* was broadly similar to that of the Prussian Chambers of Commerce and Agriculture as organizations of self-administration. Because of the technical nature of so many of the artisans' legislative demands and the competence of their new Chambers to deal precisely with so many of these matters, the legislation of July 1897 helped to maintain the traditional "technical" nature of the artisans' demands. It has been suggested that the artisans, therefore, needed far-reaching *Mittelstand* organizations much less than the retailers who had managed far fewer successes in establishing any form of official *(amtlich)* representation prior to the turn of the century and even later.[83] After 1900 there were numerous proposals and discussions on the establishment of Chambers for Workers throughout Germany, although these discussions came to nothing.[84] In 1912 even the *Reichsverband Deutscher Gastwirtsverbände* petitioned both the *Reichstag* and the *Deutscher Handelstag* to establish their own Chambers.[85] The retailers were not prepared to accept what amounted to a denial of their right to establish some form of official representation. The determination of the retailers was revealed most clearly in Hamburg and Bremon.

The Detaillistenkammer Hamburg

Although the older *Gewerbekammer* of Hamburg was (from 2 April 1900) adjusted to meet the legal specifications of the federal legislation of July 1897 on the *Handwerkskammern*,[86] the Prussian reforms of August 1897 on the Chambers of Commerce were not adopted. In Hamburg, the law of 23 January 1880 on the Chamber of Commerce remained in effect. Because the Chamber of Commerce in Hamburg had been granted certain local political rights, it was more powerful in many respects than the newly reformed Prussian Chambers of Commerce. The special political rights of the Chamber of Commerce in Hamburg consisted largely in its special relationship with local government. Not only were members of the Chamber of Commerce in an extremely privileged position in local elections to the *Bürgerschaft,* but members of the Chamber of Commerce were also very influential as advisors to the local government.[87] City hall, the Chamber of Commerce building, and the stock exchange appeared as one very large inter-connected building in which the government and the most important business activities of Hamburg were conducted.

While the Chambers of Commerce in Hamburg and Bremen[88] were more powerful than those in Prussia, they were by tradition even less accessible to the retailers. The Chamber of Commerce in Hamburg prided itself on representing not merely the larger concerns but, even more specifically, the large overseas traders and industrialists. The Chamber of Commerce in Bremen similarly considered itself the organ of the *Kaufmannschaft,* in effect, the organ of the large traders *(Grosshändler)* carrying on the tradition of the *Hansa Städte*.[89] The assumptions in Hamburg and Bremen among members of the Chambers of Commerce were that *Kaufmänner* (traders) excluded by definition *Kleinhändler* (retailers), and that *Handel* (trade) referred primarily to *Grosshandel.*

The retailers of Hamburg and Bremen claimed the right of special representation outside the existing Chambers of Commerce on the grounds that the assumptions upon which the Chambers of Commerce were based were apparent to all.[90] It was made quite clear in both cities that the retailers' claim for their own Chambers was based on the models of the Chambers of Commerce and Agriculture and the *Gewerbekammern* already in existence.[91] The struggle by retailers in Hamburg and Bremen to establish their Chambers each lasted approximately ten years. The establishment of these Chambers was viewed by the retailers as an integral part of their local activities to "protect" themselves, that is, the Chambers were seen by the retailers as local *Schutzverbände.* The particular struggles of the retailers in Hamburg and Bremen attained national significance, however, when their existence came to form an important argument in itself for at least the creation of special retailers' committees within the Chambers of Commerce.

There was some agitation among retailers' organizations in Hamburg at least as far back as 17 February 1895 for the creation of a Chamber of Commerce for the retailers of Hamburg.[92] The argument was that retailers must have an independent organization if they were to fight for themselves against the threats of various kinds from all sides. One of the reasons why so many years passed before the *Detaillistenkammer* was actually established in Hamburg was that from the very outset this question became linked with other retailers' demands, such as the abolition of the civil servant consumer co-operatives and special taxes on department stores.[93] It happened frequently that the meetings called to discuss the first question became embroiled in the second. Even among the retailers themselves, such confrontations often occurred. One meeting in late March 1895 (with 3,000 in attendance) degenerated, in the words of local newspapers, into a fiery debate between anti-Semites and Socialists. [94] Werbeck, in his role as an executive member both of the *Verein gegen Unwesen im Handel und Gewerbe* in Hamburg and of the *Central-Ausschuss Hamburger Detaillisten-Vereine,* was very much behind the drive to establish the Chamber (and, for that matter, to abolish civil servant consumer co-operatives).[95] The meetings of retailers held throughout 1895 and 1896 in Hamburg were called to protest numerous specific types of economic abuses. Almost invariably, they ended with resolutions calling for the establishment of the *Detaillistenkammer.* [96]

A distinct Chamber for retailers posed a difficult question to local government in Hamburg. That government was effectively in the hands of the 18 Senators elected from the 160 members of the "representative" body, the *Bürgerschaft.* [97] The Senate had to be convinced of the need for the new Chamber. The *Bürgerschaft* had accepted the case of the retailers from as early as 12 October 1898. As the spokesman for the Senate saw the matter, the further breaking down of economic interests into fixed corporative bodies was a bad thing—to establish a separate *Detaillistenkammer* would be to create an additional "tool of the social war".[98] It was further claimed that the men behind the drive to create the Chamber did not possess "the necessary objectivity required to lead" such an organization. The police authorities were said to have reported to the Senate's spokesman that many of the retailers were mixed up in all sorts of "turbulent public agitation", and that these retailers often went much too far in their denunciations of "department stores and consumer co-operatives".[99] Later in the same year (1899), the Senate considered that the establishment of a separate *Detaillistenkammer* was a "dangerous experiment";[100] soon even the workers would be looking for such representation.

By the end of 1899, however, the repeated entreaties of the *Bürgerschaft* could not be totally ignored as they had been from early 1897 onward.[101] At the end of 1899 the Senate continued to insist that the "interests of trade *(Handel)* are common" and that it would be folly to draw a line between wholesale trade and the *Mittelstand.*[102] The Senate, therefore, put forward a number of proposals which were intended to open the doors of the Chamber of Commerce to the retailers. The proposals were put forward with little expectation that either members of the Chamber of Commerce or the retailers would accept them. In the course of 1899 the *Bürgerschaft* had reiterated its call for a special Chamber for the retailers.[103] The retailers themselves who had formalized their demands considered inadequate any special representation within either the Chamber of Commerce or the *Gewerbekammer* (the artisans' Chamber). The basis of their special claim also indicated the extent to which their new Chamber was to become, in effect, perhaps the retailers' most important and effective protective *(Schutz)* organization. However, some of the leading retailer organizations in Hamburg were overly optimistic concerning the potential of the new Chamber.[104]

Legislation establishing a special retailers' Chamber in Hamburg could not be passed before the resistance, especially that of the Senate (and, to a lesser extent, that of the Chamber of Commerce), had been overcome. Even the various proposals to the *Bürgerschaft* of 26 May 1897 had expressed some doubt concerning the effectiveness of the Chamber to ameliorate the retailers' problems.[105] Almost exactly two years later in 1899, local newspapers were at least conceding that the Chamber might represent an important first step.[106] By that time, the question of establishing the Chamber had become very much a political question. It was queried whether in fact the Senate could continue to prevent the *Bürgerschaft* (who favoured the Chamber) from carrying out a duty which the *Bürgerschaft* considered "one of its most important tasks. . . to preserve and to foster the interests of the retailers".[107] In July 1899 the Senate was resisting. Although the

Chamber was still considered a "dangerous experiment" in November 1899, the Senate had begun to realize that the question of the establishment of the Chamber was hardly to be dismissed. From early January 1900 the Senate was tempted by the idea that since the creation of the Chamber appeared inevitable, the Senate should determine its exact function and form. After the Senate had dropped its opposition to the very principle of such a *Detaillistenkammer,* the Chamber of Commerce followed suit.[108] Only the working out of the details of the law remained. The law on the *Detaillistenkammer* was finally passed on 29 February 1904. The powerful *Central-Ausschuss Hamburg-Altonaer Detaillisten-Vereine* considered that since the new Chamber had been created, its own work was finished. The operations of the *Central-Ausschuss* formally ended in March 1905.[109]

The major substantial differences between the proposals of, for example, the *Central-Ausschuss Hamburg-Altonaer Detaillisten-Vereine,* and those of the Senate were reduced to a simple proposition. One group, the Senators, considered that it was granting a great favour to the retailers, a favour which was to be hedged with as many restrictions as possible. The other group, the retailers, was of the opinion that it was seeking its reasonable rights and was determined that it was not going to be bullied by the Senate. It was in part because of this great difference of outlook that problems which might otherwise have been easily overcome became real obstacles. Even the name of the new Chamber became such an obstacle. The Senate wanted to name the new Chamber a *Kleinhandels-kammer,* but the retailers raised the most strenuous objections. The retailers were convinced that if the Chamber were called a *Kleinhandelskammer,* it would somehow appear less important than the Chamber of Commerce which represented overseas and wholesale trade *(Gross-handel).* By insisting on the name *Detaillistenkammer* (which the Senate labelled "tasteless"),[110] retailers were indicating that they considered the social and economic function of retailing no less important than that of wholesaling or overseas trade. The obstinacy of the retailers in Hamburg concerning the name of their Chamber was an indication of their heightened consciousness and their desire to assert themselves. Retailers in Bremen, who deliberately followed the Hamburg example, avoided much difficulty when they opted for a *Kammer für Kleinhandel.*[111]

The Detaillistenkammer Hamburg: The Assessment by Retailers of its Composition and Activity.

From the very outset many retailers (certainly the great majority of those in Hamburg) were greatly disappointed with their new Chamber. This disappointment was based both on the composition of the Chamber and, stemming from that composition, on the nature and range of activity of the *Detaillistenkammer.* The establishment of the Chamber in Bremen paralleled the establishment of the Chamber in Hamburg. The disappointment of the retailers in Bremen was similar to the disappointment of the majority of retailers in Hamburg.

The Senate had ensured the conservative nature of the *Detaillistenkammer* by severely limiting the right to vote to those who possessed (among other things full citizenship of Hamburg. To obtain citizenship it was necessary to have paid taxes on an income of 1,200 Mk. (or more) for at least the five previous consecutive years. In other words, one would have to already have had the right to vote in the *Bürgerschaft* elections before one could obtain the right to vote in the elections to the *Detaillistenkammer.* The suffrage was restricted even further in 1906 when the income level was raised to 2,500 Mk.[112] On a number of occasions it was estimated that there were in Hamburg some 14,000 to 15,000 retailers who were represented in neither the Chamber of Commerce nor the *Gewerbekammer.*[113] The eligible voters never exceeded 2,073 in any year up to 1929.[114] It was found that the *Verein der Tabak- und Zigarrenladen-Inhaber* in Hamburg (with some 800 members) could muster in 1904 only 46 members who were both qualified to vote and interested.[115] In the first elections to the Chamber, there were only 1,334 retailers who were entitled to vote.* Such results of the voting restrictions had been predicted in April 1904 by a new group, the *Gesamtausschuss der Hamburg-Altonaer Gewerbeschutzvereine* (which had, incidentally, Henningsen and Werbeck on the executive). The *Gesamtausschuss* denied that the new Chamber should be properly entitled a "class representation of retailers", "because it has not been produced by a free election of retailers; in spite of some cloaking, it can only be composed according to the will of the Senate."[116]

The political activities (or non-activities) of the *Detaillisten-kammer* which most outraged the Henningsens and Werbecks were those concerning support of the idea of a special taxation on department stores. The Chamber refused to advocate any special taxes on department stores even after a special meeting between the executives of the new Chamber and the *Gesamtausschuss der Hamburg Altonaer Gewerbeschutzvereine* had been held in early July 1905. The *Detaillistenkammer* never changed this policy. The anti-Semitic *Deutsches Blatt,* commenting on the meeting of July 1905, stated that the executive of the *Gesamtausschuss* had accused the executive of the *Detaillistenkammer* of being in the service of the *Verband der Waren- und Kaufhäuser* and that a minor anti-Semitic uproar followed.[117] The *Detaillistenkammer* had been willing to consider the support of the idea of special taxes on consumer co-operatives. Nevertheless it was the view of some retailers that the Chamber was too conservative in its demands. In 1911 the *Hamburgischer Verband der Detaillisten und sonstiger Gewerbetreibenden,* an organization which had been created in 1909, complained that the *Detaillistenkammer* had recommended much too low a tax on consumer co-operatives.[118] By April 1914 there were reports in the local press that many retailers were deserting the Chamber altogether.[119]

---

*Jahresbericht der Detaillistenkammer zu Hamburg für 1905 : 5. Electors were divided into 18 groups. When certain groups had fewer electors eligible than others, their representatives were, nevertheless, elected. Because of this procedure, there were complaints that some representatives were elected by less than half the votes by which others were elected. See *HH.St.Ar.Detaillistenkammer.1.XIII.B.1.   Wahlen, Entlassung und Ersatzwahlen usw.*

The *Kammer für Kleinhandel* in Bremen was comparable in almost every respect to the Chamber in Hamburg, not excepting restrictions of the entitlement to vote. It may be said that the vast majority of the activities of the new Chambers were restricted, at the local level at least, to technical matters. Both Chambers appear to have been occupied with questions of further education among retailers, of regulations of conditions of work, and of the relationship of employer to employee. These questions were not unimportant to the retailers. The Chambers fulfilled useful, if limited, functions. The sober and unemotional approach of both Chambers to the economic problems of the retailers may have helped to create the impression of anti-climax. This impression arises from an examination of both the activities of the Chambers and the reactions of the retailers to them.[120] As early as April 1906 it was claimed not only that the *Detaillistenkammer* in Hamburg was failing to carry out the plans of the "rescuers of the *Mittelstand*", but that it had become a "bulwark" preventing the realization of these plans by engaging in strictly "practical" work.[121] The struggle to establish the Chambers had caught the imagination of the retailers. After the Chambers had come into existence, they receded into the background (neither held public meetings), part and parcel of the establishment and hardly more accessible to small retailers than the Chambers of Commerce had been. However, the establishment of both Chambers exercised an influence on retailers outside Hamburg and Bremen.

Special Representation for Retailers in Chambers of Commerce outside Hamburg and Bremen

The question of the need for special representation of retailers within Chambers of Commerce really arose at all only in Prussia, and then only after the establishment of the special Chambers in Hamburg and Bremen. In Bavaria the new law of 25 October 1889 on Chambers of Commerce made special provisions for broadening the representation of the economic interests of retailers in Chambers of Commerce and *Gewerbekammern*.[122] It is noteworthy that the reforms of the Prussian Chambers of Commerce, which came just after the new legislation on the artisans in 1897, did not mention the retailers. Wilhelm's letter of 31 July 1895 to Von Berlepsch is usually interpreted as having ordered a change in the emphasis of German (and Prussian) social policy to one oriented toward the *Mittelstand.*[123] However the letter made only brief mention of the artisans and no mention at all of the retailers.

Particularly after the creation of special Chambers in Hamburg and Bremen, retailers in Prussia could claim that their lack of official representation had become blatantly obvious. Even the largest of the retailers' national organizations was opposed to specific *Detaillistenkammern,* and at its general meeting in 1898, expressed the view that retailers should work with the already established Chambers of Commerce. Hamburg and Bremen were recognized as exceptional cases.[124] Neither the Hamburg nor the Bremen Chambers came to the assistance of their fellows in this matter. Both had claimed as a rationale for their own existences the "local peculiarities" *(örtliche Besonderheiten)* which had necessitated the creation of special Chambers.[125] It was not their wish to see special *Detaillistenkammern* established throughout Germany.

In the Prussian *Landtag* the first significant public call for more equitable representation of retailers (either within separate Chambers or through special sections within Chambers of Commerce) came from Trimborn, a deputy from the Centre party, on 27 February 1907.[126] His proposal was linked with a call for a full enquiry into the economic conditions of the retailers. The proposal was based on what were considered to have been the highly favourable results of the artisans' legislation of 1897 Trimborn visualized that the retailers' special representative body would perform five main functions. Like the *Handwerkskammern* the retailers' organization would provide a centre where further activities might be planned and executed. The organization would take over matters of education and training, organize co-operative self-help activities, set up *Einkaufsgenossenschaften,* and even regulate unfair practices within retailing. The state was to play its role—but as the Conservative member Hammer put it, a role of backing up the retailers' own endeavours.[127] Trimborn refused to accept the old argument that distinct representation of retailers would further break down society into fixed and institutionalized separate economic interests.128 In the Prussian House the matter was quietly dropped and not mentioned again until early March 1909. By 1909 the *Deutscher Handelstag* had developed a policy of its own. Its policy decision directly influenced the debate in the House.

On 29 October 1907 the *Handelstag* commission for retailing discussed the question of the establishment of *Detaillistenkammern*. The commission did not limit the discussion to Prussia, for it was assumed that any change in the Prussian legislation would have national implications. The commission decided against the establishment of both *Detaillistenkammern* and compulsory committees for retailing within Chambers of Commerce. There was some opposition to this decision. Accusations were made that not only were Chambers of Commerce incapable (as they were then constituted) of representing the retailers, but that the *Deutscher Handelstag* was similarly incapable.129

At the general meeting of the *Handelstag* in late March 1908, there was opposition to any form of special representation for retailers because this representation would lead to "a regrettable division in the representation of the interests of trade and industry". Resolutions suggesting that Chambers of Commerce voluntarily create their own commissions for retailing (composed of retailers) and that retailers be directly represented on the commission for retailing of the *Handelstag* received insufficient support and were dropped by the *Handelstag*.130

When Hammer once again brought proposals for representation of retailers in Chambers of Commerce before the Prussian House in March 1909, the impact of the decisions of the *Handelstag* was evident. After a rather complex (and questionable) series of calculations, Hammer claimed that some 1.2 million retailers in Prussia were without official local representation.131 He remarked, somewhat bitterly, that action would long since have been taken if as many workers had been without such representation.132 Hammer and Trimborn no longer insisted upon the creation of independent *Detaillistenkammern*.133 They were willing to accept the committees for retailing, although they continued to insist that these committees had to be compulsory. Hammer pointed out that only 20 of the 90 Chambers of Commerce in Prussia had voluntarily established special retailers' committees.[134] Hammer's continuing reiteration of the need for compulsory committees, although the proposal never passed the Prussian House, persuaded the Prussian government that the least it could do was to remind the Chambers of Commerce in Prussia that they did have the duty to fully represent the interests of all "traders" in their areas. The Prussian Minister of Trade sent out the reminder to the Chambers of Commerce on 29 October 1909.[135] Some Chambers of Commerce,[136] for example, the *Vereinigung von Handelskammern des niederrheinisch-westfälischen Industriebezirks,* were quick to follow up such reminders.[137]

Conclusion

The economic activities of the retailers, particularly those of the small independents, were largely limited to the local level. Many of the most pressing problems confronted the retailers as local phenomena. The organizational activities of the retailers were firmly rooted in concrete local situations. The establishment of the local *Schutzverbände* provides evidence of the existence of economic forces against which retailers wanted to be protected. At the same time, the creation of local *Schutzverbände* demonstrated that retailers were willing to join together in order to overcome their problems. The creation of all types of local *Schutzverbände* by retailers in pre-war Germany may be seen as another step in their political mobilization. The actual results, in terms of the amelioration of the economic difficulties of retailers—even in cities where retailers were (ostensibly) most successfully organized (such as in Hamburg and Bremen)—appear to have fallen far short of retailers' expectations.

The next essential step in the political mobilization of the retailers would be a slightly more complex analysis of their problems. Retailers had to realize that their own local problems were not to be overcome by agitation and activity at the local level alone. Moreover, they had to come to the realization that retailers in other centres frequently shared common problems and that only joint activity on a far wider front offered some possibility of solving their problems.

5

Schutzverbände in Retail Trade 1890-1914: Regional and National Organizations

The creation of retailers' *Schutzverbände* was a response to local problems. The results of local activity by retailers, however, even in cities where they were best organized, fell far below many retailers' expectations. Although it had been expected that the activity of retailers would have more fruitful results if retailers joined together to form larger regional and national organizations, the very strength of the local organization was one of the most important factors mitigating against the successful creation of regional and national *Schutzverbände*. In the period from 1890 to 1914 there emerged no single national *Schutzverband* which managed to win the support of retailers throughout Germany. At the national level there were almost always two or more competing organizations. At the regional and state levels numerous organizations with greatly varying aims waged competition for retailers' support. As indicated above, many retailers considered even the *Verband der Rabattsparvereine Deutschlands,* numerically the largest retailer organization in 1914, to be an organization that was to be fought in the same way as a consumer co-operative or department store.

The local *Schutzverbände,* taken together with the broader regional and national organizations, became what may be termed a veritable *Schutzverbandsbewegung.* This movement is conceived of as a pre-institutionalized form of a collective attempt by retailers to master their economic problems.[1] In the retailers *Schutzverbandsbewegung* the regional or state organizations provided the important link between the original local organizational initiatives of the retailers'

Schutzverbände and the national *Schutzverbände.* The broader activities of the *Schutzverbände* became an integral part of what contemporaries referred to as the *Mittelstandsbewegung.* Between 1890 and 1914, this latter "movement" gradually transformed itself from a pre-institutionalized form of political endeavour into a more formal and discernible party-political enterprise.

State and Regional Schutzverbände

Although one may distinguish between local, regional, and national *Schutzverbände* on the basis of obvious differences in the names of each organization, the lines which separated the various *Schutzverbände* were far more blurred than the labels attached to the organizations would suggest. Werbeck's organization, the *Verein gegen Unwesen im Handel und Gewerbe* (Hamburg), formed the central core and shared the same newspaper as the *Verein gegen Unwesen im Handel und Gewerbe für Norddeutschland.* Werbeck, in the name of both organizations, was perhaps the chief moving force behind the foundation of the national organization, the *Deutscher Bund für Handel und Gewerbe* (founded in 1899). Werbeck, who was elected to the executive of this national organization at its founding meeting, seems to have had a good deal of influence upon both the aims and the methods of the organization. There was, therefore, a considerable overlap in the structure of retailers' *Schutzverbände.* That structure was further complicated by the participation of retailers' technical organizations at all levels. However Werbeck's activities (which were by no means unique)* indicate that the lines of transmission between the local *Schutzverbände* and the regional and national *Schutzverbände* might be very direct.

As Table 2 indicates, retailers' *Schutzverbände* at the state and regional levels were—as in the case of the local *Schutzverbände*—created primarily after 1890. Only five of the

*Cf. the activities of the *Bund der Handel- und Gewerbetreibenden* (Berlin), the *Zentralvereinigung preussischer Vereine zum Schutz für Handel und Gewerbe* (Berlin), and the *Zentralvereinigung deutscher Vereine für Handel und Gewerbe* (Berlin). These organizations were effectively the creation of one man, Hugo Lissauer.

more than twenty retailers' *Schutzverbände* which were established at the state and regional levels by 1909 had existed prior to 1890. Of these five, only one had existed as early as 1884, while two had been created in 1887 and two in 1889. With only one exception *(the Detaillistenverband für Hessen und Waldeck,* created in 1895), these state and regional organizations were established when local *Schutzverbände* joined together to form the larger organization. The establishment of the state and regional organizations chronologically followed the establishment of the local *Schutzverbände.* There were at least three cross-regional areas where state and regional organizations were in some manner or other related to one another. Although a geographical principle is not used to organize the present chapter, these three cross-regional areas emerge quite distinctly in the course of the discussion. The first area rotated around a Hanover-Leipzig axis; the second area was centred in, but not confined exclusively to the Rhineland; the third area, which was not as important to the retailers' *Schutzverbandsbewegung* as either of the first two, was centred in Berlin and the Northeast.[2] In terms of the political mobilization of the retailers, these three focal areas were not of equal importance.

Table 2: Retailers' Schutzverbände at the Regional and State Levels: The Dates of their Foundation

1884   *Verband Thüringischer Kaufleute* (headquarters in varying cities)

1887   *Verband von Kaufleuten der Provinz Hannover und der angrenzenden Länder* (Hanover)
        Verband der Kaufleute der Provinz Sachsen, der Herzogtümer Anhalt und Braunschweig (Cöthen)

1889   *Verband der Vereine zum Schutz des Handels und Gewerbes für Schlesien* (Breslau)
        Verband Sächsischer Kaufleute und Gewerbetreibender (Leipzig)

1891   *Verband von Kaufleuten der Provinzen Rheinland und Westfalen und der angrenzenden Länder* (at first with headquarters in varying cities, later Barmen)

1892   *Württembergischer Schutzverein für Handel und Gewerbe* (Stuttgart)

1893   *Verband selbständiger Kaufleute und Gewerbetreibender des Grossherzogtums Baden* (headquarters in varying cities)

*1894   *Bayerischer Verband der Vereine zum Schutz für Handel und Gewerbe* (Munich, until the end of 1894)
Detaillistenverband für Rheinland und Westfalen (Barmen)

1895   *Detaillistenverband für Hessen und Waldeck* (Cassel)
Zentralausschuss Hamburg-Altonaer Detaillistenverbände (Hamburg)

1898   *Bund der Handel- und Gewerbetreibenden* (Berlin)

1900   *Verband süd- und westdeutscher Detaillistenvereine* (Frankfurt/M)

1902   *Kaufmännischer Provinzialverband zu Stettin*

1905   *Zentralvereinigung preussischer Vereine für Handel und Gewerbe* (Berlin)

1906   *Bayerischer Verband der Vereine zum Schutz für Handel und Gewerbe* (Nuremberg)

1907   *Provinzialverband der Kolonialwarenhändler Ostpreussens*
Verband der Detaillistenvereine im Grossherzogtum Hessen (Darmstadt)
Verband der selbständigen Kaufleute und Gewerbetreibenden der Pfalz (Ludwigshafen)

1908   *Verband kaufmännischer und Detaillistenvereine von Elsass-Lothringen* (Strasbourg)

1909   *Verband Mecklenburgischer Handelsvereine* (Rostock)

State and Regional Schutzverbände: From the Foundation of the First Organizations to 1895

The initiatives for the creation of state and regional *Schutzverbände,* like those for the creation of the *Verband der Rabattsparvereine Deutschlands,* came from the Hanover-Saxony area of Germany. In 1887 the *Verband von Kaufleu-*

*Source for Table 2: Wein, *Verbandsbildung,* 1968 : 42. These two organizations took decisions not to work with Schulze-Gifhorn's national organization.

ten der Provinz Hannover und der angrenzenden Länder was founded under the leadership of Senator Schulze (from Gifhorn).* The establishment of this organization was important not only because most state organizations (until 1895) followed the example of Schulze-Gifhorn's organization, but also because these organizations joined the central organization of retailers created in 1888 by Schulze-Gifhorn. The latter organization was established through the co-operation of the *Verband Thüringischer Kaufleute* (founded in 1884) and the *Verband der Kaufleute der Provinz Sachsen, der Herzogtümer Anhalt und Braunschweig* (founded in 1887). The central organization originally carried the name *Zentralvorstand kaufmännischer Verbände und Vereine Deutschlands.* Until 1895, with but two exceptions (see Table 2), the state and regional *Schutzverbände* which came into existence took decisions to work with the *Zentralvorstand.* It seems fairly certain that the *Zentralvorstand* did not play a direct role in the establishment of these early state and regional organizations, although its advice and friendly offices were probably offered.[3]

The early state and regional *Schutzverbände* did not merely represent the reaction of retailers in one area to the organizational activities of retailers in another area.[4] The larger organizations very often resembled the local *Schutzverbände* in that they were responses to localized problems. The *Centralausschuss Hamburg-Altonaer Detaillisten-Vereine* was founded in 1895 primarily with a view to the creation of a *Detaillistenkammer* in Hamburg.[5] The *Detaillistenverband für Hessen und Waldeck,* also founded in 1895, was established specifically to combat the further creation of consumer co-operatives in the area.[6] It was mentioned earlier that this latter organization was unique in establishing branches instead of being itself constituted by the coming together *(der Zusammenschluss)* of a number of already existing local organizations.

*According to Wein, *Verbandsbildung,* 1968 : 45, Schulze-Gifhorn "belonged at first to the extreme right wing of the National Liberal Party, but left when the party did not participate actively enough in the struggle against department stores and consumer co-operatives. Thereafter, he sympathized with the Free Conservative Party, although he did not become a member of it". Wein's only source was the *Kolonialwaren-Ztg.* Nr. 33, 27.4.1905.

The majority of the local *Schutzverbände* associated with the early state and regional *Schutzverbände* were made up of the organizations of the smaller retailers. The organizations of the grocers and dry-goods dealers appear to have been well represented. The available data reveals neither the nature of those local organizations nor their membership figures. Moreover, the very broad names which local organizations tended to adopt for themselves add to the uncertainty about the nature of the membership.[7] The *Centralausschuss Hamburg-Altonaer Detaillisten-Vereine* was a unique case. Of the seven local organizations associated with it in 1903, two were grocers' associations, one a delicatessen association, one of cigarette dealers and one of dry-goods. The other organizations were the Hamburg *Verein gegen Unwesen im Handel und Gewerbe* and a wholesalers' association.[8]

Although the specific occasions which prompted the creation of the early state and regional *Schutzverbände* varied considerably, after they had been established there were many obvious problems around which the activities of these *Schutzverbände* tended to gravitate. The various local archives reveal that a more or less continuous campaign was waged by these organizations against those things which retailers considered to be the economic threats to their existence. The organizations established in the period up to 1895 were particularly preoccupied with opposition to consumer co-operatives especially those of the civil servants. A long letter of 24 August 1903 was sent by the *Verband von Kaufleuten der Provinz Hannover und der angrenzenden Länder* to the governmental authorities in Hanover. The letter stated that retailers were suffering under severe pressure from two sides. On the one side, there were the pressures from the department stores, mail-order houses, and travelling salesmen. It was claimed, however, that the whole range of consumer co-operatives "very greatly threatens and burdens retail trade". The immediate object of this particular letter was to enlist the support of the head of the government in Hanover to suggest that it was not really proper for a civil servant to belong to consumer co-operatives since they were known tools of Social Democracy.[9]

Apart from such direct appeals to state and regional government, the early state and regional organizations worked very closely with the national organization founded by Schulze-Gifhorn, the *Zentralvorstand*. By 1903 five of the ten organizations listed by the Ministry of the Interior as state and regional organizations affiliated to the (then re-named) *Zentralvorstand* were listed as branch organizations.[10] The official newspaper shared by these organizations preserved the older names of the state and regional organizations after 1903,[11] but the close interrelation was implied in the common newspaper (and even in common names). The detailed discussion below of Schulze-Gifhorn's central organization implicitly covers many of the activities of the several state and regional organizations which came to be virtually branch organizations of the *Zentralverband*.

State and Regional Schutzverbände: The Post - 1895 Period

The most important development in state and regional *Schutzverbände* in the post-1895 period was the establishment of organizations which were in open conflict both with the already established state and regional *Schutzverbände* and with Schulze-Gifhorn's central organization. The first blows to the initial unity of approach and policy which characterized the earlier established state and regional organizations came from the Rhineland. The *Detaillistenverband für Rheinland und Westfalen,* established in 1894, did not formally unite with Schulze-Gifhorn's central organization. The *Bayerischer Verband der Vereine zum Schutz für Handel und Gewerbe,* which was also established in 1894, maintained a similar stance. Because of financial difficulties, the latter organization did not remain in existence. It was not until 1906 that a successful Bavarian *Verband* was created. It adopted the same policy orientation which the earlier Bavarian organization had followed.[12] Under the direction of the *Detaillistenverband für Rheinland und Westfalen,* the newspaper *Der Detaillist* was established in 1906. It was shared by the Bavarian *Verband* and other dissenting organizations such as the *Verband süd-und westdeutscher Detaillistenvereine* (with headquarters in Frankfurt a.M.), and the *Verband Kaufmännischer und Detaillistenvereine von Elsass-Lothringen.* By

1911 the organizations grouped around *Der Detaillist* were said to have some 70,000 members.[13] In contrast to most of the earlier state and regional *Schutzverbände,* the organizations around *Der Detaillist* were not formed from the ranks of the small grocers but from the generally more financially well-off textile dealers.[14] Differences in social composition between the earlier and later *Schutzverbände* were not entirely responsible for the policy differences which were to emerge. The underlying causes of these policy differences were undoubtedly far more complex.

One of the more spectacular policy differences between the earlier organizations around Schulze-Gifhorn and those around *Der Detaillist* was that which concerned the ever-present department stores and the question of their taxation. From their inception the former organizations were strong opponents of consumer co-operatives, department stores and all other types of large concerns. An integral part of their opposition was the advocacy of a special tax upon such enterprises. In the early years of its activity the *Detaillistenverband für Rheinland und Westfalen* did not openly question this policy and tended to work with Schulze-Gifhorn's central organization. In response to the increasing tempo of the demands for the special tax on department stores and to the revelation of the intentions of the Prussian government to pass such a tax, the Rhineland organization formally resolved at its meeting on 9 June 1898 to oppose a policy of taxing the department stores. The basis of the rejection of "every tax on turnovers and every special tax which burdens retail trade in general" was that such special taxation "would have a detrimental effect not only on retail trade, but also on the development of industry, the communities, and the entire state."[15] The full resolution sounded objections similar to those of the *Vereinigung von Handelskammern des niederrheinisch-westfälischen Industriebezirks*[16] rather than to those of Schulze-Gifhorn's central organization.[17] Such a policy provides some indication that the organizations around *Der Detaillist* were composed of more financially secure retailers. In spite of the fundamental differences in policy between these first two groups of regional *Schutzverbände,* there remained a considerable area of agreement. The consumer co-operatives continued to provide a common target. Although there was a shared desire to clean up all forms of "unfair competition", there were differences of opinion about what constituted the "unfair".[18] The shared views could not compensate for the great differences which had emerged over the issue of taxing the department stores.

Differences no less fundamental soon developed between Schulze-Gifhorn's central organization and the *Bund der Handel- und Gewerbetreibenden,* an organization oriented towards Berlin and environs which was established in 1898. These differences, which will be examined below within the context of splits in the national movement, appear to have been based more on personal rivalry within the leadership than on real policy differences. Whatever their bases these differences resulted in the creation of a new state organization in 1905 (the *Zentralvereinigung preussischer Vereine für Handel und Gewerbe),* and even in the creation of a new central organization in 1908 in open conflict with the central organization established by Schulze-Gifhorn.[19] The Berlin organization, as well as the relatively late emerging state and regional *Schutzverbände* of the Northeast, enter more fully therefore than the organizations around *Der Detaillist* into the history of Schulze-Gifhorn's organization.

If the Rhineland organization considered that advocacy of special taxes was more than the central organization of Schulze-Gifhorn should demand of government, there were other organizations which considered that Schulze-Gifhorn's organization was not demanding enough. One of the organizations of a more radical caste was Werbeck's Hamburg organization. In 1899 it led in the struggle for the establishment of a rival central organization, the *Deutscher Bund für Handel und Gewerbe.* By the early years of the nineteenth century therefore, the central organizations created by Schulze-Gifhorn was faced with the potential or actual competition of three other groups of organizations—there were the organizations around *Der Detaillist,* those in Berlin and the Northeast around the *Bund der Handel und Gewerbetreibenden,* and those such as Werbeck's organization, which formed the *Deutscher Bund für Handel und Gewerbe.* The disunity and conflict had been elevated to national proportions.

National Schutzverbände: 1. The Zentralvorstand kaufmännischer Verbände und Vereine Deutschlands (founded in 1888)

The *Zentralvorstand* was not the first organization to attempt the formation of a national *Schutzverband* for retailers in Germany. A *Zentralverband der Kaufleute Deutschlands*, which had been founded in Berlin in 1878, failed to win sufficient support among retailers to survive beyond 1878.[20] This initial attempt to rally the retailers may be said to have failed partly because the economic pre-conditions for such an organization did not exist in 1878. It was after 1890 that retailers in general became conscious of the economic problems which came to threaten their existence. The early years of the *Zentralvorstand* were difficult years. It was not until 6 September 1891 that the loosely organized *Zentralvorstand* was transformed into the more prepossessing *Zentralverband deutscher Kaufleute*. This same organization was subsequently transformed into the *Zentralverband deutscher Kaufleute und Gewerbetreibender* (on 27 August 1899) and still later into the *Deutscher Zentralverband für Handel und Gewerbe* (on 13 August 1907).[21]

Even after 6 September 1891 the power of the state and regional organizations affiliated to the central organization persisted. Membership resided in the state and regional organizations which decided whether to join the *Zentralverband*. Local *Schutzverbände* affiliated to the state and regional organizations had therefore merely an indirect membership in the *Zentralverband*. Some of the state and regional organizations in the course of time did decide to refer to themselves as branches of the *Zentral*.[22] (See the first five organizations listed in Table 2.) In effect, they merely formalized their earlier commitment. Some state and regional organizations affiliated to the *Zentral* decided to retain at least the independence of their name, while others, such as the Hamburg *Central-Ausschuss* and the *Berliner Bund*, gradually moved away altogether from the Schulze-Gifhorn *Zentral*. It was only after 1890, when additional state and regional organizations were attracted to the solid early core of organizations, that the existence of the *Zentralverband* became assured.

Almost immediately, it was attacked by both the radical organizations, such as the *Verein gegen Unwesen im Handel und Gewerbe* from Hamburg, and by the more conservative organizations around *Der Detaillist.*

Throughout its existence the *Zentralverband* officially maintained as its aim "the safeguarding of interests and the elevation of retailers, as well as the furthering and broadening of technical knowledge".[23] Although this general aim appears to have advocated self-help,* the *Zentralverband* from the very beginning of its activity was much more inclined towards state-help. A memorandum of 30 November 1893 of the *Zentralverband* sent to the Kaiser stated that

> *To rescue the class through self-help is almost com-*
> *pletely out of the question. Against the freedoms, which*
> *damage, even ruin, traders from fixed selling outlets,*
> *against the superior strength of* Grosskapital, *neither the*
> *individual nor an association can do anything; only the*
> *law can give sufficient protection.* [24]

The activities of the early years of the *Zentralvorstand* under Schulze-Gifhorn which were most characteristic were attacks against the consumer co-operatives and the so-called civil servant consumer co-operatives.[25] The arguments for such an orientation would have been plausible because the consumer co-operatives and several of the civil servant consumer co-operatives were the first to pose real threats to the economic existence of the retailers. In a memorandum written in 1916 on the activities of the *Zentralverband,* the *Zentralverband* reiterated that consumer co-operatives had remained throughout the period up to 1914 "the greatest pests of retail trade".[26]

From the first years of its existence the *Zentralverband* sought (not without success) various legislative enactments, particularly from the Prussian and federal German governments, which were designed to restrict the development of all types of consumer co-operatives as far as possible. The legis-

*The impression conveyed by Wein, *Verbandsbildung*, 1968 : 44-45 is that this general aim was representative of the policy orientation of the *Zentralverband.*

lative demands of the *Zentralverband* against the civil servant consumer co-operatives were very different from those against the civilian consumer co-operatives. The demands were, however, based upon the interpretation of the *Zentralverband* that the most insidious (even if unintended) result of the operation of both types of consumer co-operatives was that "the way was made clear" for Social Democracy. This result followed from the "decline of small independents". The destructive competition of the consumer co-operatives was turning the "loyal *(staatserhaltende)* classes" (including, of course, the retailers) into part of the "menacing proletariat". It was claimed that this truth had become recognized by the leaders of Social Democracy who had become "enthusiastic supporters" of consumer co-operatives.[27] In a statement representative of the views of the *Zentralverband* made in a petition of January 1891 to the Prussian Ministry of State, the *Zentralverband* claimed that its members were "not irreversible opponents" of consumer co-operatives

> *so long as they pursue their original aim, the procurement of cheaper food for the worker, as their only aim. We must expect, however, that these establishments which enjoy the same rights, accept the same duties as the other open selling outlets with which they are in competition.*[28]

This argument, which was very widely held among retailers' *Schutzverbände* at all levels, contained a number of general elements which called for state regulation in favour of independent retailers. The argument contained the necessary political element—the suggestion that Social Democracy was being favoured because market forces were permitted to operate. The statement also contained the view that retailers had been supporters of the state "as taxpayers and through their intelligence".[29] The unstated question to the governmental authorities was whether this support should go totally unrewarded. The *Zentralverband* sought nothing so radical as a demand for the complete abolition of all consumer co-operatives. Although retailers' *Schutzverbände* often campaigned for legislation on consumer co-operatives, they rarely demanded the abolition of consumer co-operatives.[30] The

Zentralverband would have been content, at least in its early years, if consumer co-operatives had been made subject to "the same duties"—that is, to pay the same taxes as independent retailers. This was the line of argument which ran through the petitions of retailers.

By claiming that consumer co-operatives should be made subject to "the same duties", the *Zentralverband* implied that all types of consumer co-operatives had an unfair advantage over independent retail trade. This unfair advantage was considered to be concerned chiefly with matters of taxation. Consumer co-operatives were not subject to taxation, and their dividends were not taxed.[31] The only "reward" which the *Zentralverband* sought from the government was an adjustment of the laws on consumer co-operatives. It was the view of the *Zentralverband* that consumer co-operatives should be treated as any other business venture. In the late 1880s and early 1890s this argument found little support outside retailers' circles. The *Zentralverband* responded using the argument of the defenders of the consumer co-operatives* by insisting that if a consumer co-operative was in fact a type of society created in order to assist its members, it should be permitted to sell to those members alone. With considerable difficulty and sometimes on curious grounds, measures were enacted by the *Reichstag* forcing the consumer co-operatives to sell to members only.

In the *Reichstag,* the chief advocate of legislatively forcing consumer co-operatives to sell to members only and, incidentally, of enforcing this restriction with legal penalties, personally favoured the existence of the co-operatives. Against the majority of his party, Wilhelm Kulemann (NL) argued that consumer co-operatives were quite clearly hurting the independent retailers and that the latter were only beginning to react. In the debate in the House, he claimed that a movement was beginning against the consumer co-operatives and that "this movement assumes a dimension which can damage the entire substance of co-operation". "I would not like to under-

---

*The chief argument of the defenders of the consumer co-operatives was that a consumer co-operative was a type of welfare society *(gemeinnützig).*

estimate", he continued, "where it will lead, if one does not give due consideration to the complaints of the independents."[32]

The first federal law forbidding consumer co-operatives to sell to non-members came into effect on 1 May 1889, albeit without the legal penalty clause suggested by Kulemann.[33] The federal authorities were subsequently persuaded to tighten up the laws on the consumer co-operatives and, specifically, to introduce Kulemann's earlier proposals on the penalty clause. After 1889 the authorities received numerous petitions from retailer *Schutzverbände,* including several petitions from the *Zentralverband.*[34] In late 1895 and early 1896, there were arguments in the *Reichstag* in favour of the penalty clause from the Centre, the Conservative, and the anti-Semitic parties. The general tone of the argument in favour of the penalty clause was either that the *Mittelstand* was being destroyed or that its continued existence was becoming impossible.[35] The anti-Semitic member Oswald Zimmermann called the consumer co-operatives "the gravediggers of our *Mittelstand*".[36] The Conservative Freiherr von Stumm-Halberg declared solemnly, "We do not fight against the consumer co-operatives, but against the abuses of the consumer co-operatives, which have developed to the disadvantage of the *Mittelstand* and the small independent."[37] The supplementary law which was passed on 12 August 1896 embodied Kulemann's earlier proposals. By the time the last of these laws came into effect, the *Zentralverband,* keeping in step with the increasing tempo of the establishment of the consumer co-operatives, had already raised its demands considerably.[38]

The viewpoint of the *Zentralverband* on civil servant consumer co-operatives was forceful from the very beginning. The *Zentralverband* desired, according to one of its petitions,[39] that the state present its "servants" with a clear ultimatum:

> *You* (Du) *are either an officer, a civil servant, or you are a retailer; in my service, you are not permitted to be both. If you are both, not only do you ruin a great number of my citizens, but eventually you will destroy the state.*[40]

The original demand of the *Zentralverband* was that the federal government forbid all its civil servants from "participating in the founding and administration" of consumer co-operatives.[41] This view remained consistent within the retailers' *Schutzverbände* and within other groups associated with the *Mittelstandsbewegung*. The argument was based in part on the view that civil servants had special connections and knowledge which should not be put at the disposal of enterprises in direct competition with independents.

By 1896 however, the *Zentralverband* was seeking both the dissolution of all existing civil servant consumer co-operatives and a law forbidding the creation of any others.[42] The *Zentralverband* even suggested that if the formation of civil servant consumer co-operatives was made necessary by the low wages of the civil servants, these wages should be raised. A rise in wages for civil servants would presumably remove the *raison d'être* of their consumer co-operatives. At almost all the annual meetings of the *Zentralverband* after 1896, there were recurrent demands for some form of curtailment of civil servant consumer co-operatives or, at least, the ending of civil servant participation in the administration of consumer co-operatives.[43] At the twenty-fifth annual meeting in Hanover on 26 August 1912, the unfulfilled demands of the *Zentralverband* were still high on its list of priorities.[44]

In the period from its foundation up to 1914, the *Zentralverband* occupied itself with a whole series of endeavours to fight what it considered to be "unfair competition". The leaders of the *Zentralverband* always spoke with great pride of the role which the *Zentralverband* had played in the enactment of the federal law against unfair competition (published on 30 May 1896). It was the *Zentralverband*, it was claimed, which had succeeded in getting the Centre Party "interested in the idea".[45] In fact, the Prussian and federal authorities had received numerous petitions seeking legislation against "unfair competition" from other *Schutzverbände* at all levels, as well as from certain Chambers of Commerce.[46] In a long memorandum of December 1894 the Prussian Ministry of Justice said that although such a law might be presented as necessary to protect the consumer, the practical difficulties of enforcing the law would be enormous. There was some opinion among both Chambers of Commerce and larger newspapers that the law was unnecessary and that it might even have some negative effects.[47]

The federal law which was passed on 27 May 1896 was aimed against only certain specific unfair practices and did not contain a statement of general principles which a court might apply to non-specified abuses.[48] From the retailers' point of view, failure of such a general principle meant that the law was of extremely limited use. Between the passage of the first law on unfair competition and the new law of 7 June 1909, numerous petitions were sent to the federal and Prussian governments by retailers' organizations which were campaigning to get the so-called general clause introduced into the law.[49] Apart from the general clause, the new law incorporated a large number of the retailers' demands which had been included in the petitions sent to the various authorities over the years. Retailers particularly welcomed specific clauses to prevent abuses in advertisements and in connection with "sales" and "selling off" *(Ausverkäufe)*. Even under the old law, retailers often pursued "unfair" practices extremely far. At the turn of the century, a two-year court case was fought by an association in Gelsenkirchen against a local business. The proprietor had displayed the sign, "50 Pf. Bazar", outside the shop, even though there were goods inside which cost more than fifty pfennigs. The firm was found guilty, forced to remove the sign, and pay the court costs.[50]

After 1900 the *Zentralverband* took up the struggle for considerable broadening of the 1896 law on unfair competition,[51] even though it had appeared initially to have been generally satisfied with the 1896 law.[52] In June 1898 Werbeck wrote to the *Verein selbständiger Leipziger Kaufleute und Fabrikanten zur Wahrung berechtigter Interessen* in the name of the *Verein gegen Unwesen im Handel und Gewerbe für Norddeutschland.* The object of the letter was to call a conference on "burning questions". The agenda was to include the laws on unfair advertising, unfair competition, and *"Grosskapital* in retail trade". An aim of the conference was to establish the *Deutscher Bund für Handel und Gewerbe.* The occasion for the first formal split in the *Schutzverbandsbewegung* was discontent with the results of the activities of the *Zentralverband* in one specific area, the matter of unfair competition. This particular split was not to be permanent; neither was it to be the last formal split away from the *Zentralverband*.

National Schutzverbände: 2. The Deutscher Bund für Handel und Gewerbe 1899 - 1907

The conference designed to lay the groundwork of the new organization was held in Leipzig on 3 and 4 October 1898. There were representatives present from some sixty-five *Schutzverbände,* Chambers of Commerce, and *Gewerbekammern* from cities all over Germany. None of the organizations around *Der Detaillist* attended. The several Rhineland organizations which had sent delegates were in no way affiliated to the *Detaillist* group. Schulze-Gifhorn was present, as well as a number of representatives of state and regional *Schutzverbände* associated with his *Zentralverband.* Hugo Lissauer, who had created the *Bund der Handel- und Gewerbetreibenden* in 1898 in Berlin, was also in attendance. In 1908 Lissauer was to establish a further rival to the *Zentralverband* at the national level. The Leipzig conference of 1898, therefore, brought together most of the chief rivals within the retailers' national *Schutzverbände.* Nevertheless the conference itself proved to be a relatively mild affair.

The chief area of conflict was that concerned with organizational questions. Although Werbeck did not deny the accomplishments of the *Zentralverband* of Schulze-Gifhorn, he noted that "the *Verband* cannot and will not carry through what needs to be done". For that very reason, it was "absolutely advisable that young blood be introduced into the movement".[53] As another delegate put it, the ideas of the *Zentralverband* "no longer coincide with those of the younger generation".[54] The *Zentralverband* could easily have satisfied the claims for greater independence to affiliated organizations demanded by those seeking to establish the new

Deutscher Bund, even though the allegations of undue centralization had been denied (notably by Lissauer himself).[55]
Differences over matters of real substance however made it
extremely difficult for Schulze-Gifhorn and his comrades to
head off the split in the movement. The underlying difference
between the *Zentralverband* and the new *Bund* was contained
in the determined statement of one delegate who claimed
that "political and religious questions ought not to restrict
the activity of our organization".[56] Rightly or wrongly, these
and other statements were taken in the press to mean that the
new organization was to pursue anti-Semitic policies and to
engage more directly in party politics.[57] According to one
account, such a policy proved a sufficient basis for the departure of Schulze-Gifhorn from the meeting.[58] However the
hesitation to become further involved in "politics" was itself
part of the basic accusation directed at the *Zentralverband,*
namely that the *Zentralverband* had failed to address itself to
those matters which were of primary importance to the retailers. As Werbeck derisively put it, the agenda of the last
meeting of the *Zentralverband* had contained twenty-five
points, most of which were of "secondary importance".[59]

In the discussion of other matters at the conference ("the
burning questions"), the basic ideology of the new *Deutscher
Bund* emerged clearly. F.W. Bargmann, who was associated
with Werbeck's *Norddeutschland* organization, gave a long
speech on *"Grosskapital* in retail trade" in which he spoke of
what he called "a basic error in the liberal economic philo-
sophy".[60] This "basic error" was the assumption that Germans wanted to buy at the cheapest prices, regardless of the
consequences. It was alleged that the German consumer
included in his calculations considerations such as whether the
Fatherland might inadvertently be damaged in some manner.
If "mindless Social Democrats" were created through the
ruination of the *Mittelstand* (which would follow if department stores were to flourish at the expense of independents),
then "cheap prices" were actually quite expensive. In view of
the need "to protect the Fatherland" from "revolutionaries",
a tax on large undertakings in retail trade should never be
considered too high. Bargmann's response to the defenders of
the department stores who claimed that the tax was a "stran-

gulation tax"* was that "it is less cruel if a few individuals are strangled through such a tax than if a mass-strangulation is set in motion on behalf of *Grosskapital*".61 The new *Bund* took a "moral" stand against *Grosskapital*. Bargmann's speech dealt with much more than his subject—"*Grosskapital* in Retail Trade"—would suggest. His own summary of that speech provides an insight into the aims, methods, and *Weltanschauung* of the new *Bund*.

> *Gentlemen! In closing permit me to give a short resumé of my address. The activity of* Grosskapital *in retail trade is only justified from a purely materialistic standpoint. The consequence of this standpoint is anarchy. In opposition to this consequence, legislation represents a protector of the national conscience, the standpoint of the moral* Weltanschauung. *We recognize in the intervention of* Grosskapital *in retailing an endangering of the endurable association of great classes of the nation* (Volk). *Therefore, right is on our side and demands of us the duty, on the one hand, to guide legislation towards orderly intervention and, on the other, to rouse to self-help the classes whose existence is threatened. We expect the legislation to take into consideration our suggestions concerning taxes on both turnovers and branch stores. The primary task of our association is and must remain above everything else the development, stimulation, and mobilization of moral forces with a view to the improvement of our business and economic relations.* 62

The conference ended with the passage of ten resolutions, many of which went far beyond the former policy of the *Zentralverband*. Two of the resolutions contained demands for the complete dissolution of all existing civil servant consumer co-operatives and for measures to prevent the establishment of others. Several of the other resolutions called for

---

*In order to discredit the demands of the retailers, the interest groups of the department stores popularized the idea that retailers wanted a "strangulation tax". See, for example, *Denkschrift des Generalsekretariats des Verbandes Deutscher Waren-· und Kaufhäuser* (Nov, 1904). Cf. the various works of Wernicke.

taxation of consumer co-operatives and department stores in all conceivable forms. Other resolutions demanded new measures to be introduced into the laws on unfair competition. Finally, a committee was elected to study the feasibility of establishing the new *Deutscher Bund für Handel und Gewerbe*.[63]

The *Bund* was formally established in June 1899 with headquarters in Leipzig. It began with some 6,500 members in 35 affiliated associations. The first chairman was Heinrich Reinhardt from Leipzig. Werbeck from Hamburg was elected to the eleven member executive. According to the official press release, the organization was to pursue the interests of members

> *in all questions. . .(whether they fall under the law of 27 May or not) which concern unfair competition, that is, the endangering of retail trade and artisanship through* Grosskapital, *for example, through department stores, consumer co-operatives, and associated organizations: in any case [the aim is] the awakening and the protection of class consciousness, class honour, and the representation of class questions in general.* [64]

This declaration of aims is interesting not only because it categorized all economic elements threatening the small independents as "unfair", but also because it explicitly or implicitly reflected the views of Werbeck's Hamburg based *Verein gegen Unwesen im Handel und Gewerbe.* By mid-1899 "malpractice", "unfair competition", and all forms of "large concerns" had become synonymous with a "hazard for trade" for members of the new *Bund.* [65]

A study of the annual general meetings of the new *Deutscher Bund für Handel und Gewerbe* indicates that the aims of the organization (and the methods suggested for the achievement of these aims) went far beyond merely "the enforcement of the clauses of the law of 27 May 1896 against unfair competition".[66] The concept of the "unfair" that was held by the new *Bund* was far more wide-ranging than the concept embodied in the law of 1896 or even that embodied in the revised law of 1909.

The first annual meeting of the new *Bund* was held on 26 June 1900 in Gera. There was discussion of certain aspects of the law of 1896, especially those aspects of the law which the *Bund* thought required revision. There was also consideration of various measures which might be taken against large concerns in retail trade, in addition to taxation measures. The *Schutzgemeinschaft für Handel und Gewerbe* in Greiz suggested the idea of publishing the names of all wholesalers and manufacturers who had recently petitioned the Prussian government to drop its proposals to pass a special department store tax.[67] The Socialist newspaper in Hamburg, the *Echo,* responded to such proposals by branding them an attempt to introduce a boycott.[68] Following its usual pattern, the *Echo* described the meeting as one animated by anti-Semitism, even though nothing specifically anti-Semitic was publicly discussed or reported. It was mentioned above that the *Mittelstand* organizations had frequently attacked the SPD for the latter's alleged advocacy of the boycott by workers. The Socialist *Echo* had, therefore, very cleverly selected a sensitive and vulnerable area in its attack on the first meeting of the new *Bund.*

The measure advocating the boycott was not passed by the *Bund* in 1900 at least in part because the *Bund* hesitated to make enemies of the wholesalers and manufacturers. It was finally decided to issue a statement to the effect that those entrepreneurs (outside of department store owners) who had petitioned the Prussian government to drop the proposed legislation on department store taxes could not have realized the full consequences of such petitions. The *Bund* promised however that in the future it would not be so understanding and would support the publication of what would amount to a boycott list.[69] In fact, it was not until after the reunification of the *Zentralverband* with the *Deutscher Bund für Handel und Gewerbe* on 13 July 1907 that the use of the boycott was recommended to a general meeting of the reunited *Verband* by its legal counsel.[70]

The chief impact of the activities of the *Deutscher Bund für Handel und Gewerbe* on the *Schutzverbandsbewegung* during the period of the independent existence of the *Bund* (from 1899 to 1907) was the radicalization of the "movement" as represented by its central organizations. This radicalization took many specific forms. At the 1901 general meeting, the *Bund* was moving far beyond matters connected with the provisions of the law on unfair competition.[71] A new and extremely radical twenty-point program was elaborated at the general meeting of 1903. In one newspaper the program was reviewed under the heading, *"Verbot, Verbot, Verbot!!!".*[72] Although several points of the new program had been designed to strengthen various provisions of the law on unfair competition, these points were scattered throughout the program. Moreover, none of these matters was mentioned before point eight. Taken together, the twenty points amounted to open advocacy of a complete reversal of the "free economy" system. The very first point claimed that the new organization perceived the true freedom of trade in the

> *protection of all national work in urban and rural centres, federal legislative organization of all employed classes with disciplinary authority against their members; under these laws, all inner matters to be self-regulated and arbitrated on the basis of legal ordinances.*[73]

The idea that "false liberalism" in the form of a "false" freedom of trade had come to dominate Germany was an idea that had been popularized in the 1870s and 1880s by well-known anti-Semites such as Otto Glagau, Adolf Stoecker, Paul de Lagarde, Adolf Wahrmund, and Eugen Dühring, as well as a host of other, less well-known figures.[74] The first point in the new program of the *Bund* anticipated the kinds of economic demands which have become associated with National Socialism.[75]

The nature of the radical protest of the *Bund* against the existing social, economic, and political system is also reflected in the other points of the new program. The second point called for "protection against the penetration of *Grosskapital* into retail trade". There were demands for the complete dissolution *(Verbot)* of all forms of civil servant consumer co-operatives (point 3) and the forbidding of the participation of civil servants in any kind of consumer co-operative (point 4). It was decided that consumer co-operatives should be given a licence to operate where a need *(Bedürfnis)* existed. They were not to be permitted to produce any goods and were to be made subject to a tax on turnover. A demand was made for the complete *"Verbot"* of all forms of dividend or dis-count giving, either by consumer co-operatives or retailers' shops (point 6). Point seven of the program demanded the introduction of a progressive nation-wide tax on turnovers (as opposed to the chaotic individual state taxes) on all large concerns *(Grossbetriebe)* in retailing, from department stores to mail-order houses. Point eight sought "more severe legal penalties for fighting unfair competition as well as a law regu-lating 'selling off' of all kinds". Several points demanded old-age and invalid insurance "for all independents of the German *Mittelstand"* (point 11) and state-supported technical schools (point 16). It was most indicative of the radical na-ture of the program that there was the claim for general, secret, legally protected, and direct suffrage in federal, state, and local elections (point 13). Immediately following this claim was the call for higher pay for federal members of par-liament (point 14). While the latter two points indicated dis-satisfaction with the existing political processes, the call for the "simplification of the rules of procedure for national and local administration" indicated some degree of dissatisfaction with the existing bureaucracy (point 18). It was thought that the problems between employers and employees could be regulated in special courts devoted to employer-employee re-lations *(Kaufmannsgerichte).*[76] The remaining points con-cerned specific requests for a revised law on unfair competi-tion. These requests, however, occupied a secondary position in the program. They were overshadowed by the much more radical demands.[77]

The anti-Semitic *Deutsches Blatt* stated that the demands of the new *Bund* had to be satisfied "so that the independent German *Mittelstand* in trade and artisanship, in the national interest, in the interest of state and monarchy will remain secure, become strengthened, grow and thrive". The *Mittel-stand,* the newspaper continued, required state support "in the battle against the damaging influence of *Grosskapital* and Social Democracy, which threatens the independent German *Mittelstand* with complete destruction".[78] The "restoration of the security of our economic existence" would come only if the demands were met. As a final touch the *Deutsches Blatt* reported that the *Bund* claimed the need for these various measures from the state "in order to be able to live and pay taxes".[79]

The *Bund* was at least partially responsible for opening the *Schutzverbände* to the artisans. The endeavours of the *Bund* to marshal the support of the artisans' organizations may have been due to the nature of the legislative demands of the *Bund* and to the type of men (Werbeck, for example) at the top in the *Bund* who were not infrequently artisans themselves. There had been a good deal of resistance, notably from *Mittelstand* organizations associated with *Schutzverbände* around *Der Detaillist,* against giving access to retailers' organizations to the artisans. The 1903 program of the *Bund* contained only one point specifically aimed at winning the support of the artisans (point 9 on the regulation of tenders). The reports of the 1904 meeting in Cologne indicate that the *Bund* was, nevertheless, turning toward the representation of artisan interests.[80] By 1904 some of the most active leaders in specific *Mittelstandsvereinigungen* were artisans. Among the various groups which considered themselves members of the *Mittelstand,* there was developing a widespread (if not a universal) opinion that greater unification of the *Mittelstand* was a necessary prerequisite to the achievement of greater concessions from government.

The *Bund* had from the outset, however, at least partially oriented itself toward the artisans. The very name of the organization emphasized trade and artisanship. At the founding conference in 1898, one resolution had been passed which attempted to head off the split with the *Zentralverband deutscher Kaufleute* by simply broadening the name of the latter organization to the *Zentralverband für Handel und Gewerbe.*[81]

The *Zentralverband* finally changed its name to the *Zentralverband deutscher Kaufleute und Gewerbetreibender* on 27 August 1899, just prior to the formal breakaway of the *Deutscher Bund.* In the period from 1899 to 1907, the years of the existence of the *Deutscher Bund,* the *Zentralverband* changed its attitudes towards broadening the organization to include other *Mittelstand* groups (especially the artisans) and towards radicalizing its policy sufficiently to regain the confidence of organizations in the *Bund.*

National Schutzverbände: 3. The Zentralverband deutscher Kaufleute und Gewerbetreibender 1899 - 1907

The immediate reaction of the *Zentralverband* to the creation of the rival *Deutscher Bund für Handel und Gewerbe* was one of deep regret.[82] The change of name of the *Zentralverband* was not really reflected in its activities until the general meeting of 1901. It was symbolic of the new trend that at the end of the discussion at the meeting on 20 August 1901, Schulze-Gifhorn formally retired as president.

At the annual meeting of 1901 the whole range of subjects with which the organization had become associated was discussed. There was a far greater preoccupation with various aspects of the law on unfair competition than there had been at the previous meetings of the *Zentralverband*. There was discussion of proposals to draw up a black list of all those firms dealing with department stores in order that these firms might be boycotted. Although the latter proposal did not become the official policy of the *Zentralverband*, individual members of the *Zentralverband* were openly encouraged to draw their own conclusions about how to proceed against firms which persisted in dealing with department stores. It seems not unlikely that in this matter the *Zentralverband* followed the lead of the *Deutscher Bund* which had held its meeting the previous year. Although there were differences in their declarations of principle, the general meetings of both organizations discussed broadly similar subjects from 1902 to 1906.[83]

The considerable broadening of the subjects discussed at the annual meetings of the *Zentralverband* was a response to the challenge of the young and vigorous *Deutscher Bund für Handel und Gewerbe*. During the period when these two leading retailer *Schutzverbände* were separated (from 1899 to 1907), differences between them persisted. The younger organization set out to resolve all the problems which had beset the *Zentralverband*, and thereby to wrest the leadership of the *Schutzverbandsbewegung* from the *Zentralverband*. At its founding conference in 1898 the *Deutscher Bund* had been bold enough to offer membership to the *Zentralverband*.

From 1900 onward the *Zentralverband,* as the older organization, adjusted to the challenge of the upstart. Burdened with
a traditional policy and approach, the *Zentralverband* had
been initially unable to make a radical aboutface. Given new
leadership and time, however, the *Zentralverband* recovered.
By the summer of 1907 it was able to make the *Deutscher
Bund* appear redundant.

National Schutzverbände: 4. The Deutscher Zentralverband für Handel und Gewerbe 1907 - 1914

The *Deutscher Bund für Handel und Gewerbe* was reunited
with the *Zentralverband deutscher Kaufleute und Gewerbetreibender* at the annual meeting of the *Zentralverband* on 12
and 13 August 1907. The new name, the *Deutscher Zentralverband für Handel und Gewerbe,* was itself testimony to the
extent to which the establishment of the *Bund* had affected
the *Zentralverband.* In 1898 the *Zentralverband* had been the
relatively modest *Zentralverband deutscher Kaufleute.* At the
meetings held in 1907 the legislative demands of the newly
confident *Zentralverband* became much bolder. President
Geest's speech was both a summary of these demands and a
statement of the success which he attributed to the *Zentralverband* from 1888. The fourteen extremely wide-ranging
legislative demands listed by Geest presented a considerable
contrast to those which had been associated with the
Zentralverband prior to 1899.

The 1907 meetings of the reunited *Zentralverband,* if they
had a single theme beyond that dealing with reunification,
centred around questions concerning employees. The subjects
chosen for discussion at the meeting may have been designed
to draw attention away from the differences still separating
the rival *Schutzverbände* and to direct attention to common
problems. However this particular policy orientation was in
part a response to developments in the employee organizations. In the period after 1900 the *Zentralverband* had turned
increasingly to the pressing question of the employer-
employee relationship.

Much to the displeasure of the *Deutsches Blatt,* which was
closely associated with the DHV, president Geest of the

Zentralverband spoke at the 1907 meeting of the need for protection "against the excessive demands of the employees".[84] The *Deutsches Blatt* was particularly outraged at the policies formulated at the 1907 meetings, especially those policies which involved the position of the *Zentralverband* on the competition clause *(Konkurrenzklausal)* and on the period of notice to be given by an employee before leaving his place of employment. These demands were seen by the DHV as attempts to tie the employee to a position of permanent subordination to the employer. The *Deutsches Blatt* was also disturbed because the *Zentralverband* supported the view that employees should work on Sundays, at least to dress shop windows. The *Zentralverband* also opposed the appointment of the trade inspectors demanded by the DHV.

As far as employers were concerned, the competition clause and the period of notice, which had been written into the commercial law code, were legally binding. The competition clause was designed to ensure that employees who were well versed in the operation of a particular enterprise should be permitted to establish a similar enterprise only after a certain fixed period of time. Employers felt that employees learned all the "business secrets" of the firms in which they apprenticed. The employees therefore would become potential competitors as soon as they had finished their apprenticeship. While the DHV wanted to abolish the competition clause altogether and to shorten the period of notice required of an employee before leaving an establishment, the *Zentralverband* insisted on the retention of both. Although the *Zentralverband* did display a willingness to modify the competition clause, it remained adamant that the former employee should not be legally permitted to establish a business similar to that of his former employer sooner than one year after he had parted from him.

According to the *Deutsches Blatt,* the *Zentralverband* had accepted and was propagating the policies of the larger concerns in retailing (especially those of the department stores and the larger specialty shops). The *Deutsches Blatt* therefore branded the employee policies of the *Zentralverband* as nothing less than "protection of the Jews" and claimed that the policies were in the "interest of *Grosskapital''*[85] In fact a local survey in Bochum in June 1907 indicated that it was the smaller retailing shops and industries which were most in favour of the retention of some form of competition clause.[86]

A growing polarization of the "old" from the "new" *Mittelstand* developed between 1890 and 1914. The meetings of the *Zentralverband* in 1907, which established a common front among retailers in opposition to the demands of the employees, reflected that development. There were signs among employee organizations as well that such a polarization was taking place.[87] The DHV in particular, as the largest employee organization in Germany, sought to head off a split by all possible means, while at the same time insisting on the fulfilment of its social-political demands. The DHV interpreted the policies of the *Zentralverband* (in fact, the policies of any organization of the "old" *Mittelstand)* on employee questions which were opposed to the policies of the DHV as a kind of "false" consciousness. According to this view, such (ill founded) policies were not in the real interests of "Christian-German" retailers, but in the interests of the *Grosskapitalisten* who merely took advantage of the "little men". *("Juda hat die Augen offen und leitet die blinden Kühe nach seinem Willen!!")*[88]

At the first annual meeting of the *Zentralverband* after the reunification, there was an attempt to broaden the "common front" through two specific decisions. The first decision was to conduct the annual meeting as a joint meeting with the *Verband der Rabattsparvereine Deutschlands.* The second decision was to reconcile the interests of the independents with those of the employees. Hennigsen's report of the meeting in the *Deutsch-soziale Blätter* emphasized the reemergence of the idea that employees ought to be considered by retailers "as assistants *(Mitarbeiter),* but not as workers *(Arbeiter)".*[89] An important aspect of the *Deutscher Bund für Handel und Gewerbe* had been to establish that

> all groups of the Mittelstand *have above all things two common enemies to fight: the ever despotic, flourishing* Grosskapital *and the similarly despotically disposed revolutionary proletariat. Both harass and pressure the* Mittelstand *in increasing measure; and against both, the*

> Mittelstand *can protect itself only by strong alliance and firm resolution.* [90]

A policy of opposition to those anxious to claim membership in the *Mittelstand,* even if in the "new" *Mittelstand,* would appear to have been in conflict with the aim to broaden the "common front". It has already been mentioned that retailers were unwilling to pay too high a price for unity with their employees.

The meetings of the *Zentralverband* in 1909 and 1910 were generally preoccupied with discussions on the *Hansa-Bund* and with the question of whether the *Zentralverband* should join the *Hansa-Bund* in order to help form a really powerful common front. The decision was taken against joining for reasons which are discussed later.

By 1911 the *Zentralverband* had not only forsaken the *Hansa-Bund,* but had also developed a rather hostile attitude toward the social-political demands of the employees. Although the *Zentralverband* had sought to avoid passing resolutions on the inflammatory question of employer-employee relations between 1908 and 1911, it had been declared at the meeting of 1909 that employees' associations were making legislative demands which could not be met.[91] In 1911 the *Zentralverband* was compelled to formulate a specific policy toward employees' demands because the proposals for special social insurance benefits for employees were scheduled for discussion in the *Reichstag* session in the autumn of that year. At the annual meeting of the *Verband der Rabattsparvereine,* there was a very long speech by C.A. Nicolaus of Bremen. Nicolaus "recognized the need" for such insurances and hinted that the state should bear the cost if it considered that additional insurance was necessary.[92] The *Zentralverband* took a slightly stronger stand against the new proposals. While the resolution passed at its annual meeting in 1911 recognized the need for special insurance, the government's proposed law was rejected "because it places great economic burdens upon the owner, without securing the expected advantages for the employees".[93] The phrasing of the resolution very carefully avoided any condemnation of the entire project. Once the new measures were passed by the government, the *Zentralverband* came to accept them as accomplished facts. At its meetings between 1911 and 1914, the *Zentralverband* did not again discuss such matters.

It has been suggested that the special insurance laws of 1911 were somehow considered by the government and the bourgeois parties as a reward to the employees for their "anti-proletarian efforts". The *Zentralverband* did not view the new law as a reward for its own not inconsiderable "anti-proletarian efforts". Nevertheless, after the new laws had come into force, they had the effect of legally recognizing and institutionalizing what had previously been primarily ideological differences between the employees *(Angestelltenschaft)* and the workers *(Arbeiterschaft)*. The *Mittelstandsbewegung* would have to face the question of the representation of the "new" *Mittelstand*. That question led to a split within the *Mittelstandsbewegung* and eventually to the decision to exclude the "new" *Mittelstand* from the movement altogether.

Except for the rather brief and fruitless endeavours of the *Zentralverband* to reverse the tide of the insurance laws for the employees, there were no novel departures in its policy, methods, or approach in the period from 1907 to 1914. After 1911, however, the *Zentralverband* received more formal recognition of its role within the then much spoken of *Mittelstandsbewegung*. At the 1912 general meeting, there was some talk of the need to introduce a certificate of qualification into retail trade.[95] Following this general meeting, the *Zentralverband* held special meetings in Berlin in order to establish who was responsible for the rising cost of living and to demand special taxes for competitors who ran large concerns.[96] In addition to carrying forward the well established policy lines, the *Zentralverband* made some attempts to bring other retailer *Schutzverbände* into its ranks.[97]

National Schutzverbände: 5. The Zentralvereinigung deutscher Vereine für Handel und Gewerbe 1908 - 1914

The split which developed within the *Zentralverband* and which ultimately led to the establishment of yet another central organization can be traced back to the creation of the *Bund der Handel- und Gewerbetreibenden* by Hugo Lissauer in Berlin in 1898. At the 1898 meeting which had been called to establish the *Deutscher Bund,* Lissauer avowed the formal affiliation of his organization to the *Zentralverband* of Schulze-Gifhorn.[98] The 1903 survey of the Federal Ministry of the Interior listed Lissauer's organization among the state and regional organizations affiliated to the *Zentralverband.* At that time the Berlin organization claimed a total membership of 7,400 in 29 associated organizations of various types.[99] In late 1905 Lissauer led his Berlin organization in the establishment of the *Zentralvereinigung preussischer Verein für Handel und Gewerbe.*[100] The press reported that the new organization embraced 48 Berlin organizations and 78 organizations based in other areas of Prussia.[101]

Because of lack of evidence, it is not possible to establish with any certainty whether Lissauer regarded this step as the first that would lead him eventually to break with the *Zentralverband.*[102] It cannot be established whether Lissauer sought merely to pursue his personal ambitions or whether he wanted to establish a solid all-Prussian organization within the *Zentralverband.* There is some evidence which suggests that Lissauer was unhappy with some of the policies of the *Zentralverband.* Lissauer appears to have regarded the establishment of the new Prussian organization not so much the first step in a break with the *Zentralverband* as rather the first step towards the conquest of the leadership of the *Zentralverband* and, therefore, of the *Schutzverbandsbewegung.* It is certain that in late 1907 he was considered a serious candidate for the presidency of the recently reunited *Zentralverband.*[103] In 1908 after he had failed to achieve this position, Lissauer established his own central organization, the *Zentralvereinigung deutscher Vereine für Handel und Gewerbe.* This organization appears to have found little success outside Berlin and the surrounding area.[104]

The chief differences in policy, approach, and social composition of Lissauer's organization were not, in themselves, important enough to have caused the split with the *Zentralverband.* Wein claims that Lissauer was interested in "the very small businesses which were extremely numerous in Berlin".[105] The only evidence which Wein presents for the different orientations of the *Zentralverband* and Lissauer's *Zentralvereinigung* are slight differences in the statements of each organization's statutes. The statutes of the *Zentralverband* were not representative of its activities. It has been claimed that Lissauer, who was Jewish, had been anxious to purge an element of anti-Semitism from the attacks of the *Zentralverband.*[106] There is little evidence, however, to suggest that the *Deutscher Zentralverband für Handel und Gewerbe* employed a policy of anti-Semitism in its attacks on department stores.* At the meetings of the *Zentralvereinigung preussischer Vereine* in 1905, it was not emphasized that the department stores *(grössere Spezial- und Fachgeschäfte)* were greater enemies of the retailers than the consumer co-operatives and that therefore the policy emphasis of the *Zentralverband* was misplaced.[107] All forms of large concerns were discussed at almost equal length, along with questions of unfair competition. The significance of the eventual split of Lissauer's organization away from the newly reunited *Zentralverband* was far less important than suggested by Wein. This particular split revealed that not only policy differences, but perhaps personal ambition as much as anything else might have led to deterioration in retailers' organizations.

Attempts at Unification of the Central Schutzverbände

Only two attempts, other than those endeavours of the *Zentralverband,* to unify the *Schutzverbandsbewegung* at the national level after the turn of the century, appear to have impressed contemporaries. The *Bund der Kaufleute,* which was established in Berlin on 25 February 1903, sought to unify not only all retailers within its organization, but other *Mittelstand* groups associated with trade not usually linked with the retailers. The other significant attempt to reconcile the differences within the *Schutzverbandsbewegung* sought to establish not an organization, but rather an *Interessengemeinschaft* (community of interests).

*There were, however, accusations that the leaders of the *Zentralverband* supported anti-Semitic parties. After 1904 and particularly after 1911, the chairmen of the *Zentralverband* participated in the activities of organizations within the *Mittelstandsbewegung* which were said to have been tinged with anti-Semitism. It should be kept in mind that Lissauer himself took part in these activities.

The organizations which were present at the founding meeting of the *Bund der Kaufleute* in Berlin claimed to represent a total of 219,000 members. These organizations, called together by the *Verband Berliner Spezialgeschäfte,* ranged from retailers' *Schutzverbände* to organizations of bank employees and even of industrialists. The *Zentralvereinigung der kaufmännischen katholischen Vereine Deutschlands* and even the *Verband reisender Kaufleute* were also represented.[108] In a sense, the attempt to unite virtually all groups associated in any way with trade into a single organization represented an attempt similar to that of the *Hansa-Bund* of 1909. The difficulty, if not the impossibility, of reconciling so many diverse interests within the *Bund der Kaufleute* was recognized by the *Deutsches Blatt* which branded the *Bund* a "stillborn child".[109]

The *Bund der Kaufleute* had been conceived as an organization to represent the interests of trade as the BdL and the CDI represented other economic interests. The *Bund der Kaufleute* resembled the *Hansa-Bund* in being animated by the consideration that the BdL had achieved too many concessions from government. In a pamphlet of 1903 the *Bund der Kaufleute* made clear its own liberal (and even specifically NL) sentiments and outlined its aims concerning the agrarian-conservative party.

> *It is, in no way, a question of fighting against the agrarian-conservative* Weltanschauung, *but rather much more a question of impregnating public institutions, the state, the parliament, with the spirit of the modern* Weltanschauung *far into the agrarian circles. In this way, these agrarian circles will become interested in the progressive cultural development. Thus will the entire national economy be led to harmonious work and manifestation of strength.*[110]

It was perhaps because the new *Bund* had been called together at the request of the financially secure owners of large specialty shops that the new organization was coloured "by the modern *Weltanschauung*".[111] Almost immediately, the new *Bund* began to complain that it was not being accepted.[112] The two leading central *Schutzverbände* of the time, and the retailers' *Schutzverbände* in general, apparently completely ignored the existence of the *Bund der Kaufleute*. The radical 1903 program of the *Deutscher Bund für Handel und Gewerbe* may have been, in part, a response to the *Bund der Kaufleute*. That program, with its marked orientation toward the small independent retailers, was a great blow to the *Bund der Kaufleute*. Although the *Bund der Kaufleute* continued to exist after 1903, it was not able to achieve the goals which it had originally set.[113]

The first meetings of the so-called *Interessengemeinschaft grosser deutscher Detaillistenverbände* took place after the *Zentralvereinigung deutscher Vereine für Handel und Gewerbe* (Lissauer's national organization) had been established. At the request of the federal government, both rival central organizations, together with some of the larger state organizations, met on 16 November 1908 in order that the government might discover the retailers' views on the proposed new law on unfair competition. It was estimated that the *Interessengemeinschaft* embraced some 16 major associations with a total membership of 100,000 on 22 November 1910. At the meeting held on 22 November 1910 even several of the organizations associated with *Der Detaillist* were present.[114] The *Interessengemeinschaft* reflected the great influence of the *Zentralverband*. Even the wording of the resolution of late 1911, which the *Interessengemeinschaft* had drawn up in opposition to the proposed employees' insurance law, resembled the wording of the resolution of the *Zentralverband*.[115]

As long as the *Interessengemeinschaft* remained a loose "community" rather than a more formal organization, its existence was as harmless as it was ineffective. In 1913 when an attempt was made to transform the *Interessengemeinschaft* into an organization, the "community" fell apart. According to one observer, the *Deutscher Zentralverband für Handel und Gewerbe* (Leipzig) was chiefly responsible for the breakdown of the *Interessengemeinschaft* because the former had sought to become and remain the sole representative of the retailers.[116] In fact the collapse of the *Interessengemeinschaft* was due not to the action of one particular organization, but to the whole range of differences in policy and approach within the "community".

Conclusion

The conflict and disunity discerned within the technical organizations in general and within the local *Schutzverbände* in particular were also present within the regional and national *Schutzverbände*. Once they had been established, state, regional, and even national central organizations were slow to develop the kind of self-sustaining momentum which characterized the trade unions of the period in Germany. Although state and regional *Schutzverbände* often provided very direct links between local and national organizational activities, there was much resistance to centralization tendencies. In terms of the achievement of specific goals, the failure of the "movement" to attain unity may be judged a real weakness.[117] On the other hand the failure to achieve unity reveals a good deal concerning the nature of the political mobilization of the retailers. Becoming "politicized", joining organizations to fight for various demands, did not have the same meaning for an independent retailer as joining a trade union had for a worker. The organizations of the retailers reflected the anti-organizational biases of their members. Even the most powerful retailers' organizations at the state, regional or national level might be easily disrupted, even at the moment (such as in 1907) when years of painstaking activity in a search of unity appeared to be reaching fruition.

Nevertheless the conflict-ridden and erratic activities of retailers' organizations at the state, regional, and national levels represented an extension of the political mobilization of the retailers in several important respects. From the point of view of the retailer, still faced at the local level with his economic problems, the efforts of his local *Schutzverbände* to carry the struggle beyond the confines of the locality required at least his tacit recognition of the need to join fellow retailers facing broadly similar problems elsewhere in Germany. The continual attempts of local *Schutzverbände* to establish regional and national organizations were an indication that retailers had come to recognize the necessity of mobilizing the support of greater numbers of their fellows. The activity of these various organizations not only broadened the consciousness of retailers throughout Germany, but opened up the possibility of the creation of a *Mittelstandsbewegung* in which the participation of retailers would be assured.

6

Independent Retailers within the Mittelstandsbewegung 1890-1914

Retailers operated within the traditional party-political context in two interrelated fashions. Retailers' organizations of all types sought specific legislative enactments either through enlisting the support of friendly bourgeois political parties or through direct appeals to various governmental bodies at the local, state, and national levels. In addition to operating on the basis of avowed (and often ephemeral) party-political neutrality however, retailers entered more self-consciously into party politics. The emergence of the retailers in various types of organizations, either in unity with other *Mittelstand* groups such as the artisans or alone, was heralded in Imperial Germany as a "movement", the *Mittelstandsbewegung*.

The Mittelstandsbewegung and the "political Mittelstandsbewegung"

Problems of definition arise whenever the term *"Mittelstand"* or *"Mittelstandsbewegung"* is used. Some writers, for example, maintain that the efforts of artisans from the early nineteenth century onward to reverse the freedom of trade laws should be considered an integral part of the *Mittelstandsbewegung*.[1] More recent works employ a definition of *Mittelstandsbewegung* which maintains that the "movement" comprised the organizational activity of artisans and retailers, regardless of whether these organizations referred to themselves as *Mittelstand* organizations.[2] Because retailers were a social group which came to conceive of itself as part of the

Mittelstand, there is some validity in suggesting that all their organizational activities were part of the *Mittelstandsbewegung.* A definition of *Mittelstandsbewegung* that includes virtually all forms of the organizational activity of retailers, whether or not these activities were considered by retailers to be *"mittelständisch",* has the advantage of emphasizing the pre-institutional nature of these activities and that of the *Mittelstandsbewegung.*

The appearance of a *Mittelstandsideologie* forming part of the rationale behind the demands of retailers for protection was related to their economic problems. As a recent study has maintained, "a specific *Mittelstandsideologie* first emerged at the beginning of the 1890s".[3] However, the *Mittelstandsideologie* (in so far as it may be viewed as a unitary phenomenon) which came to inspire specific *Mittelstand* organizations was also a reflection of the failure of other retailers' organizations to win legislative enactments deemed essential by retailers. The *Mittelstand* organizations were to carry forward the struggle for these legislative enactments. The means to be used in the achievement of these aims were most frequently conceived in terms of the "winning of political influence".[4] This more overtly politically oriented movement has been termed by several writers as the "political *Mittelstandsbewegung"* in order to distinguish it from the other organizational initiatives of the social groups within the *Mittelstand.*[5]

The activity of retailers within the "political *Mittelstandsbewegung"* and the tendency of retailers increasingly to shed the last vestiges of their party-political neutrality constituted the final step in their political mobilization. Retailers' organizational activities were transformed from a more pre-institutionalized form of political endeavour into a more formal and discernible party-political enterprise.

The First Specific Mittelstand Organizations

As early as 1890 the *Zentralvorstand kaufmännischer Verbände und Vereine Deutschlands* had suggested "the need" for the *Mittelstand* to take more active participation in elections. It was not until the 16 April 1895 meeting of the so-called *Verband deutscher Mittelstände* that this "need" found any organizational form. The moving forces behind the creation of this organization, besides the *Zentralvorstand*—which by that time had been re-named the *Zentralverband deutscher Kaufleute*—were the *Verband der Kaufleute der Provinz Sachsen, der Herzogtümer Anhalt und Braunschweig* and a number of artisans' organizations. The BdL was selected as the model for the organization. *Vorwärts* branded the program of the *Verband deutscher Mittelstände* "corporative *(zünftlerisch)* anti-Semitic".[6] The organization was a complete failure and disappeared almost immediately.

In mid-April 1895 a certain goldsmith Fischer founded a *Deutsche Mittelstandspartei* in Berlin to represent primarily the interests of retailers and artisans. Except for several specifically artisan demands in the program, this party sought legislative enactments not unlike those sought by the *Verband deutscher Mittelstände.* The Berlin *Mittelstand* party also enjoyed an extremely short existence.[7]

In April 1895 a meeting was held in Halle by one of the leading artisan organizations. At this meeting, the question of "the political representation of artisanship" was discussed. Opinions were sharply divided between those who wanted to create a special *Mittelstand* party (which would seek the support of other *Mittelstand* groups) and those who were just as satisfied with their already existing organization as they were determined to confine its activity to artisans' problems. At the meeting it was resolved to work towards greater unity among artisans. Once that goal had been achieved, demands might be made in any number of directions.[8] After the turn of the century, artisans more seriously undertook the establishment of a *Mittelstand* organization. Even after 1900 the determination to restrict their organizations to artisans persisted.[9]

In early June 1895 a Berlin based *Bund zur Hebung des Mittelstandes,* which had enjoyed a brief existence, was declared a failure by its executive. The reason given for the failure of the organization by the newly elected executive (who remained without members to lead!) was that the earlier executive had pursued "intense anti-Semitism instead of economic policies".[10] There were reports, also in June 1895, of the founding in Halle of a new *Mittelstand* party. Once again, artisans and retailers were primarily involved, and, once again, the newly founded organization achieved but a short existence.[11]

Very few writers on the subject attempt to account either for the initiative behind these early endeavours to form a *Mittelstand* party or for the causes of the failure of these attempts. Representative statements usually state that the efforts were "without success",[12] "fruitless"[13] or that they did not attain "further importance".[14] The chief reason for the failure of these initial attempts to form a *Mittelstand* party can be traced to the absence of the necessary economic pre-conditions. These economic pre-conditions for the most important group behind the *Mittelstandsbewegung* (the retailers) did not fully emerge until after the turn of the century. A good deal of space has already been devoted to demonstrating both the nature of the retailers' economic problems and the period when these problems became acute. If the economic pre-conditions for the successful organization of a *Mittelstand* party or organization were not fully developed during the 1890s, the existence of certain of the necessary political pre-conditions do (in part) account for the initial endeavours.

From the point of view of the *Mittelstand* in general and of the retailers in particular, a climate conducive to their own political organization was created by two related events. The first of these "events" concerned the reemergence of the SPD and, specifically, the passage of the Erfurt program of 1891. The other event was the adoption of a new program (the Tivoli program) by the *Deutsch-Konservative* Party in 1892.

The Erfurt program of the SPD came to serve the function of helping to create a *Mittelstandsbewegung* which was to remain steadfast in its opposition to the SPD.* *Vorwärts* had

---

*An important aspect of Bernstein's Revisionist theory involved his contention that the *Mittelstand* was not disappearing and that the continued existence of the *Mittelstand* was not necessarily in contradiction with the interests of the working class. See his *Voraussetzungen des Sozialismus*, 1911 (original ed. 1906): 51 ff. See also Gay, *Dilemma of Democratic Socialism*, 1970 : 204 ff. and the section entitled "Found: The Disappearing Middle Class". Cf. the response of the orthodox Marxist Lange, "Detailhandel und Mittelstandspolitik", 1907 : 693 ff.

considered that the various efforts by the *Mittelstand* to form political organizations in 1895 represented the final desperate attempts of the *Mittelstand* to preserve itself in the face of concentrated competition.[15] (The newspaper included the formation of the *Antisemitische Volkspartei* by Hermann Ahlwardt and Otto Böckel as another of these endeavours.) The interpretation of the inevitable decline of the *Mittelstand* was reflected in other Socialist newspapers in their reports of the activities of any *Mittelstand* organization.[16] This often hailed "prognosis of decline" had formed an important part of the new Erfurt program of the SPD passed in 1891. The SPD interpretation of political anti-Semitism was, incidentally, a corollary of the "prognosis of decline".[17] The object of both aspects of the policy was to convince the *Mittelstand* of the inevitability of its decline and to point out that it was not the Jews who were the enemies of the *Mittelstand*. The decline of the *Mittelstand* should not be blamed on the individual activities of several Jews. It was the consequence of the development of capitalism. Instead of convincing the *Mittelstand* of the inevitability of its fate, the "prognosis of decline" confirmed the anti-Socialist attitudes of the *Mittelstand* and strengthened the determination of the *Mittelstand* to resist its predicted decline.

While the SPD had spoken of the "declining middle classes",[18] the *Deutsch-Konservative* Party, in its Tivoli program adopted in December 1892, demanded "the strengthening of the urban and rural *Mittelstand*".[19] The Tivoli program was more than a reaction to what amounted to the "anti-*Mittelstand*" program of the SPD. Although the Tivoli program quite deliberately sought a social following among the *Mittelstand*, this striving was not only an attempt to win votes on the basis of opposition to SPD. The most to be expected in pursuing such a policy would be to enlist the somewhat negative support of the *Mittelstand*. The Tivoli program sought to capture the positive support of the *Mittelstand*. That positive support, it was claimed in the *Kreuz-Zeitung*, had been won by Hermann Ahlwardt in a run-off election and had been responsible for the defeat of the Conservative Party's candidate.* This defeat, which came on the eve of the Conservative Party's conference in early December 1892, impressed the delegates at the conference of the need both to accept overt anti-Semitism as part of their newly formulated program and to include points in the program designed to make the party appear the champion of the economic interests of the *Mittelstand.*** The party had already demonstrated its support (along with the Centre and the anti-Semitic parties) of the retailers in the debates on the legislative restriction of the customers of the consumer co-operatives in 1889 and early 1890. Throughout the period from 1890 to 1914 the *Deutsch-Konservative* Party insisted that it represented the interests of the *Mittelstand* in both the *Reichs-* and *Landtag* more strenuously than any other party.[20]

The *Bund der Landwirte* (BdL), created on 18 February 1893 shortly after the Tivoli meeting of the Conservative Party, was both sympathetically inclined towards the Conservative Party and determined to marshal the support of the *Mittelstand.* As one writer said of the BdL, "its concept of the protection of national work, high tariffs and conservative *Mittelstand* policies, together with the façade of a new German *völkisch* nationalism, mobilized various sections of peasant proprietors and the old *Mittelstand* against all forces

---

*The election was in *Wahlkreis* Friedeberg-Arnswalde. Ahlwardt did not win an absolute majority on the first ballot, but collected 6,901 votes compared to the 2,815 votes of the *Deutsch-Konservative Partei.* On the second ballot, he received 11,206 votes compared to the 3,306 votes of his Progressive rival. See *Neue Preussische Ztg.* 29.11.1892. The newspaper commented that the anti-Semitism would not have succeeded "if it had not struck a responsive chord in the hearts of the electorate". Although the newspaper did not, at this time, suggest that the *Deutsch-Konservative Partei* should engage in anti-Semitic campaigns, it pointed to the need to search out all the *"Schäden in unserem Volksleben".* Cf. the comments in *Köln. Ztg.* 7.12.1892.

**See esp. the speeches of Von Waldow and Adolf Stöcker at the *Deutsch-Konservativer* conference. Stöcker claimed that the party could be assured of the votes of the *Mittelstand* only if the party made it clear that it would fight for the *Mittelstand.* Throughout the meeting, Ahlwardt's success was conspicuous in the discussions. For the full account, see *Neue Preussische Ztg.* 8.12.1892. Cf. the editorial comments in the newspaper on 9.12.1892. Cf. *National Ztg.* 10.12.1892.

which were interested in a new distribution of the power relations in the German Empire".[21] The early *Mittelstand* organizations (such as the *Verband deutscher Mittelstände)* took the BdL as their model. It was not until after the turn of the century, however, that the model of the BdL was successfully used in the establishment of *Mittelstand* organizations. By that time, the necessary economic pre-conditions for the successful creation of a *Mittelstand* organization had matured. At the same time, the political climate had also taken a turn favourable to the organizational endeavours of the *Mittelstand.*

The Deutsche Mittelstandsvereinigung (DMV) 1904 - 1908

After the turn of the century, efforts were renewed to found some form of *Mittelstand* organization or party. Hanover was once again the focal point of the initiatives to form the *Mittelstand* organization. The *Mittelstandsvereinigung-Hannover* was established in October 1903.[22] It was no accident that Heinrich Beythien of the *Verband der Rabattsparvereine Deutschlands* was a leading figure behind the *Mittelstandsvereinigung-Hannover* and that he was elected to the executive. The Hanover branch of the *Zentralverband deutscher Kaufleute* was also very much behind the formation of the new *Mittelstandsvereinigung.* The latter organization was also supported by several artisan organizations, organizations of the house owners, and even those of the "new" *Mittelstand.*[23] The aim of the organization was stated to be the

> recruitment of the members of the employed German Mittelstand *with a view to the protection of their professional and class interests in national and local elections, whether it be from within the existing parties or, if need be, outside them.*[24]

Parallel to developments in Hanover, there swept all across Germany a new wave in the foundation of specific *Mittelstand* organizations with similar, clearly stated political views. Only one year after the formation of the *Mittelstandsvereinigung-Hannover,* various types of *Mittelstand* organizations or parties existed in all parts of Germany.* (In the great majority of cases, these organizations also labelled themselves *Mittelstandsvereinigungen.*) The precise relationship between the Hanover organization and the other organizations remains to be established. The *Deutsche Mittelstandsvereinigung* (DMV), which grew out of the Hanover organization, later emphasized the many successes of the original Hanover organization in creating *Mittelstandsvereinigungen* "in many parts of the German Empire".25

The *Mittelstandsvereinigung-Hannover* played a dominant role in the foundation of the DMV. Max Küster and Heinrich Beythien were the two leading executives of both the *Mittelstandsvereinigung-Hannover* and the DMV. The headquarters of the DMV was originally also in Hanover. A number of other retailers' organizations had played a role in the creation of the DMV The *Bund der Handel- und Gewerbetreibenden* in Berlin under Hugo Lissauer and the *Deutscher Bund für Handel und Gewerbe* (Leipzig) were active in the foundation of the new organization. There exists some controversy over the exact date of the founding of the DMV. One account maintains that the DMV came into existence in August 1904, another that it was formed in September 1904.26 The DMV appears, however, to have been created in October 1904.27 It can be established with certainty that the first general meeting of the DMV was held on 26 November 1904.

At the 26 August 1904 *Allgemeiner deutsche Innungs- und Handwerkertag* in Magdeburg it was decided to form a "*Mittelstand* organization free of party politics".28 According to a later statement of the DMV, the artisan organization declared that it wanted "to move closer to the foundation of a *Mittelstand* association in co-operation with all the German economic organizations".29 C. Rahardt, head of the Berlin carpenters' guild, called for the immediate foundation of a *Mittelstandsvereinigung* at the Magdeburg meeting because he had "not advanced one step forward . . . through all his artisan

Mittelstandsvereinigungen existed in Altona, Augsburg, Barth, Berlin, Burgdorf (Hanover), Frankfurt a.M., Hanover, Herne (Westphalia) and Lübeck; *Mittelstand* parties existed in Magdeburg, Munich, Nuremberg, Schönau and Strasbourg.

meetings and associations over the last decade". Max Küster of the executive of the *Mittelstandsvereinigung-Hannover,* who also spoke at the meeting in Magdeburg, persuaded the delegates at the meeting to establish a commission both to study the question further and to consult "other classes". The DMV was created in October 1904 after the work of the commission had been completed.[30]

Delegates to the first general meeting of the DMV on 26 November 1904 represented the whole range of *Mittelstand* organizations from retailers' *Schutzverbände* to house owners associations and all types of artisan organizations. The "new" *Mittelstand* was represented by a delegate from the *Deutsch-nationaler Handlungsgehilfen-Verband.* There were a number of government officials present, as well as numerous parliamentarians. There were three members of the *Deutsch-Konservative* Party (Hammer, Witt, Bruhn), one from the Centre (Erzberger), and nine members of the *Freikonservative* Party from the Prussian *Landtag* (Rewoldt, Krause, Schön, Eckert, von Woyna, Volger, Lüdes, Schmidt, and Witt).[31]

The aims of the new organization read, virtually word for word, like the aims of the *Mittelstandsvereinigung-Hannover.* The DMV was as anxious as the *Mittelstandsvereinigung-Hannover* to win the support of the "new" *Mittelstand.* Rahardt's address to the meeting emphasized that it was not only possible, but absolutely necessary, for "retailers, artisans, civil servants etc." to join together. The possibility "was never as great as it is today". The attempt to represent both the "old" and the "new" *Mittelstand* within the DMV was to lead the organization into considerable difficulty and to lead ultimately to its virtual collapse. Rahardt would, nevertheless, continue to insist that the DMV had to represent the entire *Mittelstand.* The organization of the agrarians, the BdL, was taken as the model for the new organization.

At the general meeting Dr. E. Wienbeck of the *Mittelstandsvereinigung-Hannover* spoke on the "economic aims of the DMV" :

> *In our* Mittelstandsvereinigung, *we have suggested the same approach as the representatives of trade and industry suggested some time ago, in that they, like agricul-*

*ture recently, try to influence the legislative process.
We wish to work in such a direction that, in the next
few years, politics can become labelled 'friendly to the*
Mittelstand'.[32]

Rahardt was careful to point out that the DMV should avoid
turning those political parties already favourably disposed towards the *Mittelstand* into enemies.[33] An implicit anti-Semitic and nationalistic theme ran through all the discussions.
Küster ended the meeting on a determined note: "We remain
faithful to our word and seek its realization: the *Mittelstand*
should and must remain intact for the German nation
(Volk)".[34]

The full program of the DMV with its long list of
twenty-eight legislative demands may be characterized as
the program of an organization anxious both to quell
doubts that it was primarily an artisan organization and
to win the support of other *Mittelstand* groups. In fact,
most of the first points in the program comprised a list
of virtually all the standard demands of the retailers'
Schutzverbände. Not until the ninth point was any mention
made of a specific artisan demand. Other points concerning artisan affairs were scattered throughout the remainder
of the program (points 13, 14, 18, 19, and 20). The
second point called for "protection against the penetration
of *Grosskapital* into retail trade", the third for the "restriction of the further development of consumer co-operatives
which damage the *Mittelstand*", the fourth for the abolition of all types of civil servant consumer co-operatives,
the fifth for the introduction of stronger measures against
department stores, and the sixth for "severe legal penalties
to fight unfair competition as well as the enactment of a
law to regulate 'selling off' of all kinds".

Although the retailers' *Schutzverbände* were conspicuously
absent at the founding meeting of the DMV, the program of
the DMV reflected a consciousness of the need to win the
support of the retailers. The interests of the retailers were
very much in the forefront of the program of the DMV.[35]
The largest and most important organization within the DMV
was the *Verband der Rabattsparvereine Deutschlands* under

Beythien.* By the time the second general meeting of the DMV was held in early September 1905, the number˙ of participating artisan organizations had already declined considerably. No doubt part of the cause of this decline was the development of the new *Bund der Handwerker,* an organization created in April 1904 and largely restricted to the achievement of more technical artisan demands.[36]

The political orientation of the DMV became even more clearly defined at its second general meeting. Hammer, who had been present at the first meeting, participated actively in the discussions. Within the Conservative Party in the Prussian House, Hammer was one of the staunchest supporters of the whole range of legislation favouring retailers' demands.[37] From the opening address on "the social and national importance of the *Mittelstand*", the meeting sounded a marked pro-conservative, nationalistic, anti-Semitic, and anti-SPD note. [38] The master tailor Voigt, as manager of the *Bund der Handwerker,* had participated in the founding meeting of the DMV. In mid-1905 he withdrew the support of his organization from the DMV because he considered that the latter organization had become too dependent upon the BdL.[39] *Vorwärts* joyfully reported this rupture, as well as the precise electoral districts in which the DMV had declared that it would support the candidates of the BdL in the up-coming federal elections.[40] Nothing was said at the September 1905 general meeting of the DMV to counter Voigt's charges. *Vorwärts* was not the only newspaper to substantiate the dependence of the DMV on the BdL.[41]

Max Küster of the DMV spoke at the twenty-seventh *Deutscher Haus- und Grundbesitzertag* in late 1905. The aim of his speech was to win the support of the *Deutsche Haus- und Grundbesitzervereine* for the DMV.[42] The effort was a failure, according to the newspaper of the house owners *(Das Grundeigentum),* because it appeared all too obvious that the DMV was a political party. It was a party, moreover, that "looks after the business of the BdL in the city and which pursues the same agrarian-anti-Semitic line, to be sure, under

*Krueger, *Freie Interessenvertretung,* 1908 : 231 estimated that the DMV (outside of Saxony and Thuringia) may have counted as many as 80,000 members in 1908. Such a figure seems greatly over-estimated.

a different banner". The article claimed further that "the aims and purposes" of the DMV and the BdL were the same; "both fight progress; both wish to place a stumbling block in the way of progress. . ." The house owners' organization was adamant that "such a fraternization with the BdL is only harmful to the true interests of the *Mittelstand;* it is also thoroughly unnatural".[43]

The DMV experienced difficulties almost from the very beginning. The rejection of the DMV by the *Bund der Handwerker* and particularly by the conservative *Haus- und Grundbesitzervereine* in 1905 were severe blows to the DMV. In 1906 the difficulties of the DMV were increased. From mid-January 1906 there were complaints by the executive of the DMV that the organization was running into serious financial problems. The local sections of the DMV were accused by the executive of not working hard enough on fund raising. (Seventeen local sections had participated in the late 1905 general meeting.) The executive claimed that the organization might have to fold if more money were not forthcoming.[44]

If the Munich local section of the DMV was in any way typical of the attitude of the other local sections, the DMV was already in serious trouble in 1906. The section in Munich was markedly anti-Semitic. At a meeting in early September 1906 the claim was made that all the political parties had forsaken the *Mittelstand.* The attempt by the *Mittelstand* to form its own party (the DMV) had only resulted in a disunity so bad that one half of the organization was ashamed of the other half. This disunity, it was said, made fighting the enemies of the *Mittelstand* ("the Jew in alliance with capitalism" of which he was "the most brutal representative") almost impossible. The essential task of combining the economic and political struggle, as the Christian-Social Party under Adolf Stöcker had accomplished briefly, was not being effectively carried forward. According to the police reports of subsequent meetings, the section in Munich gradually lost faith in the DMV and on 2 July 1910 dissolved itself.[45]

Even in Hanover, the original home of the DMV, a so-called *Freie Mittelstands-Einigung* was created in mid-1906 in direct competition with the DMV [46] The DMV sought without success to win the support of the new *Einigung.*[47] The reputation of the DMV in Hanover was not helped by a minor scandal involving Max Küster and his use of privileged information in the bidding for the undertaking of improvements in the city hall. Küster was replaced by Rahardt as the chairman, and the headquarters of the DMV was moved to Berlin.[48]

The decisions taken at the annual meeting of 1906 were to prove even more fateful to the continued existence of the DMV.[49] The DMV came out in open support of the BdL and the anti-Semitic and Conservative parties in the up-coming federal elections of 1907. In addition to advocating that members of the DMV support these parties, the DMV even put up candidates of its own. The message to members of the DMV was to stand up for their rights by getting out to vote. "And then have confidence in yourself and your cause. You are stronger than you think. So now, use your strength."[50] However the more overtly the call was to members of the DMV to stand up and to be counted, the more obvious the weaknesses of the organization appeared. In the 14 constituencies in which the organization put its own candidates forward, the DMV managed a total of 90,218 votes but collected no seats. In the Prussian state elections of 1908, Rahardt alone succeeded in being elected. There were no successes in other state elections.[51] The weakness of the DMV as a political party was obvious. The annual general meetings held in 1907 and 1908 immediately reflected a dissatisfaction both with the social orientation of the DMV and with its transformation from an "association free of party politics" into a political party closely tied to the BdL and the anti-Semitic parties.[52]

The annual meeting of 1907 (held in Strasbourg) was concerned chiefly with the question of the party-political activity of the DMV. The official press release stated that the DMV was to become once again "a purely economic, professional organization" and that "in principle, party politics and religious matters are excluded". This policy did not preclude "that the association, through the efforts of its members who belong to the various parties, systematically and steadily pressure the parties, in order to ultimately bring about a forceful representation of *Mittelstand* interests".[53] The presence at the meeting of a number of Conservative and anti-

Semitic politicians did not help to make this avowed policy of party-political neutrality very convincing. A contemporary wrote of the declaration that the statement should be taken to mean that "publicly, the Jews will no longer be abused; so much the more intensive will be the support for the parties which include anti-Semitism in their programs."[54]

In early 1908 the conclusion was reached by the Berlin section of the DMV that its own local executive (including the chairman, Rahardt) was tied too closely to such anti-Semitism. The Berlin section blamed the open advocacy of anti-Semitism for the poor showing of the DMV in the elections and demanded the resignation of the executive. Rahardt remained the leader of the DMV, although he had been unseated in his stronghold, Berlin.[55] These events in Berlin are an indication of the degree of dissatisfaction within the DMV concerning its policy towards party politics. In fact, a split had developed within the DMV that was concerned not only with the political activities of the DMV, but with its social orientation.

The Düsseldorf Annual Meeting (1908) of the DMV: Creation of the Mittelstandsvereinigung für Handel und Gewerbe

By the time the fifth annual meeting of the DMV took place in Düsseldorf on 20 September 1908, the two issues of the party-political activities and the social orientation of the organization could no longer be avoided. Rahardt, who was by that time an elected member of the Prussian Lower House, continued to insist that the DMV would avoid formal party politics. However, he maintained, the DMV had a natural interest in recent development: "within the political parties, our wishes are gaining recognition". Similarly, Rahardt's attitude towards the opposition within the DMV to the representation of the "new" *Mittelstand* was tempered. "We support the interests of white-collar workers, but we also hope that the white-collar workers will remember that the artisan and the retailer also have a right to live". Stocky of the Rhenish-Westphalian branch of the DMV insisted that the *Mittelstand* did not include "white-collar workers and shop assistants".[56] This advocacy of a limited definition of *Mittelstand* became known as the "Düsseldorf policy". Stocky's definition stressed that the relationship between "employees" and the development of industrialization was completely different from that between the "old" *Mittelstand* and industrialization. As he later pointed out

> *The stronger* Grosskapital, *the better are the salaries, etc. of the employees. The situation is different for the independent* Mittelstand. *The latter does not advance through the development of* Grosskapital; *rather the number of its members is continuously diminished.*[57]

The leaders of the "Düsseldorf policy" were not satisfied by Rahardt's somewhat half-hearted avowal of party-political neutrality. The Düsseldorf group seceded soon after the fifth annual meeting of the DMV. The program of the new *Mittelstandsvereinigung für Handel und Gewerbe,* as the new Düsseldorf-based organization called itself, emphasized that the new organization ought not to be viewed as a counter-organization to the DMV. The aim was rather to become an "economic organization". The party-political activity of the DMV and especially its anti-Semitism were regarded by the Düsseldorf organization as "mistakes". Similarly, it had been a "mistake" to have even attempted to represent the "new" *Mittelstand.*[58] The new Düsseldorf organization agreed that if specific candidates of the DMV had been elected in the federal or state elections, the aims of the *Mittelstand* would have received far more attention. Unfortunately, however, the political activities of the DMV had shown that there could be no assurance of success in elections. Participation in elections served only to alienate the major bourgeois political parties. It was far safer to pursue "economic" interests alone and to seek the support of all political parties. The Düsseldorf organization sought to represent the "old" *Mittelstand* (chiefly the retailers and the artisans). It "regretted" the policy of the retailers' *Schutzverbände* around *Der Detaillist* which insisted on separating the interests of retailers and artisans.[59] Although the Düsseldorf *Mittelstandsvereinigung für Handel und Gewerbe* specifically rejected party politics, it nevertheless accepted the support of political parties including the Centre, *Deutsch- Konservative,* and National Liberal Parties, as well as the recently founded *Deutsche Vereinigung.*

The latter party had broken away from the Centre in 1907.[60]

The "Düsseldorf Policy", in various forms, remained a feature of the *Mittelstandsbewegung* down to 1914.* Besides the DMV and the *Mittelstandsvereinigung für Handel und Gewerbe,* there were a number of important *Mittelstand* organizations in existence by 1908. Lack of space precludes an extensive examination of these various organizations. The *Mittelstandsvereinigung für das Königreich Sachsen,* because of the particular role of this organization in both leading another split away from the DMV and in establishing the *Reichsdeutscher Mittelstandsverband,* deserves special attention.

The Mittelstandsvereinigung für das Königreich Sachsen 1905 - 1909

The first meeting of the Saxon *Mittelstand* organization was held in Dresden on 28 November 1905. At this meeting the *Mittelstandsvereinigung für das Königreich Sachsen* was formally constituted as a branch of the DMV.** The leader of the Saxon organization was the radical anti-Semite, Theodor Fritsch, who was simultaneously an executive member of the DMV. Fritsch's anti-Semitic activities can be traced back to the early 1880s.[61] At the first meeting of the Saxon *Mittelstandsvereinigung* in November 1905, Fritsch, in line with the original policy of the DMV, maintained that the *Mittelstand* "stands in the middle, between the big capitalists and the wage earners . . . To the *Mittelstand* belong all those who feel themselves part of it."[62] He also emphasized that the new organization was not to become a new political party. "The main consideration is that the *Mittelstand* be helped." Fritsch's own direct involvement with the *Deutsch-soziale* (anti-Semitic) Party was too well known for his alleged desire

---

*The *Mittelstandsvereinigung für Handel und Gewerbe* specifically rejected the charge of the DMV that it sought merely to foster self-help and had rejected state-help. See *Westdeutsche Mittelstands-Ztg.* Nr.36, 8.5.1909, p.1. Cf. the later statements of Büttner, *Mittelstandsnot,* 1913.

**Wein, *Verbandsbildung,* 1968 : 86 suggests that the Saxon organization was "established independently of the DMV".

to remain neutral on party-political matters to be taken seriously. Fritsch had earlier claimed,

> *Anti-Semitism is only our point of departure, not our final goal. The higher and more general aim of our work is a great reform of the whole national life* (Volksleben) *— a social and moral rebirth of the nation.* [63]

The particular legislative demands of the *Mittelstandsvereinigung* under Fritsch's leadership were so wide-ranging that they won the organization in Saxony much notoriety.* In a long memorandum, the Saxon organization sought government help for the *Mittelstand* in the name of saving the nation from revolution. Unless help for the *Mittelstand* was forthcoming, "the revolutionary movement among the proletariat will grow further; and the revolution will move the closer, the more the independent *Mittelstand* disappears". Helping the *Mittelstand,* however, stemmed the tide of revolution in a more important respect:

> *A policy favouring the* Mittelstand *is at the same time the best policy for the workers. The proletarian question cannot be solved in any way other than to open up the possibility for the worker to move out of the ranks of the proletariat.* [64]

The first years of the *Mittelstandsvereinigung für das Königreich Sachsen* brought it into no conflict with the parent organization, the DMV. At the first meeting of the Thuringian *Mittelstand* organization in September 1907, Fritsch declared his solidarity with the DMV in its decision to abstain from party politics. At that meeting, he stated that the

> Mittelstandsvereinigung *has originated out of the crisis of the times, because the* Mittelstand *is most oppressed by modern economic developments. When numerous independents went bankrupt through modern develop-*

---

*The anti-Semitic candidates enjoyed some success in the federal elections of 1893. However, as one writer has pointed out, "the most notable feature of the election was the success of the anti-Semites in Saxony . . . In Saxony, where the number of Jews was negligible, an anti-Semitic vote was mainly a protest vote by the *Mittelstand* against the ineffectiveness of the traditional bourgeois parties." See Pulzer, *Rise of Political Anti-Semitism*, 1964 : 123.

ments, the necessity of joining together was recognized. 65

Although Fritsch claimed at the 1908 annual meeting of the DMV that his Saxon organization had become a "factor of importance" in Saxony, a tax on turnovers failed in the same year to pass the Saxon *Landtag.* 66

The DMV and the Saxon branch continued in their united opposition to the federal finance reform program put forward by a new Conservative-Centre alliance in 1909. The latter program openly opposed even the rather mild finance reform proposals of Chancellor Bülow. Bülow's proposals included the introduction of a direct tax in the form of an inheritance tax. This inheritance tax was to be levied only on the direct descendants to estates valued over 10,000 Mk. The bulk (four-fifths) of the tax levy required by the federal government was to come from the indirect taxes favoured by the Conservative-Centre proposal.* As early as February 1909 Dietrich Hahn of the BdL had boasted at the annual meeting of the BdL that thanks largely to the work of their organization (the BdL), the government's finance reform proposals "can be considered as good as dead".67 The DMV and associated organizations favoured the government's finance reform proposals over the Conservative-Centre counter proposals. Because these latter proposals relied completely upon the collection of indirect taxes, they would hit the *Mittelstand* far harder than the kind of mild inheritance tax proposed by the government. The response within the ranks of the *Mittelstand* was to call an *Allgemeiner Mittelstandstag* for mid-April 1909.** Some disenchantment with the Conservatives had

*The tax was to be graduated from one per cent on 10,000 Mk. to four per cent on 750,000 Mk. It has been claimed that only one-tenth "of the rural landed property" would have been subject to the tax. See Eyck, *Das persönliche Regiment Wilhelms II,* 1949 : 529. On the financial background, see esp. Witt, *Finanzpolitik,* 1970 : 199 ff. Cf. *Die Finanzreform von 1909 und die Parteien des Reichstags* (1910).

**The call was sponsored by the DMV, Fritsch's Saxon organization, the *Deutscher Zentralverband für Handel und Gewerbe,* the *Zentralausschuss der vereinigten Innungs-Verbände Deutschlands,* the *Preussischer Landesverband der Haus- und Grundbesitzer-Vereine,* the *Deutscher Beamtenbund,* and the *Innungsausschuss der vereinigten Innungen Berlins.* See *Der Fortschritt.* Nr. 7, April 1909 : 169 - 170.

been expressed by the DMV as far back as mid-1908. At that time, the executive committee of the DMV had issued a statement to the effect that "up until now, the conservative deputies of the *Landtag* have not sufficiently defended the interests of the *Mittelstand*"[68]

At the 13 April 1909 *Allgemeiner Mittelstandstag* in Berlin, Dietrich Hahn, who was present to defend the Conservative-Centre finance reform proposals, was literally shouted down. Seifert of the *Deutscher Zentralverband für Handel und Gewerbe* claimed that the meeting represented between 800,000 and 900,000 members of the *Mittelstand*. The German Empire, he continued, whose proud citizens they were, was in financial difficulty. The only acceptable solution to these difficulties was the introduction of the government's inheritance tax proposals. The message of the meeting's resolution was clear.

> *The meeting protests against the attempt to introduce an unequal distribution of the burden of taxation and demands direct taxes, which apply to property, alongside indirect taxes, which especially affect the broad mass of the people.*[69]

The 13 April 1909 *Allgemeiner Mittelstandstag,* which comprised the whole range of *Mittelstand* organizations, from the DMV to the leading national *Schutzverbände* of the retailers, expressed a rare unity of opinion in their opposition to the Conservative-Centre tax proposals.

From the point of view of the *Mittelstand,* and especially of the DMV, a Conservative-Centre coalition working for a finance reform directly opposed to the economic interests of the *Mittelstand* was particularly ironic. The Centre Party, like the *Deutsch-Konservative* Party, had always taken great pains to display its support of the *Mittelstand* and particularly that of retailers' legislative demands. The Centre's *Volksverein für das katholische Deutschland* had been created, in part, to mobilize the support of the *Mittelstand*.[70] Although the BdL sought to emphasize that all *Mittelstand* organizations did not agree with the policy statement of the *Allgemeiner Mittelstandstag,* there was no question that the policy expressed at the *Mittelstandstag* was representative of the views of the *Mittelstand.* (The BdL publicized any evidence it could find of views from *Mittelstand* organizations which questioned the policy of the *Mittelstandstag.)*[71] The really significant differences of opinion within the ranks of the *Mittelstand* began to appear only with the question of how to support the policy expressed at the *Allgemeiner Mittelstandstag.* That question presented itself in an acute fashion with the foundation of the *Hansa-Bund.*

The Hansa-Bund and the Development of New Cleavages in the Mittelstandsbewegung

On 12 June 1909 the *Hansa-Bund für Gewerbe, Handel und Industrie* was founded in Berlin as a direct response to the Conservative-Centre finance reform plans and as a counterweight to the BdL.[72] The powerful economic interest groups which were responsible for calling the new *Hansa-Bund* into existence included the CDI and the *Centralverband des Deutschen Bank- und Bankiergewerbes.*[73] The list of speakers at the founding meeting included some of Germany's most prominent *Grosskapitalisten.* There were Jacob Riesser, Emil Rathenau, Emil Kirdorf, and Hermann Wirth (of the CDI), to name but a few.

The unity of opinion among *Mittelstand* organizations in opposition to the Conservative-Centre finance reform proposals made it possible for many *Mittelstand* organizations to join with the *Grosskapitalisten* in the protest meeting sponsored by the *Hansa-Bund* in mid-June 1909.[74] From the point of view of the *Mittelstand* organizations the protest meeting of 12 June 1909 was simply a logical extension of their own *Allgemeiner Mittelstandstag* of 13 April 1909, with the not insignificant weight of the *Grosskapitalisten* added for good measure. The *Grosskapitalisten* sought in the protest meeting of 12 June 1909 and in the establishment of the *Hansa-Bund* a mass base especially important in the election plans which they were already formulating. Because the *Hansa-Bund* sought to unite so many economic interests under one roof, the organization attempted to form a program of "strict neutrality on questions of social policy where conflicting interests are present among the organizations represented in it or among its members".[75] · Retailers' organizations were being asked to join an organization to which· the *Verband Deutscher Waren- und Kaufhäuser* and (in the person of Dr. Hans Crüger) the *Allgemeiner Verband der auf Selbsthilfe beruhenden Erwerbs- und Wirtschaftsgenossenschaften* belonged. It is surprising that so many retailers' organizations responded to the call.[76]

In general, however, the reaction to the *Hansa-Bund* both among retailers' organizations and among *Mittelstand* organizations (such as the DMV) was very mixed. The DMV under Rahardt elected to join the new *Bund,* but left it open for its own corporative members to make their own decisions. From the outset, the *Mittelstandsvereinigung für Handel und Gewerbe* (Düsseldorf) had sought to maintain a neutral position in relation to the *Hansa-Bund.* Beythien's *Verband der Rabattsparvereine Deutschlands* had said that the "inner contradictions" of the *Hansa-Bund* would lead to its downfall and that the *Verband* could not possibly join.[77] In early November 1909 the *Zentralvereinigung deutscher Vereine für Handel und Gewerbe* (Lissauer's Berlin based organization) still maintained "a cautious attitude towards the *Hansa-Bund".*

On 20 June 1909 (or just over one week after the founding of the *Hansa-Bund),* there was a meeting of the *Mittelstandsvereinigung für das Königreich Sachsen* under Fritsch in Dresden. At this meeting, it was decided not to join the *Hansa-Bund.*[78] The verdict of the Dresden meeting was that

> *The whole* Hansa-Bund *is based on hotchpotch, on a union of contradictions. It wants to unite the contradictory interests of the large industrialist with the artisan, the large banker with the little retailer . . . The organization can only create confusion.*[79]

The Dresden meeting, with the active support of the *Deutscher Zentralverband für Handel und Gewerbe,* reaffirmed the earlier stand against the Conservative-Centre finance reform proposals and demanded the inheritance tax. The *Mittelstand* organ-

izations* at Dresden demonstrated, therefore, that they were
not about to return to the fold of the Conservatives and the
BdL. On 6 September 1909 there was a meeting of the executive of the *Mittelstandsvereinigung für das Königreich Sachsen*
in Leipzig. At the meeting it was formally declared that the
DMV, in joining the *Hansa-Bund,* had lost the confidence of
the Saxon branch. Other organizations belonging to the DMV
followed this lead.[80] By the end of September 1909 Fritsch
was already suggesting that the *Hansa-Bund* should be re-
named the *"Grosshandelsbund".*[81]

Under the leadership of the *Mittelstandsvereinigung für das
Königreich Sachsen,* there was a meeting on 22 November
1909 in Leipzig to discuss the relationship of the *Mittelstand*
to the *Hansa-Bund* and to discuss forming a *"Zentralausschuss
des deutschen Mittelstandes".*[82] The participating organizations included many which had already left the DMV and
others which clung to the hope that Rahardt and the DMV
would reverse the policy of joining the *Hansa-Bund.* Stocky
from the Dusseldorf *Mittelstandsvereinigung* attended, along
with the leading lights of the *Mittelstandsbewegung* in
Saxony.** Rahardt, who was invited to address the meeting,
neither convinced his audience to support the *Hansa-Bund* nor
reversed his own policy in favour of the *Hansa-Bund.* In spite
of his policy position, Rahardt was elected to the newly
formed *Zentralausschuss,* albeit in a minor capacity. Felix
Höhne of Leipzig was elected as chairman and Stocky as
secretary. Fritsch and Seifert were also elected to the eight
man executive. (Seifert, the chairman of the *Deutscher
Zentralverband für Handel und Gewerbe,* and his prede-
cessor, Hugo Geest, were accused by a contemporary

---

*Besides the already mentioned organizations, the following participated in the
Dresden meeting: the *Verband Sächsischer Kaufleute,* the *Gau Sachsen der
Rabatt-Spar-Vereine,* the *Sächsischer Innungs-Verband,* the *Verband Sächsischer
Haus-und Grundbesitzer-Vereine,* and the *Verband Sächsischer Gewerbe- und
Handwerker-Vereine.*

**Seifert of the *Deutscher Zentralverband für Handel und Gewerbe* was
present, as well as Felix Höhne of Leipzig (later chairman of the *Reichsdeutscher Mittelstandsverband),* Fritsch, and Ludwig Fahrenbach (later
general secretary of the *Reichsdeutscher Mittelstandsverband).*

of being anti-Semitic and of working for the election of *"Mittelständler* and anti-Semites". The *Zentralverband,* the leading national *Schutzverband* of the retailers, was labelled "an economic-political auxiliary of the reactionary parties".)[83] The primary task of the *Zentralausschuss* executive was to transform "the fragmented German *Mittelstand* into a real unity". Henceforth the DMV was to be referred to by the *Zentralausschuss* and the *Mittelstandsvereinigung* in Saxony as the "Berlin DMV". Its right to call itself the "German" *Mittelstandsvereinigung* was rejected because "the 'German' *Mittelstands-Vereinigung* is restricted primarily to Berlin".[84] As if to formalize the break that had developed between the Berlin leadership of the DMV and the new *Zentralausschuss des deutschen Mittelstandes,* the sixth general meeting of the DMV, which convened on 28 November 1909, issued a resolution stating that "co-operation" of the DMV and the *Hansa-Bund* "is in the best interests of the *Mittelstand".*[85]

The immediate significance of the *Hansa-Bund* for the DMV was that it led directly to the virtual breakdown of the latter organization without, however, effectively turning the DMV away from its earlier conservative orientation. Of the 33 members of its newly elected governing council in 1910, only one has been termed even "left liberal".[86] The continuing efforts of the *Hansa-Bund* to win the broad support of the *Mittelstandsbewegung* (including efforts to win over the "new" *Mittelstand)* achieved little or no success.[87] The failure to win that support has been considered an important factor in the swift decline of the *Hansa-Bund.*[88] While the existence of the *Hansa-Bund* had in the end brought the continued existence of the DMV into doubt, opposition to the *Hansa-Bund* within the *Mittelstand* had helped to crystallize opinion within the *Mittelstandsbewegung* well to the right of the DMV. This crystallization of opinion within the *Mittelstandsbewegung* initially took the nebulous form of the *Zentralausschuss des deutschen Mittelstandes,* was transformed slightly into the *Mittelstandsbund für Handel und Gewerbe* (in early 1910), and led ultimately to the formation of the largest *Mittelstand* organization of the period from 1890 to

1914, the *Reichsdeutscher Mittelstandsverband* (founded in mid-1911). The founding of the *Hansa-Bund** did not represent, as some writers have maintained, "a symptom of the tendency towards the lessening of radicalism in the *Verbandsbewegung* of retail trade and of the *Mittelstand* in general".[89]

The immediate object of the founding of the *Hansa-Bund*, as well as that of the protest meeting which the *Bund* had sponsored on 12 June 1909, namely, the forestalling of the passage of the Conservative-Centre finance reform bill, was not achieved. The bill was passed on 24 June 1909. Within the *Reichstag*, the old Bülow-Bloc (Bülow, as he had promised, resigned over the issue) no longer existed. The "Blue-Black Bloc" or a Conservative-Centre coalition, took the place of the old bloc, one formed by Progressives, National Liberals and Conservatives. In the stage between the dissolution of one coalition and the emergence of the other, high hopes were held by people, such as Friedrich Naumann, for a new coalition "from Bebel to Bassermann". Although these hopes were never realized, some left-wing National Liberals and even some long-time Marxists (Franz Mehring, for example) were tempted by the idea of such an anti-Conservative coalition.[90] In the years leading up to the *Reichstag* elections of 1912, the various bourgeois political parties sought to broaden their mass bases, and without exception adopted programs designed to enlist the support of the *Mittelstand* for which the *Hansa-Bund* had striven without success.

---

*Winkler, *Mittelstand*, 1972 : 55 maintains that the *Mittelstand* organizations which did decide to join the *Hansa-Bund* represented the "left-wing" of the *Mittelstandsbewegung*. It is equally valid to suggest that the *Mittelstand* organizations which did not join the *Hansa-Bund* represented something like a "right-wing" within the *Mittelstandsbewegung*. In terms of a discernible *Mittelstandsbewegung*, however, the "right-wing" grew in political significance (*en passant* capturing the leadership of the *Mittelstandsbewegung*) while the "left-wing" merged into the steadily declining force that was the *Hansa-Bund*.

The Reichsdeutscher Mittelstandsverband (RDMV) 1911 - 1914: From the Zentralausschuss des deutschen Mittelstandes to the Mittelstandsbund für Handel und Gewerbe

The *Zentralausschuss des deutschen Mittelstandes,* which had been created on 22 November 1909, was considered to be the committee necessary to lay the groundwork for a new national *Mittelstand* organization. The *Mittelstandsvereinigung für Handel und Gewerbe* (Düsseldorf) was particularly pleased to report that the *Zentralausschuss* had come to accept the "Düsseldorf policy"—"that an association of the *Mittelstand* if it is supposed to be useful, must restrict itself to the interests of trade and artisanship".91 The *Zentralausschuss* met in Leipzig on 16 January 1910 in order to establish a more formal organization. Rahardt of the DMV, who remained on the executive of the *Zentralausschuss,* wrote to inform the *Zentralausschuss* that "from the very beginning" he had not intended to participate in the meetings.92 The definitive break with the DMV coincided with the appearance of a new organization, the *Mittelstandsbund für Handel und Gewerbe,* which had grown out of the *Zentralausschuss.* The executive included familiar faces; Höhne was chairman and Stocky was secretary; Fritsch and Seifert were also members of the executive. The only new member of the executive was Nagler from the *Bayrischer Handwerkerbund.* A meeting was called to take place in Düsseldorf in August or September 1910.93

Membership in the new organization, as Stocky might have hoped, was not open to organizations of the "new" *Mittelstand.* Every conceivable organization of *"Handel und Gewerbe"* and these words were now identified primarily with retailers and artisans, was invited to join. Emil Lederer wrote at the time of the *Mittelstandsbund:*

> *According to its entire construction and activity, it is, at present, primarily a representation of retail trade (as indeed above all, postulates of retail trade stand in the foreground of German* Mittelstand *politics) even if it also strives to become the central point of the* Mittelstandsbewegung *for all of Germany.*94

As usual, "party politics and religious matters" were to be "kept well out of the activity of the *Mittelstandsbund*". It was even emphasized that "the new organization will place the greatest emphasis upon guiding the *Mittelstand* towards self-help".[95]

The meetings of the *Mittelstandsbund* which were held in the autumn of 1910 in the Rhineland (at Düsseldorf and Cologne) were marked notably by discussion of the the retailers' economic problems. Dr. August Engel, who was from 1909 director of the *Deutsche Vereinigung*, spoke at Cologne on 18 October 1910. The object of his speech was to outline the economic conditions and development tendencies in retail trade. He concluded that retailers could overcome their economic problems only by joining "class organizations" and by seeking legislative help. There was also talk of the need to found *Einkaufs-genossenschaften*, an old idea favoured by Engel. A resolution was passed asking governments in Germany to forbid civil servants from participating in consumer co-operatives. A wide range of retailers' economic problems was discussed, including the law on unfair competition. Although a number of artisan questions was also discussed, these questions took second place to those concerning the retailers.[96] The next meeting of the *Mittelstandsbund* was not scheduled until the autumn of 1911. By mid-1911, however, the *Reichsdeutscher Mittelstandsverband* had been founded.

The RDMV: Mittelstand Mobilization opposed to the DMV and Hansa-Bund Alliance

During the relatively short period of the controversy over the finance reform bill, the power constellation of Imperial Germany, as represented by the alliance of large industry and agriculture and backed by the government, appeared to have collapsed. "The Prussian-German system of government" had been based on "co-operation of those who were loyal to the state and against revolution, consolidation of the productive classes *(produktive Stände)*, protection of national work, in particular of agriculture and the *Mittelstand*".* The *Mittelstand* had been expected to perform the function of helping to maintain the *status quo*. After the Conservative-Centre finance reform proposals had been introduced, the *Mittelstand* and even the large industrial concerns, together with their interest groups, questioned a *status quo* over which agricultural interests had far too much control. The finance bill was in the economic interests of neither the *Mittelstand* nor the large industrialists (let alone those of the working classes). Momentary short-run economic conflicts of interest were reflected in the breakdown of the political relationship between the *Mittelstand* (even the *Mittelstandsvereinigung für das Königreich Sachsen,* normally pro-BdL), great industry, and the government-backed agricultural interests. This economic and political breakdown took a more positive form with the creation of the *Hansa-Bund,* an organization designed to mobilize the anti-Conservative phalanx. The patent failure of this organization to stop the passage of the finance bill provided an indication of the power of the agricultural interests.

It was not long before the demonstration of the political power of these interests made separation from them over a short-run economic issue appear foolhardy to large industry's most powerful interest group, the CDI. By mid-1911 the rupture of the CDI with the *Hansa-Bund* had begun. After the departure of the CDI and the failure of the *Hansa-Bund* to attract the main *Mittelstand* organizations, the *Hansa-Bund* became "primarily an organization for the interests of banks and semi-finished and manufacturing industries".[97] The CDI left the *Hansa-Bund* to return to a mutually beneficial alliance with agriculture.

---

*This statement was a succinct and concrete expression of the *Sammlungspolitik*. See *B.Dahlem. Pr.Staatsministerium. Rep.90. Nr.306, Vertrauliche Besprechung des Königl. Staatsministerium.* 19.4.1898. The meeting was attended by Hohenlohe, Miquel, Thielen, Borse, Von Hammerstein, Schönstedt, Von der Recke, Brefeld, Von Gossler, Von Posadowsky, Von Bülow, and Tirpitz. For the problems of interpretation of the *Sammlungspolitik*, see esp. Stegmann, "Zur Genesis der Miquelschen Sammlungspolitik, 1890-1897" (1973) and Schmidt, "Innenpolitische Blockbildung am Vorabend des Ersten Weltkrieges " (1972).

Some *Mittelstand* groups, especially those under the leadership of the Saxon *Mittelstandsvereinigung*, had been realistic enough to limit their protests against the Conservative-Centre tax proposals short of joining the *Hansa-Bund*. There was a recognition that the long-run economic interests of the *Mittelstand* would not be served by such a gesture. Faced with the *fait accompli* of the new finance bill, even if it were not in the short-run in the economic interests of the *Mittelstand*, the *Mittelstand* groups around the Saxon *Mittelstandsvereinigung* did not dwell on the immediate reversal. They turned once again to search for allies who shared their interests in a maintenance of the *status quo.*

From the point of view of the *Mittelstand* organizations outside the now virtually powerless DMV, the creation of the *Reichsdeutscher Mittelstandsverband* (RDMV) was to be a positive expression of their desire to channel the forces at the centres of power into a direction more favourable to *Mittelstand* economic interests. Regarded from the point of view of an organization such as the BdL, the return to the fold (after temporary, but harmless, vacillation) of the great majority of the *Mittelstand* organizations might be welcomed in the hope of broadening the mass base of the BdL. At the beginning of 1911 Theodor Fritsch first outlined the rationale behind the events which led up to the founding of the RDMV. His "thoughts" ("Thoughts on the *Mittelstands-Bewegung*") also provides a clear insight into the ideological and political considerations which were to play such a dominant role in the activities of the *Verband*. Because of their importance, these "thoughts" deserve closer analysis.

Fritsch recognized that German society had become politicized, that certain economic interest groups had organized themselves and that they wielded considerable political influence. The *Mittelstandsmann*, because his motto was "live and let live" was an ideal citizen and alone remained without a "powerful association". Both *Grosskapital* and the "propertyless proletariat", who were organized,

> *represent extremes, and extremes are somewhat unnatural and unhealthy. A state consisting only of* Grosskapitalisten *is as unthinkable as a state consisting only of*

> *proletarians. But a state consisting only of men of the* Mittelstand *is indeed possible; and it would perhaps represent the best and most durable form of society.* [98]

As he was to say in 1911, the *Mittelstandsbewegung* was not to be an extension of the "egoistic class struggle". Rather, the *Mittelstandsbewegung* was to introduce "a new social principle", one of "organic harmony". "The will to harmony, love must inspire us, not competitive jealousy and hatred."[99] The class struggle would end, and the state would be rescued. With such aims in view, it was therefore extremely important to foster the *Mittelstand.*

There was no question that the *Mittelstand* needed help and protection, for Fritsch claimed, "the *Mittelstand* must perish through the continuation of present conditions". These "present conditions" referred chiefly to the development of *Grosskapital.* It followed that "he who wished to pursue a serious policy for the *Mittelstand,* must restrain the power of *Grosskapital* . . . He who protects the *Mittelstand,* protects the state, morality and culture." Fritsch considered that the demands of the *Mittelstand* were not a mere extension of the interest-group mania to the *Mittelstand,* although he believed that the "protection" of the *Mittelstand* had to take the concrete form of legislative enactments. These enactments were claimed not out of mere economic self-seeking; much more significant considerations underlay the demands of the *Mittelstand.* With such a view of the importance of the *Mittelstand* to the very survival of the state, it also followed that any social policy had to begin with the *Mittelstand.* Fritsch was realistic enough to realize that the state, as it existed, responded only to political pressure. In order to apply that pressure and to put its case forward, the *Mittelstand* had to organize.

Fritsch's thoughts at the beginning of 1911 on the kind of organization required by the *Mittelstand* were still not fully developed. He was certain that none of the already existing *Mittelstand* organizations was sufficient in itself. He envisaged some form of "voluntary parliament of the *Mittelstand . . .* Every *Mittelstand* corporation should send their representatives there, in order to put forward their point of view and demands." Whatever specific form this new organization was to take, it would "not encroach upon the activity of the already existing technical organizations and associations, but rather take an interest in their legitimate desires, in order to represent them in a general way with more force". Once the *Mittelstand* was willing to organize in some such fashion, and once government was responsive, the *Mittelstandsbewegung* would secure "a peaceful development" and "settle the existing tensions of the nation *(Volk)*".[100]

In early April 1911 a meeting of the executive of the *Mittelstandsvereinigung für das Königreich Sachsen,* under the chairmanship of Fritsch, called for the foundation of what was to become the RDMV. It was also agreed to send two memoranda to the federal government outlining the most important demands of the *Mittelstand.* Both memoranda were written by Dr. Eberle. Both reflected a concern for the problems of the retailers.[101] There was already an indication of the dominant (although by no means exclusive) role that finding solutions to retailers' problems was to play in the activities of the RDMV.* The appeal for the foundation of the new organization reflected, virtually word for word, Fritsch's "thoughts" on the organization of the *Mittelstand.* The committee to prepare for the foundation of the organization included Fritsch, Höhne, Ludwig Fahrenbach (director of the Saxon *Mittelstandsvereinigung),* and Max Conradt (leader of the Silesian *Mittelstandsvereinigung).*[102] The new organization was to be the "voluntary parliament", envisaged by Fritsch as "a *Verband* of *Verbände".* The new organization was not to indulge in party politics in any way.[103] *Vorwärts* caustically commented that the latter policy (which the newspaper did not believe for one moment would be followed) was "about like a sword without a blade".[104] The new organization was formally founded in Leipzig on 17 July 1911.

There was a consciousness at the founding meeting that the new organization would be immediately considered both a

*Lederer, "Sozialpolitische Chronik. Mittelstandsbewegung", 1912 : 929, stated that the RDMV "is for the most part a representation of retail trade".

child of the BdL and a response by the latter organization to the efforts of the *Hansa-Bund* to win the support of the *Mittelstand*. Höhne insisted at the meeting that such a charge had no foundation and even went so far as to say that it would be wrong for the new organization to have close relations with the BdL. A formal resolution was passed which denied any connection between the foundation of the RDMV and the BdL. Dr. Eberle, who also addressed the meeting, was more open on the question of future alliances. His point of departure was that the *Mittelstand* had only one "absolute enemy" and that that enemy was the SPD. The extent to which the bourgeois political parties would be viewed with favour would depend upon their willingness to help the *Mittelstand*. The general secretary of the *Mittelstandsvereinigung für das Königreich Sachsen,* Fahrenbach, agreed that the *Mittelstand* (which, in any case, did not have a hope of winning a majority at the polls) had to work with all its "friends".[105]

In spite of the strenuous denials of the new organization, the *Hansa-Bund* from the outset considered the RDMV to be "a new branch" of the BdL.[106] That charge had been formally rejected at the founding meeting of the RDMV on 17 July 1911 as "a frivolous accusation".[107] Although no documents appear to have survived which indicate that the BdL even financially supported the foundation of the RDMV, both organizations shared a hatred of the *Hansa-Bund* and a fear of the SPD. The BdL, in spite of having supported the DMV only to see it join the ranks of the *Hansa-Bund,* was doubtless still interested in enlisting the support of the *Mittelstand* and in creating a counter-organization by the *Mittelstand* to both the DMV and the *Hansa-Bund.* The establishment of the RDMV was, therefore, not an unhappy event for the BdL.[108] Subsequent events were to reveal that the natural affinity (one based upon both common ideological presuppositions and shared enemies) between the RDMV and BdL was to produce an alliance between them even though the organizations which formed the core of the RDMV had been strenuously opposed to the finance reform bill backed by the BdL. By 1913 the CDI was to become an open ally to both the BdL and the RDMV. The RDMV was forced, therefore, to alter its definition of *Grosskapital*, for surely the CDI was the organization of *Grosskapital par excellence*. The RDMV came to insist that the real *Grosskapitalisten* who were the enemies of the *Mittelstand* were those *Grosskapitalisten* within the *Hansa-Bund*. Ideological purity was one thing, but practical politics something else!

The first general meeting of the RDMV was held in Dresden in late September 1911. Once again the ideology running through the meetings reflected views similar to those outlined by Fritsch at the beginning of the year. Höhne, the newly elected chairman, spoke of the two main enemies of the *Mittelstand* in a fashion in which anti-Semites of varying colours had spoken of the Jews and their alleged influence.[109]

> *The one enemy is the golden, the other the red international. The Moloch of capital with its whole egoistic thoughtlessness, burdens . . . the* Mittelstand. *Social Democracy, on the other hand, is very anxious to cut the ground from under our feet, and, dear God, it must be said that our whole economic development in combination with legislation has led to the point where Social Democracy, in many areas, has succeeded.*[110]

Eberle, who had also been elected to the executive of the RDMV, said:

> *The delegates of the* Mittelstand *from all over Germany are also in Dresden in order to close ranks for the struggle against Social Democracy. They are there in order to set the German citizens against the international Social Democracy.*[111]

This kind of ideological basis and political orientation would have been pleasing to the Conservative members of the *Reichstag* (Malkewitz, Rieseberg, and Hanisch) who took part in the meeting. The honorary chairman was the mayor of Dresden, Beutler, who was at the same time member of the *Deutsch-Konservative* Party.[112]

The conservative character of the new organization was most evident in the composition of the executive board (with 9 members), the executive committee (with 24 members), and the general committee (with 100 members). Within this somewhat cumbersome executive were included the leaders of virtually all the *Mittelstand* organizations opposed to the DMV and the *Hansa-Bund*. The executive of the *Mittelstands-vereinigung für das Königreich Sachsen* which had played a leading role in the foundation of the RDMV was heavily represented in the executive at all levels. Seifert of the *Deutscher Zentralverband für Handel und Gewerbe* was elected to the executive committee, as well as Nicolaus of the *Verband der Rabattsparvereine Deutschlands*. Stocky of the *Mittelstandsbund für Handel und Gewerbe* (Düsseldorf) was an active participant in the meeting which formulated the statutes of the RDMV and was elected to the executive board. Nevertheless, Stocky declared that he could "not give a definite promise of membership", but could "almost for sure hold out a prospect of membership".[113] Stocky was very likely not unhappy to learn that the organization was not to represent the employee organizations. Höhne had branded the latter organizations prior to the founding meeting as "our direct opponents".[114]

The RDMV was received with some scepticism by a number of *Mittelstand* groups. Although many artisan organizations elected to join the RDMV, the important *Zentral-Ausschuss der Vereinigten Innungs-Verbände Deutschlands* had been against the idea of the RDMV from the beginning.[115] The *Mittelstandsbund für Handel und Gewerbe* later decided not to join the RDMV. The Düsseldorf organization continued to insist that the time had not been ripe for a national organization such as the RDMV. Such an organization, the Düsseldorf organization was convinced, should not be imposed from above, but had to originate from below when "inner necessities" within the *Mittelstand* would cry out for the creation of a national organization.[116] Unsympathetic newspaper reports suggested that as many as 350 associations of various social groups had refused to join the RDMV. However, that figure probably included many smaller organizations still associated with the DMV or the *Hansa-Bund*.[117]

From the beginning there was considerable speculation about the relationship between the RDMV and various established interest groups. Newspapers reported the charge that the BdL, which reputedly owned the *Mittelstands-vereinigung für das Königrech Sachsen*, also stood behind the RDMV.[118] There seemed some agreement, among the newspapers of a liberal or Socialist cast, that the new organization would be necessarily "agrarian-anti-Semitic".[119] Soon, however, a new rumour began to circulate in the press. The suggestion was that the RDMV was being financed by industrialists from Rhineland-Westphalia. These industrialists were said to have provided 100,000 Mk. in five instalments of 20,000 Mk.[120] Even an antagonist of the RDMV, who was willing to print the rumour, admitted that no solid proof existed.[121] Subsequent research has added no evidence to support the original rumours.*

The RDMV: The Federal Elections of 1912 and the Rise of the Kartell der schaffenden Stände

The RDMV was aware of the dangers to its existence of open political participation or alliance. The public disavowal of any party-political interests (apart from the safe declaration of opposition to the SPD) 'had of course become a traditional policy with the foundation of new *Mittelstand* organizations. Initially at least the RDMV expressed an open determination to seek fulfilment of its "economic" program which was to be strenuously separated from "political" participation of any kind.

In a letter to the Saxon government on 30 November 1911 the RDMV sought the advice of the government about the best means of approach to all the candidates of the bourgeois political parties in the up-coming federal elections. The RDMV stressed that it would carry out a survey of the policies of all bourgeois parties on the economic interests of the *Mittelstand* and simply publish the results. Not only would

*Kaelble, *Industrielle Interessenpolitik*, 1967 : 133, suggests that the CDI supported the RDMV "since 1911"; Stegmann, *Erben Bismarcks*, 1970 : 331, states that the CDI had financially supported the RDMV "since its foundation" (cf. p.251). Stegmann appears to have based this conclusion on the newspaper articles of the period. Cf. Fischer, *Krieg der Illusionen*, 1969 : 60 and Puhle, *Agrarische Interessenpolitik*, 1966: 162 - 163.

the organization not put forward its own candidates (as the DMV had done previously), but it would show no public favour to any party. The letter sought "reassurances" from the federal government that after members of the RDMV had fulfilled their "damned duty and obligation towards the Fatherland", some government official would not subsequently brand the "economic" RDMV a "political" organization. The RDMV sought these "reassurances" in return for helping to mobilize the *Mittelstand* for any party other than the SPD. A denunciation of the RDMV as "political", it was emphasized, would harm the organization considerably.[122] The letter indicated the fear within the RDMV in late 1911 of forming any open alliances. It would appear questionable, on the basis of this "secret" letter to the Saxon government, that either the BdL or the CDI were at that time even financially supporting the RDMV. When financial support was forthcoming (as it was later), the BdL insisted on some form of public disclosure.

Presumably "reassurances" were obtained from the federal government in answer to the letter of 30 November 1911 from the RDMV,[123] for the organization as promised issued its electoral manifesto in mid-December. The manifesto listed the familiar demands of the *Mittelstand*. There was a call for "effective taxation of department stores and all consumer co-operatives and branch stores", as well as the demand for "improvement of the law against unfair competition".[124] On the basis of some 350 answers received from the various candidates, the Conservatives, the National Liberals, the Centre, the *Reichspartei*, and the *Wirtschaftliche Vereinigung* were said by the RDMV to be inclined to support the manifesto of the RDMV. "Almost all candidates of these groups who responded [to the survey] maintain a favourable attitude." The *Fortschrittliche . Volkspartei,* although the RDMV received few answers from them, wanted to assure the RDMV that they were "true friends of the *Mittelstand*". On several points, however, the *Fortschrittliche Volkspartei* was said by the RDMV "to be soft".[125]

The *Fortschrittliche Volkspartei,* as the left-liberal successor to Eugen Richter's doctrinaire liberalism, maintained, in accordance with Richter's beliefs, that modern economic developments would not hurt the "skilled trader". A policy of taxing department stores, for example, would simply not work if the aim of the taxation was to help the independent retailers. Self-help alone could help the retailers in their competitive economic struggle.[126] The RDMV urged the members of the *Mittelstand* to draw their own conclusions.

Only one imperative found its way into the published survey of the RDMV.

> *Only national candidates are to be supported! No vote of the* Mittelstand *may be given to the fatherlandless Social Democracy!*[127]

The appeal to the *Mittelstand*, the opposition to the SPD, and the support of "national candidates" by the RDMV sounded the same note as the appeals of the *Reichsverband gegen die Sozialdemokratie*. The DMV also reminded its members that in the election "the enemy is to the left and to be sure very left".[128]

One of the surprising features of the survey by the RDMV was that the National Liberals were implicitly recommended by the RDMV. The National Liberal Party had only very slowly adopted a *Mittelstand* policy.[129] The demands of the *Mittelstand* won limited support at the National Liberal conference of 1906. By 1907 the party appeared more worried about the *Mittelstand*, specifically the DMV and its association with the BdL, than about formulating a *Mittelstand* policy of its own.[130] After the breakdown of the Bülow-Bloc in 1909, and probably out of consideration of the threat of Social Democracy, the party began to seriously re-think its *Mittelstand* policy. That policy had previously hardly gone beyond recommending self-help measures. At the National Liberal conference in 1910 held in Cassel, the *Mittelstand* policy of the party was given serious attention for the first time.

At the National Liberal conference, Dr. Schroeder gave a long address, the aim of which was to mobilize the *Mittelstand* into the ranks of the National Liberals. With an eye to the next federal elections, Schroeder pointed out that the SPD alone was opposed to the *Mittelstandsbewegung* and that the

National Liberals could ill afford to go on ignoring the *Mittelstand*. The SPD, he claimed, was opposed to the *Mittelstandsbewegung*.

> *Because the broad groups of the* Mittelstand *are a bulwark against the red flood of Social Democracy, the latter has no interest whatever in the preservation of the* Mittelstand; *on the contrary, Social Democracy does everything it can to destroy the* Mittelstand.[131]

It followed that

> *in order to hinder the achievement of this aim, all bourgeois parties* must *pursue a* Mittelstand *policy, whether they wish to or not.*[132]

Schroeder put forward specific legislative proposals favouring the *Mittelstand*. (He included the "new" *Mittelstand* within his definition of the *Mittelstand*.) The party's policy towards the retailers, for example, consisted in granting virtually all the traditional demands of the retailers. Higher taxes on department stores were to be introduced, laws on unfair competition were to be tightened, laws forbidding civil servants participation in consumer co-operatives were to be introduced. In its electoral appeal the party also emphasized that the finance reform bill of 1909 had been passed over the objections of the National Liberal Party.[133] The RDMV received favourable responses from National Liberal candidates in the survey which the RDMV had carried out before the 1912 federal elections. According to one analysis, the National Liberal party was rewarded for that policy at the polls in 1912 by the *Mittelstand*.[134]

In spite of all the efforts to mobilize the support against the SPD in the federal elections of 1912, and in spite of an electoral alliance between the SPD and the *Fortschrittliche Volkspartei* which lost the SPD far more than it gained, the SPD emerged from the elections with the largest number of deputies (110).[135] At the previous federal elections (held in 1907), the SPD had elected 43 deputies. In 1912 the *Deutsch-Konservative* Party elected 43 (in 1907, 60), the *Frei-*

konservative Party 14 (in 1907, 24), the National Liberal Party 45 (in 1907, 54) and the Centre Party a respectable 91 (in 1907, 105). Although the SPD had fallen far short of a majority in the *Reichstag*, the balance of power had been shifted to the left and away from the "Blue-Blacks", the Conservative-Centre alliance responsible for pushing through the finance reform bill of 1909. If such a development represented only a half-victory for the SPD, it was a complete defeat for the parties openly opposed to the SPD.[136]

The RDMV insisted that 103 members of the bourgeois parties which had been elected to the *Reichstag* had agreed to the election manifesto of the *Verband*. These included 36 members of the *Deutsch-Konservative* Party, 25 National Liberals, 21 from the Centre, 7 members of the *Frei-konservative* Party, and 8 members of the *Wirtschaftliche Vereinigung*.[137] Even one member of the left-liberal party was said to have been "friendly to the *Mittelstand*". The RDMV reported that 5 other members of the *Reichstag* were also "sympathetic". The RDMV liked to label these 103 members of the *Reichstag* a "majority friendly to the *Mittelstand*". However there was no rescuing a victory from such an obvious defeat. For the first time the *Verband* began to suggest a form of alliance with "the industrial associations which are also heavily threatened by Social Democracy". This extra-parliamentary alliance would also include "agriculture".[138]

Even before the second general meeting of the RDMV in mid-September 1912, the CDI and the BdL had moved closer together and had sought agreement on possibly financing the RDMV. The CDI was prepared to pay 15,000 Mk. per year over the next three years if the BdL agreed to do the same. In answer to this proposal, the BdL appeared to agree provided that

> we really can energetically unite the productive classes *(*produktive Stände*) and, thereby, confront our enemies as a united power in future elections.*[139]

Because the BdL had once backed the DMV only to see it later join the *Hansa-Bund*, the BdL was now more cautious.

> *We must naturally have certain guarantees, that the*
> *RDMV is not as powerful as the (DMV) was earlier, that*
> *one will not accept our support and then go one's own*
> *way or even follow another who offers more.* [140]

In fact, the BdL wanted a signed guarantee and wished to meet with both the CDI and RDMV before the general meeting of the RDMV scheduled for September 1912. The meeting between the three organizations was to decide what form, if any, the public declaration of the "co-operation" was to take. As no formal declaration appeared at this time, it seems not unlikely that the RDMV raised some objections to any public admission of its alliance. The way had to be prepared carefully before such a public statement. Without such careful preparation, the statement would have confirmed the rumours which had surrounded its affiliations, and thereby damaged the reputation of the RDMV.

The general meeting of the RDMV in 1911 had emphasized the need to win governmental support for any open alliance. Fahrenbach and Höhne, in a letter of 19 February 1912 to the Chancellor Bethmann-Hollweg, responded to the Chancellor's call of 16 February 1912 for the formation of some type of alliance against Social Democracy. The leaders of the RDMV said that they too were interested in an "association (*Sammlung*) of all those loyal to the state". They said that they had been already working

> *several months in co-operation with an influential*
> *association of industry for the creation of a loose interest*
> *group (*Interessengemeinschaft*) of all independent pro-*
> *ductive classes (*produktive Stände*). The success of these*
> *endeavours to fight against the process of dissolution in*
> *society is satisfactory. One may hope, therefore, that, in*
> *the future, the clearly recognized community of social*
> *interests will eliminate petty party squabbling throughout*
> *the nation.* [141]

The first significant public step toward open avowal of the alliance came at the general meeting of the RDMV in mid-

September 1912. Dr. Eberle, successor to Höhne as chairman of the RDMV, emphasized in a speech that the causes of the "misery of the *Mittelstand*" were to be found in part in the disunity within the *Mittelstandsbewegung*. The obvious way to help the *Mittelstand* was to create a central organization, the aim of which would be to give all groups an opportunity to come together and to present their opinions.[142] Dr. Alexander Tille, legal representative of the chamber of commerce in Saarbrücken and long associated with the CDI, also spoke at the meeting. Tille had shown an interest in creating some form of "corporative parliament" along the lines earlier visualized by Bismarck.[143] His ideas on a so-called *Gewerbebund* had been publicized in the newspaper of the RDMV in July 1912.[144] His speech at the general meeting of the RDMV in September 1912 was an elaboration on his earlier theme. According to Tille, "the common interests of independents" might be summarized as "Fatherland", "corporative social order", and "economic peace".[145] In order to protect and foster these "common interests", a *Gewerbebund* or association "based on a corporative principle" had to be formed.[146] Dr. Tille's speech was by no means received in the press with universal accord. The anti-Semitic *Deutschsoziale Blätter*, in part because of its close ties with the DHV, did not feel overly sympathetic. This newspaper insisted only that the *Mittelstandsbewegung* must remain anti-Semitic ("*antisemitisch sein, oder sie wird nicht sein*").[147] The newspaper of the *Mittelstandsbund für Handel und Gewerbe* was even more sceptical of Tille's suggestion.[148]

In his review of the general meeting of the RDMV in 1912 Fahrenbach insisted that the politics of the *Mittelstand* had to change orientation because "negative defence is giving way to the positive appreciation of the achievements of modern economic development".[149] At a committee meeting of the RDMV in November 1912 Eberle insisted that the demands of the RDMV could not be accomplished by open political participation, but by enlisting the support "of the entire independent *Mittelstand*".* Within the RDMV there was evidently a determination to push forward the plans for an open alliance outside the federal parliament and to tie the fate of the RDMV to what its executive considered the centres of power. The BdL and CDI had both demonstrated how much could be accomplished by taking to the offensive.

Although the CDI represented none other than the *Gross-kapitalisten* despised by the leaders of the RDMV, and especially by Fritsch, the *Hansa-Bund* was easily transformed into the representative of the "real" *Grosskapitalisten*. In the period up to 1914, anti-Semites of varying opinions liked to distinguish between "useful" and "harmful" capital. The "useful" was that type of capital which was put into agriculture or industry; the "harmful" capital was to be found at the stock exchanges and such places.[150] When the CDI left the *Hansa-Bund*, the character of the *Hansa-Bund* changed. The *Hansa-Bund* could then be viewed as the organization representative of "harmful" *Grosskapital*. Because the *Hansa-Bund* had turned to attracting the white-collar workers, it could earn the hatred of the RDMV on that count as well.[151] By June 1914 the RDMV had refined its earlier hatred of *Grosskapital*. By that time, the organization opposed "speculative *Grosskapital* of the bank and stock-exchange world", as well as that of the "department stores". This "speculative *Grosskapital*", it was claimed by the RDMV, was represented by the *Hansa-Bund*.[152] The BdL, like the other partner in what was to become the *Kartell der schaffenden Stände* had helped to push forward a finance reform bill directly opposed to the economic interests of the *Mittelstand* (and opposed to the interests of the CDI). The very fact that the CDI and the BdL were soon after renewing

Deutsch-soziale Blätter. 30.11.1912. Cf. *Neue Wege. Aus Theodor Fritsch's Lebensarbeit*, 1922 : 280 ff. In this speech to the congress of the *Wirtschaftliche Vereinigung*, Fritsch suggested that it would take far too long for the anti-Semites to win "two hundred seats" in the federal parliament. "I am convinced that we shall realize our aims more quickly if we attempt to turn all existing political parties towards anti-Semitism." The primary aim was "to break the harmful influence of Jewry through legislation, in short, to push through anti-Semitic legislation".

friendship was reason enough for the RDMV to reconsider its own policy towards both. By the summer of 1913 the scene was finally set for the foundation of the *Kartell.*

Unification of the Mittelstandsbund für Handel und Gewerbe with the RDMV and the Emergence of the Kartell der schaffenden Stände

Within the *Mittelstandsbewegung* itself the way toward the foundation of the *Kartell* was cleared by a somewhat surprising decision of the *Mittelstandsbund für Handel und Gewerbe* (Düsseldorf) taken at the conference (the *Westdeutscher Mittelstandstag*) on 27 April 1913. This meeting had been called to see if it were possible to unite the Düsseldorf organization with the RDMV. There was open scepticism that the *Mittelstand* in the Rhineland was prepared for such a step. Much to the satisfaction of the leaders of both organizations, the conference was extremely well attended. At this conference in Cologne, the decision was taken to transform the Düsseldorf organization into the "committee for Rhineland and Westphalia as a part of the RDMV". A further meeting was called for 18 May 1913 to give the organizations concerned sufficient time to work out the details.[153]

At the second conference on 18 May 1913 there was a willingness on the part of the Düsseldorf organization to reverse its policy towards joining the RDMV. That aboutface was justified because it was considered by the central committee of the Düsseldorf organization "as the best way, perhaps the only possibility" by which the independent *Mittelstand* could influence "the legislation and administration of the German Empire and the individual states".[154] Even more significant in terms of the emergence of the *Kartell* was a statement which indicated that *Grossindustrie* and the independent *Mittelstand* shared common economic interests.

> *Concentrated large industry dominates, directly or indirectly, the entire economy so that the independent* Mittelstand *is closely associated with the interests of industry. In earlier times these groups were mostly*

hostile and mistrustful toward one another. But one gradually came to see that ultimately co-operation was advisable out of mutual interests, and that it is possible for both sides to derive benefits.

The "inner necessity" that drove these groups, particularly in the Rhineland, was "the danger of a Social Democratic majority". The decision was taken at the meeting to create a committee, the aim of which was to work towards a "community of economic interests between the independent *Mittelstand* and industry and agriculture".155 Other important *Mittelstand* organizations, such as the *Verband der Rabatt-sparvereine Deutschlands*, responded favourably to these decisions.156 The idea of forming a front against Social Democracy greatly impressed the *Niedersächsischer Schutz-verband für Handel und Gewerbe* at its meeting in late June 1913, a meeting held in conjunction with the RDMV.157

Parallel to the closing of the ranks within the *Mittelstands-bewegung* around the RDMV, the CDI and BdL were concluding their plans for the public foundation of the new *Kartell*. In early July 1913 a meeting of the RDMV, the BdL, the *Christlicher Bauernverein*, and the CDI came to full agreement on the foundation of the *Kartell*. The chief driving forces from industry which sought to enlist the BdL in the venture came from the Rhenish and Westphalian industrialists (Alfred Hugenberg and Emil Kirdorf), as well as the successor to Tille, Max Schlenker from the Saar industrialists.158 In mid-June 1913 there was an attempt to win the support of the Pan-German League (*Alldeutscher Verband*). Wangenheim of the BdL sought to extend what was to be the *Kartell* to all "national forces outside parliament".159 Such a *Kartell*, according to Wangenheim, might even become "a great organization against Democracy".160 It has been suggested that the chairman of the Pan-German League, Heinrich Class, shared views similar to those of Fritsch on the *Mittelstand* and that their conception of the ideal nation was one consisting entirely of "men from the *Mittelstand*".161 Although there was much agreement on all sides for the Pan-German League to join the *Kartell*, only a "loose bond" developed between the two in the period before 1914.*

In preparation for its announcement of the *Kartell* at its third annual meeting, the RDMV published an important article by one of its leading functionaries, Walter Graef, in July 1913. Graef elaborated the themes raised at the second conference (*Westdeutscher Mittelstandstag*) of 18 May 1913. The really significant additional point adopted by Graef was that the new *Kartell* was to be both a counter-weight to the "democratic wave" and a form of organization to fight "*Spekulantentums*" or mobile *Grosskapital*. In other words, Graef echoed Wangenheim's views as Wangenheim had presented them in mid-June. The specific aims mentioned in Graef's article later appeared as the program of the *Kartell*. Graef did consider that the RDMV had played the all-important role of providing a bridge between industry and agriculture.162

The third general meeting of the RDMV took place in Leipzig from 22 to 25 August 1913. Among the more interesting representatives at the meeting were General von Liebert (chairman of the *Reichsverband gegen die Sozialdemokratie*),163 a host of Conservative members of the *Reichs-* and *Landtag*, Ferdinand Schwieghoffer (*Geschäftsführer* of the CDI), Henning aus dem Winkel, and Secretary Hempel (both of the BdL). The "economic community of interests", as formulated by the executive committee of the RDMV and adopted by the *Kartell,* was designed to lead to four specific goals;

1. Co-operation of the three groups, the independent *Mittelstand*, industry and agriculture, for reciprocal economic support and struggle against the abuses in the organism of our economic life
2. Maintenance of authority in all economic enterprises
3. Protection of national work, securing of fair prices,

*Stegmann, "Machteliten", 1972 : 373. Cf. Class, *Wider den Strom*, 1932 : 272. Class seemed genuinely interested in the idea "of a general co-operation of all national forces outside parliament". According to Class, the BdL (Wangenheim) never followed up the promise of 1913, although the Pan-German League had been not unwilling to participate in such a *Kartell*.

and protection of the willingness to work
4. Struggle against Social Democracy and false Socialist teachings.[164]

Schwieghoffer of the CDI pointed out that the overriding consideration on which industry, agriculture, and *Mittelstand* could all agree was "the maintenance of the existing social and economic order". He was of the opinion that although there were undoubted differences of interest among the three groups (in certain "details"), these differences receded into the background when compared to the larger considerations.[165] However the conflicts of interest in certain "details" could, for example, make it difficult even to broaden the *Kartell* to include industrialists who were not already members of the CDI. At a meeting of the *Bund der Industrieller* on 11 September 1913 it was declared that the *Bund der Industrieller* would not co-operate with the BdL in any form of *Interessengemeinschaft*. The *Bund der Industrieller* which after the CDI was the leading national organization of the industrialists, embraced primarily light and manufacturing industries.[166] At the 11 September 1913 meeting of the *Bund der Industrieller*, the BdL in particular was branded "a danger to German economic life". The BdL was, according to the chairman of the *Bund der Industrieller*, "never suitable as a partner for us industrialists".[167]

The organizational difficulties implicit in even attempting to unite so many diverse social groups within a specific organization was avoided by limiting the new creation to a *Kartell*. This *Kartell* looked very much like the "voluntary parliament" outlined earlier by Fritsch, but on a far greater scale. As in any cartel, each organization, as a member of the cartel, was to work on the unique problems which confronted it. Only when "economic" questions arose which were of concern to all three groups were there to be direct consultation and co-operation.[168] Rahardt was strongly opposed to the new *Kartell*.[169] Stresemann was said to have renamed the *Kartell der schaffenden Stände* the *"Kartell der raffenden Hände"* (*Kartell* of grasping hands). The *Kartell* was, in fact, a type of *Interessengemeinschaft*, albeit one with a great deal of potential influence. It was pointed out at the time that the *Kartell* might not last long because the natural economic conflicts between industry and artisanship and between industry and agriculture would inevitably emerge.[170]

While it has been suggested that the BdL was more satisfied than any of the other parties with the *Kartell*,[171] the *Mittelstand* groups had most to gain. Before the formation of the *Kartell*, the *Mittelstandsbewegung* had far less influence than either the BdL or the CDI. These latter organizations, with their affiliates, had already demonstrated at various times the kind of political power they could command. The *Mittelstand* organizations around the RDMV sought a share of that power through participation in the *Kartell*. The importance of the *Kartell* and the advantages of having a place within it were recognized immediately by *Mittelstand* organizations and formed, in part, the basis of the unification of the *Mittelstandsbewegung* with the RDMV as its core. Old enemies among retailers' organizations, for example, saw the great advantage of linking their fate to the RDMV and, in turn, to the BdL and the CDI. Both the *Deutscher Zentralverband für Handel und Gewerbe* (Leipzig), the *Zentralvereinigung deutscher Vereine für Handel und Gewerbe* (Berlin), and even the *Detaillistenverband von Rheinland und Westfalen* (*Der Detaillist* group), agreed to join the RDMV. The *Verband der Rabattsparvereine Deutschlands*, whose representatives, Nicolaus and Beythien, were active participants in the founding of the RDMV and the *Kartell*, was also a member.[172] The various strands of the *Schutzverbandsbewegung* came together once again. Even if their alliance within the *Kartell* left the differences between them unresolved, there was now a real incentive to work together in the company of other interest groups with direct lines to the centres of power.

The RDMV attached great importance to the establishment of the *Kartell*.

> *In reality, it is here for the first time that the* Mittelstand *as an accepted public power was recognized. Here were offered prospects and possibilities for development about which the* Mittelstand *had earlier hardly ventured to dream.*[173]

Under such circumstances the RDMV could not understand why any *Mittelstand* organization would not seek to participate in such a "community" (*Gemeinschaft*).

> *It is therefore not understandable that a small, ill-led part of the independent* Mittelstand *still stands aloof in this relationship and sees an encroachment of its own interests in the common endeavour* (Gemeinschaftsarbeit*).* 174

In early 1914 the RDMV reported that both the federal government and the "parties of order" were already displaying far more sympathy for the need to keep the *Mittelstand* in existence than ever before. The newspaper of the RDMV quoted from a long speech of Dr. Delbrück of the Federal Ministry of the Interior in an article entitled "Free rein for *Mittelstand* politics". Delbrück was quoted as saying that far greater emphasis had to be placed on the *Mittelstand* because

> *the process of dissolution of the old independent* Mittelstand *is progressing and, thereby, the buffer between capital and the revolutionary workers is disappearing; one day, some extreme occasion must bring about the great social revolution as the hour of death of our national body politic (*Volkskörper*).* 175

The preservation of the *Mittelstand* had become identified with continuing existence of Imperial Germany's society.

There has been some controversy concerning the actual "practical importance" of the *Kartell*. While some writers have considered the *Kartell* little more than a "declaration of sympathy" (*Sympathieerklärung*),176 others have seen it as a very significant symptom of the reemergence of the "agrarian-great industrial *Bund*"177 and, therefore, a positive indication that the "power elites"178 were willing to work together to retain their social order. It is beyond the scope of the present study to attempt to assess the practical political consequences of the *Kartell* in terms of its political importance to agriculture (the BdL) or to industry (the CDI). Although the *Kartell* may not have been politically strong enough to achieve all the legislative goals which its members had demanded, the *Kartell* with the co-operation of the federal government was at least able to stem the democratic tide and to see the division of power in Germany remain virtually unchanged in the face of the SPD challenge. The *Kartell* was something of a victory for the RDMV and for the retailers. While the RDMV may be considered the pawn in the power game, the RDMV at least won formal recognition from those wielding great influence in Imperial Germany. At the beginning of 1913 the RDMV counted "just over" 500,000 members. By the beginning of 1914 the figure had increased to 630,000.[179] The demands of so many "little men", which had begun as local, sporadic, and isolated protests, had been elevated to the national level.

Conclusion

The participation of retailers within the "political *Mittel-standsbewegung*" represented the logical extension of their political mobilization. No *a priori* competition for power or the capture of institutionalized positions of authority is implied in the process of political mobilization. However, retailers, faced with growing economic problems in the period from 1890 to 1914, were somewaht reluctantly driven into a competition for power. Their pre-institutionalized struggle was transformed into a more obvious party-political activity. Particularly within the "political *Mittelstandsbewegung*", retailers grew increasingly conscious both of the problems they shared, not only with other retailers, but also with other groups within that movement. At the same time retailers became conscious of the unique character of their economic problems. The very existence of the "new" *Mittelstand* came to pose a political problem for the "old" *Mittelstand*. Because the "new" *Mittelstand* identified ideologically with the "old" *Mittelstand*, the former group could be used politically by the latter. The inherent economic conflicts of interest between the two groups made positive political co-operation difficult, and in the end, impossible.

The "political *Mittelstandsbewegung*" also vacillated in its attitude towards other economic interest groups which did not share the economic problems of the *Mittelstand*. The conflicts of interest between industrialists' interest groups and the *Mittelstand* initially ruled out political alliance between them. Even the agrarians, with whose *Weltanschauung* and ideology the *Mittelstand* could identify, proved in the struggle over the finance reform bill of 1909 to be unreliable allies. The more the "political *Mittelstandsbewegung*" was driven into competition for political power, the more obvious it became that a formula had to be found which permitted both a *rapprochement* with the agrarians and co-operation with the industrialists. From the point of view of the "political *Mittelstandsbewegung*" (which after 1911 in particular was virtually synonymous with the RDMV), two political considerations interacted and produced the necessary basis for co-operation with both agrarians and industrialists.

The first consideration was that in a competition for power it made no sense for the *Mittelstand* to cut itself off from the centres of power, the agrarian-industrial alliance. The second factor was the growing realization on all three sides that although separated on short-run (and even some long-run) conflicts of interest, all three groups had an overriding interest in the preservation of the power structure of Imperial Germany which was being threatened by rising Social Democracy. The *Mittelstand* could offer, its numbers to an alliance designed to stem the democratic tide and thereby share in the political power of the most powerful social groups in Germany. Retailers working within the "political *Mittelstandsbewegung*" won more formal recognition from the bourgeois political parties, the powerful interest groups, and government for their economic problems. They were at least promised solutions to their problems. In return retailers took their place among the forces that sought to preserve the *status quo*. They had, to be sure, been given up for lost by the SPD both economically and even politically. Retailers rejected the parties seeking social or political change and sided instead with parties which could not only preserve the *status quo*, but assure retailers a place within it.

EPILOGUE: 1914-1939

Recent studies of the Nazi seizure of power at the local level have emphasized that the winning of the *Mittelstand* was an extremely important factor in the Nazi successes of 1930 and 1933. In spite of the influx of workers into the NSDAP from 1930, the *Mittelstand* in Bavaria, it has been claimed, "continued to provide the main strength of the activist element" within the movement.[1] The decisive importance of winning the *Mittelstand* in Lower Saxony has been similarly demonstrated.[2] The NSDAP was able to exploit the "crisis of the *Mittelstand*" by carefully tailoring its propaganda in such a fashion that it could present itself as the saviour of the *Mittelstand*.[3] The small independent retailers, whose economic position was extremely precarious, proved particularly susceptible

The retailers, like other social groups in Germany, supported the decision of the central authorities during the initial stages of the First World War.[4] From the very outset of what was expected to be yet another quick victory for the German forces, however, there was a general concern among retailers of the direct implications of the war for them. Even before the introduction of rationing (from 15 January 1915) and the fixing of maximum prices of goods sold through retail outlets, prosperous retailers, such as those represented in the *Detaillistenkammer* in Hamburg, expressed anxiety at the economic implications of mobilization. Many employees and even some owners of retail establishments were being called to the colours. On a practical level, it was considered necessary to find credit support for retailers at home who were short of working capital or who were caught undercapitalized because their credit customers were unable to pay off debts. In the spirit of the *Burgfrieden*, there was at least initially an expressed desire to keep as many employees as possible working when business activity was cut back and to pay part of the salaries of employees who were at the front.[5]

With the reluctant adoption by the central government of a policy which has been branded as "war socialism", with an increasing inflation, a growing shortage of consumer goods, and more price fixing, retailers came under considerable economic pressure. Developments such as the direct distribution of goods by government and large concerns very often exercised additional pressure when consumption in general was already shrinking. In this period of general insecurity, however, the retailers, in so far as they were co-opted by the state to distribute the goods which were available, were given a measure of security. Nevertheless, with the gradual development of a shortage of goods, there developed both a black market and a partial return to barter exchange; both worked to undermine the economic position of the small independent retailer.[6]

Perhaps one of the most insidious effects of the war, and its accompanying inflation and shortage of consumer goods, was the growing opinion among the general population that the retailers were directly responsible. On 22 January 1915 a meeting was held by leading retailer organizations in order to publicize the real causes of price increases and shortages. The meeting, called by Beythien of the *Verband der Rabattspar-vereine Deutschlands*, was attended by representatives of the RDMV, as well as those of most of the retailers' national *Schutzverbände*. Beythien outlined the impact of the war on small retailers and took particular pains to point out how consumer co-operatives were taking advantage of the situation to broaden their enterprises. Help and understanding for the plight of retailers was demanded of the public and government.[7]

While the government sought to continue its support of the *Mittelstand* in general[8] and, early in the war, even "feared an alienation" of the *Mittelstand*,[9] the ever increasing demands of the war effort were soon to lead to the virtual abandonment of the *Mittelstand.* As Rathenau,* initially the chief organizer of Germany's economy during the war, stated in 1917, "the economic task is no longer a private one, it is the task of the community".10 The war effort was causing great hardship among the German people. Dissatisfaction among the population (as consumers) could not be minimized if the government appeared to protect the interests of retailers over those of the population as a whole. Retailers' wishes were, therefore, to be subordinated to the war effort. Even before the demands on the wartime economy had been formalized with the introduction of Hindenburg's Program on 5 December 1916 (the law on *Vaterländischer Hilfsdienst*), retailers had set about to unify their organizations into a single central organization (*Spitzenverband*).

As retailers struggled to create a single and united *Spitzenverband* which would fight for their interests, there reappeared the old cleavage between those demanding more extreme protectionist measures and those (the organizations representing the larger and economically more secure retailers) with a more "liberal" economic orientation. The latter group, led by the department store owners' organization, formed the short-lived *Bund deutscher Kleinhandelsverbände* at the end of 1915. The two leading retailer *Zentralverbände* (the one from Berlin and the other from Leipzig) decided to join the organization. This decision was an indication of how the adverse economic impact of the war upon all retail trade drove some erstwhile enemies into a common organization. In the same year, 1915, a more extreme protectionist group of retailers' organizations, including Beythien's organization and the RDMV, formed the *Reichsausschuss für den Kleinhandel* with headquarters in Hanover.11 Even under the extreme pressure of war and, eventually, under the pressure of the Hindenburg Program which extended the army's political

---

*Rathenau's general coordinating of the economy was to provide something of an organizational model for the running of the economy after 1933. In the Third Reich, the reluctance of the government to continue the support of the *Mittelstand* was to be justified in almost exactly the same terms.

power to all aspects of the economy, the extreme protectionist wing of the retailers' movement persisted. Furthermore, it began to search for allies at the top whose political power it could tap to its own advantage.

In late 1917 the foundation of the *Deutsche Vaterlandspartei* presented the extreme protectionist retailers with the opportunity to find such allies. The *Vaterlandspartei* has been described as heir to the *Kartell* of 1897 and the *Kartell der schaffenden Stände* of 1913[12] and has been characterized as an "early fascist" phenomenon.[13] How far the retailers' organizations which favoured the *Vaterlandspartei* also supported the war aims and the other policies of the party is difficult to establish. One writer suggests that the coincidence of views on other political matters was considerable.[14] Fritsch claimed that the creation of the new party was necessary in order "to recruit all honourable Germans" to fight against "un-German and anti-German machinations".[15] Whatever reservations retailers' organizations such as the RDMV may have had, retailers were attracted by the obvious advantages of belonging to such a powerful party whose political weight they might hope to use for their own purposes. (The *Vaterlandspartei* counted one million members in 1918.) Although it was inspired by the military,[16] the party, in a manner similar to that of the old *Kartell* of 1913 gave retailers a direct line to the sources of power in the state. The manner in which various organizations of the "old" and "new" *Mittelstand* reacted to the creation of the *Vaterlandspartei* serves to highlight the extent to which the two had grown apart during the war. Even the right-radical DHV, for example, did not elect to join the new party.[17] The polarization of the "old" from the "new" *Mittelstand*, already pronounced before the war, continued during the war. The eventual defeat of the Central Powers destroyed the hopes of the "new" cartel (the *Vaterlandspartei*) not only in the realm of foreign affairs, but also in that of domestic affairs. While dreams of conquest abroad were dashed, defeat was accompanied by revolution at home.

The precise relationship of the retailers to the Weimar state, like their role in the revolution of 1918/1919, requires further research. There have been some suggestions that in Hamburg, for example, the retailers and their organizations helped to "tame" the revolution. The Constitution of the new Republic promised "to protect the independent *Mittelstand* in agriculture, industry, and trade"[18] but, as the SPD and liberal parties had said before 1914, not at the expense of the general population. What was unstated, in fact, was that the free market economy was to be left to work more or less on its own, even if it spelled the doom of the *Mittelstand*. In Imperial Germany, the small independent had been protected by favourable legislation from precisely this kind of economic development. In the new Republic, the *Mittelstand* was "socially isolated". Moreover the old political allies on whom it had depended for special legislative treatment were in disarray.

The national organizations of the retailers, particularly their most active party-political organizations such as the DMV and the RDMV, did not survive the war intact. Rahardt, who had been largely responsible for the decision of the DMV to join the liberal *Hansa-Bund* prior to 1914, did participate in the DDP (the liberal party) after the war. Some ex-leaders of the RDMV appear to have taken part in the activities of the heir to the old Conservative Party (and *Vaterlandspartei*)[19], the DNVP. The powerful *Zentralverband der deutschen Haus- und Grundbesitzer*, which had prior to 1914 opposed the policies of the RDMV and the *Kartell* of 1913, also initially went over to the ranks of the DNVP. After the 1921 Prussian *Landtag* elections, however, the *Haus- und Grundbesitzer* organization helped to establish an independent party, the *Wirtschaftspartei*, which became known as the *Reichspartei des deutschen Mittelstandes* from 1925. This party, it should be emphasized, associated itself with but few of the elements of the "political *Mittelstandsbewegung*" of the pre-1914 days.[20] While there was a continuity between the older *Mittelstandsbewegung* and the post-war variety, it would be a mistake to assume that the *Wirtschaftspartei* was the custodian of that continuity.

If the conservative, or more generally the non-working class political parties (*bürgerliche Parteien*), were more or less in retreat immediately after the war and the upheaval of 1918/1919, they were by no means defeated. Furthermore, these parties, virtually all of which were the old Imperial political parties with new names, had not abandoned the *Mittelstand*. The *Mittelstand* policy which each had to some extent developed before the war, soon reemerged. Transformed party names could not conceal the continuity between the old conservative parties and the DNVP, for example. It was no accident that the DNVP member of the Weimar constitutional committee, von Delbrück, had defended the *Mittelstandsartikel* (article 164) of the Weimer constitution.[21]

In the period from the revolution to the catastrophic inflationary collapse of 1923, the DNVP was not the only political party to put forward as a political slogan the need to foster and to aid the *Mittelstand*. Its program was unique, however, in so far as it harked back to the social-protectionist ideology of Theodor Fritsch and the RDMV in the period before 1914.[22] The early (1920) program of the NSDAP proclaimed the advantages for the state of a "healthy" *Mittelstand* and went on to demand the immediate takeover of the large department stores. These stores would be let to small independents at low rents.[23] Non-working class parties, especially the right-wing parties, were therefore actively seeking the support of the retailers from the very beginning of the Weimar Republic. While there were only a few organizational continuities between retailers' organizations and specific political parties, parties of the right sought to take advantage of the peculiar ideology of retailers.

In the immediate post-war period, a whole series of organizations which labelled themselves *Mittelstand* parties existed in Berlin, Brunswick, Breslau, Cologne, and also in several states, including Bavaria, Mecklenburg, and Pomerania. Further research may establish the relationship of these and other organizations to their precursors in the pre-1914 period. Certain specific retailer *Schutzverbände* did survive the war, along with various "technical" organizations of the retailers. One of the most important of these organizations was the old *Verband der Rabattsparvereine Deutschlands*. Its development into a full-fledged *Schutzverband* is suggested by its new name, the *Verband der Handelsschutz- und Rabattsparvereine*. On 19 March 1919 a new *Hauptgemeinschaft des deutschen Einzelhandels* (Berlin) was founded. Some idea of the policy and social composition of the organization may be inferred from the decision of the *Verband der Handelsschutz- und Rabattsparvereine* (which had always been extremely protectionist and representative of the smaller retailers) not to join the *Hauptgemeinschaft*, but to link its fate with another organization, the *Reichsschutzverband für Handel- und Gewerbe* (Brunswick).[24]

The old split in the retailers' *Schutzverbandsbewegung* of the pre-1914 period was apparently duplicated in the early years of the Weimar Republic. The more extreme social-protectionist wing seems to have survived and to have continued its militant and uncompromising attitude towards such retail distribution outlets as the department store, the mail-order house, and the consumer co-operative. This wing of the retailers' movement, which appears to have benefited after 1918 by the influx of members from the new recruits to "independent" retailing, had traditionally been open to the appeals of the more right-wing parties and interest groups. It was this segment of the retailers' movement which initially continued its support of the conservative DNVP, for example. The more liberal (and economically secure) wing, while it too had briefly flirted with the DNVP, turned with other *Mittelstand* groups, such as the powerful Berlin-based *Haus- und Grundbesitzer Verband*, towards the creation of the *Wirtschaftspartei*.

If the political mobilization of the retailers in the pre-1914 era of general "prosperity" had been occasioned in the last analysis by their growing sense of "economic despair", postwar economic developments could not but have deepened that sense of despair. Most works on post-1918 Germany employ the statistics contained in the censuses of 1907 and 1925 and do not investigate statistics for the years between 1907 and 1925. The considerable non-statistical evidence suggests that the chronic problems of the small retailers of the pre-1914 period were considerably exacerbated in the period up to 1923. The old "numbers problem" appears to have become even more acute. Demobilized soldiers returning from the front, peasants driven from the land, and various old-age pensioners sought to establish their own small businesses. These new recruits lacked training and capital, but their very existence posed a competitive threat to already established small firms. In addition the larger retail distribution outlets, such as the department stores and consumer co-operatives, were better equipped to meet the ever worsening economic situation. In spite of the general increase in small firms the larger outlets increased in numbers and turnover even faster. Smaller firms had to contend with the steady influx of small competitors, and as the level of inflation steadily rose, they were left unprotected from the process of concentration from above.[25]

The great inflation, which had its roots in the finance policies of the government during the war, really began to set in from mid-1921. People lost faith in money; real goods and property alone continued to be valued. The picture has often been painted of the worker, being paid daily, running to the retailer to purchase as many commodities as possible before his wages were devalued with the afternoon quotation of the mark. The attention of the population, and particularly that of the small independent, with his traditional suspicion of "mobile capital", was directed towards the mysterious workings of the monetary system. The small independents were thrust into a situation where they lost ground with every sale. Credit dealing, on which so many small retailers had depended for their living before the war, no longer made any economic sense. Each sale of goods by the retailer must have been made with the sure knowledge that he was becoming impoverished by the transaction. As a recent account suggests, "the post-war period with its runaway inflation seems to have hurt the self-employed *Mittelstand* much more than the war".[26]

After 1919 the retailers, especially the less economically secure retailers, and the *Mittelstand* in general turned to the right for solutions to their problems in a pattern similar to that which had made itself apparent before 1914. How far this disposition had favoured the various right-wing outbursts of the period from 1919 to the beginning of the stabilization phase at the end of 1923, such as the Kapp Putsch and Hitler's Beer Hall Putsch, remains to be established. There is no doubt that while the attitudes of members of the *Mittelstand* varied toward the NSDAP, for example, the Nazis had found it "easiest" to win over the retailers.[27]

During the period from 1924 to 1933 the small retailers seem to have most readily opted for the Nazi Party when other social groups (even the peasants of Bavaria, for example) proved more reluctant to make that step. While the Nazi Party directed much attention to the *Mittelstand*, the social-political program of the party contained a mixture of conflicting, if not contradictory, principles. Nazi propaganda and practice before 1933 shows that the party did not aspire to become the political representative of the *Mittelstand* alone. Such an approach would have reduced the NSDAP to yet another splinter party within the existing social-political system. Hitler was determined from the beginning to attain the leadership of Germany. In his attempts to win power through the ballot box, it would not have been politically sound to restrict the appeal of the party to the *Mittelstand*, even if he employed the widest possible definition of *Mittelstand*. Nevertheless, at least before the depression hit Germany from 1929 onwards, party membership and electoral support came from this social group, if only because the party could win little working class support.[28] Moreover many elements of the Nazi ideology could be traced back to the *Mittelstandsideologie* as it had developed in the late nineteenth century.

The ideology of any particular social movement not only refers to the set of beliefs which mobilizes people into action, but contains a diagnosis (what is wrong) and a prognosis (what must be done) and identifies the agents to carry out the job. At least the diagnostic and prognostic elements of the ideology of the pre-1914 "political *Mittelstandsbewegung*" and those of the post-war ideology of the NSDAP contained some similarities. The small retailers had sought to form various alliances from the 1890s onwards which would aid them in their precarious economic position. After 1926 the Nazi Party (and Hitler) came to appear as the only party which proposed to transform society and to guarantee the retailers a place within it. The Nazi Party convinced the retailers of the need not just of collective action, but of a specific form of collective action which could be represented as a logical and total extension of the kinds of activities characteristic of the retailers' movement prior to 1914.

National Socialism, as Sigmund Neumann wrote in 1932, was "a protest movement". It was "protest against the November Revolution and parliamentarianism, protest against the defeat and Versailles, protest against the economic system and protest against the domination of rationalism and materialism".[29]

The retailers proved ready to accept the radical proposals of the NSDAP not only because the proposals were an alternative to a left-wing revolution, but because the retailers' own sense of deepening economic despair demanded such a radical course. The economic position of the "politically homeless" retailers did not improve in the period of stabilization from 1924 to 1929. This period, when compared with the period after the war (from 1919 to 1923) and with the period when the depression struck (after 1929), may well be labelled a period of prosperity. However it was also the period when economic "rationalization" proceeded almost unhindered. For the small independent retailers, this rationalization meant the further development of the larger distribution outlets and the situation in which small retailers were faced with formidable competitors. Geiger suggested that even in 1925 almost 45 per cent of those engaged in retailing were living on "proletarian" incomes.[30] The cleavage between the retailers' estimation of their social importance (always an essential ingredient of their ideology) and the manifest decline of their actual economic position was widening, not narrowing, even before 1929.[31] The growing consciousness of this cleavage led retailers to seek a "bulwark against the pressing proletarianization, for a resolution of the discrepancy between economic position and social-ideological claim".[32] In short, the greater the despair of the "little men" grew, the more prepared they were to accept radical alternatives. The Nazi Party not only represented that radical alternative, but appeared to share many ideological affinities with the old *Mittelstandsbewegung*. Geiger, writing in 1932, claimed that after 1930 the Nazi Party put aside its hope of conquering the working class "from within" and "became a pronounced *Mittelstand* party".[33] Neumann, writing in the same year, said that the party was "first of all the party of the *Mittelstand*". The NSDAP was supported more and more by the *Mittelstand* out of the fear that under "organized 'late-capitalism'", its economic basis was being eroded.[34] Other contemporaries and many commentators since have tended to agree with the thesis put forward by Geiger and Neumann. Lasswell spoke of the Nazi movement as "a desperate reaction of the lower middle classes". More recently, Lipset has suggested that fascism represents the "extremism of the centre".[35]

The Nazi Party was not content to rest its fate on ideological affinities. Through specific units it sought to mobilize retailers from a latent strength into the ranks of the activist party faithful. Numerous other political parties, after all, also sought the support of the *Mittelstand* and set forth concrete proposals for the legislative protection of the retailers. (The 1926 program of the *Reichspartei des deutschen Mittelstandes*, for example, contained eight specific points directed at gaining the support of the retailers.) The great difference between the Nazi Party and other parties which sought the support of the *Mittelstand* was that the Nazi Party promised not merely to alleviate specific evils, but to transform and revolutionize the entire society. In the 1920s Nazi propaganda was carried to the retailers through specific *Kampfbünde*. These included such organizations as the *Kampfgemeinschaft gegen Warenhäuser und Konsumvereine*, a *Kampfbund für Erhaltung des Mittelstandes*, and an *Arbeitsgemeinschaft deutscher Geschäftsleute*.[36] Some local members of the party, such as those in Lower Saxony, were very enthusiastic about establishing such organizations and contrary to party policy, permitted *Mittelstand* organizations to join *en bloc* instead of joining as individuals.[37] In December 1932 the party created a uniform *Mittelstand* department (the *N.-S. Kampfbünde des gewerblichen Mittelstandes*) with branches in the various districts. This department employed as functionaries men who were already well known activists in the *Mittelstandsbewegung*. The department had one unique feature: it drew up lists of artisans and retailers who were party members and encouraged the party faithful to frequent their shops. Members (or their families) who shopped in department stores or consumer co-operatives were threatened with expulsion.[38] The Nazi Party appeared to have already begun to implement its program even before the seizure of power.

Throughout the period of its struggle for control of the state up to 1933, the Nazi Party sought to present itself as the saviour of the *Mittelstand*. The "negative" outlook traditionally associated with the *Mittelstandsbewegung* involves their hostility to organized (particularly Socialist organized) labour on the one side and their hostility to large capital (especially to "mobile capital") on the other. While there were real differences within the party on these issues before 1933, this outlook was, at least initially, also associated with the NSDAP. The *Mittelstand* responded to political parties which promised to improve its economic position. Several local studies of the NSDAP have shown that in the 1930s racialism had to be linked with concrete economic issues before it could play any significant role in bringing about the electoral success of the party. It was decided even to play down the anti-Semitism in certain areas where anti-Semitism could not be linked with specific economic facts for fear of alienating potential, but cautious Nazi voters.[39]

Recent works have explored the differences between the "social promises" of the Nazi Party before 1933 and their non-fulfilment.[40] Briefly stated, the "middle class socialism" propagated by the NSDAP formed only part, and not the most important part, of the Nazi ideology. Racialism and imperialism were shown after 1933 to have been higher on the Nazi list of priorities. Racialism could, at least initially, be integrated into "middle class socialism" in so far as the Jews could be attacked as department store owners or as the holders of "harmful" capital. (In fact, even from 1934, the department stores "enjoyed a discreet but perceptible official rehabilitation".)[41] However, Hitler's imperialist aims were not really compatible with "middle class socialism". To achieve these aims, Hitler needed a modern, efficient, and highly industrialized state — the exact opposite of the fairy-tale society which the *Mittelstand* desired. Retailing, like every other branch of the economy after 1933, was "coordinated". A new *Gesamtverband des deutschen Einzelhandels* was soon created under new leadership to replace the *N.-S. Kampfbünde des gewerblichen Mittelstandes*. The new organization was to embrace all retail trade, including department stores (which were not confiscated and rented out to small independents). By 1938, maintenance of the standard of living of the entire population was listed by the Adolf-Hitler-Spende as the top priority. It was stated that small shopkeepers could not fulfil the economic task of distributing goods to the consumer as efficiently as larger retail outlets. In early 1939 the *Völkischer Beobachter* declared

> *A* Mittelstand *ideology is no basis for the construction of a national economy which is supposed to be an economy of the people (*Volk*). The extreme protection of the* Mittelstand, *which is the basis of* Mittelstand *ideology, presupposes that the people is itself incapable of constituting a* Mittelstand. *The extreme protection of an existing* Mittelstand *implies the erection of an effective barrier against all those who want to enter the* Mittelstand *from below. And second, the representatives of the* Mittelstand *ideology do not wish to place the* Mittelstand *at the service of the people, but rather the people at the service of the* Mittelstand.[42]

These words harked back to those of Rathenau in 1917. The interests of the German people, it was claimed, could not be sacrificed on behalf of a small segment of society.*

---

*For a more detailed analysis of the economic position and the political activity of the retailers during this period, see the author's forthcoming article "German Shopkeepers and the Rise of National Socialism".

CONCLUSION

The economic position of independent retailers was conditioned both by the retail market in general and by specific economic factors which operated within that market. Between 1871 and 1914 Germany's retail market expanded greatly, and thereby provided the possibility for an ever-increasing proportion of the population to occupy itself in retailing. There were scarcely any threats to the economic position of the retailers implicit in an expanding retail market. Independent artisans, on the other hand, because they were producers of wares rather than simply final sellers to the consumer, were adversely affected by virtually all the factors which worked towards the expansion of the retail market. The economic position of the retailers became endangered, however, by the development of various forms of concentrated competition. The competition of large concerns presented itself all the more forcefully to independent retailers because retailers were frequently ill-equipped to meet that competition. The expansion of the retail market had encouraged ever greater numbers to establish their own shops. The new recruits to retailing frequently possessed neither the necessary qualifications nor the capital and, although they came to pride themselves on being independent *Mittelständler*, could be classified as "proletarians" on the basis of their income. While independent retailers had to contend with the competition of large concerns in retailing, they were confronted, as employers, with the economic and social demands of their own employees. Independent retailers, faced with a deteriorating competitive position, were anxious to preserve the

210

political support of their employees, but they were increasingly unable to pay for that support by granting the reforms demanded by those employees. Although the latter identified ideologically with the independent retailers, they gradually disqualified themselves as political allies by their insistence on reforms. Employees too became politically mobilized in the period from 1890 to 1914.

Retailers' organizations of all types, whether they are classified as technical (*Fach*) organizations, *Schutzverbände* or as distinct party-political enterprises, represented the response of the retailers to the imperative "organize or perish". Retailers' organizations of all types served to articulate the interests of retailers and, according to the rationale underlying the organization, sought fulfilment of the economic or "political" demands of their members. Initially retailers' organizations were responses to local problems. Local organizations, even in cities such as Hamburg where retailers were more conscious of their problems and well organized to combat them, did not fulfil the expectations of many of their members. The frustration or non-fulfilment of the interests articulated by retailers' local organizations formed an important element in the process which led to the establishment of regional and national organizations after 1890. In the period from 1890 to 1914, in spite of certain legislative "successes", retailers became more conscious of what they came to consider their precarious economic position. The activities of their most politically active organizations at all levels, the *Schutzverbände*, served both to heighten the retailers' awareness of economic threats and to demonstrate conspicuous failures in checking them. Between 1890 and 1914 a *Schutzverbandsbewegung* embracing local, regional, and national *Schutzverbände* developed among independent retailers in Germany. This "movement" was gradually transformed from a more pre-institutionalized form of collective attempt by retailers to secure their economic position into an integral part of what contemporaries referred to as the *Mittelstandsbewegung*. Particularly after 1900 a more formal and discernible party-political enterprise, the "political *Mittelstandsbewegung*" appeared. These movements developed within the context of frustrated interest articulation and the growing consciousness among retailers that their organizations were not achieving the reforms considered essential to the security of the economic position of retailers. Retailers and their organizations turned to more overt political activities.

Although political factors, particularly the rise of Social Democracy from 1890 onwards, inclined most bourgeois political parties and government towards open sympathy for the "political *Mittelstandsbewegung*", economic and social conflicts within that movement prevented it from becoming a united political force. Within the "political *Mittelstandsbewegung*", there were varying conceptions of which social groups were entitled to refer to themselves as *Mittelständler*. These differences were, to some extent, overcome by excluding the "new" *Mittelstand* from the most important organizations within the "political *Mittelstandsbewegung*". The problems posed by economic differences within the abbreviated *Mittelstandsbewegung*, a movement in which retailers then provided the driving force, were resolved by concentrating upon common enemies. Because Social Democracy was high on the list of enemies of more influential interest groups and political parties, an alliance between these latter groups and the *Mittelstand* could, even in the face of obvious conflicts of economic interest, be established. By mid-1913 that alliance was institutionalized with the formation of the *Kartell der schaffenden Stände*. Although the alliance was the product of a whole series of decisions and calculations which were reached at the "macro-political" level, it reflected (in fact, was possible at all) because certain processes at the "micro-political" level had culminated at the same time.[1]

Retailers responded to the economic threats to their existence by creating organizations which were designed to overcome these threats. At the same time, the existence of these organizations created possibilities for their exploitation. Retailers' organizations not only served the function of articulating the interests of retailers, but were themselves used by governments, political parties, and even other interest groups to provide political support. It may be said that these institutions not only capitalized upon the politically mobilized retailers, but fostered the organization of retailers as well.

In recent years there has been much discussion about the various defensive strategies of government (in concert with bourgeois political parties and the more powerful interest groups of industrialists and agrarians) which were designed to prevent changes in the distribution of power within Imperial Germany.[2] While the "tactics" varied — so the argument runs — between men in positions of authority (whether Bismarck, Miquel, Bülow, Tirpitz, or Wilhelm II), the strategy remained unchanged. If one tactic (such as imperialism) failed, others (such as anti-Semitism or anti-Socialism) filled the gap. The retailers, in fact the *Mittelstand* in general, appear, according to this interpretation, to have been merely the pawns in the power game. Whether it was a question of positive means of integration (state or interest group fostering of enthusiasm for imperialism or for the creation of a fleet), or negative means (anti-Semitism, anti-Socialism, or even, paradoxically, anti-*Grosskapitalismus*), the *Mittelstand* was to be "integrated", that is, to come to identify its own fate with an unchanging *status quo*. According to this view, authority legitimation was not something that just happened. It was the result of a permanent and persuasive effort conducted through a multitude of agencies and deliberately intended to create what Talcott Parsons calls a "national supra party consensus" based on "higher order solidarity".[3]

Perhaps it is because these arguments have been based upon studies of the established authorities that there is a tendency to attribute to the "establishment" far greater powers of manipulation than it possessed (or even needed to possess!). It is easy to over-emphasize the manipulative force of the established authorities because, certain setbacks notwithstanding, their tactics and over-all strategy appear to have worked. The arguments remain incomplete, however because, for the most part, they pay so little attention to the social and political processes at the micro-political level. A study of micro-politics does not attempt to refute the arguments of those who have studied macro-politics. It seeks rather to investigate the behaviour of one of the groups usually considered the objects of influence. Micro-politics and macro-politics are not distinct entities; on the contrary, they interact with each other. In pre-1914 Germany the retailers and the *Mittelstand* developed into "loyal classes". The development was channelled in that direction both by the absence of the possibility of choosing from alternatives, and by the provision by the state of the material basis for the integration of retailers.

It has been maintained that the establishment of organizations and associations of all kinds performs the important social and political function of working towards a reduction of the inner social tensions within the social, economic, and political sub-systems of society.[4] More recently, it has been suggested that the social-psychological satisfaction which both members and leaders of the SPD derived from the existence of their organization in pre-1914 Germany led them to fear for the destruction of that organization to the point where they became "negatively integrated".[5] As another writer puts it, this fear produced, especially after 1890, the paradox of an avowed revolutionary party becoming one of the pillars of the state.[6] While the unyielding political structure of pre-1914 Germany forced Social Democratic workers into "negative integration", the retailers sought more "positive integration". The *Mittelstand*, which was promised no distinct place in the egalitarian society propagated by the SPD, might look forward only to a loss of independence. Whether the *Mittelstand* had calculated where its interests lay correctly, or whether it suffered under the delusion of "false consciousness", it was not open to the appeals of Social Democracy. The retailers did not seek to change the power constellation of Imperial Germany; they sought the kinds of reform which were designed to assure retailers a place within it.

The demands of the retailers for state-help, no less than their own self-help endeavours, worked in the direction of adaptation to the existing society rather than that of revolution. The established authorities found retailers' demands considerably easier to satisfy than those of Social Democracy. The limited "successes" and the promise of other reforms operated as a kind of safety-valve which helped to reduce or neutralize inner social tension. As the retailers' temporary vacillation over the finance reform bill in 1909 indicated, retailers' support of established authority was not inevitable. That support was assured only so long as the interests of the established authorities coincided with those of the retailers. An integral aspect of the political mobilization of the retailers was the development of their political consciousness. To be politically conscious "is to see a political meaning in one's own insecurities and desires, to see oneself as a demanding political force, which, no matter how small, increases one's hopes that expectations will come off".[7] For the retailers, alliance with, rather than opposition to, the established authorities promised retailers that their expectations and hopes would be realized.

The *Mittelstandsideologie*, in so far as it may be referred to as a unitary phenomenon, reflected the social, economic, and political views of the *Mittelstand*, and particularly those of the retailers. That ideology was a reflection of the *mittelständische Weltanschauung* and the product of an appraisal by the *Mittelstand* of the political possibilities with which they were faced. As such a product, that ideology (and even the evolution of the concept of *Mittelstand*) worked in the direction of the integration of the *Mittelstand* within the existing society. The all-important characteristic of that ideology — implicit in the very word *Mittelstand* — was the expression of a determination to remain in the middle, that is, not to decline into the lower *Stand*. Ultimately, it was a combination of fear and hope (together with the absence of plausible alternative courses of action) which led retailers to seek alliances with established authorities. Retailers feared that they might lose their independence and sink into what they considered the faceless proletariat. Economic problems, albeit problems with fairly simple legislative solutions, helped to mobilize independent retailers and to transform them into ideal allies for political institutions and elites who had similar long-term outlooks and who were willing to pay for retailers' support with reforms. Not only would these reforms not disturb the power constellation of Imperial Germany, but they would tie the retailers solidly to it.

Perhaps it was merely a dream for a solution of the insoluble that ultimately led retailers into the ranks of the Nazi Party. "Rationally", it may be said, the small independents ought to have accepted the inevitability of their fate, economic decline. The only "logical" solution to the retailers' discontent was acceptance of the diagnosis: terminal disease. Within the social-political world of Weimar Germany, there simply did not exist institutionalized means of solving the problems of the retailers (particularly given their swollen numbers and the poor quality of the new recruits). Retailers turned to the support of a party which militantly rejected the existing society. The Nazi Party proclaimed that it would create an idyllic world, purged of all those threats to the economic existence of the small independent. The new order would not "rationalize" the "healthy" elements (the *Mittelstand*) out of existence; it would rather create a new world around them. If society as constituted was not compatible with the *Mittelstand*, society would have to change, not the *Mittelstand*. While retailers in other societies and at different times might secretly share the dream of transforming society in a fashion promised by National Socialism, nowhere else and hardly at any other time did the opportunity to attempt such a transformation present itself. However, in the Weimar Republic, burdened as it was from the outset and uneasily accepted as it remained, the "conservative revolution" (*Revolution von rechts*) of which some thinkers had only dared dream was offered by the Nazi Party. To an ever growing percentage of the population, Hitler made that kind of "revolution" appear not only feasible, but logically necessary.

NOTES

Introduction

1. A.Rosenberg, "Faschismus als Massenbewegung" (1968) p.75 ff.

2. Stegmann, *Erben Bismarcks* (1970) p.17. Cf. Winkler, *Mittelstand* (1972) p.18. The latter work has been based almost exclusively upon sources for the artisans.

3. Cf. the essays in Bell (ed.), *Radical Right* (1964); Lipset, *Political Man* (1963) esp. pp.127-182; Winkler, "Extremismus der Mitte? " (1972) pp.175-191; Mills, *White Collar* (1951 ff.)

4. See the claims in Wehler, *Bismarck und Imperialismus* (1969) p.464 ff.

5. *Der Detaillist.* Nr.29, 18.7.1908.

6. Büchner, "Warenhaussteuer" (1928) pp.889-890.

7. Siegfried, *Tableau Politique* (1913) p.431. Cf. Guyot, *Commerce et Commerçants* (1909) and Lecordier, *Classes Moyennes* (1950).

8. Campbell, "Mouvement Poujade" (1957) pp.363-364.

9. See esp. Hays, *Response to Industrialism* (1957) p.48 ff. and Boorstin, *The Americans* (1973) p.89 ff.

10. Hofstadter, *Age of Reform* (1956) p.131 ff. Note the comments on Hofstadter's thesis in Hays, op.cit., p.198

11. Hofstadter, "Pseudo-Conservative Revolt" in Bell (ed.), op.cit. p.84. See the highly critical review of this collection of essays in Wilson, *Social Movements* (1973) pp.62-63. Wilson points out the fallacies of inferring the social bases of social movements from their ideologies.

12. Kühnl, Rilling, Sager, *Die NPD* (1969) pp.220, 269.

13. Cf. Hood and Yamey, "Middle-Class Cooperative Retailing Societies in London" in Tucker and Yamey (eds.), *Economics of Retailing* (1973) p.140 ff. Cf. the continual and largely fruitless efforts of grocers to win government support for their claims outlined in *The Grocer* (London) and Nossiter, "Shopkeeper Radicalism" (1972) p.437.

14. Levy, *Retail Trade Associations* (1942) pp.17-18.

15. Yamey, "United Kingdom" in Yamey (ed.), *Resale Price Maintenance*

(1966) p.251 ff.

16. Boggis, "The European Economic Community" in ibid. p.186. Cf. the hypothesis put forward on the growth of Poujadism in S.Hoffmann, *Le Mouvement Poujade* (1956) p.190 and Duverger et al. (eds.), *Les Elections du 2 Janvier 1956* (1957) p.61 ff. See also Anderson, *Conservative Politics in France* (1973) p.276 ff.

17. Wehler, op.cit., p.473.

18. Wehler, "Probleme des Imperialismus" in *Krisenherde* (1970) pp.131-132.

19. Winkler, *Mittelstand*, op.cit., p.54.

20. This fact is not denied by the better books on pre-war political anti-Semitism. Cf. Massing, *Rehearsal for Destruction* (1967); Pulzer, *Rise of Political Anti-Semitism* (1964); Wawrzinek, *Entstehung der deutschen Antisemitenparteien* (1927).

21. On Belgium, see the reports in *The Grocer:* 24.10.1936. On Great Britain, see 2.3.1935 and Freedmann, *Minority in Britain* (1955) p.212 ff.

22. On the etymology, see Puhle, *Agrarische Interessenpolitik* (1966) p.98 ff.

23. See esp. Stern, *Politics of Cultural Despair* (1965) p.7 ff. Cf. Mohler, *Konservative Revolution* (1950); von Klemperer, *Germany's New Conservatism* (1957); Dahrendorf, *Gesellschaft und Demokratie* (1965) chaps. 3 and 4.

24. Mosse, *Germans and Jews* (1971) p.16. For an explanation of "*völkisch*", see his *Crisis of German Ideology* (1964) p.4 ff. Cf. Bracher, *Die deutsche Diktatur* (1969).

25. Note the comment in Laqueur, *Young Germany* (1962) p.5.

26. Stern, op.cit., p.19.

27. Sombart, *Deutsche Volkswirtschaft im 19. Jahrhundert* (1903) p.537 ff.

28. Marbach, *Theorie des Mittelstandes* (1942) p.280. Cf. Grünberg, *Mittelstand* (1932) p.163 ff.

29. Cf. Engelsing, "Lebenshaltung" (1956) pp.73-107; Lederer and Marschak, "Der neue Mittelstand" (1926) pp.120-141. There were real economic advantages within large industrial concerns associated with the status of *Angestellte* (employees); see esp. Kocka, *Unternehmensverwaltung und Angestelltenschaft* (1969) p.463 ff.

30. Noakes, *Nazi Party in Lower Saxony* (1971) p.108. Cf. Schweitzer, *Big Business in the Third Reich* (1964) p.60 ff.

31. Cf. Massing, op.cit., p.209 and Lebovics, *Social Conservatism* (1969) p.9.

Chapter 1

1. See the useful introductory model in Alexander, *Retailing in England* (1970) p.3 ff.

2. On the periodization of Germany's economic growth, see esp. Hoffmann, "The Take-Off in Germany" (1963), pp.95-118. Cf. Kellenbenz, "Von den Wirtschaftsstufentheorien" (1964) passim. A useful and succinct introduction is Böhme, *Prolegomena zu einer Sozial- und Wirtschaftsgeschichte Deutschlands* (1968) passim.

3. Hoffmann, Grumbach, Hesse, *Wachstum der Deutschen Wirtschaft* (1965) pp.391-393.

4. Ibid., pp.352-353.

5. Bry, *Wages in Germany* (1960) p.17. Cf. Wagenführ, *Industriewirtschaft* (1933) p.16.

6. See the discussion of the problem in Wehler, "Probleme der modernen Wirtschaftsgeschichte" in *Krisenherde*, op.cit., p.291 ff. and the massive literature cited there. Cf. W.Fischer and Czada, "Wandlungen in der deutschen Industriestruktur" in Ritter (ed.), *Entstehung und Wandel der modernen Gesellschaft* (1970) pp.116-165.

7. Sombart, *Deutsche Volkswirtschaft* (1903) op.cit., p.258. Cf. Neuhaus, "Berufliche und soziale Gliederung der Bevölkerung" (1926) p.369.

8. See, for example, Bechtel, *Wirtschaftsgeschichte Deutschlands* Bd. 3 (1956) pp.323, 462.

9. Quoted in Pohle, "Neuere Entwicklung des Kleinhandels" (1901) p.9.

10. This tendency is very widespread. See, for example, Lebovics, "'Agrarians' versus 'Industrializers'" (1967) p.37. Cf. Gellately, "Emergence of Political Anti-Semitism" (1970) p.68 ff.

11. Hoffmann, Grumbach, Hesse, op.cit., pp.172-173. In all cases, the 1913 boundaries apply.

12. Köllmann, *Bevölkerung und Raum* (1965) pp.92-93.

13. Köllmann, "Industrialisierung, Binnenwanderung und 'Soziale Frage'" (1959) pp.45-70. Cf. the very complete figures given in Hoffmann, Grumbach, Hesse, op.cit., pp.179-180.

14. Schmoller, *Grundriss der Volkswirtschaftslehre* Bd.2 (1923) p.39.

15. Cf. Sombart, *Der moderne Kapitalismus* Bd.2, 1 Halbband (1924) pp.452-454; Kanter, *Entwicklung des Handels mit gebrauchsfertigen Waren* (1902) p.142; Reemsten, "Der moderne Detailhandel" (1913) passim. See Bücher, *Entstehung der Volkswirtschaft* Bd.1 (1922) p.91 ff.

16. Krüer, *Markthallen* (1914) pp.104-105. See also *Statistisches Jahrbuch Deutscher Städte* (1892) p.102 ff.; (1900) pp.338-352; (1904) pp.412-419.

17. Krüer, op.cit., pp.74-75, 86-89. See the generally informed remarks of visitors from Great Britain in Ashley, *Progress of the German Working Classes* (1904) p.21, and Dawson, *German Life in Town and Country* (1901) p.43 ff.

18. See the bibliography in Hobsbawm, *Labouring Men* (1968) pp.124-125.

19. Hoffmann, Grumbach, Hesse, op.cit., pp.622-625, 630-633, 656-657.

20. Ibid., pp.428-431. Calculation of this "production" is based on production and consumption indices. The "production" apparently includes both retail and wholesale trade. For their definition of the "production of trade", see pp.426-427.

21. These figures have been calculated from Bry, op.cit., pp.18, 23 and Hoffmann, Grumbach, Hesse, op.cit., pp.428-431.

22. Hoffmann, Grumbach, Hesse, op.cit., p.445.

23. Cf. the calculations of Kuczynski, *Geschichte der Lage der Arbeiter in Deutschland* Bd. 1 (1947) p.176 ff; Hoffmann and Müller, *Das deutsche Volkseinkommen* (1959) p.14 ff; Phelps Brown and Hopkins, "The Course of Wage Rates in Five Countries" (1950), pp.226-296; Bry, op.cit. passim. The most recent and persuasive is Desai, *Real Wages in Germany* (1968) esp. pp.97-105.

24. Desai, op.cit., p.101. After 1895 there was net immigration for the first time; see Köllmann, *Bevölkerung und Raum,* op.cit., p.94.

25. For complete figures on the railroads, see Sombart, *Deutsche Volkswirt-*

schaft im 19. Jahrhundert und im Anfang des 20. Jahrhunderts (1923) p.493. Cf. Landes, *Unbound Prometheus* (1969) pp.154-155, 193-196, 242-244.

26. These price declines had enormous repercussions for German society, economy, and politics. See esp. Wehler, *Bismarck und Imperialismus* op.cit., p.87 ff. and Böhme, *Deutschlands Weg zur Grossmacht* (1966) p.341 ff.

27. Sombart, *Deutsche Volkswirtschaft* (1903) op.cit., p.580, Appendix 24.

28. Bücher, op.cit., Bd.1 p.122.

29. Ibid., p.125. Cf. Sombart, *Deutsche Volkswirtschaft* (1903) op.cit.,p.452. Cf. Mottek, *Wirtschaftsgeschichte Deutschlands* Bd.1 (1959) pp.183-184 and van der Borght, *Handel und Handelspolitik* (1902) p.63 ff.

30. See esp. Hirsch, "Der moderne Handel" (1925) p.7 ff. Cf. Sartorius von Waltershausen, *Deutsche Wirtschaftsgeschichte* (1920) p.26 ff. See the figures in Hoffmann, Grumbach, Hesse, op.cit., pp.656-657.

31. Pohle and Muss, *Das deutsche Wirtschaftsleben* (1930), p.122 ff. Cf. Pohle, "Kleinhandel", op.cit., p.6.

32. Dawson, *The German Workman* (1906) p.13. Cf. Rosenberg, "Zur sozialen Funktion der Agrarpolitik" *Probleme der deutschen Sozialgeschichte* (1969) pp.51-80.

33. Hoffmann, Grumbach, Hesse, op.cit., pp.399-400. Cf. Wiedenfeld, "Transportwesen" (1930) esp. p.131.

34. Cf. Winkler, "Der rückversicherte Mittelstand" (1971) p.166 and Rosenberg, *Grosse Depression* (1967) p.102.

35. Landes, op.cit., pp.233-234. For a presentation and critique of the various theories on the "economic nature" of the depression, see p.232 ff. In spite of the widespread acceptance of Rosenberg's thesis (by Winkler, Wehler, Böhme), no one has related the "depression" to the urban *Mittelstand*.

36. Rosenberg, *Grosse Depression,* op.cit., p.38.

37. Ibid., pp.42, 45. Rosenberg says that although figures on unemployment have not been researched sufficiently to draw firm conclusions (p.48), it was in the course of the period from 1873 to 1896 that "pauperism came to an end". On the period after 1900, see Kuczynski, *Geschichte der Lage der Arbeiter unter dem Kapitalismus* Bd.4 (1967) p.315 ff.

38. Rosenberg, *Grosse Depression,* op.cit., p.51 ff.

39. Ibid., p.56.

40. Ibid., p.53.

41. These publicists, both those active prior to the "crash" in 1873 and those active afterwards, are analysed in Gellately, op.cit., p.44 ff.

42. Cf. Spiethoff, *Die wirtschaftlichen Wechsellagen* Bd.1 (1955) p.147; Rosenberg, *Grosse Depression,* op.cit., p.53; Desai, op.cit., p.44.

43. Wehler, *Bismarck und Imperialismus,* op.cit., pp.62-64.

44. Landes, op.cit., p.236. Cf. Wagenführ, op.cit., p.13.

45. Schmoller, *Zur Geschichte der deutschen Kleingewerbe* (1870) passim. Cf. his later talk in *Verhandlungen des 8. Evangelisch-sozialen Kongresses* (1897) pp.159-160.

46. The conclusions have been based on a study of the massive research project of the *Verein für Sozialpolitik*. See *Schriften des Vereins für Sozialpolitik,* Bde. 62-70 (1895-1897) passim. Also see Bd.76 (1898) esp. pp.16-34, for K.Bücher's paper. Bücher was the general editor of the work on the artisans. Cf.

his *Entstehung der Volkswirtschaft*, op.cit., passim, and Brentano, *Ueber die Ursachen der heutigen socialen Noth.* (1889) esp. p.13 ff.

47. See for example a contemporary textbook, Lexis, *Allgemeine Volkswirtschaftslehre* (1910) p.93.

48. Helfferich, *Deutschlands Volkswohlstand* (1914), p.40 ff. emphasizes that the "decline" was relative to population growth, and only rarely in absolute terms. Cf. Schmoller, *Verhandlungen des 8. Evan.-soz. Kongresses,* op.cit., passim. See also Stieda, "Handwerk" (1910) passim, and his *Lebensfähigkeit des deutschen Handwerks* (1897) passim.

49. Hamburg (from 1904) and Bremen (from 1906) had specific Chambers for retailers. Winkler, *Mittelstand,* op.cit., p.215 fn.46, denies their existence.

50. For an analysis of the debates concerning *Gewerbefreiheit* in the North German Confederation, *Stenographische Berichte über die Verhandlung des Reichstages des Norddeutschen Bundes 1867-1870,* see Gellately, op.cit., pp.43-65.

51. See esp. von Gerber, *Der Ruin des Mittelstandes von einem Mann aus dem Volke* (1891) pp.7-8; this work was highly anti-Semitic. Cf. the following: Glagau, *Des Reiches Noth* (1879) p.168 ff., and his *Börsen- und Gründungs-Schwindel in Deutschland* (1877) pp.xxxvii-xxxviii, 21 ff.; Wilmanns, *Die "goldene" Internationale* (1876) pp.1-2. Cf. the "social conservatives", Wagener, *Erlebtes* (1884) passim and Meyer, *Politische Gründer und die Corruption in Deutschland* (1877) esp. p.180 ff. See also Lagarde, "Diagnose" (1874) *Deutsche Schriften* (1892) p.94.

52. On the earlier period, esp. 1848, see Noyes, *Organization and Revolution* (1966) esp. pp.28-29. On the general problem, see Stieda, "Handwerk", op.cit., pp.377-393. A recent work, Hamerow, *Social Foundations of German Unification* (1969), p.44 ff., sets the artisan within the social structure of Germany and continues his earlier work, *Restoration, Revolution, Reaction* (1958).

53. It was sometimes suggested by politicians that the artisans really did not want compulsory guilds. See for example the report in *Nordwestdeutsche Handwerks-Ztg.* Nr.49, 13.12.1913, p.208. It is well known, however, that even after the legislation of 1897, the artisans continued to advocate further legislation for compulsory guilds.

54. See esp. Bücher, *Entstehung der Volkswirtschaft* Bd.1 op.cit., p.91 ff. and Sartorius von Waltershausen, op.cit., p.29 ff. Von Lehe, *Märkte Hamburgs* (1966) passim, is also useful.

55. See for example Noyes, op.cit., passim and Hamerow, *Restoration* op.cit., esp. pp.30-35, 102 ff. Cf. Bücher, *Entstehung der Volkswirtschaft* Bd.2 op.cit., pp.385-399.

56. This conclusion is based (in part) on a survey of the massive compilation *Verzeichnis der im Deutschen Reiche bestehenden Vereine gewerblicher Unternehmer zur Wahrung ihrer wirtschaftlichen Interessen* Reichsamt des Innern (ed.) (1903) passim. For the contrary opinion, see esp. the works of Winkler, op.cit.

57. Mills, op.cit., p.24. See also his "The Middle Classes in Middle-Sized Cities" in *Power, Politics and People* (1967) pp.274-291. Cf. Hays, op.cit., p.54 ff.

58. Heberler, *Der Deutsche Verband für das kaufmännische Bildungswesen* (1936) p.9 ff.

59. Ehlers, "Binnenhandel" in Zorn and von Berger et al., *Deutschland unter Kaiser Wilhelm II* Bd.2 (1914) pp.723-724.

60. *Westdeutsche-Mittelstands-Ztg.* Nr.6, 6.1.1909, pp.1-2.

61. Lederer, "Sozialpolitische Chronik. Mittelstandsbewegung" (1910) p.974.

62. Ibid. Cf. the views of Wegener, *Freiheitskampf des Mittelstandes* (1906) esp. p.85 ff.

Chapter 2

1. See esp. Stegmann, op.cit., p.113 ff. Cf. Naumann, *Die politischen Parteien* (1910) p.108 ff. In 1890, the SPD received, for the first time, the greatest number of votes in a *Reichstag* election, though, because of the existence of latter day "rotten boroughs", the party did not succeed in electing a proportionate number of deputies.

2. *DZA 1, Reichsamt des Innern, 6318. Besprechung am 9. Juni 1914 wegen Veranstaltung einer Erhebung über die Verhältnisse des kaufmännischen Mittelstandes.*

3. Ibid., pp.6-7.

4. See for example the survey of Bavaria by Adlmaier and Bahnbrecher, *Lage des bayerischen Kleinhandels* (1909) p.22 ff., henceforth cited as *Lage des Kleinhandels I.*

5. *DZA 1, 6318, Besprechung,* op.cit., pp.13-14.

6. Schmoller, *Grundriss der Volkswirtschaftslehre,* op.cit., p.39.

7. Sombart, *Deutsche Volkswirtschaft im 19. und 20. Jahrhundert,* op.cit., p.200.

8. Ibid.

9. For the 1861 and 1882 figures, see Rathgen, "Handelspolitik" (1906/1907) p.169; for those of 1895 and 1907, see Sombart, *Deutsche Volkswirtschaft im 19. und 20. Jahrhundert,* op.cit., p.220.

10. For a summary of the relevant national statistics, see *Statistik des Deutschen Reichs, Bd. 220/221* (1914) p.1* ff.

11. *Die Lage des Kleinhandels in Deutschland* (2 Bde. 1899/1900), henceforth cited as *Lage des Kleinhandels II* and *III.* For Celle, see *III* p.61. Cf. Stumpf, *Bericht über die am 9. Dezember 1895 zu Osnabrück gepflogenen Verhandlungen* (1896) for the contemporary discussion that preceded these surveys.

12. *Lage des Kleinhandels III* p.100.

13. Ibid. p.123.

14. *Lage des Kleinhandels II* p.55.

15. Ibid. p.159.

16. Ibid.

17. *Lage des Kleinhandels III* pp.21-25.

18. *Lage des Kleinhandels II* p.114.

19. *Kolonialwaaren-Kleinhandel und Konsumvereine. Untersuchungen.* (1901) p.17, henceforth cited as *Lage des Kleinhandels IV.*

20. Schmoller, *Grundriss der Volkswirtschaftslehre,* op.cit., p.40.

21. *Statistik des Deutschen Reichs, Bd.220/221,* op.cit., pp.152-153.

22. Cf. Mataja, "Kleinhandel" (1910) pp.874-880; Lexis, op.cit., p.93; Landwers, *Lage des Kleinhandels* (1905) p.2.

23. See for example Troeltsch, "Über die neuesten Veränderungen im deutschen Wirtschaftsleben" (1899) esp. p.95.

24. Hirsch, op.cit., p.223 ff.

25. See for example *Lage des Kleinhandèls II* pp.101 ff., 146, 168; *Lage des Kleinhandels III* pp.100-101.

26. *Lage des Kleinhandels II* p.35. Cf. *II* p.81; *Lage des Kleinhandels IV* p.57.

27. *Lage des Kleinhandels III* p.5 ff.

28. See for example *Lage des Kleinhandels II* pp.88-89. Cf. *Lage des Kleinhandels III* p.82.

29. *HH. St.Ar. Gerichtsvollzieherwesen, Nr.25. Jahresberichte, statistische Übersichten, 1882-1934.* Cf. *Statistisches Handbuch für den Hamburgischen Staat. Ausgabe 1920* (1921) p.396.

30. *Lage des Kleinhandels II* p.88.

31. Ibid., pp.56-57, 88-89. Cf. *Lage des Kleinhandels III* pp.92 ff., 107.

32. Sombart, *Deutsche Volkswirtschaft* (1903), op.cit., p.255.

33. Geiger, *Soziale Schichtung des deutschen Volkes* (1932) p.73.

34. See *Cd. 4032, Cost of Living in German Towns* (1908), esp. pp.1-38, 367-381.

35. See esp. *Lage des Kleinhandels III* pp.85-91.

36. See for example *HB.HK.Ar., Kl.2 , Rundschreiben, Verein Berliner Kaufleute und Industrieller* (16.4.1907).

37. See esp. the campaign in Hamburg, *HH.St.Ar. PP. S6750.* In Hamburg, all the local newspapers carried whole pages devoted to the Tietz campaign, beginning esp. from 29.11.1898. See also *HH.C.* 7.3.1901, *HH.F.* 7.3.1901; *Neue HH. Ztg.* 23.10.1901.

38. *DZA 1, 6318, Besprechung,* op.cit., p.11.

39. For a brief introduction to the history of the consumer co-operative movement in Germany, see Staudinger, *Konsumgenossenschaft* (1908) p.40 ff.

40. On Schulze, see his *Schriften und Reden* (5 Bde. 1909/1913), esp. Bd.5 for the biography by Thorwart. Cf. Pfeiffer, *Über Genossenschaftswesen* (1863) and V.A.Huber, *Selbsthilfe der arbeitenden Klassen* (1848).

41. Kaufmann, *Kurzer Abriss der Geschichte des Zentralverbandes* (1928) p.8.

42. Kulemann, *Genossenschaftsbewegung. Erster Bd. Geschichtlicher T.* (1922) p.31.

43. Cf. the treatment in Wein, *Verbandsbildung* (1968) pp.33-35.

44. Kaufmann, op.cit., p.330.

45. See esp. Cassau, *Konsumvereinsbewegung. Schriften des Vereins für Sozialpolitik. Untersuchungen über Konsumvereine, Bd.150, IV T.* (1924) p.5.

46. See the full tables in Kaufmann, op.cit., p.330.

47. See the detailed tables in Kulemann, op.cit., p.84.

48. Ibid. There was a total of 1,197 consumer co-operatives listed.

49. Ibid., pp.31-32.

50. Birnie, *Economic History of Europe* (1966) pp.168-169.

51. Cassau, op.cit., pp.6, 120 ff.

52. Ibid, p.122. Cf. Kaufmann, *Stellungsnahme der Sozialdemokratie zur Konsumgenossenschaftsbewegung* (1911) p.5 ff. Kaufmann was general secretary of the *Z.d.K.*

53. Cassau, op.cit., p.7.

54. Ibid., p.125. Cf. *Bundesarchiv Z.Sg.1.130. Handbuch für nichtsozialdemokratische Wähler* (1911) pp.336-356 for a discussion of the SPD and its connection with the consumer co-operative movement.

55. Tables on all the various states of Germany are given in Kaufmann,

Kurzer Abriss, op.cit., p.332.

56. Schmoller, *Grundriss der Volkswirtschaftslehre,* op.cit., p.40.

57. For a summary, see Büchner, op.cit., p.887 ff. Excerpts from and commentaries on the department store taxes of the individual German states can be found in Wernicke, *Das preussische Warenhausgesetz* (1913) passim.

58. See for example Dortmund *WWAr.K.2, Nr.1267, Bd.2 Plenarsitzung 22.3.1899 HK. Bochum, Schrift-Bericht.*

59. See the survey carried out by Lux, *Studien über die Entwicklung der Warenhäuser* (1910) p.8 and Göhre, "Warenhaus" (1907) p.90. Wein, op.cit., p.32 confuses the figures; the figures he adopts (from Hirsch, op.cit., p.239) refer only to the number of department stores "subject to the department store tax" in Prussia, and not, as he suggests, to those in all of Germany.

60. Wernicke, *Kapitalismus und Mittelstandspolitik* (1907) p.545.

61. Mataja, *Grossmagazine und Kleinhandel* (1891) p.17 ff.

62. See the testimony given by Tietz in Wernicke, *Kapitalismus und Mittelstandspolitik,* op.cit., pp.545-549.

63. See Göhre, op.cit., passim, for a detailed account of Wertheim.

64. Messow, *Schaden im Detailhandel und die Warenhäuser* (ca. 1900) p.4.

65. Büchner, op.cit., p.891.

66. Lux, op.cit., p.8.

67. Nieschlag, "Versandgeschäfte in Deutschland" (1936) p.10 ff.

68. Sombart, *Deutsche Volkswirtschaft* (1903), op.cit., p.266.

69. Hirsch, op.cit., p.247.

70. See the figures in Schmoller, *Grundriss der Volkswirtschaftslehre,* op.cit., pp.40-41.

71. On the hawkers, see esp. Stieda "Hausiergewerbe" (1899) and the extensive *Schriften des Vereins für Sozialpolitik,* Bde. 77-81 (1898/99) passim.

72. See Sombart's remarks in *Deutsche Volkswirtschaft* (1903), op.cit., p.267.

73. Ibid. Cf. *Lage des Kleinhandels I* p.3 ff.

74. This was the argument, for example, of Richter, *Politisches ABC Buch* (1898) pp.83-84.

75. Mataja, "Abzahlungsgeschäfte" (1909) p.15.

76. See esp. Kaufmann, *Kurzer Abriss,* op.cit., p.30.

77. See for example, *HH.St.Ar.PP.S6750.* See the reports in the following: *Mitteilungen der Centralvereinigung deutscher Vereine für Handel und Gewerbe* 15.9.1911; *Deutsche Nahrungs- und Genussmittel Ztg.* 14.10.1910 and 17.5.1913; *Detaillist und Publikum,* esp. 27.4.1912 and 12.4.1913; *Die Blumenschmuckkunst* 6.6.1906; *Westdeutsche Mittelstands Ztg.* Nr.55, 7.8.1909.

78. See for example *B.Dahlem. Pr.Justizministerium. Rep.84a, III, Nr.10479.* Note esp. Crüger, *Zur Kritik der Agitation gegen die Konsumvereine* (1899) passim. Crüger was legal representative of the *Allgemeiner Verband.*

79. See esp. Sombart, "Entwicklungstendenzen im modernen Kleinhandel" *Zweiter Verhandlungstag (26.9.1899) des Vereins für Sozialpolitik. Schriften des Vereins für Sozialpolitik,* Bd.87 (1900) pp.137-160. Cf. Rathgen's speech, pp.161-180 and Wirminghaus, "Wirtschaftliche Verhältnisse und Entwicklungstendenzen im Kleinhandel" (1910), pp.32-60.

80. See Rathgen's complaint on this point in *Verhandlungen des Vereins für Sozialpolitik* (1899), op.cit., p.161.

81. See esp. *Lage des Kleinhandels II* pp.5, 146.
82. Crüger, "Einfluss der Konsumvereine auf der Preisbildung des Kleinhandels" *Zweiter Verhandlungstag des Vereins für Sozialpolitik (1899)*, op.cit., pp.155-184.
83. See the detailed charts given in ibid., p.180 ff.
84. Lexis, "Der breslauer Konsumverein und die Kleinhandelspreise" *Schriften des Vereins für Sozialpolitik*, Bd.37 (1888) pp.181-200.
85. Cf. Schmitz, *Lage des Lebensmitteldetailhandels* (1906) p.49; Nientimp, *Kolonialwarenhändler wehrt euch!* (1913) p.6 ff.
86. *Lage des Kleinhandels II* pp.37-38, 133. Cf. *Lage des Kleinhandels III* p.73. On the general picture, see *Lage des Kleinhandels II* p.258 ff. "Verhältniss zwischen Versandgeschäfte und Kleinhandel . . ·. in den kleinen Städten und Dörfern". See also Hübner, *Zur Lage des Kleinhandels* (1902) p.66 ff.
87. See for example *Lage des Kleinhandels II* pp.37, 172-173.
88. Cf. Wernicke, *Kapitalismus und Mittelstandspolitik*, op.cit., p.531 ff. and his *Wirtschaftliche und soziale Bedeutung der Warenhäuser* (1904) passim.
89. See Bayerdörffer, op.cit., p.138 who doubts that lower prices actually resulted.
90. See for example *Lage des Kleinhandels II* pp.9-10, 101-106, 234-257.
91. *HH.St.Ar.PP. S18649, Detaillist und Publikum.* 25.11.1911.
92. See esp. Rassow and Born (eds.), *Akten zur Staatlichen Sozialpolitik* (1959) pp.1-5 and Born, *Staat und Sozialpolitik* (1967) p.98. For an interesting collection of documents on the "new course" see Ritter (ed.), *Historisches Lesebuch* (1967) p.264 ff. and Kotowski, Pöls, Ritter (eds.), *Das Wilhelminische Deutschland* (1965) p.6 ff.
93. Lederer, *Privatangestellten* (1912) pp.158-159. Cf. the later work, Lederer and Marschak, op.cit., passim, and Schuon, *Der Deutschnationale Handlungsgehilfen-Verband* (1914) pp.238-241.
94. Schuon, op.cit. Cf. also Lederer, *Privatangestellten,* op.cit., pp.158-159. Founded in 1897, the ZHGD stood as the 11th largest (of the 16 at the head of) white-collar organizations in 1910.
95. Kocka, "The First World War and the 'Mittelstand'" (1973) pp.101-123, esp. 103.
96. *Merkuria* Nr.5, 2.2.1908, pp.33-34.
97. Cf. Lederer, *Privatangestellten* op.cit., passim. For a recent study of the DHV, see Hamel, *Völkischer Verband und Nationale Gewerkschaft* (1967) passim. This organization sought to retain its position within the *Mittelstandsbewegung.* Its leaders were among the most prominent anti-Semites in pre-war Germany. See esp. Schack, *Wie und was wir geworden sind.* (1903) passim.
98. *HH.St.Ar.PP. S4013,* Bd.1; *SA28,* Bd.5; *S7751.* See the earlier attempts, reported in the *Volks Ztg.* 19.4.1898, of some people with a dual membership in the DHV and the VDH at the 16th annual meeting of the VDH. Cf. *B.Tagebl.* 25.4.1908 and 27.4.1908, *Volks Ztg.* 27 and 28.4.1908 on a more serious attempt by both. It was reported then that some in the VDH considered the DHV "little more than the recruiting school of the anti-Semites". Cf. *Vorwärts.* 29.4.1908. See the later opinion of the VfH von 1858 in *HH.F.* 16.11.1910. The further meeting of 7.12.1912 was boycotted by the important DHV. See the *Frank Ztg.* 8.12.1912 and *B.N.Nach.* 14.12.1912.
99. *HH.St.Ar.PP. S7751.* Cf. *National Ztg.* 21.8.1894; *Volks Ztg.* 20.8.1894;

B.Tagebl, 20.8.1894. See the earlier report in *HH.F.* 6.8.1894. The DHV newspaper *Deutsche Handels-Wacht.* 15.9.1896 accused the VDH of being as backward as the VfH von 1858 and in the paper 24.2.1901 accused them both of "social-political dilettantism".

100. *Der angebliche Ruin des Kleinhandels. Flugschrift Nr.5 DHV* (1899) pp.4, 19-20.

101. *HH.St.Ar.PP. S12369* and *Neue HH.Ztg.* 11.11.1904

102. See Wilhelm's decree of 29.3.1890 in Ritter, *Lesebuch,* op.cit., pp.264-265. It suggests the extent to which the "new course" was engineered by Wilhelm under no popular pressure.

103. For the full reports, see *HH.St.Ar.Senatsakten, Cl.1, Lit.T. No.8, Vol.65, Fasc.3. Deutsches Reich-Arbeiterstatistik.* Bde.1-23 (1892-1894); Bde.25-29 (1896). *Inv.1-6.* Cf. esp. *Cl.1, Lit.T. No.8, Vol.65, Fasc.5* which contains the *Drucksachen der Kommission für Arbeiterstatistik. Verhandlungen. Protokolle über die Verhandlung der Kommission* (1895 ff.); see also *Fasc. 4 and 9.*

104. *HH.St.Ar.PP. S2869,* Bd.2. Cf. the summaries of *HH.F.* 12.7.1893 and *Volks Ztg.* 30.6.1893; Oldenburg "Statistik der socialen Lage der deutschen Handlungsgehilfen"(1893) pp.1231-1250.

105. See the details in Göhre, op.cit., passim.

106. Oldenburg, "Die heutige Lage der Commis" (1892) p.793.

107. Lederer, *Privatangestellten,* op.cit., pp.85-86.

108. Kocka, "Mittelstand", op.cit., p.103.

109. Oldenburg, "Statistik der socialen Lage", op.cit., p.1243. Cf. Krueger, *Wirtschaftliche und soziale Lage der Privatangestellten* (1912) esp. pp.125-144. The department stores were not much better at providing opportunities for their staff to acquire further training. See *HH.St.Ar.PP. S6747.* See the comments of a leading women's group in *Neue HH.Ztg.* 14.2.1903.

110. Lederer, *Privatangestellten,* op.cit., pp.207-208. For information on most of these demands, see *Handwörterbücher der Staatswissenschaften.*

111. *Der Detaillist* Nor.40, 2.10.1909. See also Kocka, "Mittelstand", op.cit., p.120 who mentions briefly that the wartime polarization of the *Mittelstand* had really begun prior to the war.

112. Cf. Lederer, "Sozialpolitische Chronik. Mittelstandsbewegung", op.cit., p.974. For the later period, esp. the Third Reich, see the comments of Uhlig, *Warenhäuser im Dritten Reich* (1956) p.50 and Buchner, *Warenhauspolitik und Nationalsozialismus* (1930) passim.

Chapter 3

1. Some insight into the relationship of "structural changes" in German society and interest group activity is given in Nipperdey, "Interessenverbände" (1961) passim and esp. Born, "Der soziale und wirtschaftliche Strukturwandel Deutschlands am Ende des 19. Jahrhunderts" (1963) pp.271-284.

2. See for example Puhle, op.cit., and Kaelble, *Industrielle Interessenpolitik* (1967) passim.

3. The interest groups of the agrarians prior to the BdL and the industrialists prior to the CDI have been studied in a broadly similar fashion. See Lambi, *Free Trade and Protection* (1963) passim and Hardach, *Bedeutung wirtschaftlicher*

Faktoren (1967) passim. On the later period, see esp. Stegmann, op.cit., p.59 ff.'
Cf. Barkin, *Controversy over German Industrialization* (1970) passim.

4. See Stegmann, op.cit. esp. pp.32 ff. and 113 ff. Cf. Böhme, *Deutschlands Weg zur Grossmacht*, op.cit., p.575; F.Fischer, *Krieg der Illusionen* (1969) p.58 ff.

5. The concept of "organize or perish" was introduced first in the works of Emil Lederer. See for example "Die wirtschaftlichen Organisationen" (1913) pp.132-138. Cf. Schürholz, *Entwicklungstendenzen im deutschen Wirtschaftsleben* (1922) p.35 ff. For a more recent version, applied to the United States, see Hays, op.cit., p.48 ff. Cf. Puhle, "Parlament, Parteien und Interessenverbände" (1970) pp.344-346.

6. The idea of establishing a substitute for parliament *("Parlamentsersatz")* in Germany is examined in Böhme, *Deutschlands Weg zur Grossmacht*, op.cit., p.575 ff. and Stegmann, op.cit., p.113 ff. Note the extensive literature quoted in both. Cf. Puhle, "Interessenverbände" op.cit., p.343 and Weber, "Parlament und Regierung" (1958) pp.294-394.

7. Wein, op.cit., pp.15-27. Cf. Lampert, "Strukturwandlungen des deutschen Einzelhandels" (1956) and Puderbach, "Entwicklung des selbständigen Mittelstandes" (1967) passim. Wein's typology is largely accepted by Winkler, *Mittelstand,* op.cit., p.46 ff.

8. Wein, op.cit., p.21 ff.

9. For information on the activities of the technical organizations, see the archives of the various Chambers of Commerce.

10. *Colonial- und Fettwaren- Ztg.* 21.9.1901.

11. *HH.St.Ar.PP. S8113.* See also *S15672* and the comments in *Vorwärts* on the ironmongers' meeting 22.5.1901.

12. *HH.St.Ar.PP. S15113.* See esp. the statutes of 1913 of the *Verband deutscher Detailgeschäfte der Textilbranche.*

13. Cr. *Bay.Haupt.St.Ar.M.Wi. 1457* and *NS.St.Ar.Hann.80. Hann.II, Nr.1295.*

14. Wein, op.cit., p.209 ff.

15. *Festschrift 1870-1970. Einhundert Jahre Berufsorganisation des Lebensmittel-Einzelhandels* (1970) p.24.

16. For the general picture, see Bredek, "Entwicklungstendenzen in den genossenschaftlichen Selbsthilfebestrebungen" (1960) passim. Cf. Wein, op.cit., p.143.

17. See for example Dursthoff, *Lage des Kleinhandels und die Begründung von Einkaufsgenossenschaften* (1903) p.3.

18. *HH.St.Ar.PP. SA692.* Cf. Wein, op.cit., pp.232-233.

19. Wein, op.cit., p.238.

· 20. Landwers, op.cit., p.3.

21. Engel, *Detaillisten-Fragen* (1907) p.91. Cf. Dursthoff, op.cit., p.14.

22. Cf. *Festschrift Berufsorganisation Bremen,* op.cit., p.11 ff.; Wein, op.cit., p.158; Winkler, *Mittelstand,* op.cit., pp.48, 214. In June 1967, some 40,000 individual retailers counted themselves as members of *Edeka.*

23. For a brief account, see Wein, op.cit., p.159. Cf. Biller, *Kolonialwaren, Kleinhandel und Einkaufsvereine* (1913) esp. p.3 ff. Biller was director of the *Verband deutscher kaufmännischer Genossenschaften e.V.* (Berlin).

24. Engel, op.cit., p.95.

25. *Konsumvereine und Einkaufs-Genossenschaften, deren Schäden und Vorschläge zur Abstellung derselben* (1901) p.4. See *HB.HK. Kl.2.*

228 The Politics of Economic Despair

26. Borgius, "Wandlungen im modernen Detailhandel" (1899) p.79.

27. See for example Nientimp, op.cit., p.45 ff.

28. See for example *HH.St.Ar.PP. S12340*, the *Wirtschaftlicher Schutzverband Hamburg*. Cf. the *Schutzverbands-Mitteilungen*. Nr.25, 10.2.1907 with its specific appeal to the retailers.

29. See *HH.F.* 20.9.1905 for a report of the meeting of the *Schutzverband*, "Der Mittelstand im Kampfe mit dem Umsturz".

30. *HH.C.* 29.8.1907. See esp. *HH.St.Ar.PP. S15113.*

31. *HH.C.* 29.8.1907; *HH.N.* 1.2.1908. For the general picture, see esp. Lederer, *Die wirtschaftlichen Organisationen* (1913) p.105 and Kocka, "Mittelstand", op.cit., p.120.

32. *HH.N.* 5.11.1908.

33. Meetings had been held in Nov. 1908 and Aug. 1909. See esp. the full report of *HH.N.* 5.11.1908 and *HH.C.* 11.8.1909. On the wholesalers, see *HH.N.* 1.2.1908. For an example of the reaction among other retailers to such discussions, see *HH.N.* 5.2.1911; *HH.C.* 5.2.1911; *G.A.* 3.2.1911.

34. Lemmel, *50 Jahre Geschichte* (1922) p.4.

35. *Festschrift zum 40. jähr. Stiftungsfest* (1912) passim. For a full account of the voting system of the *Bürgerschaft* in Hamburg, see Bagge, *Bürgerschaftswahlen* (1906) passim.

36. *HH.St.Ar.PP. S13841* and *SA1442*. See for example the *Hamburger Verband der Detaillisten und sonstigen Gewerbetreibenden* or the *Zentralvereinigung preussischer Vereine für Handel und Gewerbe*.

37. *Verzeichnis der bestehenden Vereine gewerblicher Unternehmer*, op.cit., p.353. Although, in a sense, this organization had ceased to be a *Schutzverband* and had become a technical organization, it retained its membership in the *Zentralverband deutscher Kaufleute*.

38. Ibid., p.39.

39. *HB.HK.Kl.2*, esp. letters of the *Verband deutscher Detailgeschäfte der Textilbranche* 9.12.1908, and of the *Detaillistenverband der Bekleidungsindustrie und verwandten Branchen e.V.* 17.7.1912. Cf. *Dortmund WWAr. K2, Nr.1071, Nr.1226.*

40. See esp. Winkler, *Mittelstand*, op.cit., p.47.

41. For a full report of the *Verbandstag*, see *Deutsche Rabattsparvereins-Ztg.* Nr.7, 2 Ausgabe (Juli 1910) pp.73-88.

42. *DZA 1, 6318, Besprechung*, op.cit., p.59.

43. Winkler, *Mittelstand*, op.cit., p.48.

44. See esp. Faucherre, *Die Händler-Rabattsparvereine* (1912) p.79. See the report of the annual meeting of the *Zentralverband*, 12.8.1907. The president of the *Zentralverband* (Geest) claimed, with some pride, that the *Rabattsparvereine* had developed "in the circles of members of the *Zentralverband*". See *HH.C.* 14.8.1907. Cf. *Echo.* 25.8.1904, where the support of *Rabattsparvereine* and *Einkaufsgenossenschaften* by the annual meeting of the *Zentralverband* was contrasted with the opposition of the *Zentralverband* to all consumer co-operatives.

45. Beythien, *Rabattsparvereine der Kaufleute* (1913) pp.97-99.

46. *Konsumvereine und Einkaufs-Genossenschaften*, op.cit., p.10.

47. See for example Büchler, *Rabattsparvereine* (1910) passim. Cf. Suchsland,

Schutz- und Trutzwaffen (1904) p.5 ff. Suchsland was one of the more important ideologues of the *Mittelstandsbewegung* and very much in favour of establishing further *Rabattsparvereine*. See also his *Los von der Konsumvereine und Warenhäusern* (1906) passim.

48. See the circular of the organization in *HB.St.Ar.Senats Reg. V2, Nr.395,* of 1.1.1914. Cf. *Reichsdeutsche Mittelstandsblätter.* Nr.9, Sept. 1914, p.6.

49. *DZA 1, 6318, Besprechung,* op.cit., p.59 ff.

50. Kandt, "Über verschiedene Prämien-Sparsysteme" (1907) pp.337-368. Cf. Elster, "Rabattsparvereine" (1911) pp.1-5.

51. See the account of *Händlerstolz* in Faucherre, op.cit., pp.1-49.

52. For complete statistics, see ibid., p.52.

53. *Jahresbericht der Handelskammer zu Hannover für das Jahr 1901* (1901) p.6.

54. See *HB.HK. 6.12. Gewerbekammer.1.K.9. Flugblatt. 10.9.1895.* For the statistics, see *HB.St.Ar.Senats Reg. V2, Nr.167.* Cf. *HB.HK.Kl.13.*

55. Winkler, *Mittelstand,* op.cit., p.48.

56. Cf. Faucherre, op.cit., p.79 and Beythien, op.cit., pp.59-85.

57. Beythien, op.cit., p.15 ff. Cf. his *Entwicklung des gemeinnützigen Rabattsparvereins-Wesens* (1907) passim.

58. *HH.St.Ar.PP. S5916.* For full reports of the meeting in Leipzig, see *HH.F.* 6. and 7.8.1902.

59. Beythien, *Rabattsparvereine der Kaufleute,* op.cit., p.15 ff.

60. *HH.St.Ar.PP. S7011.* See the *Flugblatt.* 21.3.1914, "Ein ernstes Wort zur rechten Zeit!"

61. Weber, *Wirtschaft und Gesellschaft* (1927) esp. p.26 ff. Cf. Michels, *Zur Soziologie des Parteiwesens* (1925) passim.

62. See the sources listed above, chap.3, note 48.

End of June of the Year	Verbandsvereine	Collective members
1904	62	12,000
1905	143	27,428
1906	186	33,691
1907	215	41,741
1908	262	50,423
1909	305	54,773
1910	340	57,508
1911	370	61,500
1912	425	65,733
1913	circa 467	circa 70,400
1914 (beginning)	503	73,495

63. *Deutsche Rabattsparvereins-Ztg.* Nr.1 (Jan.1913) p.4.

64. Beythien, *Rabattsparvereine der Kaufleute,* op.cit., p.55. Cf. *HH.N.* 26.2.1914 for a report of the rejection of the idea of founding a member union by the *Hamburger Drogisten-Verein.*

65. See copies of the statutes in *HB.St.Ar.Senats Reg. V2, Nr.349.*

66. On the Handelstag, see *Der Deutsche Handelstag* 2 Bde. (1911/1913) passim and Gensel, *Der Deutsche Handelstag* (1902) passim.

67. *HH.HK.Ar.80.A.2.h.3.* See *Deutscher Handelstag. Bericht über die Sitzung der Kommission betr. Kleinhandel vom 17.-18. Sept. 1906* pp.16-24. Cf.

Deutscher Handelstag. Bericht über die Sitzung des bleibenden Ausschusses (3.-4. Dez. 1906) passim.

68. Beythien, *Rabattsparvereine der Kaufleute*, op.cit., p.29 ff.

69. Ibid., p.92 ff.

70. *NS.St.Ar. Hann.80.Hann.II, Nr.1093.*

71. See for example Biller, op.cit., passim.

72. Beythien, *Rabattsparvereine der Kaufleute*, op.cit., p.43 ff. Earlier, there had been some acceptance among members of the *Verband der Rabattsparvereine Deutschlands* of the need to create *Einkaufsgenossenschaften*. See Beythien's report in *Entwicklung des gemeinnützigen Rabattsparvereins-Wesens*, op.cit., pp.36-37.

73. Faucherre, op.cit., p.87.

74. For a list of examples indicating the very positive effects of the local establishment of *Rabattsparvereine*, see Beythien, *Rabattsparvereine der Kaufleute*, op.cit., p.59 ff and Landwers, op.cit., p.18 ff.

75. See *HH.St.Ar.PP. V618* for examples of the activity of this organization.

76. *HH.N.* 19.5.1908. See also the lists of the activities of the *Kammer* given on the 25th anniversary in *Die Detaillistenkammer Hamburg 1904-1929* (1929) p.29.

77. *Der Weckruf!* (Dez. 1906). Cf. *Mitteilungen. Verein gegen Unwesen im Handel und Gewerbe*, 15.7.1906 and the earlier views of the *Central-Ausschuss* at the meeting of 5.11.1896 in *HH.F.* 8.11.1896. See also *HH.St.Ar.PP. V1034* and *HH.N.* 21.5.1912. Cf. the letter of *HK* Bochum to *Handelskammern* throughout Germany where it was suggested that *Rabattsparvereine* were too susceptible to misuse to be of real value to retailers. Cf. the letters of *HK* Berlin of 3.4.1901 and 4.6.1901 in *Dortmund WWAr. K2, Nr.430.*

78. The allegation that the *Freie Vereinigung* represented so few members was made by the *Rabattsparvereine Deutschlands*. See *HB.HK.Kl.2*, esp. *Entgegnung des Verbandes der Rabatt-Spar-Vereine Deutschlands (e.V.) Sitz in Bremen auf die von einer Anzahl Münchener Geschäftsinhaber gemachten Vorschläge zur Besteuerung der Rabattgewährung durch die Detailgeschäfte* (Juni 1909).

79. Ibid.

80. *Neue HH.Ztg.* 12.1.1904 and *HH.N.* 19.2.1904. See also *HH.St.Ar.PP. S11810.* Cf. the reports of the anti-*Rabattsparvereine* meetings in Munich and Düsseldorf 25.6.1909 carried in *Der Detaillist.* Nr.27, 3.7.1909.

81. *HH.St.Ar.PP. V618.* At a meeting of the *Central-Ausschuss* in Hamburg 6.1.1896, the question was raised "By what means can discount malpractice be taxed?", but even the *Rabattsparvereine* were opposed to such malpractice.

82. The announcements of the meetings are to be found in *HH.St.Ar.PP. S7011.* Cf. the coverage of the meeting in *HH.F.* 27.3.1914; *G.A.* 26.3.1914; *Der Weckruf!* (April 1914); *Neue HH.Ztg.* 29.3.1914. The meeting was held at the *Detaillistenkammer.*

Chapter 4

1. Cf. Deutsche Auslands-Arbeitsgemeinschaft Hamburg (ed.), *Hamburg* (1912) passim; Baumann, *Bevölkerung Hamburgs* (1919) passim; Mauersberg, *Wirtschafts- und Sozialgeschichte* (1960) passim.

2. For documentation of the *Zollanschluss*, see *Dokumente zur Geschichte der HK Hamburg* (1965): 153-166.

3. See the testimony in *Die Detaillistenkammer Hamburg*, op.cit., pp.3-4.

4. Rieger, Mendel, Postelt, *Die hamburger Konsumgenossenschaft "Produktion"* (1949) p.89 ff. and Ahrens, "Das sozialistische Genossenschaftswesen in Hamburg" (1970) passim.

5. For the employers and their organizations, see *HH.St.Ar.PP. S6810, S8610, S12340,* and Hoebel, "Das organisierte Arbeitgebertum in Hamburg-Altona" (1923) passim.

6. For the working classes and their organizations in Hamburg, see the works of Laufenberg, *Geschichte der Arbeiterbewegung Hamburgs* (1931) and *Die Hamburger Revolution* (1919) passim. Cf. Schult, *Geschichte der Hamburger Arbeiter* (1967) passim.

7. *Verzeichnis der bestehenden Vereine gewerblicher Unternehmer* op.cit., p.22 ff.

8. Ibid., p.78 ff.

9. Ibid., p.60 ff.

10. Ibid., p.26 ff.

11. Ibid., p.331 ff. The organization in question was the technical organization, the *Verband selbständiger deutscher Konditoren.*

12. Ibid., p.72 ff.

13. Winkler, *Mittelstand*, op.cit., p.48 says that the *Schutzverbände* were "typical products of the depression" of 1873-1896.

14. Wein, op.cit., p.38. Wein's chart leaves the distinct impression that local *Schutzverbände* were created more or less evenly from 1861. He concedes that the 1880s, 1890s, and even early 1900s saw the greatest number of local *Schutzverbände* come into existence (p.39).

15. Cf. *Dortmund WWAr. K2, Nr.1552,* letters of various organizations from 14.7.1897 ff. See also *St.Ar.München. Polizei-Direktion. Verz. 24.a.1.48.7b* and the meeting of retailers covered in the *M.N.N.* 23.7.1892.

16. *HH.St.Ar.PP. V827, Polizei Schrift* 30.1.1904.

17. *IIII.St.Ar.PP. S4293* and *V488,* 2 Bde. See the police file on Werbeck, *S3618.*

18. See the newspaper of the *Verein, Der Weckruf!* (Mai 1913).

19. *Verzeichnis der bestehenden Vereine gewerblicher Unternehmer* op.cit., p.73 ff.

20. The statutes were printed in *Deutsches Blatt.* 24.12.1893.

21. *Deutsches Blatt.* 13.2.1894. On the organizations, see the massive collections of police reports in *HH.St.Ar.PP. V299* (4 Bde.), *S4296* (5 Bde.) and *S7488.*

22. *HH.F.* 13.1.1894.

23. *HH.St.Ar.PP. S4293. Flugblatt Nr.2 Verein gegen Unwesen im Handel und Gewerbe* (n.d., ca. Feb. 1894).

24. On the identification of the Jew with immorality and the German with the best of morals, see the collection of documents, Boehlich (ed.), *Berliner Antisemitismusstreit* (1965) passim. See also Krausnick et al., *Anatomie des SS-Staates* (1965) esp. chap. 1.

25. See the massive collection in *HH.St.Ar.PP. S4293, V488,* and *S3618.*

26. See *HH.St.Ar.PP. V488*, Bd.1, for the police accounts of Werbeck's public verbal duel with *Bankhaus* Kirsch in the early part of 1892. See also *HH.St.Ar.PP. S4293, Amtsgericht Hamburg. Nr.134* (Juni 1911). Cf. *Der Weckruf!* for the summer months of 1910.

27. See the reports of the stormy meetings in *G.A.* 17.11.1901 and *HH.F.* 18.11.1901. *Echo.* 11.12.1901 was happy at Werbeck's difficulties. *HH.C.* 10.12.1901 and *HH.N.* 11.12.1901 both pointed out that the numbers opposed to Werbeck within the organization were small. Cf. *Mitteilungen. Verein gegen Unwesen im Handel und Gewerbe* (Mai 1902) for the somewhat mild reply of Werbeck.

28. See *Bay.Haupt.St.Ar.M.H.14617*, esp. the *Denkschrift* to the session of the *Bundesrat* of 1877-1888 (16.4.1878). Cf. the later discussion of the bill on *Wanderlager und Warenauktion* in *Bay. Kammer der Abgeordneten*, esp. 303 *Sitzung* 29.9.1897, p.1 ff; 324 *Sitzung* 5.10.1897, p.499 ff. On the second reading, see 333 *Sitzung* 18.11.1897, p.709 ff. Cf. *HH.St.Ar.376-16. Handwerks-kammer, XVIII.A.7*, esp. the petitions of the *Verein gegen Unwesen* (HH.) 16.11.1900 and 6.6.1901 and *Mitteilungen des Senats an die Bürgerschaft* 4.12.1901, p.667 ff.

29. *HH.St.Ar.PP. V488*, Bd.1.

30. *Mitteilungen. Verein gegen Unwesen im Handel und Gewerbe* (April 1903).

31. A list of the "successes" of the *Verein* for the year 1906 is given in *Verein gegen Unwesen im Handel und Gewerbe e.V. Ein Mahnwort.*

32. *HH.St.Ar.PP. S4293.*

33. For the numerous petitions sent to the federal and Prussian ministries on the question of civil servant consumer co-operatives, see *B.Dahlem. Pr. Justizministerium. Rep.84a, 3.Generalakten.3. Nr.10479, 10481.* See *HH.C.* 5.3.1895 on the meeting called by the *Verein gegen Unwesen;* for a copy of the *Flugblatt* for the meeting, see *HH.St.Ar.PP. V488*, Bd.1.

34. *HH.St.Ar.PP. V323*, Bd.1. Cf. *Bay.Haupt.St.Ar.M.H.Nr.11358* for a petition of 10.5.1890 of the *Verein Berliner Kaufleute der Kolonialwaren-Branche* which did demand the dissolution of all civil servant consumer co-operatives. One of the organizations sharing more radical views was an organization with which Werbeck was directly linked.

35. See *Mitteilungen. Verein gegen Unwesen im Handel und Gewerbe* (Nov.1903) where twelve factors allegedly behind the operation of the department stores were listed.

36. Ibid., (April 1903).

37. Ibid., (Juni 1903).

38. *HH.St.Ar.PP. S6750.* Cf. *Deutsches Blatt.* 2.12.1903 and *Deutsch-soziale Blätter.* 10.12.1903; *HH.F.* 29.11.1903 and *Mitteilungen. Verein gegen Unwesen im Handel und Gewerbe* (Dez.1903). Cf. the anti-Semitic views on department stores in *Aufklärungsschriften des Reichsverbandes der deutsch-sozialen Partei (HH).* (Dez.1906).

39. *Mitteilungen. Verein gegen Unwesen im Handel und Gewerbe* (Juli 1903).

40. Ibid., (Mai 1905).

41. Ibid.

42. See the work of Wehler, *Bismarck und Imperialismus*, op.cit., p.454 ff. and

Berghahn, *Der Tirpitz-Plan* (1971) p.15 ff.

43. For a summary of the activities of the *Verein*, see *HH.St.Ar.PP. V498*.
44. See the police reports in *HH.St.Ar.PP. V825*.
45. At the meeting of 1900, the *Deutscher Handelstag* favoured an increase in the fleet and expressed its hope that the *Reichstag* would vote the necessary funds. See *26. Vollversammlung des Deutschen Handelstags in Berlin am 6. und 7. April 1900. Steno Bericht.* (1900) p.7. See also Kehr, *Schlachtflottenbau und Parteipolitik* (1930) p.208 ff.
46. Winkler, *Mittelstand,* op.cit., p.61.
47. *HH.St.Ar.PP., V618; Flugblatt,* 4.12.1903.
48. *Deutsches Blatt.* 13.2.1894.
49. *HH.N.* 19.10.1909, *HH.F.* 19.10.1909, *Kolonial- und Warenhandel Ztg.* (HH.) 23.10.1909. For the economic reasons given for the opposition of the *Verband* to the SPD, see *HH.N.* 21.11.1909. According to the political police, only the moderate retailers were represented on the executive of the *Verband;* see *HH.St.Ar.PP. SA1442.*
50. *Deutsches Blatt.* 31.8.1901. See also *HH.St.Ar.376-16. Handwerkskammer. XVIII.H.7.*
51. *Israelitisches Familienblatt.* 4.6.1903. The Berlin newspaper, *Die Post.* 19.9.1903, reported on the activities of the *Verband.* Although the anti-SPD activities were praised, no mention was made of the *Verband* as an anti-Semitic organization.
52. *HH.St.Ar.PP. S11980.* See also *Volks Ztg.* 11.4.1904.
53. See the letter to the editor in *Israelitisches Familienblatt.* 27.4.1908. According to the anti-Semitic *Die Abwehr.* 15.9.1891, anti-Semites were thenceforth forbidden to hold public meetings in Hamburg; see *HH.St.Ar.PP. S2424,* Bd.1.
54. Hamel, op.cit., p.69 ff.
55. For extensive files collected by the police on Raab, see *HH.St.Ar.PP. S4302.*
56. For the police files on Henningsen, see *HH.St.Ar.PP. S7916.* See also Henningsen, *Beiträge zur Warenhaus-Frage!* (1906) p.16.
57. *Echo.* 27.9.1894. See the articles by Werbeck in *Die Abwehr.* 2.7.1893; 6.8.1893; 5.11.1893; in *Deutsches Blatt.* esp. 7.2.1894; 7.5.1902; 25.6.1902; 23.12.1904; 9.5.1908.
58. *HH.St.Ar.PP. V600.* See esp. *Polizei Schrift* on the statutes, the original meeting, and a breakdown of the social composition of the executive. The *Verein* was addressed on 23.10.1894 by Steigner and on 8.5.1894 by Raab. On Steigner (of the DHV), see *PP. S4493.*
59. *HH.St.Ar.PP. V827.*
60. *Echo.* 19.3.1904. *Echo* was not the only local newspaper to brand Henningsen anti-Semitic. See for example *HH.C.* 12.1.1904 where he is referred to as "the well-known anti-Semitic agitator". Henningsen was editor of the *Aufklärungsschriften des Reichsverbandes der deutschsozialen Partei* and very frequent contributor to *Deutsches Blatt.* He was politically active outside Hamburg for the anti-Semitic party, esp. in the period after 1900. See *HH.St.Ar.PP. S7916.* See his unfavourable review of the later attempt to found the *Kartell der schaffenden Stände* in *Deutsch-soziale Blätter.* 25.9.1912.

234 The Politics of Economic Despair

61. *Echo.* 2.7.1905. See also *HH.St.Ar.PP. V825* on the *Gewerbeschutzverein.*
62. *HH.St.Ar.PP. V618.* See the *Bürgerschaft* elections in *HH.F.* 13.2.1898 and HH.F. 30.6.1900. Cf. the *Reichstag* elections of 1903 reported in *Delicatessen und Kolonialwaren Anzeiger.* 2.5.1903. Cf. *HH.N.* 15.6.1903; *HH.N.* 25.9.1903; *G.A.* 26.9.1903. Cf. *HH.St.Ar.PP. V827, Flugblatt* (1903) of the *Vereinigte Schutzvereine zur Bekämpfung der Warenhäuser* Hamburg.
63. *Deutsches Blatt.* 27.8.1896.
64. *HH.St.Ar.PP. S5580, Polizei Schrift.* 7.6.1896. Cf. *HH.C.* 8.6.1896 and *HH.F.* 15.7.1896.
65. *Echo.* 13.2.1898.
66. *Der Elbwart.* 15.6.1911. Such sentiments were expressed by many retailers' organizations much earlier and the passage quoted sums up very widely held views.
67. *Dortmund WWAr. K2, Nr.1552.* The call for greater unity among retailers tended to come from regional and national organizations.
68. Although Wein, op.cit., does not mention this aspect of the retailers' activities, he would probably include them in his typology under what he terms *"die alten Standesvereine",* pp.36-37.
69. See Maresch, "Handelskammern" (1910) pp.295-301 and Wirminghaus, "Handelskammern" (1923) pp.69-82.
70. *Die Handelskammern, Ihre Organisation und Tätigkeit* (1906) p.13.
71. Ibid., pp.13-20.
72. *Stenographische Berichte über die Verhandlungen des (Preussischen Haus der Abgeordneten.* 59 *Sitzung* (24.4.1896) esp. p.1877, henceforth cited as *Preus.Abg.Haus, Steno. Berichte.*
73. Von Altrock, "Landwirtschaftskammern" (1923) pp.220-229.
74. For a copy of the letter, see Hohenlohe-Schillingsfürst, *Denkwürdigkeiten* (1931) pp.86-87.
75. Stegmann, "Wirtschaft und Politik nach Bismarcks Sturz" (1973) pp.161-184.
76. There exists a considerable controversy over the dating of this "reorientation". See, apart from the works of Stegmann, comments on some of the literature in Barkin, op.cit., pp.274-275, fn.1.
77. *Preus.Abg.Haus, Steno.Berichte.* 101 *Sitzung* (23.7.1896) pp.3290-3291. The *"Sammlung"* was designed to rally all the anti-SPD forces. Berghahn, "Kaiserreich in der Sackgasse" (1971) p.497 ff. suggests that there were two *"Sammlungen",* a *"kleine Sammlung"* (suggested by agrarians and heavy industry) and a *"grosse Sammlung"* (suggested by Tirpitz and Bülow).
78. *Preus.Abg.Haus. Steno. Berichte.* 59 *Sitzung* (24.4.1896) p.1867 ff.; 91 *Stizung* (25.5.1897) p.2933 ff.; 94 *Sitzung* (29.5.1897) p.3061 ff.
79. *Die Handelskammern. Ihre Organisation und Tätigkeit,* op.cit., p.15.
80. *Reichstag. Steno.Berichte (1895/1896): Anlageband.* Bd.6, Nr.713, esp. p.3796; Bd.7, Nr.819, p.4261 ff.; Bd.7, Nr.906, p.4497 ff. The original form of the proposal (Nr.713) was modified considerably by the great debates over the artisans' bill; the final form of the bill was far more explicit on the question of the exclusion of retailers (and, indeed, of "unorganized" artisans) from the *Handwerkskammern.* The debates in the *Reichstag* are far too long to be listed

here. See *Reichstag. Steno. Berichte (1895/1897). Sitzungen* Nr.201, 202, 203, 224, 225, 227, 228, 230, 232, 234. Cf. *NS.St.Ar.Des.122a.XXXIII.Nr.8. Vol.1.* and *Hannoversche Handwerker-Ztg.* 27.8.1898. See also *NS.St.Ar.Hann.80. Hann.II.Nr.1229.Vol.2, Jahresbericht der Gewerbekammer* (1890) esp. pp.29-37.

81. See *Protokoll über den 1. Deutschen Handwerks- und Gewerbekammertag Berlin, am 15.-17. Nov. 1900* inclusive to *Protokoll über den 16. Deutschen Handwerks- und Gewerbekammertag Mannheim am 27.-29. Juli 1914,* 16 Bde. Cf. *Jahresberichte der Hamburgischen Gewerbekammer* (1900 ff.) passim.

82. See Hampke, "Gewerbekammern" (1909) pp.993-1006 for a convenient summary.

83. Winkler, *Mittelstand,* op.cit., p.49.

84. See the great number of pertinent documents given in Rassow and Born, op.cit., p.344 ff. On the failure, see Born, *Staat und Sozialpolitik,* op.cit., p.233. Cf. Stegmann, *Erben Bismarcks,* op.cit., p.415 ff.

85. See *HH.HK.Ar.80.H.13* for copies of the petition.

86. The *Gewerbekammer* was further reorganized from 4.10.1907. See Hampke, op.cit., p.995 and *Die Handelskammern. Ihre Organisation und Tätigkeit,* op.cit., p.32. Cf. *NS.St.Ar.Hann.80.Hann.II.Nr.1051.* Bd.1, *Katechismus der Handwerks-Organisation auf Grund des Gesetzes vom 26. Juli 1897* (1898) passim.

87. See the massive work of Baasch, *Die Handelskammer zu Hamburg* (1915) passim. For a copy of the law of 23.1.1880, see *Dokumente zur Geschichte der HK Hamburg,* op.cit., pp.146-152.

88. *Die Handelskammern. Ihre Organisation und Tätigkeit,* op.cit., pp.34-35.

89. *De Koopman tho Bremen* (1951) passim.

90. See the long article in *Bremer Nachrichten.* 18.10.1900.

91. *HB.St.Ar.3. Senats Registratur.H.1. Nr.149. Bericht der Kommission wegen Detailhandel* (11.11.1900). See *HH.F.* 2.9.1896 for a report of a meeting of the chief movers behind the establishment of the *Detaillistenkammer* in Hamburg.

92. *HH.St.Ar.Detaillistenkammer.1.Organisation und Tätigkeit. XIII.B.1 (1) Errichtung einer HK für den Kleinhandel.* Cf. the even earlier call in Bremen (1893); see *Erster Jahresbericht der Kammer für Kleinhandel zu Bremen für 1907/1908* (1908) p.8.

93. See for example *HH.HK.Ar.102.1.A.1.* See also *Bericht des von der Bürgerschaft am 26.Mai 1897 niedergesetzten Ausschusses, Nr.37* (Juni 1898), esp. pp.38-42 for Raab's address. The secretary of the *Gewerbekammer* in Hamburg, much to the chagrin of Herr Werbeck, declared his opposition both to the idea of a special *Detaillistenkammer* and to a tax on department stores (*Umsatzsteuer*). See Werbeck's signed article in *HH.F.* 1.1.1899. Cf. *HH.N.* 22, 24, and 26.1.1899.

94. Cf. *HH.C.* 20.3.1895; *Echo.* 22.3.1895; *HH.F.* 23.3.1895; *Deutsches Blatt.* 23.3.1895.

95. *Mitteilungen. Verein gegen Unwesen im Handel und Gewerbe für Norddeutschland* (Dez. 1896); Cf. *HH.St.Ar.Detaillistenkammer.1.XIII. B.1. Flugblatt* (31.9.1895).

96. *HH.St.Ar.PP. V488,* Bd.1; *V618.*

97. See Bolland, op.cit., passim.

98. *HH.St.Ar.Senatsakten.C1.XI.Generalia,   Nr.2.Vol.44   Fasc.26   Inv.6. Drucksache für die Abt.1 des Senates. 5* (Juni 1899).

99. Ibid.

100. *HH.St.Ar.Detaillistenkammer.1.XIII.B.1* Bd.2 *Drucksache für die Senats-Sitzung.* 18.11.1899.

101. *HH.HK.Ar.102.1.A.1.* passim.

102. *HH. St. Ar. Senatsakten. C1. XI. Generalia. Nr. 2. Vol. 44 Fasc. 26 Inv. 6. Drucksache fur die Abt.1 des Senats. 5* (Juni 1899).

103. See esp. Raab's proposals in *2. Sitzung der Bürgerschaft zu Hamburg am 18. Jan.1899. Steno. Berichte,* pp-32-42. The establishment of the *Kammer* was linked with the introduction of taxes on department stores. See also the *3. Sitzung der Bürgerschaft (25.Jan.1899)* pp.49-61 and *4.Sitzung (1.Feb.1899)* pp.69-90. Raab remained the champion of the department store tax in the *Bürgerschaft.*

104. *Mitteilungen. Verein gegen Unwesen im Handel und Gewerbe* (August 1899). The statement was the basis *(Begründung)* of the law on the *Detaillisten-kammer* put forward by the *Central-Ausschuss Hamburg-Altonaer Detaillisten-Vereine.*

105. *HH.St.Ar.Detaillistenkammer.1.XIII.B.1.* Bd.1, passim.

106. See for example *HH.F.* 17.5.1899; *HH.N.* 17.5.1899. The increasingly favourable reaction to the idea of the *Detaillistenkammer* may be said to have been due, in part, to the very sober pamphlet of Dr.Mannhardt, *Zur Frage einer amtlichen Vertretung des Kleinhandelsstandes (Detaillistenkammer)* (1899) published at this time in Hamburg. Mannhardt made the not unimportant point that there was the need to keep the proposals for the establishment of the *Kammer* free from other "fantastic suggestions" (p.12).

107. Quoted in *HH.F.* 17.5.1899 and *HH.N.* 17.5.1899. The statement had been sent by the *Bürgerschaft* to the Senate on 10.5.1899.

108. *HH.St.Ar.Detaillistenkammer.1.XIII.B.1.* Bd.2. *Drucksache für die Senats-Sitzung.* 12.1.1900. See also *Drucksache.* 27.3.1900. See the letter of the *HK* 28.7.1900.

109. See *HH.C.* 21.3.1905.

110. *Auszug aus dem Protokolle des Senats.* 29.11.1901. This document also contains a good statement of many of the other differences between the proposals of the Senate and the wishes of the retailers' organizations.

111. *HB.St.Ar.6.12. Gewerbekammer.1.K.10.* and *HB.St.Ar.Senats Registratur. H.1.Nr.149.* It is evident that both the retailers and the authorities in Bremen deliberately followed the example of Hamburg.

112. Albrecht, *Das Hamburger Bürgerschaft-Wahlgesetz* (1906) p.9. Cf. *HH.HK.Ar.102.1.A.2* and *Handbuch für die Mitglieder der Detaillistenkammer* in Hamburg (1904) pp.7-8.

113. *HH.HK.Ar.102.1.A.1.Bericht* 26.5.1897, op.cit., p.2.

114. *Die Detaillistenkammer Hamburg,* op.cit., p.12.

115. See the reports in *HH.C.* 2 and 5.6.1904.

116. *HH.C.* 16.4.1904. Cf. *Neue HH.Ztg.* 24.5.1904; *HH.F.* 25.4.1904; *Deutsches Blatt.* 25.5.1904.

117. *Deutsches Blatt.* 1 and 29.7.1905. Cf. the earlier report in *Deutsches Blatt.* 24.8.1904. See also *HH.F.* 2.7.1905; *Echo.* 2.7.1905; *HH.C.* 28.7.1905; *Hammerbrooker Ztg.* 3.8.1905; *HH.N.* 18.8.1905. In 1908, Wernicke, the General Secretary of the *Verband der Waren- und Kaufhäuser,* pointed out that several department store owners were working in several committees of the *Detaillistenkammer* in Hamburg. The aim of Wernicke's book, printed in 1908, like that of so many of his books, was to demonstrate that the conflict of interests between department store owners and independent retailers was disappearing. See his *Wandlungen und neue Interessen-Organisationen* (1908) p.52 ff. Cf. his *Warenhaus, Industrie und Mittelstand* (1911) p.83 ff. In the *Deutsche Rabattsparvereins-Ztg.* Nr.11, (Nov.1907, p.98, Wernicke was branded "the famous apostle of the department stores".

118. *HH.St.Ar.PP. SA1442.* Cf. *HH.F.* 22.10.1911 and the report in the *Deutsche Nahrungs- und Genussmittel-Ztg.* 20.4.1912.

119. *HH.N.* 21.4.1914; *HH.C.* 22.4.1914; *HH.F.* 23.4.1914.

120. *Sitzung der Detaillistenkammer. Über die Vollversammlung der Detaillisten-kammer* (1907 ff.). The records appear to have survived only in *HH.HK.Ar.Abt.102.*

121. *National Ztg.* 11.4.1906. Cf. the later comments of *G.A.* 8.1.1909.

122. *Die Handelskammern. Ihre Organisation und Tätigkeit,* op.cit., pp.20-22.

123. See for example Born, *Staat und Sozialpolitik,* op.cit., pp.124-125.

124. *Mitteilungen des Zentral-Verbandes Deutscher Kaufleute und Gewerbetreibender* (Sept. and Okt. 1898) Nr.1 and 2. Cf. *Köln.Ztg.* 16.8.1898.

125. Note even *Mitteilungen. Verein gegen Unwesen im Handel und Gewerbe* (Aug.1899). See *HB.St.Ar.6.12 Gewerbekammer.1.K.10* for the report of the Gewerbekammer Dresden on their meeting of 24.4.1913.

126. *Preus.Abg.Haus, Steno. Berichte.* 21 *Sitzung.* (27.2.1907) p.1506 ff.

127. Ibid., 22 *Sitzung* (28.2.1907) p.1588.

128. Ibid., pp.1605-1606.

129. *Deutscher Handelstag. Bericht über die Sitzung der Kommission betr. Kleinhandel* (29.10.1907) p.4.

130. *34.Vollversammlung des Deutschen Handelstags in Berlin am 20. und 21. März 1908. Steno.Bericht.* (1908) p.32 ff.

131. *Preus.Abg.Haus, Steno.Berichte.* 46 *Sitzung.* (5.3.1909) p.3404 ff.

132. Ibid., p.3409.

133. Ibid., p.3415.

134. Ibid., p.3431.

135. Ibid., 36 *Sitzung.* (8.3.1910) pp.2862, 2922. See the comments of *Die Post.* 9.3.1910 and *Köln.Ztg.* 9.3.1910. For a copy of the "reminder", see *Dortmund WWAr. Repositur Nr.15a (HK* Dortmund). The wording very carefully avoided giving the impression that the *HK* were under any compulsion to create committees for retailing.

136. See for example Beutin, *IHK zu Hagen* (1956) p.104. Cf. *Dortmund WWAr. K3, Nr.262.* See the complaints of retailers in *Herforder Ztg.* 8.3.1902.

137. *Preus.Abg.Haus, Steno-Berichte.* 36 *Sitzung* (8.3.1910) pp.2917-2918.

Chapter 5

1. See Heberle, "Social Movements" (1968) pp.438-444 and his earlier *Social Movements* (1951) passim.

2. Cf. Wein, op.cit., p.38.

3. Krueger, *Die freien Interessenvertretungen* (1908) p.221 ff.

4. Cf. the impression given in Wein, op.cit., pp.39-42.

5. *HH.HK.Ar.80.J.39.1.* Note also *HH.N.* 23.2.1895.

6. For the petition of April 1895 from the Hesse and Waldeck organization, see *B.Dahlem. Pr.Justizministerium. Rep.84a, III Nr.10479.*

7. See for example *Handbuch wirtschaftlicher Verbände und Vereine* (1919) p.82 ff. and Krueger, *Freie Interessenvertretung,* op.cit., passim.

8. *Verzeichnis der bestehenden Vereine gewerblicher Unternehmer* , op.cit., p.30.

9. *NS.St.Ar.Hann.80.Hann.II.Nr.1287.*

10. *Verzeichnis der bestehenden Vereine gewerblicher Unternehmer,* op.cit., p.39.

11. *Deutsche Rundschau.* Nr.35., 1.9.1913.

12. Leopold, *Stellung wirtschaftlicher Interessenvertretung (Bayern)* (1915) p.1 ff. Cf. *Bay.Haupt.St.Ar.M.Wi. 2011* and *2016.*

13. The membership figures on the organizations sharing the common newspaper were given in *Der Detaillist* 1911. The figures were printed on the leading page of each issue.

14. Wein, op.cit., pp.40-41.

15. For a copy of the protest which was sent to the Prussian authorities, see *Dortmund WWAr. K2, Nr.212.* Bd.2.

16. For a report of a meeting of 23.3.1899 of the *Vereinigung von Handelskammern,* see ibid. Cf. the *Schrift* report of 22.3.1899 of the sitting of *HK.* Bochum.

17. *Mitteilungen des Zentral-Verbandes Deutscher Kaufleute.* Nr.1 and 2 (Sept. and Okt. 1898).

18. See for example *Der Detaillist* Nr.21, 22.3.1910 and Mr.49, 4.12.1910

19. *HH.St.Ar.PP. S13841.*

20. Wein, op.cit., pp.43-44.

21. *HH.St.Ar.PP. S5916* and *S7270.* Cf. Brauer, "Mittelstandspolitik" (1927) p.389 ff.

22. *Verzeichnis der bestehenden Vereine gewerblicher Unternehmer,* op.cit., p.39.

23. Ibid.

24. Centralverband deutscher Kaufleute, *Denkschrift über die Lage des Kleinhandels und Gewerbes* 30.11.1898.

25. See for example *Bericht über die Generalversammlung des Centralvorstandes Kaufmännischer Verbände und Vereine Deutschlands am 8.Sept.1899 zu Leipzig.* Cf. the *Berichte* for 1901 and 1902 in *HB.HK.C4.*

26. *Denkschrift über die wirtschaftliche Bedeutung des Einzelhandels und die Tätigkeit des Deutschen Zentralverbandes für Handel und Gewerbe (ca. 25.5.1916)* p.6.

27. See the petitions in *B.Dahlem. Pr.Justizministerium. Rep.84a. 3.General-*

akten.3. Nr.10479 and *10481,* esp. that of 30.5.1890.

28. For a copy of the petition of 5.1.1891, see *Dortmund WWAr. K2, Nr.1267.*

29. Ibid.

30. Cf. even the most radical of the demands made by the central organizations of the retailers. See *Deutsches Blatt.* 11.7.1903.

31. See for example Crüger, "Konsumvereine" (1923) pp.875-879.

32. *Reichstag. Steno.Berichte.* 45 *Sitzung* (23.8.1889) p.1045. For an account of his reasoning at the time, see Kulemann, *Politische Erinnerungen* (1911) esp. pp.92-97.

33. Cf. *Reichstag. Steno.Berichte.* 46 *Sitzung* (26.3.1899) p.1057 ff.; 52 *Sitzung* (4.4.1889) p.1288 ff. on the failure of the clause on legal penalties *(Strafbestimmungen).*

34. See *B.Dahlem. Pr.Justizministerium. Rep.84a. 3.Generalakten. 3.Nr.10479* esp. the petition of 10.11.1895 from the *Zentralverband* and the petition of 22.2.1896 from the *Central Ausschuss hiesiger kaufmännischer, gewerblicher und industrieller Vereine.*

35. *Reichstag. Steno.Berichte.* 8 *Sitzung* (14.12.1895) p.136 ff. and esp. pp.147-148.

36. Ibid., p.149.

37. Ibid.,86 *Sitzung* (7.5.1896) p.2195.

38. Vorstand des Zentralverbandes deutscher Kaufleute, *Denkschrift über die gegenwärtige Lage der Handels- und Gewerbetreibenden* (Dez.1896) esp. p.14.

39. For the petition of 5.1.1891, see *Dortmund WWAr. K2, Nr.1267.*

40. Ibid. Cf. *HB.HK.C4. Bericht über die Generalversammlung des Centralvorstandes,* 8.9.1889, op.cit.

41. See esp. *B.Dahlem. Pr. Justizministerium. Rep. 84a. 3. Generalakten. 3. Nr.10479* for the petition of May 1890.

42. *Denkschrift, 1896,* op.cit., p.16. Cf. *Generalanzeiger für Lübeck.* 30.12.1896.

43. This statement has been based on a study of the annual and general meetings of the *Zentralverband* between 1889 and 1914.

44. Cf. *Frank.Ztg.* 29.8.1912 and *HH.C.* 29.8.1912.

45. For the report by the president of the *Zentralverband* to the annual meeting of 12.8.1907, see *HH.C.* 14.8.1907.

46. *B.Dahlem. Pr.Ministerium des Auswärtigen. III.Nr.1123.* Cf. *Bay.Haupt. St.Ar.M.H.14490; 14491* contains an important petition of 26.12.1897 from the *Zentralverband. Dortmund WWAr. K2, Nr.1241* contains many petitions from various *HK.*

47. Cf. the petition of Nov.1895 from the *HK.* Magdeburg of Nov. 1895 in *B.Dahlem. Pr.Justizministerium. Rep.84a. 7. Wirtschaftsangelegenheiten. Nr.5791.* Cf. the petition of Jan.1896. and the opinions of the *M.N.N.* 21.3.1896 and *Köln.Ztg.* 16.4.1896. For the legal opinion see *Wirtschaftsangelegenheiten. Nr.5790.*

48. See the arguments in *Reichstag. Steno.Berichte.* 7 *Sitzung* (13.12.1895) p.107 ff. and 8 *Sitzung* (14.12.1895) p.131 ff.

49. See the petitions in *B.Dahlem. Pr.Justizministerium. Rep.84a. 7. Wirtschaftsangelegenheiten. Nr.5791-5793.*

50. See *St.Ar.Münster. Reg.Arnsberg.1.G.Nr.9* for a letter of 7.4.1900 from

240   The Politics of Economic Despair

the *Landrat* of the *Landkreis* Gelsenkirchen.

51. See for example the annual meeting of 1903 in *HH.F.* 6 and 7.8.1902.

52. The *Denkschrift* of 1896 op.cit. did not mention any single point in the law of 1896 which was considered to require revision.

53. *Bericht über die Conferenz der Delegierten kaufmännischer und gewerblicher Vereine Deutschlands am 3. und 4. Oct. 1898 in Leipzig* p.19.

54. Ibid., p.20.

55. Ibid. Wein, op.cit., p.46 makes only a short reference to this break and misses the significance of the rupture within the *Zentralverband.*

56. *Bericht über die Conferenz . . . am 3. und 4. Oct. in Leipzig,* op.cit., p.16.

57. See esp. *HH.F.,* 6.10.1898 and *Deutsches Blatt.* 8.10.1898.

58. *HH.F.* 6.10.1898.

59. *Bericht über die Conferenz . . . am 3. und 4. Oct. in Leipzig,* op.cit., p.19.

60. Ibid., p.43.

61. Ibid.

62. Ibid., pp.47-48.

63. Ibid., p.54 ff.

64. *HH.C.* 22.6.1899. Cf. *HH.F.* 21.6.1899 and *Mitteilungen. Verein gegen Unwesen im Handel und Gewerbe Hamburg* (Juli 1899).

65. Werbeck boasted of his influence in *Mitteilungen. Verein gegen Unwesen u.s.w.* (Juli 1899).

66. This primary aim is suggested by Wein, op.cit., p.46.

67. Deutscher Bund für Handel und Gewerbe (Leipzig). *Bericht über die erste Hauptversammlung 26. Juni 1900 zu Gera* p.9. Cf. *HH.F.,* 28.6.1900.

68. *Echo,* 1.7.1900.

69. See the press release in *HH.F.,* 26.6.1900.

70. See the report of the 28.7.1908 meeting in Bremen in *Deutsch-soziale Blätter.* 5.8.1908. For additional comment see *Bremische Ztg.* 26.7.1908 and *HH.F.,* 29.7.1908.

71. For a full account of the meetings in 1901, see *Mitteilungen. Verein gegen Unwesen im Handel und Gewerbe Hamburg* (Juli and Aug. 1901) Cf.*HH.F.* 25.6.1901 and *Neue HH.Ztg.* 25.6.1901.

72. *G.A.,* 13.7.1903.

73. *Deutsches Blatt* 11.7.1903.

74. See Glagau, "Liberale Freiheiten" in *Des Reiches Noth,* op.cit., p.168 ff.; Stoecker, *Christlich-Sozial* (1890) pp.31-32; Lagarde, op.cit., pp.246, 311 ff.; Wahrmund, *Gesetz des Nomadtums* (1887) p.121 ff.; Dühring, *Judenfrage* (1881) p. 11 ff., 103 ff.

75. See esp. Schoenbaum, *Hitler's Social Revolution* (1967) p.66 ff.

76. The *Kaufmannsgerichte* came into existence on 1.1.1905. For details, see Krahmer, "Kaufmannsgerichte" (1910) pp.816-822.

77. Werbeck claimed that he had suggested the radical first point. See *Mitteilungen. Verein gegen Unwesen im Handel und Gewerbe Hamburg* (Dez. 1903).

78. *Deutsches Blatt* 11.7.1903.

79. Ibid.

80. *Köln.Ztg.,* 12.2.1904.

81. *Bericht über die Conferenz . . . am 3. und 4. Oct. in Leipzig,* op.cit., p.56.

82. *Mitteilung des Zentralverbandes deutscher Kaufleute* Nr.3, Nov.1899. Cf. *HH.St.Ar. 376-16 Handwerkskammer VIII.A.9.*

83. For a full report of the meeting see *HH.N.* 22.8.1901. For the meetings of 1902, see *HH.F.* 6 and 7.8.1902; for those of 1903, see *HH.N.* 5.8.1903 and *HH.C.* 6.8.1903; for those of 1904, see *HH.F.* 24.8.1904 and *Neue HH.Ztg.* 24.8.1904; for those of 1905, see *B.Tagebl.* 16.8.1905 and *Norddeut.A.Ztg.* 17.8.1905; for those of 1906, *HH.F., HH.N., HH.C.* 8.8.1906.

84. *HH.C.* 14.8.1907.

85. *Deutsches Blatt.* 24.8.1907.

86. *Dortmund WWAr. K2, Nr.265.* "Survey, 24.6.1907" of *HK* Bochum.

87. The great majority of court cases brought before the *Kaufmannsgerichte* involved action of the employee against the employer. See *Das Kaufmannsgericht* (1905 ff.) passim. Cf. *B.Dahlem. Pr.Justizministerium. Rep.84a. Bd.5. 7. Wirtschaftsangelegenheiten. Nr.11450-11453; Rep.84a.Bd.3 Generalakten.3. Nr.898-904* and *922.*

88. On the evolution of the policy of the DHV, see esp. *Neunter Deutsche Handlungsgehilfentag. Verhandlungsschrift* (1905) pp.41-59 and *Die Konkurrenzklausal* (1911) passim.

89. *Deutsch-soziale Blätter.* 5.8.1908. Cf. *Bremische Ztg.* 26.7.1908 and *HH.F.* 29.7.1908.

90. *Der Mittelstand. Nachrichten* Nr.1 (1906).

91. *Frank.Ztg.* 9.11.1909 and *B.N.Nach.* 10.11.1909.

92. *Deutsche Rabattsparvereins-Ztg.* Nr.9 (Sept. 1911) pp.137-138.

93. For the resolution see *B.N.Nach.* 16.8.1911. Cf. 15.8.1911.

94. Kocka, "Mittelstand", op.cit., p.104. Cf. his *Unternehmensverwaltung und Angestelltenschaft*, op.cit., p.517. See *Der Kampf um die Reichsversicherungs-Ordnung* (1911) passim.

95. *Frank.Ztg.* 29.8.1912. Such a demand was usually associated with the artisans.

96. *B.N.Nach.* 29 and 30.10.1912. See also *Frank.Ztg.* 29.10.1912. Cf. *Mitteilungen der Centralvereinigung deutscher Vereine für Handel und Gewerbe Berlin* 15.9.1911 "The present agitation against the retailers."

97. See esp. *Deutsche Rundschau.* Nr.35, 1.9.1913 and the resolution of the 26th annual meeting on unity with the *Zentralvereinigung deutscher Vereine für Handel und Gewerbe.* Cf. *Die Post.* 4 and 5.11.1913. Cf. *Frank.Ztg.* 5.11.1913.

98. *Bericht über die Conferenz . . . am 3. und 4. Oct. in Leipzig*, op.cit., pp.19-20.

99. *Verzeichnis der bestehenden Vereine gewerblicher Unternehmer*, op.cit., p.59.

100. *HH.St.Ar.PP. S13841.*

101. *HH.C.* 7.11.1905.

102. This view is held by Wein, op.cit., pp.48-49, who suggests that the Prussian organization represented the first step in the split of the *Zentralverband* Leipzig.

103. *Deutsches Blatt.* 24.8.1907.

104. Kulemann, *Genossenschaftsbewegung*, op.cit., p.128.

105. Wein, op.cit., pp.48-49.

106. W.Rubens, *Der Kampf des Spezialgeschäftes gegen das Warenhaus (mit*

besonderer Berücksichtigung der Zeit von 1918 bis 1929} Dissertation-Köln, 1929 p.23, quoted in ibid. p.49. Note should be taken of the dates covered by Ruben's study.

107. *HH.C.* 7.11.1905. Cf. the report of the 1910 meeting of the Prussian organization in *Frank.Ztg.* 26.10.1910. Wein, op.cit., p.49, claims that Lissauer wished to redirect the policy orientation of the *Zentralverband.*

108. *Volks Ztg.* 26.2.1903 and 3.3.1903.

109. *Deutsches Blatt.* 28.2.1903.

110. *Der Bund der Kaufleute. Seine Grundgedanken und seine Ziele* (1903) p.30; cf. pp.21-26.

111. Ibid., p.33.

112. *G.A.* 13.3.1903 and *HH.F.* 7.4.1903.

113. Cf. Stieda "Mittelstandsbewegung" (1905) p.9.

114. Lederer, "Sozialpolitische Chronik.Mittelstandsbewegung" (1910) p.980. See *Deutsche Mittelstands-Ztg.* Nr.45. Beiblatt. 6.11.1910 for a complete list of organizations present.

115. *Rundschau für Handel und Gewerbe* (Nov.1911). Cf. *Der Detaillist.* Nr.5, Jan.1911.

116. Leopold, op.cit., p.5.

117. Cf. Janssen, *Was der Detaillistenstand selbst tun muss!* (1911) pp.7-8. Janssen was chief executive of the *Verein zum Schutz für Handel und Gewerbe Barmen.*

Chapter 6

1. See for example Biermer, "Mittelstandsbewegung" (1910) pp.734-762. In 1905 Biermer had considered that the *Mittelstandsbewegung* represented "a serious danger to our present society": see his *Sammlung* (1905) p.222. Cf. the other negative reviews of the *Mittelstandsbewegung* in Pesl, "Mittelstandsfragen" (1926) pp.70-119; Brauer, op.cit., p.368 ff.; Wernicke, *Kapitalismus und Mittelstandspolitik* op.cit., p.375 ff.; Müffelmann, op.cit., p.15 ff.

2. Cf. Winkler, *Mittelstand,* op.cit., p.46 ff.

3. Stegmann, *Erben Bismarcks,* op.cit., p.40.

4. Müffelmann, op.cit., p.97. Cf. Puhle, "Parlament", op.cit., p.345 and Sternberger, "Staat der Gegenwart" (1952/1953) p.204 ff.

5. See for example Müffelmann, op.cit., p.93 ff. and esp. Bürger, *Die politische Mittelstandsbewegung* (1912) passim. A number of recent works have relied extensively upon Bürger's study. Bürger, who was director of the *Verein zur Abwehr des Antisemitismus,* opposed the "political *Mittelstandsbewegung"* chiefly because of the anti-Semitism within that movement. Cf. his *Antisemiten Spiegel* (1911) and *Die Agrardemagogie* (1911).

6. *Vorwärts.* 17.4.1895. At the meeting of 16 April 1895, the decision was taken to vote for the candidates of the BdL in "elections".

7. *Vorwärts.* 18.4.1895.

8. See *Bay.Haupt.St.Ar.M.H.Nr.14709. Protokoll über die Verhandlung des VIII. Allgemeinen deutschen Handwerkertages und des X.Delegiertentages des Allgemeinen deutschen Handwerkerbundes zu Halle. 21.-24.April 1895* (1895) p.137 ff. A representative of the *Deutsch-Soziale Partei* (Landemann-Berlin) was

particularly in favour of a specific *Mittelstandspartei* (pp.143-144).

9. See *HH.St.Ar.PP. S11980*. Cf. Biermer, "Mittelstandsbewegung" op.cit., p.739.

10. *Vorwärts*. 14.6.1895.

11. *Deutsches Blatt*. 10.6.1895.

12. Müffelmann, op.cit., p.97.

13. Winkler, *Mittelstand*, op.cit., pp.51, 216.

14. Wein, op.cit., p.84.

15. *Vorwärts*. 18.4.1895.

16. Cf. the account in *Echo*. 14.9.1897 on a small organization in Charlottenburg, the *Volkswohlstandspartei*. Cf. the non-Socialist accounts in *HH.C*. 12.9.1897 and *National Ztg*. 11.8.1897.

17. For the SPD interpretation of anti-Semitism, see esp. Bebel's speech to the Berlin *Parteitag* of 1892 in *Handbuch der sozialdemokratischen Parteitage*. Schröder (ed.) (1910) pp.35-36.

18. See the Erfurt program in Kautsky, *Texte* (1968) p.117. Kautsky spoke of the "natural necessity" of the "decline". Cf. the letter of Bernstein to Auer in 1899 quoted in Gay, op.cit., pp.213-214. "Above all, I fight against the conception that there exists an automatic, self-executing process ... of liquidation of those middle classes and professional groups." Cf. Marx's analysis in Marx-Engels, "Manifest der Kommunistischen Partei" in their *Werke* Bd.4 (1972) p.472.

19. Salomon, *Die deutschen Parteiprogramme* 2 H. (1907) p.73.

20. See esp. *Konservatives Handbuch* (1892-1911) and *Konservativer Kalender* (1913) esp. pp.49-63, 93-94; cf. Stillich, *Die politischen Parteien* Bd.1 (1908) p.155 ff.

21. Stegmann, *Erben Bismarcks*, op.cit., p.38. The initial program of the BdL did not mention the *Mittelstand*. See Salomon, op.cit., p.76 ff.

22. *HH.St.Ar.PP. S4961;* the proclamation of 12.10.1903 was printed in *HH.N*. 13.10.1903. Cf. the report in *Echo*. 16.10.1903.

23. *Echo*. 19.10.1903 reported that the NL newspaper, the *Hannoversche Courier*, opposed the foundation of the new organization because such an organization, far from helping to realize the aims of the *Mittelstand* "would only lead to a further fragmentation".

24. Müffelmann, op.cit., p.97.

25. *DZA 1, Reichsamt des Innern, 6300 and 6311; Reichskanzlei, Nr.2255*. See *Sitzungs-Bericht über die 1. Generalversammlung der DMV* (1904) p.VII.

26. Cf. Bürger, *Mittelstandsbewegung*, op.cit., p.8 and Stegmann, *Erben Bismarcks*, op.cit., p.44.

27. See the full account in *Köln.Ztg*. 29.11.1904.

28. The *Zentralausschuss der vereinigten Innungsverbände Deutschlands* also issued a call for the foundation of a *Mittelstandspartei* at the Magdeburg meeting. See *HH.F*. 16.8.1904. Cf. *Köln.Ztg*. 29.11.1904; *HH.F*. 29.11.1904; *G.A*. 29.11.1904.

29. *Sitzungs-Bericht über die 1. Generalversammlung der DMV*, op.cit., p.VII. Cf. *Echo*. 8 and 9.9.1904.

30. *Köln.Ztg*. 29.11.1904. Cf. *HH.N*. 29.11.1904; for the Socialist critique, see *Vorwärts*. 28.11.1904.

31. See *Sitzungs-Bericht über die 1. Generalversammlung der DMV*, op.cit.,

244   The Politics of Economic Despair

p.67 ff. for a complete list.

  32. Ibid., p.24.

  33. Ibid., p.45.

  34. Ibid., p.49.

  35. See the impression conveyed in the *Köln.Ztg.* 29.11.1904. For the full program, see *HH.C.* 30.11.1904. Cf. the comments in *HH.Neueste Nachrichten.* 30.11.1904. *Echo.* 1.12.1904 characterized the program as "a motley mixture of totally contradictory demands". The *G.A.* 29.11.1904 branded the DMV "a new establishment of conservatives and anti-Semites". The *Kölnische Volkszeitung.* 29.11.1904 claimed that "because the whole 'movement' is contaminated by its association with reactionary forces, it will damage rather than help the *Mittelstand*". Cf. *Vorwärts.* 28.11.1904.

  36. *HH.St.Ar.PP. S11980; Volks.Ztg.* 11.4.1904; *B.N.Nach.* 27.2.1911.

  37. *B.Dahlem. Pr.Justizministerium. Rep.84a.Bd.5. Wirtschaftsangelegenheiten. Nr.883-884.* Cf. *Rep.84a.5.Finanzen.Nr.9020-9021.*

  38. *Sitzungs-Bericht über die 2. Generalversammlung der DMV* (1905) p.11.

  39. On the BdL, see *HH.St.Ar.PP. S5915.* Cf. *Korrespondenz des Bundes der Landwirte.* Nr.30, 19.4.1905 p.95.

  40. *Vorwärts.* 15.7.1905. The newspaper published the list of the 23 electoral districts in which the DMV was to support the BdL.

  41. Cf. *HH.C.* 25.10.1905 and Bürger, *Mittelstandsbewegung,* op.cit., p.12.

  42. On the house owners' organizations, see Krueger, *Freie Interessenvertretung,* op.cit., p.232 ff. Cf. *Bay.Haupt.St.Ar.M.Inn.Nr.73534, 73535.* Although there has been little written on the house owners' organizations, there is a consensus on their substantial political power and influence.

  43. *Das Grundeigentum,* quoted in full in *HH.Neueste Nachrichten.* 31.12.1905.

  44. Cf. *Vorwärts.* 19.1.1906 and *HH.C.* 28.1.1906. According to Bürger, *Mittelstandsbewegung,* op.cit., p.13, the party circular of 12.1.1906 stated that Küster had personally born the costs of keeping the DMV in operation and that he was no longer willing or able to continue to support the organization financially.

  45. *M.N.N.* 8.9.1906; *Deutsches Volksblatt.* 9.9.1906; *Münchener Ztg.* 10.9.1906. *St.Ar.München. Polizeidirektion München. AR 550.* Cf. *Polizei Schrift* 8.10.1906 and 2.7.1910.

  46. *HH.N.* 24.8.1906 and *Echo.* 25.8.1906. Cf. *Korrespondenz des Bundes der Landwirte.* Nr.58, 4.10.1906, pp.207-208. The aims of the new organization were described as "exclusively economic".

  47. See the brief account in Wernicke, *Kapitalismus und Mittelstandspolitik,* op.cit., p.383.

  48. On the "scandal", see Bürger, *Mittelstandsbewegung,* op.cit., pp.13-15.

  49. See *HH.St.Ar.PP. S14519* and *HH.C.* 4.10.1906; *HH.F.* 8.10.1906.

  50. See the electoral circular in *HH.C.* 31.12.1906. Cf. *Berliner Volkszeitung.* 12.1.1907 where the DMV was described as a disguise for the *Deutsch-Konservative Partei.* Stöcker's earlier "Berlin movement" has been described in similar terms. See Frank, *Hofprediger Adolf Stoecker* (1935) p.79 ff.

  51. Bürger, *Mittelstandsbewegung,* op.cit., pp.16-17. Puhle, *Agrarische Interessenpolitik,* op.cit., p.165 ff. gives a detailed examination of the electoral activities of the BdL.

52. *Berliner Volkszeitung.* 12.1.1907.

53. The full resolution was printed in *HH.C.* 10.9.1907. Cf. *Echo.* 11.9.1907.

54. Bürger, *Mittelstandsbewegung,* op.cit., p.21.

55. *Israelistisches Familienblatt.* 27.4.1908.

56. See the official report in *B.Tagebl.* 20.9.1908 and *B.N.Nach.* 21.9.1908. The *Rheinisch-Westfälischer Landesverband* of the DMV was founded at the end of 1906.

57. *Westdeutsche Mittelstands-Ztg.* Nr.6, 6.1.1909, pp.1-2.

58. *Frank.Ztg.* 13.12.1908.

59. *Westdeutsche Mittelstands-Ztg.* Nr.8, 27.1.1908, p.1.

60. On the *Deutsche Vereinigung,* see *Bürgerliche Parteien* Bd.1, (1968) p.629 ff. The organization was formally constituted on 15 Jan. 1908 in Cologne. *See HH.St.Ar.PP. S15829. Was will die Deutsche Vereinigung?* (1908) p.15. The aims of the organization included "the preservation of a lively and productive *Mittelstand"* and "the struggle against Social Democracy". Cf. *Köln.Ztg.* 16.1.1908.

61. See Wawrzinek, op.cit., p.56 ff. on Fritsch and his early association with the anti-Semitic *Deutsche Reformpartei* and the Chemnitz *Verein zur Wahrung der Interessen Handels- und Gewerbetreibender.* Cf. Phelps, "Theodor Fritsch und der Antisemitismus" (1961) p.442 ff.

62. Fritsch's speech to the Nov. meeting was published as a pamphlet, *Mittelstand, Kapital-Herrschaft, Monarchie* (1917); see pp. 18, 21, 23.

63. *Bericht über den deutsch-sozialen (antisemitischen) Parteitag zu Leipzig am 18. und 19. Mai 1891* (1891) p.13.

64. *DZA 1, Reichsamt des Innern, 6305. Denkschrift der Mittelstands-Vereinigung* (1907) p.23. See the review in Wernicke, *Kapitalismus und Mittelstandspolitik,* op.cit., p.973 ff.

65. *DZA 1, Reichsamt des Innern, 6305. Nachrichten des Landes-Verbandes Thüringen der DMV.* Nr.3 (Okt. 1907).

66. *B.Tagebl.* 20.9.1908. Cf. *Der Fortschritt.* Nr.2 (Nov. 1908) pp.27-29; *Merkuria.* Nr.50, 13.12.1908. pp.400-401; Wernicke, *Preussisches Warenhaussteuergesetz,* op.cit., p.182.

67. The proposals were introduced into the *Reichstag* by the government only on 3.11.1908. For Hahn' comments at the 16th annual meeting of the BdL, see the full report in *Korrespondenz des Bundes der Landwirte.* Nr.14, 22.2.1909, pp.55-72. Cf. Witt, *Finanzpolitik* (1970) pp.256-259.

68. Bürger, *Mittelstandsbewegung* op.cit., p.23. Rahardt eventually left the *Deutsch-Konservative Partei* to join the *Freikonservative Fraktion* in the Prussian *Landtag.* See *Der Elbwart.* Nr.18, 15.9.1910, p.212 and *Deutsch Mittelstands-Ztg.* Nr.10, 5.3.1911.

69. *Der Fortschritt.* Nr.8 (Mai 1909) pp.202-207. Cf. *Deutsche Rabatts-parvereins-Ztg.* Nr.5 (Mai 1909) p.43.

70. Cf. *Die Sozialpolitik der deutschen Zentrumspartei* (1903) p.89 ff. and (1910) p.97 ff. See also *Bundesarchiv. Z.Sg.1.108. Deutsche Zentrumspartei. Tätigkeitsberichte der Reichstagsfraktion* (1903-1904) p.96 ff.; (1904-1905) pp.161-169; (1907) pp.68-69; (1912) pp.154-157. Cf. Luebbering, *Was können wir im Volksverein tun zur Hebung des Kleinhandels* (1912) and Bachem,

Vorgeschichte, Geschichte und Politik der deutschen Zentrumspartei (Bd.9. 1932) p.206 ff.

71. See for example *Korrespondenz des Bundes der Landwirte.* Nr.36, 27.5.1909, pp.153-154. Cf. *Konservative Partei und die Reichsfinanzreform 1909* (1909) passim.

72. On the *Hansa-Bund,* see *Bürgerliche Parteien,* Bd.2 (1970) pp.201-215. Cf. the reports in *Frank.Ztg.* 14.6.1909; *HH.C.* 14.6.1909; *B.Tagebl.* 15.6.1909; *Neue HH.Ztg.* 15.6.1909. The latter commented: "In the first instance, the new *Bund* will see to establish itself as a counterweight to the BdL." Cf. *Schulthess' Europäischer Geschichtskalender. Neue Folge.* 1909 (1910) pp.198-201.

73. See the circular of 26.6.1909 in *HH.HK.Ar.V145,* Bd.1; cf. *HH.St.Ar.PP. S17000* and *V976.*

74. Cf. *Stenographischer Bericht über die Verhandlung am 12.6.1909 im Circus Schumann in Berlin betr. die Reichsfinanzreform und Gründung des Hansabundes* (1909) passim. A full list can be found in Stegmann, *Erben Bismarcks,* op.cit., p.179. Cf. *DZA 1, Reichskanzlei 1422-1424* for a list of retailers' organizations.

75. *Wirtschafts-Politisches Handbuch des Hansa-Bundes* (1910) pp.72-74.

76. *DZA 1, Reichskanzlei 1422-1424.* Cf. the review of Brandt, "Der Hansabund" (1909) pp.348-361.

77. See the anti-Semitic attack on both the *Hansa-Bund* and the DMV in *Deutsch-soziale Blätter.* 16 and 19.6.1909. Cf. *Westdeutsche Mittelstands-Ztg.* Nr.49, 26.6.1909, p.1 and Nr.36, 5.9.1909, p.7.[7] See also *Deutsche Rabattspar-vereins-Ztg.* Nr.7 (Juli 1909) p.59. and *Mitteilungen vom Hansa-Bund für Gewerbe, Handel und Industrie.* Nr.14, 9.11.1909.

78. See esp. Seifert's views on the *Hansa-Bund* in *Korrespondenz des Bundes der Landwirte.* Nr.42, 25.6.1909, pp.179-180. For the similar negative response of Fritsch, see *Neue Preussische Ztg.* 19.6.1909.

79. *Der Fortschritt.* Nr.10 (Juli 1909) p.266. Cf. *Deutsch-soziale Blätter.* 30.6.1909.

80. Cf. *B.N.Nach.* 12.9.1909; *HH.C.* 15.9.1909; *HH.N.* 2.10.1909; *G.A.* 6.10.1909.

81. *Korrespondenz des Bundes der Landwirte.* Nr.57, 23.9.1909 pp.235-236.

82. *Der Fortschritt.* Nr.2 (Nov. 1909) p.39. Cf. *Echo.* 4.11.1909.

83. Bürger, *Mittelstandsbewegung,* op.cit., p.41. Without denying or confirming Bürger's allegations (for which he provides no proof), it should be remembered that Bürger was the director of the *Liga zur Abwehr des Antisemitismus.* The chief tactic of this organization was to publicly discredit anti-Semitism and anti-Semites. See Schorsch, *Jewish Reactions to German Anti-Semitism* (1972) p.79 ff.

84. *Der Fortschritt.* Nr.3 (Dez. 1909) pp.68-71.

85. *B.N.Nach.* 29.11.1909. Eschenburg, *Das Kaiserreich* (1929) p.264 states that the *"Mittelstandsvereinigung"* left the *Hansa-Bund* in November 1909.

86. Stegmann, *Erben Bismarcks,* op.cit., p.182. Cf. the contrary opinions of Winkler, *Mittelstand,* op.cit., p.55; Bürger, *Mittelstandsbewegung,* op.cit., pp.30-31. See *Deutsche Mittelstands-Ztg.* Nr.35,28.8.1910.

87. *Mittelstandskongress des Hansa-Bundes* (1911) p.25 ff. Cf. Wernicke,

"Mittelstandskongress" (1911) pp.642-643 and *Mitteilungen vom Hansa-Bund*. Nr.36, 13.7.1910.

88. Eschenburg, op.cit., p.264.

89. Wein, op.cit., p.129. Cf. the views of F.Fischer, op.cit., p.60.

90. Cf. Heuss, *Friedrich Naumann* (1968) p.290 ff. and Schorske, *German Social Democracy* (1972) pp.157-165.

91. *Westdeutsche Mittelstands-Ztg.* Nr.71, 27.11.1909.

92. *Der Fortschritt.* Nr.5 (Feb. 1910) pp.137-138.

93. See ibid. for a complete list of the members of the executive.

94. Lederer, "Sozialpolitische Chronik. Mittelstandsbewegung" (1910) p.677. Lederer maintained that the *Mittelstandsbund* was created at the end of 1909.

95. *Der Fortschritt.* Nr.5 (Feb. 1910) pp.137-138.

96. *Bericht über den 2. Mittelstandskursus des Deutschen Mittelstandsbundes für Handel und Gewerbe (Sitz Düsseldorf) zu Köln, am 12.- 16. Sept. 1910* (1911) p.62 ff. Cf. *Frank.Ztg.* 20.9.1910.

97. Eschenburg, op.cit., p.264. On the departure of the CDI, see Stegmann, *Erben Bismarcks*, op.cit. pp.239-243. Cf. *Dortmund WWAr. K2, Nr.548*, circular of 8.7.1911.

98. *Der Fortschritt.* Nr.4 (Jan. 1911) pp.109-110.

99. *Hammer. Blätter für deutschen Sinn.* Nr.224, 15.10.1911: "Der organische Staats-Gedanke und der Mittelstand."

100. *Der Fortschritt.* Nr.4 (Jan. 1911) pp.109-110. The new *Mittelstand* organization would be limited to the representation of retailers, artisans, and house owners. See Nr.5 (Feb.1911) pp.139-141 and Nr.6 (März 1911) pp.170-171.

101. *B.N.Nach.* 5.4.1911. Cf. the response of the DMV in *Deutsche Mittelstands-Ztg.* Nr.17, 23.4.1911. which suggested that the time was "not yet ripe" for such an organization. See also *B.N.Nach.* 21.5.1911.

102. See their ideas on the problems confronting the *Mittelstand* in *Der Fortschritt.* Nr.9 (Juni 1911) pp.264-267.

103. *Nordwestdeutsche Handwerks-Ztg.* Nr.21. 27.5.1911, p.104. Cf. *Norddeut. A.Ztg.* 20.6.1911.

104. *Vorwärts.* 3.7.1911.

105. *Neue Preussische Ztg.* 19.7.1911. Cf. *B.N.Nach.* 19.7.1911 and *Nordwestdeutsche Handwerks-Ztg.* Nr.31, 16.9.1911, p.150.

106. *Frank.Ztg.* 22.7.1911.

107. *Neue Preussische Ztg.* 19.7.1911.

108. *Agrarisches Handbuch* (1911) pp.739-748. Cf. the report of the 18th annual meeting of the BdL in *Korrespondenz des Bundes der Landwirte.* Nr.13, 20.2.1911, p.44 ff.

109. Cf. Wilmanns, op.cit., p.58 ff.; Ahlwardt, *Der Verzweiflungskampf* (1890) p.198 ff.; Dr.Capistrano (Böckel), *Die europäische Judengefahr* (1886) p.3. See the remarks attributed to Böckel in Curtius, *Der politische Antisemitismus* (1911) p.98.

110. *Bericht über den Ersten Reichsdeutschen Mittelstandstag abgehalten zu Dresden vom 23.-25. Sept. 1911,* p.25.

111. Ibid., p.13.

112. For a full list of the politicians present, see Stegmann, *Erben Bismarcks*,

op.cit., p.252. Cf. *Neue Preussische Ztg.* 23.9.1911.

113. *Bericht über den 1. Reichsdeutschen Mittelstandstag,* op.cit., p.38.

114. *Frank.Ztg.* 24.9.1911. The newspaper reported Höhne's remark of 23.9.1911. Höhne was quoted as stating that "the employees' organizations ought not to be permitted to become members. We do not want them; we want only the independent *Mittelstand.* The employee organizations are our direct enemies."

115. For a more positive response to the creation of the RDMV, see *Nordwestdeutsche Handwerks-Ztg.* Nr.31, 12.8.1911, p.150 and **Nr.38,** 30.9.1911, pp.185-186.

116. Wiedermann, *Der Reichsdeutsche Mittelstands-Verband!* (1913) p.27 ff. Cf. Bürger, *Mittelstandsbewegung,* op.cit., p.47. See the similar views of Rahardt of the DMV in *Deutsche Mittelstands-Ztg.* Nr.17, 23.4.1911 and Nr.42, 15.19.1911.

117. Cf. *Frank.Ztg.* 26.9.1911; *B.N.Nach.* 25.9.1911; *National Ztg.* 29.9.1911.

118. *Frank.Ztg.* 29.9.1911.

119. *Konsumgenossenschaft Rundschau* (HH) 30.9.1911 and *National Ztg.* 27.9.1911.

120. Cf. *B.N.Nach.* 10.10.1911; *Vossische Ztg.* 11.10.1911; *Frank.Ztg.* 14.10.1911.

121. Bürger, *Mittelstandsbewegung,* op.cit., p.48.

122. *DZA 1, Reichsamt des Innern. 6306.* "secret" letter to *Ministerial-Direktor* Heink 30.11.1911.

123. A meeting was later held between the RDMV and the Federal Ministry of the Interior to discuss the problems of the *Mittelstand.* See *B.N.Nach.* 25.4.1912.

124. Cf. *HH.N.* 12.12.1911 and *B.N.Nach.* 13.12.1911.

125. *Westdeutsche Mittelstands-Ztg.* Nr.2, 13.1.1912 and *B.N.Nach.* 8.1.1912.

126. Cf. Bayer, *Liberale Kleinhandelspolitik* (1912) p.50 ff. and *Politisches A.B.C.-Buch* (1892, 1893, 1898, 1903). See also *Bundesarchiv. Z.Sg.1.46. Der Siebente Parteitag der Freisinnigen Volks-Partei. 1907* (1909) pp.89-95.

127. *Westdeutsche Mittelstands-Ztg.* Nr.2, 13.1.1912.

128. *Deutsche Mittelstands-Ztg.* Nr.45, 5.11.1911.

129. *Politisches Handbuch für Nationalliberale Wähler* (1897) had no section covering the *Mittelstand.*

130. *Politisches Handbuch der Nationalliberalen Partei* (1907) pp.563-658, 753-765.

131. *Zwölfter allgemeiner Vertretertag der NL Partei am 1. und 2. Oktober 1910* (1910) p.89. Cf. *HH.St.Ar.PP. V982,* Bd.4 and *Bundesarchiv. Z.Sg.1.74.*

132. *Zwölfter Nationalliberaler Parteitag,* op.cit., p.89.

133. Ibid., pp.99-107. Cf. *Taschenbuch für Nationalliberale Wähler* (1911) pp.136-137; *HH.St.Ar.PP. S5809,* Bd.1; *National Ztg.* 25.10.1911.

134. Ecker, *Der Mittelstand* (1914) pp.3, 12.

135. See esp. the analysis in Schorske, op.cit., p.233; cf. *Vorwärts.* 26.1.1912.

136. Cf. Schwarz, *MdR* (1965) p.807 and Treue, *Parteiprogramme* (1961) p.389. See the comments in *Norddeut.A.Ztg.* 10.4.1912.

137. The *Wirtschaftliche Vereinigung* had direct connections with the RDMV, through Walter Graef, for example. See *HH.St.Ar.PP. S11890.* Cf. *Deutschsoziale Blätter.* 2.1.1907.

138. *Der Fortschritt.* Nr.5, Feb. 1912,   p.145 ff. Cf. *Nordwestdeutsche*

Handwerks-Ztg. Nr.6, 10.2.1912 and the response of the BdL at their annual meeting in *Korrespondenz des Bundes der Landwirte.* Nr.10, 19.2.1912, p.37 ff.

139. Wangenheim to Endell. 3.8.1912, published in *Anlage* 13, Puhle, *Agrarische Interessenpolitik,* op.cit., p.323.

140. Ibid.

141. *DZA 1, Reichsamt des Innern. 6308.* Letter of Höhne and Fahrenbach to Bethmann-Hollweg. 12.2.1912. Cf. Miquel's earlier call in *Die Post.* 3.5.1899.

142. *Bericht über den Zweiten Reichsdeutschen Mittelstandstag abgehalten zu Braunschweig vom 14. bis 17. September 1912* p.5.

143. See Tille, *Berufsstandspolitik des Gewerbe- und Handelsstandes* (1910 ff.). For Bismarck's ideas on a *"berufsständisches Parlament",* see Augst, *Bismarcks Stellung zum parlamentarischen Wahlrecht* (1917) passim. The connection between Bismarck's ideas and those of Tille has been extensively explored by Stegmann, *Erben Bismarcks,* op.cit.

144. *Der Fortschritt.* Nr.10 (Juli 1912) p.304 ff.

145. *Bericht über den 2. Reichsdeutschen Mittelstandstag,* op.cit., p.23.

146. See ibid., p.32 and Tille, *Die gemeinsamen Interessen der selbständigen Gewerbetreibenden* (1912) passim.

147. *Deutsch-soziale Blätter.* 25.9.1912.

148. *Westdeutsche Mittelstands-Ztg.* Nr.38, 21.9.1912. Cf. *Nordwestdeutsche Handwerks-Ztg.* Nr.39, 5.10.1912, pp.180-182; *Frank.Ztg.* 17.9.1912; *B.N.Nach.* 17.9.1912; *Neue Preussische Ztg.* 16 and 17.9.1912.

149. *Nordwestdeutsche Handwerks-Ztg.* Nr.41, 19.10.1912, pp.191-192, "Neue Wege in der Mittelstandspolitik".

150. See for example Fritsch, *Neue Wege* (1922) p.7 ff. and Massing, op.cit., p.277.

151. See the new *Richtlinien des Hansa-Bundes* in *HH.St.Ar.PP. S17000,* Bd.3. On the second *Hansa-Tag,* see *HH.F.* 19.11.1912; *Frank.Ztg.* 18.11.1912; *National Ztg.* 19.11.1912.

152. *Reichsdeutsche Mittelstands-Blätter.* Nr.6, Juni 1914, p.2.

153. *Westdeutsche Mittelstands-Ztg.* Nr.18, 3.5.1913. Cf. *Der Fortschritt.* Nr.7 (April 1913) p.217. Among the guests of honour at the meeting were representatives of the CDI, the BdL, and the *Volksverein für das katholische Deutschland.*

154. *Reichsdeutscher Mittelstandsverband. Landes-Ausschuss für Rheinland und Westfalen. Verhandlungen des 2. Westdeutschen Mittelstandstages zu Essen-Ruhr am 18. Mai 1913* pp.25-34.

155. Ibid. Cf. *Westdeutsche Mittelstands-Ztg.* Nr.21, 24.5.1913.

156. *Deutsche Rabattsparvereins-Ztg.* (April 1913) 2 Ausgabe p.57.

157. *Verhandlungs-Bericht des 2. Niedersächischen Mittelstandstages in Hannover am 29. und 30. Juni 1913* pp.3-5. See *HH.St.Ar.PP. V1034.*

158. Cf. Stegmann, *Erben Bismarcks,* op.cit., pp.355-356 for full details.

159. Ibid., p.356.

160. Wangenheim to Class. 30.7.1913, quoted in ibid., p.361.

161. Pulzer, op.cit., p.238.

162. *Der Fortschritt.* Nr.10, Juli 1913, p.306 ff.

163. On this organization, see *HH.St.Ar.PP. S11792* and *S1480.* See its favourable reaction to the founding of the *Kartell* in *HH.N.* 30.10.1913. Its

definition of "a thorough-going policy for the *Mittelstand*" insisted on the "preservation of the old and creation of new independent existences"; this was "in the end the best social policy and the most promising means of overcoming Social Democracy".

164. *Bericht über den Dritten Reichsdeutschen Mittelstandstag abgehalten zu Leipzig vom 22. bis 25. August 1913* p.67.

165. Ibid., pp.70-71.

166. *Bürgerliche Parteien*, Bd.1 op.cit., p.119.

167. *Schulthess' Europäischer Geschichtskalender. Neue Folge* 1913 (1915) p.310. '

168. Cf. the analysis in *Vorwärts*. 26.8.1913. Cf. *HH.C.* 29.8.1913 and *HH.N.* 29.8.1913.

169. *Vorwärts*. 9.11.1913.

170. Cf. Lederer, "Sozialpolitische Chronik. Mittelstandsbewegung" (1913) p.1018 ff.

171. Puhle, *Agrarische Interessenpolitik*, op.cit., p.163.

172. *Westdeutsche Mittelstands-Ztg.* Nr.39, 27.9.1913.

173. *Reichsdeutsche Mittelstands-Blätter.* Nr.1 (Jan. 1914) p.5.

174. Ibid.

175. Ibid., Nr.2 (Feb. 1914) p.1.

176. See for example Kaelble, op.cit., p.134 and Winkler, *Mittelstand*, op.cit., p.53.

177. F.Fischer, op.cit., p.58.

178. Cf. Stegmann, "Machteliten", op.cit., passim.

179. *Reichsdeutsche Mittelstands-Blätter.* Nr.1 (Jan. 1914) p.6.

Epilogue

1. Pridham, *Hitler's Rise to Power* (1973) pp.188-189.

2. Noakes, op.cit., p.246 ff.

3. Cf. Bullock, *Hitler* (1965) p.216.

4. *Deutsche Rabattsparvereins-Ztg.* Nr.8, Aug. 1914, p.111.

5. *Vollversammlung der Detaillistenkammer HH. (8.8.1914). Niederschrift.*

6. Brauer, op.cit., p.396. Cf. Meerwarth et al., *Einwirkung des Krieges* (1932) p.103 ff.

7. *Neue HH. Ztg.* 23.1.1915.

8. Kocka, "Mittelstand", op.cit., p.115.

9. Feldman, *Army, Industry and Labor in Germany* (1966) p.101.

10. Quoted in Bruck, *Social and Economic History of Germany* (1938) p.141.

11. Cf. Wein, op.cit., pp.242-244 and Becker, *Denkschrift über die wirtschaftliche Bedeutung des Einzelhandels* (1916) p.4 ff.

12. Stegmann, *Erben Bismarcks*, op.cit., pp.499-500.

13. Wehler, "Probleme des Imperialismus" in *Krisenherde*, op.cit., pp.131-132.

14. Stegmann, *Erben Bismarcks*, op.cit., p.512.

15. *Hammer.* Nr.349, Jan. 1917, pp.1-4.

16. Stegmann, *Erben Bismarcks*, op.cit., p.511. Cf. Feldman, op.cit., pp.429-430

17. Stegmann, *Erben Bismarcks*, op.cit., p.510 and "Machteliten", op.cit.,

p.385 ff.

18. Dürig and Rudolf (eds.), *Texte zur deutschen Verfassungsgeschichte* (1967) p.157.

19. Neumann, *Die deutschen Parteien* (1932) p.60.

20. Schumacher, *Mittelstandsfront und Republik* (1972) pp.20-21.

21. Winkler, *Mittelstand*, op.cit., pp.73-74.

22. Treue, op.cit., p.116. For a brief summary of the policies "friendly to the *Mittelstand*" of the other parties, see Schumacher, op.cit., p.47 ff. and Winkler, *Mittelstand*, op.cit., p.121 ff.

23. Treue, op.cit., p.147.

24. Wein, op.cit., p.246.

25. Uhlig, op.cit., p.25. Cf. Meerwarth, op.cit., p.103 ff. and Westrap, *Rede über Mittelstand* (1920) p.4 ff.

26. Kocka, "Mittelstand", op.cit., p.122.

27. Winkler, *Mittelstand*, op.cit., p.165. Cf. p.81.

28. Winkler, "Extremismus der Mitte? " op.cit., passim.

29. Neumann, op.cit., pp.73-74.

30. Geiger, op.cit., p.72 ff.

31. Note esp. Allen, *Nazi Seizure of Power* (1965) p.24, who points out that after 1929 even the threat of economic decline was frequently sufficient to mobilize "businessmen" into the Nazi ranks.

32. Bracher, *Auflösung der Weimarer Republik* (1957) pp.163-164.

33. Geiger, op.cit., p.119.

34. Neumann, op.cit., p.78.

35. Lipset, *Political Man*, op.cit., p.138 ff. Cf. the critique of A.Rosenberg, op.cit., passim.

36. Bracher, Sauer, Schulz, *Nationalsozialistische Machtergreifung* (1960) p.191.

37. Noakes, op.cit., pp.128, 170-171.

38. Cf. Bracher, Sauer, Schulz, op.cit., p.637 and Noakes, op.cit., p.171. See *NSDAP Hauptarchiv. Reel 42, Folder 860* for a copy of the certificate of admission to a *Kampfgemeinschaft*.

39. Cf. Pridham, op.cit., p.238 ff. and Noakes, op.cit., p.209. The latter states that "anti-Semitism, as articulated by the NSDAP, was in the first place an appeal to economic interest. There were thousands of small shopkeepers who were threatened by department stores of which a considerable number were in Jewish hands, quite apart from the rivalry of ordinary Jewish shopkeepers." Noakes quotes statistics which show that "79 per cent of the turnover in department stores in Germany" took place in stores owned by Jews.

40. Cf. Schweitzer, op.cit., and Schoenbaum, op.cit. See also Mason, "Primacy of Politics" (1969) pp.165-195.

41. Schoenbaum, op.cit., p.143.

42. Quoted in Uhlig, op.cit., p.189.

Conclusion

1. For further discussion of the concept of micro-politics and its function in the process of legitimation, see Miliband, *State in Capitalist Society* (1972)

p.161 ff.

2. There are important variations in the interpretation of the defensive strategies *(Krisenstrategien)* and the importance attributed to the role they played in German domestic politics leading up to 1914. The underlying thesis stems in large measure from Kehr's works which postulate the "primacy of domestic politics" as opposed to the older school of interpretation which stressed the "primacy of foreign policy". Cf. the works by Kehr, H.Rosenberg, Wehler, Böhme, Berghahn, and Stegmann. Critics who suggest that the importance of the *Sammlungspolitik* (as put forward esp. by Stegmann and Böhme) has been overrated because the *Sammlungspolitik* allegedly achieved so little forget, perhaps, how successful that policy was in terms of helping to conserve the distribution of power in Imperial Germany. For a summary, see Scheideler, "Parlament, Parteien und Regierung 1890-1914" (1971) p.16 ff.

3. See Miliband, op.cit., p.163. Cf. Korsch, *Marxismus und Philosophie* (1923) who emphasized the importance of the intellectual and ideological apparatus of bourgeois society and the role of that apparatus in the hegemony of the ruling class. Cf. Kühnl, *Formen bürgerlicher Herrschaft* (1971).

4. Stein, "Pauperismus und Assoziation" (1936).

5. Groh, *Negative Integration und revolutionärer Attentismus* (1973) p.36 gives his definition of negative integration.

6. Sauer, "Problem des deutschen Nationalstaates" (1966) p.434. Cf. Groh, op.cit., p.36. For substantive, logical, and ideological criticism of functionalism, see esp. Cohen, *Modern Social Theory* (1968).

7. Mills, *White Collar*, op.cit., p.327.

BIBLIOGRAPHY

Unpublished Sources

1.   Deutsches Zentralarchiv, Abt.1: Potsdam

Reichskanzlei

Nr. 14??/4	Hansabund, 1909-1918
Nr. 2255	Mittelstandsvereinigungen, 1905-1917

Reichsamt des Innern

Nr. 6297-6310	Die Hebung der wirtschaftlichen Lage des Handwerks, Kleingewerbes und Kleinhandels (Mittelstandsbewegung), 1880-1915
Nr. 6311-6312	Pressestimmen hierzu, 1894-1906
Nr. 6313-6318	Erhebungen über die Verhältnisse des kaufmännischen Mittelstandes, 1904-1914

2.   Geheimes Staatsarchiv Berlin-Dahlem

Rep. 84a: Preussisches Justizministerium
Bd.3 Generalakten. 3. Zivilrecht und Zivilrechtsgang

Nr. 898-904	Deutsches Handelsgesetzbuch, 1871-1923
Nr. 922	Material aus kaufmännischen und anderen Kreisen zum Handelsgesetzbuch, 1896-1934
Nr. 923	Äusserungen der Presse über das Handelsgesetzbuch, 1896-1925

Nr. 924   Berichte betr. das Handelsgesetzbuch,
                                1899-1922
Nr. 984   Deutscher Industrie- und Handelstag,
                                1904-1934
Nr. 4990 Bd.1   Konkurs- und Vergleichsstatistik,
                                1894-1913
Nr. 10440   Abgrenzung des Kleingewerbes,
                                1898-1924
Nr. 10441   Dgl.- Gutachtliche Berichte, 1899
Nr. 10479-10480   Konsumvereine, 1890-1913
Nr. 10481   Dgl.- Gutachtliche Berichte
Nr. 10488-10496   Erwerbs- und Wirtschaftsgenossens-
                                chaften, 1888-1920
Nr. 10500   Gutachtliche Äusserungen über das
                                Genossenschaftswesen bsw. das
                                Genossenschaftsregister, 1891-1927
Nr. 10506   Generalberichte betr. die Erwerbs- und
                                Wirtschaftsgenossenschaften

Bd.5 Finanzen

Nr. 9020-9022   Besteuerung der Warenhäuser, Bazare,
                                Versandgeschäfte usw. (Betriebssteuer,
                                Umsatzsteuer), 1896-1919

Bd.5. 7. Wirtschaftsangelegenheiten

Nr. 881-884   Handelskammern, 1869-1917
Nr. 5790-5794   Bekämpfung des unlauteren
                                Wettbewerbes, 1894-1924
Nr. 5797   Dgl.- Äusserungen der Presse, 1896-1931
Nr. 5798   Dgl.- Gutachtliche Berichte, 1901-1902
Nr. 5799   Dgl.- Generalberichte, 1902-1905
Nr. 9246-9573   Kaufmannschaften (verschiedentlich)
Nr. 11373-11378   Verhältnisse der Handwerker und
                                Innungen, 1887-1934
Nr. 11379   Dgl.- Petitionen, 1896-1906
Nr. 11450-11452   Kaufmännische Schiedsgerichte,
                                1894-1928
Nr. 11453   Dgl.- Äusserungen der Presse, 1897-1926

Rep.90: Preussisches Staatsministerium

Nr. 306-307   Wahlbeeinflussung, 1883-1919

Nr. 1651-1658   Gewerbeordnung für das Deutsche
                             Reich, 1867-1935
Nr. 1659-1665   Handelsgesetzbuch, 1860-1923

*Preussisches Ministerium des Auswärtigen. III. Teilnahme am
Preussischen Staatsministerium*

Nr. 1123   Bekämpfung des unlauteren
                             Wettbewerbs in Handel und Verkehr,
                             1894-1910
Nr. 1135   Handelskammern
Nr. 1141   Gewerbe-Betrieb im Umherziehen,
                             1896-1911
Nr. 1146-1147   Sonntagsruhe im Handel- und Gewerbe-
                             Betriebe, 1894-1913
Nr. 1165   Warenhäuser, Versandgeschäfte.
                             Konsumvereine, Schutz des
                             Kleinhandels, 1899-1916

Hauptabteilung XII: Zeitgeschichtliche Sammlung

IV   Vaterländische und Völkische Parteien,
                             Wirtschaftliche Vereinigung, Deutscher
                             Mittelstandsbund, Christliche Gruppen,
                             Deutsche Reform Partei, Antisemitische
                             Volkspartei

3.   **Bundesarchiv Koblenz**

Zeitgeschichtliche Sammlung (Zg.1)

46   Deutsche Freisinnige Partei, 1884-1910
52   Deutsche Volkspartei, 1873-1897;
                             Fortschrittliche Volkspartei, 1910-1915
70   Konservative Parteien, 1879 ff.
74   Nationalliberale Partei
108   Deutsche Zentrumspartei, 1882 ff.
130   Der Reichsverband gegen die
                             Sozialdemokratie, 1907 ff.
145   Volksverein für das katholische
                             Deutschland, 1894, ff.

228	Deutschnationaler Handlungsgehilfen-Verband
289	Hansa-Bund, 1911-1934
E.73	Christlich-Soziale Partei
E.115	Bund der Landwirte
E.146	Deutsch-Hannoverische Partei
E.165	Deutscher Antisemiten-Bund

4.   Bayerisches Hauptstaatsarchiv München

Staatsministerium für Handel, Industrie und Gewerbe (MH)

MH. 11310	Erhebungen über die Verhältnisse des Kleinhandels, 1897
MH. 11358	Konsumvereine, usw., 1883-1893
MH. 11359	Zentralverband deutscher Konsumvereine, 1904-1914
MH. 11382	Der deutsche Verband kaufmännischer Vereine, 1891-1900
MH. 11383	Verein zur Vertretung wirtschaftlicher Interessen, 1901-1913
MH. 11384	Kaufmännischer Verein München von 1873, 1903-1917
MH. 11385	Gründung eines Verbandes "Deutscher Waren- und Kaufhäuser", 1903
MH. 14490-14494	Gesetz gegen den unlauteren Wettbewerb in Handel und Gewerbe, 1893-1916
MH. 14496	Vollzug des Gesetzes gegen den unlauteren Wettbewerb in Handel und Gewerbe, 1897-1912
MH. 14497-14499	Den unlauteren Wettbewerb betr. (Gesetz v. 27.5.1896), 1894-1904
MH. 14506	Unlauterer Wettbewerb; hier das sogen. Coupon-System, 1905-1906
MH. 14509-14511	Unlauterer Wettbewerb; hier Missbräuche auf dem Gebiete des Ausverkaufswesens, 1902-1903
MH. 14600-14602	Gesetz; die Besteuerung des Gewerbebetriebs im Umherziehen und dessen Vollzug betr. (Hausierhandel), 1878-1909
MH. 14616	Geschäftsverkehr der Wanderlager und Warenauktion, 1879-1905

MH. 14617	Der Gewerbebetrieb im Umherziehen; hier die Wanderlager und Warenauktion und deren Besteuerung, 1876-1896
MH. 14633	Märkte: Generalia, 1849-1904
MH. 14655	Statistische Erhebung über die seitherige Wirkung des Handwerker- gesetzes vom 26. Juli 1897 betr., 1904
MH. 14659	Bayerische Handwerkskammertage und Konferenzen der bayerischen Handwerks- kammern, 1901-1908
MH. 14660	Handwerks- und deutsche Gewerbe- kammertage, 1893-1913
MH. 14661	Verhältnisse des deutschen Handwerks, 1891-1892
MH. 14669	Befähigungsnachweis für das Handwerk, 1884-1904
MH. 14709	Bayerischer Handwerkerbund, 1883-1905

Staatsministerium des Innern (MInn)

MInn. 54468	Entwurf eines Warenhaussteuer- Gesetzes, 1907-1910
MInn. 71542	Generalversammlung der katholischen Vereine Deutschlands; deutsche und bayerische Katholikentage; Zeitungs- berichte, 1889-1911
MInn. 73534-73535	Haus- und Grundbesitzervereine, 1893-1929
MInn. 73586	Nürnberg. Verein Merkur, Kaufmännischer Verein, 1905-1919

Staatsministerium für Wirtschaft (MWi)

MWi. 956	Handwerkskammer für Oberbayern, 1905-1928
MWi. 1452	Handwerkerbund, 1909-1919
MWi. 1457	Verband deutscher Gewerbe-Vereine, 1892-1909
MWi. 1576	Forderungen des Handwerks im Allgemeinen, 1905-1944
MWi. 2009	Verein bayerischer Geschäftsreisender, 1905-1917
MWi. 2010	Verband deutscher Handlungsgehilfen Leipzig, 1909-1917

MWi. 2011	Verein Merkur in Nürnberg, 1904-1917
MWi. 2014	Verband reisender Kaufleute Deutschlands, 1906-1926
MWi. 2015	Verband katholischer kaufmännischer Vereinigungen Deutschlands, 1910-1932
MWi. 2016	Katholischer kaufmännische Verein "Hansa" in München, 1905-1915
MWi. 8339-8341	Warenhaussteuer und Filialsteuer, 1908-1940

5.   Staatsarchiv München

Polizeidirektion München

AR 550	Ortsgruppe München der deutschen Mittelstandsvereinigung, 1906-1910
AR 613	Deutsch-Sozialer Verein, später Antisemitische Volkspartei, 1891-1897
AR 621	Verband süddeutscher Konsumvereine, 1878-1915
AR 630	Deutscher Kellnerbund, Bezirksverein München, 1879-1905
AR 633	Deutscher Antisemitenbund in München 1892-1899. (Seit 1893, Deutsch-soziale, antisemitische Partei in Bayern)
AR 635	Nationalliberaler Arbeiter- und Angestellten Verein München, 1913-1917
AR 744	Allgemeiner deutscher Handwerkerbund, 1885-1901
AR 746	Soziale Vereinigung des neuen Mittelstandes, 1908-1917
RA 41420-41422	Reichstagswahlen, 1903, 1907, 1912
RA 57814	Die antisemitische Bewegung 1892-1922
RA 57855	Verein der Haus- und Grundbesitzer Deutschlands, 1893-1905
Verz. 24a 1.48.7b	Sonntagsruhe, 1892-1903
Verz. 24a 1.49.7a	Sonntagsruhe im Handelsgewerbe, 3Bde, 1904-1916
Verz. 24a.111	
240	Deutschnationaler Handlungsgehilfen-Verband, 1897-1919
257	Verband deutscher Handlungsgehilfen, 1890-1933

300   Bayerischer Arbeitgeberverband des
                             Transport-, Handels- und Verkehrgewerbes,
                             1907-1915
304   Landesverband Bayern im Verband d.
                             Handelsschutz- und Rabattsparvereine,
                             1913-1934

6.   **Staatsarchiv Bremen**

Senats Registratur.3.H.

149   Kammer für Kleinhandel, Nr.2-15
290   Eingabe des Deutschen Handelstages,
                             betr. Förderung des Kleinhandels usw.

Senats-Registratur.3.V2

Nr. 167   Verein Bremer Ladeninhaber und
                             Gewerbetreibender, 1896 ff.
Nr. 349   Das Gesetz des Rabatt-Spar-Vereins
                             "Brema", 1903 ff.
Nr. 395   Verband der Rabatt-Spar-Vereine
                             Deutschlands, 1904 ff.
Nr. 519   Rabatt-Spar-Verein "Union"
Nr. 607   Tagungen des Deutschen Zentralverbandes
                             für Handel und Gewerbe und des
                             Verbandes der Rabatt-Spar-Vereine in
                             Bremen, 1908

Gewerbekammer. 6.12

1.K.9   Kleingewerbliche Fragen: Wanderlager,
                             Abzahlungsgeschäfte, Wucher, unlauterer
                             Wettbewerb
1.K.10   Kleinhandelskammer

Polizeidirektion. 4.14

111. A.27   Gewerbekammer
111. A.28   Kammer für Kleinhandel

V. Gewerbepolizei

A.4. LA   Sonntagsruhe im Handelsgewerbe
A.4. T   Strassen- und Hausierhandel

VIII. Sitten- und Kriminalpolizei

F.26   Bekämpfung des unlauteren Wettbewerbs

IX. Bau- und Feuerpolizei

D.1.i.   Kontrolle und Bestimmungen für
                 Warenhäuser

XII. Politische Polizei

A.2 BG   Diverse politische Vereine und Verbände.
                 Wichtige Akten über die Gründung der
                 einzelnen Verbände
A.2 BL   Diverse Vereinigungen und Verbände
A.2 BM   Diverse politische Vereine
A.2 BM(4)   Deutscher Reform Verein zu Bremen,
                 1890 ff.
A.2 BM(14)   Verband der Tapezierer und verwandten
                 Berufsgenossen Deutschlands (Filiale
                 Bremen)

7.   Archiv der Handelskammer Bremen

Congress, Vereine und Verbände

C.3   Kaufmännische Vereine, verschiedenes,
                 1884-1943
C.4   Deutscher Verband kaufmännischer
                 Vereine, 1869 ff.
C.10   Hansa Bund für Gewerbe, Handel und
                 Industrie, 1909-1920

Kleinhandel

K1.2	Verschiedenes, 1895 ff.
- K1.3	Kleinhandelskammer, 1895 ff.
K1.4	Ladenschluss. Kommission für Kleinhandel, Handelstag
K1.11	Ausschaltung des Einzelhandels, 1912 ff.
K1.13	Rabattsparvereinswesen

Einzelhandel Abteilung

Protokolle der Kammersitzungen, 2 Bde. 1907-1918 (unpublished)

8.   Archiv der Handelskammer Bielefeld (WWAr. in Dortmund K3)

Nr. 4	Ladenschluss und Sonntagsruhe, 1899-1920
Nr. 5	Ausverkauf und Reklame und deren gesetzliche Regelung, 1901-1917
Nr. 68	Vereinigung Niedersächsischer Handelskammern, 1910-1915
Nr. 214	Hansa-Bund, 1910-1916
Nr. 215	Hansa-Bund, 1909
Nr. 262	Blenden der Schaufenster, 1901-1905
Nr. 263	Bestechung von Angestellten, 1905-1914

9.   Archiv der Handelskammer Bochum (WWAr. in Dortmund K2)

Nr. 1030	Kaufmännische Schiedsgerichte, 1897-1902
Nr. 1214	Dgl. 1900-1903
Nr. 379	Dgl. 1901-1913
Nr. 295	Gewerbe- und Kaufmannsgerichte, 1913-1924
Nr. 38	Gewerbeordnung, 1856-1895
Nr. 894	Dgl. 1890-1895
Nr. 58	Dgl. 1897-1913
Nr. 715	Dgl. 1913-1914

Nr. 1241	Gesetzentwurf zur Bekämpfung des unlauteren Wettbewerbs, 1894-1896
Nr. 1240	Unlauterer Wettbewerb, Ausverkäufe, 1912-1914
Nr. 1234	Unlauterer Wettbewerb, Ausverkäufe, 1910-1912
Nr. 606	Gerichts- und Konkursstatistik, 1903-1914
Nr. 1097	Einführung von Handelsinspektionen, 1903-1907
Nr. 1068	Sonntagsruhe, 1891-1895
Nr. 228	Sonntagsruhe, 1906-1914
Nr. 26	Ladenschluss (Allg.), 1899, 1902-1905
Nr. 1278	Ladenschluss, 1905-1911
Nr. 1277	Ladenschluss, 1911-1914
Nr. 1071	(Achtuhr) ladenschluss, 1904-1912
Nr. 1226	Einführung des Achtuhrladenschlusses in der Stadt Bochum, 1907-1913
Nr. 1267	Warenhäuser, Konsumvereine und sonstige grosskapitalistische Betriebe im Kleinhandel. Abzahlungsgeschäfte, 1863-1896
Nr. 212	Dgl. 1897-1902
Nr. 59	Dgl. 1903-1914
Nr. 966	Rabattsparverein, Gauverband Rheinland-Westfalen, 1914-1917
Nr. 430	Kleinhandel, 1896-1914
Nr. 1283	Dgl. 1912-1926
Nr. 1216	Ausschluss vom Verbot des Detailreisens, 1896
Nr. 984	Unfallversicherung des Kleinhandels. Detailberufsgenossenschaft, 1912-1914
Nr. 1085	(Hausierhandel), Wanderlager und Abzahlungsgeschäfte, 1886-1887
Nr. 202	Handwerk, 1897-1903
Nr. 96	Dgl. 1900-1913
Nr. 485	Kleinhandelsausschuss, 1907-1913
Nr. 285	Schaffung von Kleinhandelsausschüssen, 1908, 1909-1910
Nr. 1552	Kaufmännische Vereine des Bezirks, 1897-1907
Nr. 265	Kaufmännische Angestellten, 1907
Nr. 1249	Kaufmännische Angestellten, 1907-1913
Nr. 1286	Bestechung von Angestellten, 1905-1910

Nr. 831	Deutscher Handelstag, 1859-1896
Nr. 106	Dgl. 1897-1900
Nr. 830	Dgl. 1900-1902
Nr. 226	Dgl. 1903-1905
Nr. 534	Dgl. 1906
Nr. 92	Dgl. 1910-1911
Nr. 481	Dgl. 1912-1913
Nr. 467	Dgl. 1914-1917
Nr. 548	Hansa-Bund, 1911-1913

10. Archiv der Handelskammer Dortmund (WWAr. in Dortmund K1)

Nr. 27	Kleinhandelsausschuss, 1909-1918

11. Staatsarchiv Hamburg

Senatsakten

C1 1 Lit.T.No.8.vol.65	
Fasc.3.Inv.1-9	Deutsches Reich-Arbeiterstatistik, 1892 ff.
Fasc.9.Inv.1	Deutsches Reich Gewerbewesen, 1901-1907
C1.VII.Rf.Nr.174b	Deutscher Handwerks- und Gewerbekammertag, vol.1-25b, 1900-1914
C1.VII.Rf.Nr.176	Verband deutscher Gewerbevereine und Handwerkervereinigungen, vols.1-4, 1900-1914
C1.VII.Rf.Nr.197	Deutscher Handelstag, vols.1-16, 1901-1914
C1.VII.Rf.Nr.485	Deutscher Zentralverband für Handel und Gewerbe, vols.1-2, 1914-1917
C1.XI.Gen.Nr.2.vol.126	Denkschrift des Hamburger Gewerbevereins zur Hebung des Gewerbestandes, 1909

Senatsakten, Deputation für Handel, Schiffahrt und Gewerbe,2

Detaillistenkammer. 1 Organisation und Tätigkeit.B

XIII.B.1(1)	Errichtung einer Handelskammer für den Kleinhandel, Bd.1, 1895-1898; Bd.2 1898-1918
1A	Konstituieren und Organisation der

1C

                Detaillistenkammer und deren Befugnis
und Zuständigkeit, 1904-1922
Sammlung der vorzulegenden
Tagesordnungen der Versammlungen der
Detaillistenkammer, Bd.1, 1904-1918

1b3

                Wahlen, Entlassung und Ersatzwahlen
der Mitglieder der Kammer, der
Ausschüsse

1H

                Budget und Abrechnung der Detaillisten-
kammer, 1908-1922

Gerichtsvollzieherwesen

Nr. 25

                Jahresberichte, statistische Übersichten,
1882-1934

Handwerkskammer. 376-16

IV.A.2

                Wanderlager und Waaren-Auctionen,
1877-1922

IV.B.6

                Die Sonntagsruhe im Handelsgewerbe,
1890-1912

VI.A.12

                Das Gesetz zur Bekämpfung des
unlauteren Wettbewerbs, 1893-1931

VI.B.11

                Regelung der Ausverkäufe auf Grund
des Gesetzes gegen den unlauteren
Wettbewerb, 1909-1930

VI.C.8

                Verfolgung unlauterer Wettbewerbs-
handlungen, 1912-1929

VII.A.6

                Bestimmungen betr. die Beschäftigung
von Gehülfen und Lehrlingen in Gast-
und in Schrankwirtschaften, 1901-1907

VIII.A.8

                Geschäftsbetrieb der Consum-Vereine
und die Besteuerung derselben, 1888-1911

VIII.A.9

                Die Besteuerung der Waarenhäuser und
Grossbazare, 1896-1912

XII.1

                Misstände im Zahlungsverkehr. Regelung
des Kreditwesens, 1909-1931

XVIII.A.7

                Besteuerung des Wanderlagerbetriebs in
Hamburg, 1880-1902

XVIII.D.23

                Verein deutscher Arbeitgeberverbände,
1905-1918

XVIII.E.4

                Akte betr. den Internationalen Verband

	zum Studium der Verhältnisse des Mittelstandes, 1904-1932
XVIII.F.21	Gutachten und Auskünfte für den Hansa-Bund, 1912-1917
XVIII.F.28	Deutscher Zentralverband für Handel und Gewerbe, e.V. (Leipzig), 1908-1917
XVIII.H.7	Wirtschaftlicher Schutzverband Hamburg, 1904-1914
XIX.1	Akte betr. Kommission der Deutschen Handelstages betr. Kleinhandel, 1908-1924

Institution von Handwerk und Gewerbe. A
Gewerbe- und Handwerkskammer

| 1.7A | Handwerkskammer. Organisation und Tätigkeit. Errichtung der Handwerkskammer, 1895-1903 |

Polizeibehörde- Politische Polizei (PP.)

S675	"Juden raus"
S1581	Fachvereine und Innungen, 1888
S2364	Verein zur Abwehr des Antisemitismus, 1891-1918
S2424	Antisemitische und christlich-soziale Vorträge in Hamburg, 1888-1907
S2649SA	Deutsche Detaillisten Verbände
S2869	Bd.1 Arbeiterstatistik, Kommission für Arbeiterstatistik-Allgemeines, 1892-1901
	Bd.2 Komm. für Arbeiterstatistik: Erhebungen über die Verhältnisse im Handelsgewerbe, Ladenschluss, 1892-1901
	Bd.3-Bd.7, Dgl.
S3846	Hamburgische Gewerbe-Ztg.
S4013	Deutschnationaler Handlungsgehülfen Verband, 3.Bde. 1895-1920
S4293	Verein gegen Unwesen im Handel und Gewerbe, e.V., 1893-1920
S4295	Deutscher Reformverein zu Hamburg, 1882, 1894-1899
S4296	Antisemitischer Wahlverein von 1890, Deutschsoziale Reformpartei

	Bd.1 Hauptakten mit Versammlungs-berichten und Flugschriften, 1891-1899
	Bd.2 Zeitungsausschnitte, 1892-1899
	Bd.3 Deutsch-soziale Reformpartei; Parteitage, 1895-1899
	Bd.4 Deutsch-soziale Reformpartei, mit Flugschriften, 1900-1905
	Bd.5 Deutsch-soziale Partei, Deutsch-völkische Partei, 1906-1918
S4635	Verein für Sozialpolitik, 1894-1918
S4666	Akte betr. Berufs- und Gewerbezählung, 1894-1917
S4961	Verband deutscher Mittelstände-Deutsche Mittelstandspartei, 1895 ff.
S4985	Deutscher Volksverein. Wirtschaftlicher Verband freiheitlicher Antisemiten, 1895-1896
S5081	Deutsch-nationaler Arbeiterbund, 1895-1914
S5193	Verband Deutscher Gewerbe Verein, 1895-1908
S5272	Gesetz über den unlauteren Wettbewerb, 1895-1910
S5580	Liga zur Herbeiführung des Achtuhr-Schlusses in sämmtlichen kaufmännischen Betrieben, 1896-1897
S5666	Reichstagswahlen 1898, Vol. IIa, Versammlungen
S5720	Bd.1 Organisation des Handwerks, 1893-1896
	Bd.2 Dgl. 1897-1899
	Bd.3 Dgl. und Handwerks- und Gewerbe-kammertage 1900-1912
	Bd.4 Arbeiterkammer usw. 1898-1908
	Bd.5 Dgl. 1909-1918
	Bd.6 Detaillistenkammer, 1900-1918
	Bd.7 Kaufmannsgerichte, 1902-1915
	Bd.8-Bd.10 Handwerk, verschiedenes, 1902 ff.
S5809	Nationalliberale Partei, 2Bde., 1896-1918
S5915	Bund der Landwirte, 1897-1918
S5916	Zentralverband deutscher Kaufleute

	und Gewerbetreibender, 1896-1909
S6747	Kaufmännischer und gewerblicher Hülfsverein für weibliche Angestellten, 1898 ff.
S6750	Auseinandersetzungen um Warenhäuser und Konsumvereine, Bd.1, 1897-1898 bis Bd.5, 1912-1918
S6810	Arbeitgeber Verbände in Deutschland, 2Bde., 1898-1912
	Bd.3 Arbeitgeber-Verband Hamburg-Altona, 1890-1913
S7011	Rabatt-Sparvereine, 1913-1918
S7270	Deutscher Bund für Handel und Gewerbe, 1898-1917
S7488	Antisemitischer Verein "Quittungsmarke"
S7751	Verband deutscher Handlungsgehülfen zu Leipzig, 1894-1918
S8113	Verband deutscher Eisenwaaren-Händler, 1900-1917
S8232	Verband Nordwestdeutscher Konsumvereine, 1900-1902, 1908-1918
S8261	Wirtschaftlicher Schutzverband, 1900-1912
S8610	Vereine zur Vertretung wirtschaftlicher Interessen, ca. 1901-1918
S10696	Bund der Kaufleute, 1903, 1910
S11699	Allgemeine Ztg. Gewerbeschutz-Ztg.
S11795	Reichsverband gegen die Sozialdemokratie, Bd.1, 1904-1907; Bd.2, 1908-1918
S11809	Wirtschaftliche Vereinigung, 1903-1912
S11810	Allgemeiner Verein der Gewerbetrei-benden Deutschlands, 1904
S11980	Bund der Handwerker, 1904-1911
S12340	Wirtschaftlicher Schutzverband Hamburg, 1904-1914
S12369	Verband deutscher kaufmännischer Vereine, 1904-1914
S13841	Zentralvereinigung preussischer Vereine für Handel und Gewerbe, 1905-1914
S14412	Handels- und Gewerbe-Kammertage, 1906-1918
S14519	Freie Mittelstandsvereinigung, 1906 ff.
S14980	Hamburgischer Verband zur Bekämpfung

	der Sozialdemokratie, 2 Bde., 1907-1915
S15113	Abnehmerverband des deutschen
	Textilgewerbes, 1907-1917
S15627	Der Verband deutscher Damen- und
	Mädchenmäntelfabrikanten, 1907-1912
S15829	Deutsche Vereinigung, 1907 ff.
S16625	Hanseatische Detaillisten-Ztg., 1909
S17000	Hansabund für Gewerbe, Handel und
	Industrie mit Zweigverein Hamburg,
	1909-1921
S17389	Konservative Vereinigung
S17723	Verband deutscher Gewerbe- und
	Kaufmannsgericht, 1910, 1913
S18068	Verband der Detaillisten- und Handels-
	Vereine Schleswig-Holsteins
S18262	Reichsdeutscher Mittelstandsverband
S18649	Ztg. "Detaillist und Publikum.
	Deutsche Einkaufs-Ztg."
S18964	Verband deutscher Gewerbevereine
	und deutscher Handwerkervereini-
	gungen, 1912-1913
S19735	Hamburgisch-Konservative Vereinigung
SA28	Verein für Handlungs-Commis von
	1858 in Hamburg (Kaufmännischer
	Verein) Bd.1 (1879-1880) bis Bd.6.
	(1912-1914)
SA692	Verband der Porzellen-, Steingut- und
	Glaswarenhändler — Grossisten und
	Detaillisten — von Hamburg, Altona
	und Umgegend, e.V., 1900-1918
SA1442	Hamburgischer Verband der Detaillisten
	und sonstiger Gewerbetreibenden,
	1909-1914
SA1480	Zentralausschuss handelsgewerblicher
	Vereine Hamburgs, 1909-1911
Ver.299	Bd.1 Antisemitischer Wahlverein von
	1890, 1890-1894
	Bd.2-Bd.3 Antisemitischer Wahlverein
	von 1890. Seit 2.11.1894, Deutsch-
	soziale Reformpartei. Seit 28.10.1898,
	Deutschsozialer Reformverein Hamburg.

	Seit 23.2.1900, Verband Nordmark der deutsch-sozialen Reformpartei.
	Bd.4 Verband Nordmark der deutsch-sozialen Reformpartei
Ver.323	Hamburger Gewerbeverein, Bd.1, 1878-1899 Bd.2, 1899 ff.
Ver.328, Vol.VI	Sozialdemokratischer Verein für den Zweiten Hamburger Wahlkreis. No.37, 1911
Ver.488	Verein zur Beseitigung schwindelhaften Auktionen und zur Hebung des Gewerbestandes, 2 Bde., 1892-1918
Ver.498	Verein der selbständigen Geschäftstreibenden von Hamburg, St.Pauli, und den Vororten, 1892-1894, 1898
Ver.562	Deutscher Reformverein zu Hamburg, 2Bde., 1893-1898
Ver.600	Verein zur Hebung der christlichen Geschäfte und des Handwerkerstandes, 1894-1895
Ver.618	Central-Ausschuss Hamburg-Altonaer Detaillisten-Vereine, 1895-1905
Ver.825	Gewerbe Schutzverein Hamburg. Seit Mai 1905, Gewerbeverein zu Barmbeck, 1903-1915
Ver.827	Schutzverein zur Bekämpfung der Warenhäuser Hamburg, 1904-1914
Ver.976	Hamburger Zweigverein des Hansabundes, 1909-1916
Ver.982	Liberaler Reichstagswahlverein
Ver.1020	Hamburgisch-Konservative Vereinigung
Ver.1034	Niedersächsischer Schutzverband. Ortsgruppe Hamburg

Personalia

S3939	Hermann Ahlwardt, 5Bde.
S7916	Johann Henningsen
S17548	Johannes Hirsch
S4302	Friedrich Carl Ernst Raab
S5260	Karl Wilhelm Fritz Schack
S4493	Wilhelm Ludwig Steigner
S3618	Amandus Karl Eduard Werbeck

12.   Archiv der Handelskammer Hamburg

Aktenabteilung 102. Detaillistenkammer

Sitzungen der Detaillistenkammer 1907 ff. (unpublished)

A.1	Verhandlungen über die Errichtung der Detaillistenkammer bis zum Erlass des Gesetzes, betr. die Detaillistenkammer vom 29.2.1904
A.2	Der Ausschuss zur Errichtung der Detaillistenkammer und der Konstituierun der Kammer am 10.9.1904
5.5 ff.	Geschäftsbedingungen für Kolonial-warenhandel usw.

Aktenabteilung V

145.1-145.2	Hansa Bund für Gewerbe- Handel- und Industrie. Satzung, Mitgliederliste, Anschrift, 1909-1915 Bd.2 Werbung von Mitgliedern, 1909
5.	Verein der Butter-, Käse- und Fettwarengrosshändler zu Hamburg von 1893 e.V., 1895-1935
21.	Verein der Gerbstoffhändler in Hamburg e.V.
50.	Verein der am Kaffeehandel beteiligten Firmen
95.	Verein der Cacaohändler in Hamburg
436	Verein Creditreform Hamburg-Leipzig
808	Deutscher Verband für das Kaufmännisch Bildungswesen, Allgemeines

Aktenabteilung 11   Warenhandel

Aktenabteilung 80

A.	Deutscher Handelstag
A2.h.3	Sitzungen des bleibenden Ausschusses des Deutschen Handelstages
H.13	Errichtung von Kammern für das Gastwirtsgewerbe

J.39.1   Anregungen auf Errichtung einer
                              Detaillistenkammer in Hamburg,
                              1895-1899
J.39.3   Wahlaufsatz und Wahlen zur
                              Detaillistenkammer, 1904-1932
J.39.6   Anfragen und Auskünfte über die
                              Detaillistenkammer, 1905-1933

13.   Niedersächsisches Staatsarchiv Hannover

Hannover 80. Hannover II   Landrostei und Regierung Hannover

Nr. 1030   Die Kaufmannsgerichte nach dem
                              Gesetz vom 6.Juli 1904, 1904-1924
Nr. 1051   Die Errichtung von Handwerkskammern
                              sowie die Umgestaltung des Innungs-
                              wesens nach dem Gesetz vom. 26.7.1898
Nr. 1052   Dgl. 1898-1905
Nr. 1053   Versammlungen der Innungsobermeister
                              und Innungsvorstände und deren
                              Verhandlungen, 1905-1911
Nr. 1093   Die Kolonialwarenhändlerinnungen zu
                              Hannover, 1892-1929
Nr. 1215   Die Verbände von Kaufleuten,
                              Handlungsgehilfen und gehilfinnen,
                              sowie von sonstigen
                              Gewerbetreibenden, u.ä., der Deutsch-
                              nationaler Handlungsgehilfen-Verband,
                              1892-1915
Nr. 1224   Der Verband deutscher Gewerbevereine
                              und Handwerksvereinigungen,
                              1901-1913
Nr. 1225   Der Verein hannoverscher Wirte,
                              1902-1905
Nr. 1228   Die Errichtung von Gewerbekammern
                              für die Regierungsbezirke der Provinz
                              Hannover, 1884-1888
Nr. 1229   Dgl. 1889-1895
Nr. 1287   Die Abänderung des Gesetzes über die
                              Erwerbs- und Wirtschaftsgenossenschaften
                              vom 1.Mai 1889, sowie über den
                              Geschäftsbetrieb von Konsumanstalten

	Vom 12. Aug.1896, auch Rabattsparverein 1896-1905
Nr. 1289	Der Verband nordwestdeutscher Konsum vereine, insbes. sein Statut und seine Verbandstagungen, 1892-1908
Nr. 1295	Der Verband deutscher gewerblicher Genossenschaften, 1904-1917
Nr. 1301	Der Verband hannoverscher gewerblicher Genossenschaften, 1911
Nr. 1302	Der Niedersächsische Schützverband für Handel und Gewerbe, 1911

Hannover. Des.122a. Oberpräsidium Hannover. XXXIII.

Nr. 8	Die Organisation des Handwerks: Errichtung von Handwerkskammern, Bd.1, 1893-1894
Nr. 9	Dgl. 1897-1902
Nr. 26	Der Stand der Gewerbeförderung im Königreich Preussen
Nr. 27	Reiseberichte über die Förderung des Gewerbes und über den gewerblichen Unterricht im Auslande, 1907
Nr. 28	Die Einwirkung des Krieges auf Handel und Gewerbe (verschiedenes)
Nr. 63-64	Die Errichtung von Gewerbekammern, 1883-1893
Nr. 88	Die Erwerbs- und Wirtschaftsgenossenschaften, 1889-1893

14.   Staatsarchiv Münster

Regierung Arnsberg 1.G

Nr. 9	Bekämpfung des unlauteren Wettbewerbs, 1900-1910
Nr.10	Dgl. 1910-1911
Nr.11	Dgl. 1912-1936

Regierung Arnsberg. 1.Pa

Nr. 383	Antisemitische Bewegung, 1901-1920

Regierung Münster. Abt. VII

Nr. 90	Verein der Deutschkonservativen für den Nördlichen Industriebezirk, 1914
Nr. 5808	Die Sonntagsruhe in den gewerblichen Betrieben, 1892-1894
Nr. 5835	Dgl. 1901-1912
Nr. 4114	Dgl. 1911-1922

15. NSDAP Hauptarchiv (Hoover Institution Microfilm Collection), Institute of Contemporary History, London

Reel 42 Folder 860   Kampfbund des gewerblichen Mittelstandes

Published Sources

1.   Newspapers

Berliner Neueste Nachrichten
Berliner Tageblatt
Berliner Volkszeitung
Bremer Nachrichten
Bremische Zeitung
Deutsches Blatt
Deutsch-soziale Blätter
Deutsches Volksblatt
Frankfurter Zeitung
Generalanzeiger für Lübeck
General Anzeiger (Hamburg)
Hamburger Echo
Hamburger Nachrichten
Hamburger Neueste Nachrichten
Hamburgischer Correspondent
Herforder Zeitung für Stadt
und Land
Israelitisches Familienblatt
Kölnische Volkszeitung
Kölnische Zeitung
Münchener Neueste Nachrichten
Münchener Zeitung
Nationalzeitung
Neue Hamburger Zeitung
Neue Preussische Zeitung
   (Kreuz-Zeitung)
Norddeutsche Allgemeine Zeitung
Die Post
Volks Zeitung
Vorwärts
Vossische Zeitung
Weser Zeitung

2.   Zeitschriften, Mitteilungen, Trade Papers

Die Abwehr
Aufklärungsschriften des Reichsverbandes der deutsch-sozialen Partei
Die Blumenschmuckkunst
Colonial- und Fettwaren- Zeitung
Delicatessen und Kolonialwaren Anzeiger

Der Detaillist. Offizielles Organ des Detaillisten-Verbandes von Rheinland-Westfalen usw.

Detaillist und Publikum

Deutsche Handels-Wacht. Zeitschrift des deutsch-nationalen Handlungsgehilfen Verbandes

Deutsche Mittelstands-Zeitung. Amtliches Nachrichtenblatt der Deutschen Mittelstandsvereinigung

Deutsche Nahrungs- und Genussmittel-Zeitung

Deutsche Rabattsparvereins-Zeitung. Mitteilungen des Verbandes der Rabattsparvereine Deutschlands

Deutsche Rundschau. Offizielles Organ des Deutschen Zentralverbandes für Handel und Gewerbe

Deutsche Wirtschafts-Zeitung

Der Elbwart

Der Fortschritt. Nachrichten der Mittelstands-Vereinigung im Königreich Sachsen

Die Geschäftswehr

Der Geschäftsfreund. Konfektions-Zeitung

Gewerbliche Mittelstands-Korrespondenz

The Grocer (London)

Der Handelsstand. Zeitschrift des Vereins für Handlungs-Commis von 1858

Hansa-Bund. Offizielles Organ des Hansabundes für Gewerbe, Handel und Industrie

Hammer. Blätter für deutschen Sinn

Hammerbrooker Zeitung

Handlungsgehilfen-Blatt

Kaufmännische Rundschau

Kolonial- und Fettwaren- Handel Zeitung

Kolonialwaren-Zeitung. Kaufmännisches Fachblatt für die Interessen des gesamten Detailhandels

Konsumgenossenschaftliche Rundschau

Korrespondenz des Bundes der Landwirte. Als Manuskript gedruckt

Korrespondenz des Reichsverbandes gegen die Sozialdemokratie

Der Manufakturist

Merkuria. Organ des Verbandes kathol. kaufm. Vereinigungen Deutschlands und seiner Hilfskassen

Der Mittelstand. Nachrichten des Deutschen Bundes für Handel und Gewerbe

Mitteilungen der Centralvereinigung deutscher Vereine für Handel und Gewerbe

Mitteilungen der Zentralvereinigung deutscher Vereine für Handel und Gewerbe (nur nach 1914)

Mitteilungen des Internationalen Verbandes zum Studium der Verhältnisse des Mittelstandes

Mitteilungen des Zentral-Verbandes Deutscher Kaufleute

Mitteilungen für die Vertrauensmänner der Fortschrittlichen Volkspartei

Mitteilungen. Verein gegen Unwesen im Handel und Gewerbe, Hamburg

Mitteilungen vom Hansa-Bund für Gewerbe, Handel und Industrie

Nordwestdeutsche Handwerks-Zeitung

Reichsdeutsche Mittelstands-Blätter

Rundschau für Handel und Gewerbe

Schutz und Trutz. Offizielle Mitteilungen des Vereins zum Schutz für Handel und

Gewerbe Barmen
Der Weckruf! Organ des Vereins gegen Unwesen im Handel und Gewerbe
Westdeutsche Mittelstands-Zeitung. Offizielle Organ der Mittelstandsvereinigung
    für Handel und Gewerbe, Sitz Düsseldorf

3.   Versammlungsprotokolle, Denkschriften u.ä.
Auszug aus dem Protokolle des Senats (Hamburg)
Becker, Ernst. *Denkschrift über die wirtschaftliche Bedeutung des Einzelhandels
    und die Tätigkeit des Deutschen Zentralverbandes für Handel und Gewerbe,
    e.V. Sitz Leipzig* (n.p. n.d. 1916)
*Bericht über den Ersten Reichsdeutschen Mittelstandstag abgehalten zu Dresden
    vom 23-25.Sept.* 1911. Hrsg. vom Reichsdeutschen Mittelstands-Verband
*Bericht über den Zweiten Reichsdeutschen Mittelstandstag abgehalten zu
    Braunschweig vom 14.bis 17.September 1912.* Hrsg. von dem Reichsdeutschen
    Mittelstands-Verband in Leipzig
*Bericht über den Dritten Reichsdeutschen Mittelstandstag abgehalten zu Leipzig
    vom 22.bis 25.August 1913.* Hrsg. vom Reichsdeutschen Mittelstands-Verband
*Bericht über den deutsch-sozialen (antisemitischen) Parteitag zu Leipzig am
    18.und 19.Mai 1891* (Leipzig 1891)
*Bericht über die Conferenz der Delegierten kaufmännischer und gewerblicher
    Vereine Deutschlands am 3.und 4.October 1898 in Leipzig*
Bericht über die Generalversammlungen des Zentralverbandes deutscher Kaufleute
    (teilweise) 1889 ff.
*Bericht über die Verhandlung in der Konferenz des Hauptverbandes deutscher
    gewerblicher Genossenschaften 13.und 14.Mai 1904*
Der Bund der Kaufleute. Seine Grundgedanken und seine Ziele (Berlin 1903)
Denkschrift betreffend Errichtung einer Kleinhandels-Berufsgenossenschaft. Hrsg.
    vom Detaillistenverband von Rheinland und Westfalen und von der Vereinigung
    von kaufmännischen und gewerblichen Vereinen des Handelskammerbezirks
    Bochum (Barmen-Bochum 1912)
Denkschrift der Mittelstands-Vereinigung (2 Aufl. Leipzig 1907)
Denkschrift der *Mittelstandes-Vereinigung (Schutzverein für Handel, Handwerk
    und Gewerbe) für Odenkirchen und Umgegend* (Odenkirchen 1911)
Denkschrift *des Generalsekretariats des Verbandes Deutscher Waren- und
    Kaufhäuser* (Nov. 1904)
*Denkschrift über die gegenwärtige Lage der Handels- und Gewerbetreibenden im
    deutschen Mittelstande und Vorschläge zur Besserung dieser Verhältnisse*
    (Dez. 1896), Vorstand des Zentralverbandes deutscher Kaufleute
Denkschrift über die Lage des Kleinhandels und Gewerbes. Centralverband
    deutscher Kaufleute (30 Nov. 1893)
*Denkschrift über die wirtschaftliche Bedeutung des Einzelhandels und die
    Tätigkeit des Deutschen Zentralverbandes für Handel und Gewerbe e.V.*
    (n.d. circa 25.Mai 1916)
*Deutscher Bund für Handel und Gewerbe (Leipzig), Bericht über die erste
    Hauptversammlung 26.Juni 1900 zu Gera*
Deutscher Handelstag. *Bericht über die Sitzung des bleibenden Ausschusses des
    Deutschen Handelstages*
————————. *Bericht über die Sitzung der Kommission betr. Kleinhandel*

—————————. *Vollversammlungen des Deutschen Handelstages. Steno-graphische Berichte* (teilweise ab 1890)

Drucksache für die Senats-Sitzungen (Hamburg)

Freisinnige Partei. *Der Erste Parteitag der Freisinnigen Volkspartei* (1893) – *Der Siebente Parteitag der Freisinnigen Volkspartei* (1907)

—————————. *Die Freisinnige Volkspartei im Preussischen Landtag in den Sessionen 1889-1901* (Berlin 1902)

—————————. *Was will die Freisinnige Volkspartei? Erläuterung des Eisanacher Programs* (Berlin 1902)

—————————. *Zu den Reichstagswahlen. Ein freisinniges Merkbüchlein* (Berlin 1898)

Hansa-Bund. *Der Mittelstandskongress des Hansa-Bundes vom 5. und 6.November 1911 in Berlin.* Hrsg. vom Hansa-Bund (Berlin 1911)

—————————. *Stenographischer Bericht über die Verhandlung am 12.6.1909 im Circus Schumann in Berlin betr. die Reichsfinanzreform und Gründung des Hansabundes* (Berlin 1909)

Das Kaufmannsgericht. Monatsschrift zur allgemeinen Eröterung von Rechtsfragen unter besonderer Berücksichtigung der Tätigkeit der Kaufmannsgerichte (1905 ff.)

Kolonialwaaren-Kleinhandel und Konsumvereine. Untersuchungen unter Mitwirkung der Handelskammern Brandenburg, Nordhausen, Hildesheim und Hilburghausen. Hrsg. von der Handelskammer für das Herzogthum Braunschweig (Leipzig 1901)

Die Konservative Partei und die Reichsfinanzreform 1909 (Berlin 1909)

Die Lage des Kleinhandels in Deutschland. Ergebnisse der auf Veranlassung von Handelskammern, Handels- und Gewerbekammern und von Vereinen angestellten Erhebungen. Hrsg. von der Handelskammer zu Hannover (2 Bde. Berlin 1899-1900)

Nationalliberale Partei. *Protokolle von Delegierten- und Parteitagen* (1896 ff.)

Protokoll über den 1.Deutschen Handwerks- und Gewerbekammertag (16 Bde. 1900-1914)

Protokoll über die Verhandlungen des VIII. Allgemeinen deutschen Handwerkertages und des X. Delegiertentages des Allgemeinen deutschen Handwerkertages zu Halle. 21-24.April 1895 (München 1895)

Reichsdeutscher Mittelstandsverband. Landes-Ausschuss für Rheinland und Westfalen. Verhandlungen des 2.Westdeutschen Mittelstandstages zu Essen-Ruhr am 18.Mai 1913

Schriften des DHV. Bechly, Hans. *Die Deutschnationale Handelungsgehilfenbewegung und die politischen Parteien* (Hamburg 1911)

—————————. *Die Konkurrenzklausal und die Verbesserungsvorschläge des preussischen Handelsministers*

—————————. Schack, Wilhelm. *Wie und was wir geworden sind (1893-1903). Festschrift zum 2.September 1903* (3 Aufl. Hamburg 1903)

—————————. *Verhandlungsschrift über den*
4. Dt. Handlungsgehilfentag 1899
7. Dt. Handlungsgehilfentag 1902
8. Dt. Handlungsgehilfentag 1903
9. Dt. Handlungsgehilfentag 1905

10. *Dt. Handlungsgehilfentag 1907*

11. *Dt. Handlungsgehilfentag 1909*

12. *Dt. Handlungsgehilfentag 1911*

——————————. *Was wir wollen! Ziele und Aufgaben der Deutschnationalen Handlungsgehilfen-Bewegung, Bd.3 der Schriften des DHV* (4 Aufl. Hamburg 1912)

Schriften des Vereins für Sozialpolitik. *Bd.36* R.van der Borght, *Der Einfluss des Zwischenhandels auf die Preise* (Leipzig 1888)

——————————. *Bd.37 Untersuchungen über den Einfluss der distributiven Gewerbe auf die Preise* (Leipzig 1888)

——————————. *Bd.38 Verhandlungen des Vereins für Sozialpolitik* (Leipzig 1889)

——————————. *Bde.62-70 Untersuchungen über die Lage des Handwerks in Deutschland mit besonderer Rücksicht auf seine Konkurrenzfähigkeit gegenüber der Grossindustrie* (Leipzig 1895-1897)

——————————. *Bd.76 Verhandlungen des Vereins für Sozialpolitik* (Leipzig 1898)

——————————. *Bde.77-81 Untersuchungen über die Lage des Hausiergewerbes in Deutschland* (Leipzig 1898-1899)

——————————. *Bd.87 Verhandlungen des Vereins für Sozialpolitik* (Leipzig 1900)

——————————. *Bd.151 Untersuchungen über Konsumvereine* (Leipzig 1915-1924)

Schulthess' Europäischer Geschichtskalender

Sitzungen der Bürgerschaft zu Hamburg. Stenographische Berichte

Sitzungs-Bericht über die 1.Generalversammlung der Deutschen Mittelstandsvereinigung am 26.und 27.Nov. 1904 in Berlin. Schriften der Deutschen Mittelstandsvereinigung Heft 1 (Hannover 1904)

Sitzungs-Bericht über die 2.Generalversammlung der Deutschen Mittelstandsvereinigung am 3, 4.und 5.September 1905 in Frankfurt a.Main. Schriften der Deutschen Mittelstandsvereinigung Heft 2 (Hannover 1905)

Stenographische Berichte über die Verhandlung der Bayerischen Kammer der Abgeordneten

Stenographische Berichte über die Verhandlung des (Preussischen) Haus der Abgeordneten

Stenographische Berichte über die Verhandlungen des Reichstages (mit Anlagebände)

Stenographische Berichte über die Verhandlungen des Reichstages des Norddeutschen Bundes

Stumpf, F. *Bericht über die am 9.Dezember 1895 zu Osnabrück gepflogenen Verhandlungen Deutscher Handels-Körperschaften betr. die Bedrängnisse des Kleinhandels und die Mittel zur Abhilfe derselben* (Osnabrück 1896)

Verband deutscher Gewerbevereine und Handwerkerinnungen. Hauptversammlungen 1900-1905

Verhandlungsbericht vom 1.niedersächsischen Mittelstandstag am 25, 26, und 27.März 1911 in Braunschweig

Verhandlungsbericht vom 1.niedersächsischen Mittelstandstag am 25, 26, und 29. und 30. Juni 1913

Was will die Deutsche Vereinigung? Deutsche Zeitfragen. Heft 1 Hrsg. von der Deutschen Vereinigung (Bonn 1908)

Was will die Mittelstandsbewegung? Nach der Denkschrift der Mittelstandsvereinigung im Königreich Sachsen bearbeitet. H.V.S.F.R.K. Nr.171 (1908)

Zentrums Partei. Luebbering, Heinrich. *Was können wir im Volksverein tun zur Hebung des Kleinhandels* (Mönchengladbach, 1912)

――――――― . *Tätigkeitsberichte der Reichstagsfraktion*

4.   Handbücher, Dokumentesammlungen u.ä.

Das A.B.C. Buch für freisinnige Wähler. Ein Lexikon parlamentarischer Zeit- und Streitfragen (Berlin 1889, 1890, 1892, 1896, 1898, 1903)

Acht Gutachten über die Sonntagsruhe im Handelsgewerbe erstattet von Gehilfinnen (Jena 1905)

Adlmaier, K. and Bahnbrecher, Frz.H. *Die Lage des bayerischen Kleinhandels* (München 1909)

Agrarisches Handbuch. Hrsg. vom Bund der Landwirte (3 Aufl. Berlin 1911)

Eine Aufklärungsschrft für die konservativen Wähler (Berlin 1911)

Der Berliner Antisemitismusstreit. Böhlich, Walter (ed.) (Frankfurt a.M. 1965)

Christlich-soziales Handbuch für Jedermann (5 Aufl. 1901 ff.)

Die Detaillistenkammer Hamburg 1904-1929 (Hamburg 1929)

Dokumente zur Geschichte der Handelskammer Hamburg. Hrsg. von der Handelskammer zu ihrem dreihundertjährigen Jubiläum am 19. Januar 1965 (n.p. n.d.)

Dürig, Günter and Rudolf, Walter. *Texte zur deutschen Verfassungsgeschichte* (München-Berlin 1967)

Erster Jahresbericht der Kammer für Kleinhandel zu Bremen für 1907/1908 (Bremen 1908 ff.)

Die Finanzreform von 1909 und die Parteien des Reichstags. Hrsg. vom Sozialdemokratischen Parteivorstand (Berlin 1910)

Fischer, Wolfram. *Quellen zur Geschichte des deutschen Handwerks* (Berlin-Göttingen-Frankfurt a.M. 1957)

Fritsch, Theodor. *Antisemiten-Katechismus. Eine Zusammenstellung des wichtigsten Materials zum Verständnis der Judenfrage* (25 Aufl. Leipzig 1893)

――――――― . *Handbuch der Judenfrage* (Leipzig 1935)

Handbuch der Fortschrittlichen Volkspartei Württembergs zu Reichstagswahl 1912 (Stuttgart 1912)

Handbuch der sozialdemokratischen Parteitage von 1863 bis 1909. Bearbeitet von Schröder, Wilhelm (München 1910)

Handbuch der sozialdemokratischen Parteitage von 1910 bis 1913. Bearbeitet von Schröder, Wilhelm (München n.d.)

Handbuch für die Mitglieder der Detaillistenkammer in Hamburg (Hamburg 1904)

Handbuch für nichtsozialdemokratische Wähler. Hrsg. vom Reichsverband gegen die Sozialdemokratie (Berlin 1911)

Handbuch wirtschaftlicher Vereine und Verbände des Deutschen Reiches. Hrsg. vom Hansa-Bund für Gewerbe, Handel und Industrie (2 Aufl. Berlin 1919)

Jahrbuch. Verband der Rabattsparvereine Deutschlands (Bremen 1908-1909 ff)

Jahresberichte der Detaillistenkammer zu Hamburg (Hamburg 1905 ff)

Jahresberichte der Hamburgischen Gewerbekammer (Hamburg 1900 ff.)

Jahresberichte der Handelskammer zu Hannover für das Jahr 1901 (Hannover 1901 ff.)

Die Handelskammern. Ihre Organisation und Tätigkeit. Bericht an der Internationalen Handelskammer-Kongress in Mailand 1906. Erstattet von den Aeltesten der Kaufmannschaft von Berlin (Berlin 1906)

Der Kampf um die Reichsversicherungs-Ordnung. Hrsg. vom Sozialdemokratischer .Parteivorstand (Berlin 1911)

Katechismus des Bundes der Landwirte (Berlin 1901)

Kautsky, Karl. *Texte zu den Programmen der deutschen Sozialdemokratie 1891-1925.* Langner, Albrecht (ed.) (Köln 1968)

De Koopman tho Bremen. Ein Fünfhundertjahr-Gedanken der Handelskammer Bremen (Bremen 1951)

Konservativer Kalender. Hrsg. vom Hauptverein der Deutsch-Konservativen Partei (Berlin 1913)

Konservatives Handbuch (Berlin 1892, 1894, 1898, 1911)

Kotowski, Georg: Pöls, Werner; Ritter, Gerhard A. (eds.) *Das Wilhelminische Deutschland. Stimmen der Zeitgenossen* (Hamburg-Frankfurt a.M. 1965)

Krueger, Hermann. *Die freien Interessenvertretungen von Industrie, Handel und Gewerbe in Deutschland insbesondere die Fach-, Zweck- und Zentralverbände gewerblicher Unternehmer,* Inaugural-Dissertation-Berlin (Berlin 1908)

Neue Wege. Aus Theodor Fritsch's Lebensarbeit. Eine Sammlung von Hammer-Aufsätzen zu seinem siebzigsten Geburtstage, Lehmann, Paul (ed.) (Leipzig 1922)

Politisches Handbuch der Nationalliberalen Partei (Berlin 1897, 1907, 1910)

Politisches Handbuch für Nationalliberale Wähler (2 Aufl. Berlin 1897)

Rassow, Peter and Born, Karl Erich (eds.) *Akten zur Staatlichen Sozialpolitik in Deutschland 1890-1914* (Wiesbaden 1959)

Ritter, Gerhard A. (ed.) *Historisches Lesebuch 2, 1871-1914* (Frankfurt a.M. 1967)

Salomon, Felix. *Die deutschen Parteiprogramme* (2 Bde. Leipzig-Berlin 1907)

Schraepler, Ernst. *Quellen zur Geschichte der sozialen Frage in Deutschland* (2 Bde. Berlin-Göttingen-Frankfurt a.M. 1955-1957)

Schwarz, Max. *MdR. Biographisches Handbuch der Reichstag* (Hannover 1965)

Der soziale Zentrumsgedanke (Mönchengladbach 1907, 1911)

Die Sozialpolitik der deutschen Zentrumspartei. Gesammelte sozialpolitischen Flugblätter des Volksvereins für das katholische Deutschland (Mönchengladbach 1903, 1910)

Stürmer, Michael (ed.) *Bismarck und die preussisch-deutsche Politik* (München 1970)

Taschenbuch für Nationalliberale Wähler. Hrsg. vom Centralbureau der Nationalliberalen Partei Deutschlands (Berlin 1911)

Treue Wolfgang. *Deutsche Parteiprogramme 1861-1961* (3 Aufl. Berlin-Göttingen-Frankfurt a.M. 1961)

Verzeichnis der im Deutschen Reiche bestehenden Vereine gewerblicher Unternehmer zur Wahrung ihrer wirtschaftlichen Interessen. Hrsg. vom Reichsamt des Innern (Berlin 1903)

Wirtschafts-Politisches Handbuch des Hansa-Bundes (n.p. 1910)

5.   Assorted Sources and Literature (to 1918)

Adler, Georg. *Der Kampf wider den Zwischenhandel* (Berlin 1896)

——————— . *Über die Epochen der deutschen Handwerkerpolitik* (Jena 1903)

Ahlwardt, Hermann. *Judenflinten, Ansichten eines Deutschen Waffenoffiziers* (Berlin 1892)

——————— . *Der Verzweiflungskampf der arischen Völker mit dem Judentum* (Berlin 1890)

Albrecht, Carl. *Das Hamburger Bürgerschaft-Wahlgesetz vom 5.März 1906 im Hinblick auf die Neuwahlen 1907* (Hamburg 1906)

Der angebliche Ruin des Kleinhandels durch den Ladenschluss. Flugschrift Nr.5 der Berufsgenossenschaft Deutschnationaler Handlungsgehilfen-Verband (Hamburg 1899)

Die Antisemiten im Reichstag (Berlin 1903)

Ashley, W.J. *The Progress of the German Working Classes* (London 1904)

Augst, Richard. *Bismarcks Stellung zum parlamentarischen Wahlrecht* (Berlin 1913)

Baasch, Ernst. *Die Handelskammer zu Hamburg; im Auftrage der Handelskammer bearbeitet* (2 Bde. Hamburg 1915)

Bagge, H. *Die Bürgerschaftswahlen im Stadtgebiete nach dem hamburgischen Wahlgesetz vom 5.März 1906* (Hamburg 1906)

Bahr, Hermann. *Der Antisemitismus; Ein internationales Interview* (Berlin 1884)

Bamberger, Ludwig, *Erinnerungen* (Berlin 1899)

Bayer, H.G. *Liberale Kleinhandelspolitik* (Berlin-Schönberg 1912)

Bebel, August (ed.) *Die Sozialdemokratie im deutschen Reichstag, 1871-1893* (Berlin 1909)

Bernstein, Eduard. *Die Voraussetzungen des Sozialismus und die Aufgabe der Sozialdemokratie* (Stuttgart 1911 original ed. 1906)

Beythien, Heinrich. *Die Entwicklung des gemeinnützigen Rabattsparvereins-Wesens und seine Einwirkung auf die wirtschaftliche Lage des Detailhandels* (Bremen 1907)

——————— . *Die Rabattsparvereine der Kaufleute und Gewerbetreibenden* (Bremen 1913)

Biermer, Magnus. "Mittelstandsbewegung" in Conrad, J. et al. (eds.) *Handworterbuch der Staatswissenschaften* (Bd.6, 3 Aufl. Jena 1910), pp.734-762

——————— . *Die Mittelstandsbewegung und das Warenhausproblem* (Giessen 1905)

——————— . *Sammlung nationalökonomischer Aufsätze und Vorträge* (Giessen 1905)

Biller, K. *Kolonialwaren, Kleinhandel und Einkaufsvereine. Vortrag auf dem 7.Verbandstage des Verbandes bayrischer Kaufleute der Kolonialwarenbranche am 14.Sept. 1913* (n.p. n.d.)

Böckel, Otto. *Zolltarif und Handelsvertragspolitik: Wirtschaftspolitische Darlegungen* (Berlin 1903)

——————— . (As Dr.Capistrano). *Die europäische Judengefahr* (Cassel 1886)

Böttger, Hugo. "Die Forderungen des gewerblichen Mittelstandes und der Reichstag" *Nationalliberale Blätter* Nr.50 (14.12.1913), pp.1015-1020

—————————. *Vom alten und neuen Mittelstand* (Jena 1901)

—————————. *Zur Bekämpfung des unlauteren Wettbewerbs* (Braunschweig 1895)

Borght, Richard van der. *Grundzüge der Sozialpolitik* (Leipzig 1904)

—————————. *Handel und Handelspolitik* (2 Aufl. Leipzig 1907)

Borgius, Walter. "Wandlungen im modernen Detailhandel" *Archiv für soziale Gesetzgebung und Statistik* vol.13 (1899), pp.41-84

Brandt, L.O. "Der Hansabund, seine Ziele und Gegner" *Die Grenzboten* Nr.34. 19.8.1909, pp.348-361

Braun, Adolf. *Die Warenhäuser und die Mittelstandspolitik der Zentrumspartei* (Berlin 1904)

Braun, Max. *Adolf Stöcker* (Berlin 1912)

Brennende Fragen: Hrsg. Thomas Frey (Theodor Fritsch) (Leipzig 1885-1890)

Brentano, Lujo. *Ueber die Ursachen der heutigen socialen Noth. Ein Beitrag zur Morphologie der Volkswirtschaft. Vortrag gehalten beim Antritt des Lehramts an der Universität Leipzig am 27.April 1889* (Leipzig 1889)

Büchler, M. *Die Rabattsparvereine, das wirksamste Selbsthilfemittel zur Hebung des kaufmännischen Mittelstandes* (Ettelbrück 1910)

Bueck, H.A. *Die Organisation der Arbeitgeber* (Berlin 1904)

Bürger, Curt. *Die Agrardemagogie in Deutschland* (Gross-Lichterfelde 1911)

—————————. *Antisemiten-Spiegel. Die Antisemiten im Lichte des Christentums, des Rechtes und der Wissenschaft* (Berlin-Frankfurt a.M. 1911)

—————————. *Die politische Mittelstandsbewegung* (Gross-Lichterfelde 1912)

Büttner, M. *Die Mittelstandsnot und die Selbsthilfe im Kleinhandel und Kleingewerbe* (n.d. n.p. Gelsenkirchen 1913)

Busch, Moritz. *Tagebuchblätter* (3 Bde. Leipzig 1899)

Buschmann, Johannes. *Kleinhandel und Kultur* (München 1908)

Calwer, Richard. "Der Handel" *Bd.8 Die Gesellschaft* (Frankfurt a.M. 1907)

Cost of Living in German Towns. Cd.4032 (Board of Trade London 1908)

Crüger, Hans. *Aus Vergangenheit und Gegenwart der Deutschen Genossenschaften* (Berlin 1899)

—————————. *Die Erwerbs- und Wirtschafts-Genossenschaften in den einzelnen Ländern* (Jena 1892)

—————————. *Zur Kritik der Agitation gegen die Konsumvereine* (Berlin 1899)

Curtius, Lorenz. *Der politische Antisemitismus von 1906-1911* (München 1911)

Dawson, W.H. *German Life in Town and Country* (London 1901)

—————————. *The German Workman* (New York 1906)

Der Deutsche Handelstag 1861-1911. Hrsg. vom Deutschen Handelstag (2 Bde. Berlin 1911, 1913)

Dix, Arthur. *Der Bund der Landwirte* (Berlin 1909)

Dühring, Eugen. *Die Judenfrage als Racen- Sitten- und Culturfrage, mit einer weltgeschichtlichen Antwort* (Karlsruhe 1881)

Dursthoff, H.M. *Die Lage des Kleinhandels und die Begründung von Einkaufsgenossenschaften* (Oldenburg 1903)

Ecker, Alexander. *Der Mittelstand und die politischen Parteien* (Essen-Ruhr 1914)

Ehlers, Otto. "Der Binnenhandel" in Zorn, Philipp and v.Berger, Herbert et al.

282   The Politics of Economic Despair

Deutschland unter Kaiser Wilhelm II (Bd.2 Berlin 1914), pp.714-731

Elster Alexander. "Rabattsparvereine" in Conrad, J. et.al. (eds) *Handwörterbuch der Staatswissenschaften* (Bd.7, 3 Aufl. Jena 1911) pp.1-5

Engel, August. *Detaillisten-Fragen. Neue Aufgaben des Kleinhandels. Nr.33 Soziale Tages-Fragen.* Hrsg. vom Volksverein für das katholische Deutschland (2 Aufl. Mönchengladbach 1907)

Engels, Friedrich. *Herrn Eugen Dührings Umwälzung der Wissenschaft (Anti-Dühring)* in Marx, Karl and Engels, Friedrich. *Werke* (Bd.20 Berlin 1972)

Erhardt, Max. *Die Warenhaus-Umsatzsteuer. Eine Besprechung der Regierungsvorlage und der Denkschrift des Bundes der Handel-und Gewerbetreibenden zu Berlin* (Berlin 1900)

Faucherre, Henry, *Die Händler-Rabattsparvereine. Studie über die praktischen Probleme der Mittelstandsbewegung* (Jena 1912)

Fest-Ausgabe zum 10.jährigen Jubiläum des Verbandes Deutscher Waren- und Kaufhäuser Berlin (Berlin 1913)

Festschrift zum 40.jähr. Stiftungsfest des Vereins der Kolonialwarenhändler von 1872 Hamburg (Hamburg 1912)

Fischer, R.J. *Der mittelständische Handel vor seinem Untergang?* (Augsberg n.d.)

Frank, Ludwig. *Die bürgerlichen Parteien des Deutschen Reichstags* (Stuttgart 1911)

Frantz, Constantin. *Der Nationalliberalismus und die Judenherrschaft* (München 1874)

───────── . *Der Untergang der alten Parteien und die Parteien der Zukunft* (Berlin 1878)

Fritsch, Theodor. *Mittelstand, Kapital-Herrschaft, Monarchie* (3 Aufl. Leipzig 1917)

Gensel, J. *Der Deutsche Handelstag in seiner Entwickelung und Tätigkeit, 1861-1901* (Berlin 1902)

Gerber, Dr. von. *Der Ruin des Mittelstandes von einem Mann aus dem Volke* (9 Aufl. Dresden 1891)

Glagau, Otto. *Der Börsen- und Gründungs-Schwindel in Berlin* (Leipzig 1876)

───────── . *Der Börsen- und Gründungs-Schwindel in Deutschland* (Leipzig 1877)

───────── . *Deutsches Handwerk und historisches Bürgertum* (Osnabrück 1879)

───────── . *Des Reiches Noth und der neue Culturkampf* (Osnabrück 1879)

Göhre, Paul. "Das Warenhaus" *Bd.12 Die Gesellschaft* (Frankfurt a.M. 1907)

Goldschmidt, Ernst Friedrich. *Die deutsche Handwerkerbewegung bis zum Sieg der Gewerbefreiheit* (München 1916)

Graetzer, Rudolf. *Die Organisation der Berufsinteressen* (Berlin 1890)

Gravelli, A. *Zum Kampf gegen die Waarenhäuser. Eine Zeit- und Streit-Frage* (Dresden 1899)

Hamburg. Senat. *Hamburgisches Staatshandbuch* (Hamburg 1881 ff.)

Hamburgisches Staats-Handbuch (Hamburg 1890 ff.)

Hampke, Thilo. *Der Befähigungsnachweis im Handwerk* (Jena 1892)

───────── . "Gewerbekammern" in Conrad, J. et al. (eds.) *Handwörterbuch der Staatswissenschaften* (Bd.4 3 Aufl. Jena 1909), pp.993-1006

————————. *Handwerker- oder Gewerbekammern* (Jena 1893)

Harms, Bernard. *Arbeitskammern und Kaufmannskammern* (Tübingen 1907)

————————. *Ist das deutsche Handwerk konkurrenzfähig* (Leipzig 1900)

Helfferich, Karl. *Deutschlands Volkswohlstand 1888-1913* (Berlin 1914)

Henningsen, J. *Beiträge zur Warenhaus-Frage!* (Hamburg 1906)

Hoschke, Heinrich. *Das Detaillisten-Kaufhaus. Ein Beitrag zur Detailhandelsfrage* (Dresden 1906)

Huber, F.C. *Warenhaus und Kleinhandel* (Berlin 1899)

————————. *Zur Handwerkerfrage* (Stuttgart 1896)

Huber, Victor Aimé. *Die Selbsthilfe der arbeitenden Klassen durch Wirtschaftsvereine und unsere Ansiedelung* (Berlin 1848)

Hübner, Friedrich. *Zur Lage des Kleinhandels.* Inaugural-Dissertation-Heidelberg (Heidelberg 1902)

Hugenberg, A. *Bank- und Kreditwirtschaft des deutschen Mittelstandes* (München 1906)

Janssen, J. *Was der Detaillistenstand selbst tun muss!* (Barmen 1911)

Jünger, Karl. *Katholisch-sozialistische Mittelstandsbewegung. Eine Gefahr im deutschen Katholizismus* (Bonn 1918)

Kaiserliches statistisches Amt. *Die deutsche Volkswirtschaft am Schlusse des 19. Jahrhunderts* (Berlin 1900)

————————. *Statistik des Deutschen Reichs, Bd.220/221. Berufs- und Betriebszählung vom 12.Juni 1907. Gewerbliche Betriebsstatistik — Abt. VIII. Gliederung und Verteilung der Gewerbebetriebe im Deutschen Reiche. Zusammenfassende Darstellung* (Berlin 1914)

————————. *Statistisches Jahrbuch für das Deutsche Reich* (Berlin 1886 ff.)

Kandt, Mortiz. "Über verschiedene Prämien-Sparsysteme und ihre volkswirtschaftliche Bedeutung" in *Festgaben für Wilhelm Lexis zur siebzigsten Wiederkehr seines Geburtstages* (Jena 1907), pp.337-368

Kanter, Hugo. *Die Entwicklung des Handels mit gebrauchsfertigen Waren von der Mitte des 18.Jahrhunderts bis 1866 zu Frankfurt a.M.* (Tübingen-Leipzig 1902)

Kaufmann, Heinrich. *Die Stellungsnahme der Sozialdemokratie zur Konsumgenossenschaftsbewegung* (2 Aufl. Hamburg 1911)

Körner, Hermann. *Die Warenhäuser, ihr Wesen, ihre Entstehung und ihre Stellung im Wirtschaftsleben* (Tübingen 1908)

Krahmer, Dr. "Kaufmannsgerichte" in Conrad, J et al. (eds.) *Handwörterbuch der Staatswissenschaften* (Bd.5 3 Aufl. Jena 1910), pp.816-822

Krüer, Hermann. *Die Markthallen und ihre Hilfskräfte als Faktoren der Lebensmittelversorgung in unseren Grossstädten* (Berlin 1914)

Krueger, Hermann Edwin. *Die wirtschaftliche und soziale Lage der Privatangestellten. Schriften der Gesellschaft für soziale Reform* (Zweiter Teil Jena 1912)

Kulemann, Wilhelm. *Politische Erinnerungen. Ein Beitrag zur neueren Zeitgeschichte* (Berlin 1911)

Lagarde, Paul de. *Deutsche Schriften* (Göttingen 1892)

Lambrechts, Hector. *Warenhäuser und Konsumvereine vom sozialen Standpunkt betrachtet,* in *Jahrbuch. Verband der Rabattsparvereine Deutschlands* (Bremen 1913)

Landwers, Richard. *Die Lage des Kleinhandels und die Gründungen der Rabatt-*

Sparvereine und Einkaufs-Genossenschaften Inaugural-Dissertation-Heidelberg (Berlin 1905)

Lange, Paul. "Detailhandel und Mittelstandspolitik" in *Neue Zeit* 25 (1907), pp.693 ff.; 730 ff.; 764 ff.

――――――― . *Handlungsgehilfenbewegung und Sozialpolitik* (Hamburg 1908)

Lederer, Emil. *Die Privatangestellten in der modernen Wirtschaftsentwicklung* (Tübingen 1912)

――――――― . "Sozialpolitische Chronik. Angestelltenorganisationen" *Archiv für Sozialwissenschaft und Sozialpolitik* XXXIV (1912), pp.336-360.

――――――― . "Sozialpolitische Chronik. Mittelstandsbewegung" *Archiv für Sozialwissenschaft und Sozialpolitik* XXXI (1910), pp.970-1000.

――――――― . "Sozialpolitische Chronik. Mittelstandsbewegung" *Archiv für Sozialwissenschaft und Sozialpolitik* XXXV (1912), pp.913-938.

――――――― . "Sozialpolitische Chronik. Mittelstandsbewegung" *Archiv für Sozialwissenschaft und Sozialpolitik* XXXVII (1913), pp.1005-1026.

――――――― . *Die wirtschaftlichen Organisationen* (Leipzig 1913).

――――――― . "Die wirtschaftlichen Organisationen" in Sarason, D. (ed.) *Das Jahr 1913, ein Gesamtbild der Kulturentwicklung* (Leipzig-Berlin 1913), pp.132-138.

Leopold, Max. *Die Stellung wirtschaftlicher Interessenvertretung zu Fragen des Detailhandels, mit besonderer Berücksichtigung des Bayerischen Verbandes der Vereine zum Schutz für Handel und Gewerbe* (Nürnberg 1915).

Lexis, Wilhelm. *Allgemeine Volkswirtschaftslehre* (Berlin-Leipzig 1910).

Lux, Käthe. *Studien über die Entwicklung der Warenhäuser in Deutschland* (Jena, 1910).

Mannhardt, W. *Zur Frage einer amtlichen Vertretung des Kleinhandelsstandes (Detaillistenkammer)* (Hamburg 1899).

Maresch, Rudolf. "Handelskammern" in Conrad, J. et al. (eds.) *Handwörterbuch der Staatswissenschaften* (Bd.5, 3 Aufl. Jena 1910), pp.295-301.

Marx, Karl and Engels, Friedrich. "Manifest der Kommunistischen Partei" in Marx, Karl and Engels, Friedrich. *Werke* (Bd.4 Berlin 1972).

Mataja, Viktor. "Abzahlungsgeschäfte" in Conrad, J. et al. (eds.) *Handwörterbuch der Staatswissenschaften* (Bd.1, 3 Aufl. Jena 1909), pp.13-20.

――――――― . *Grossmagazine und Kleinhandel* (Leipzig 1891).

――――――― . "Kleinhandel" in Conrad, J. et al. (eds.) *Handwörterbuch der Staatswissenschaften* (Bd.5, 3 Aufl. Jena 1910), pp.874-880.

Messow, Paul. *Die Schäden im Detailhandel und die Warenhäuser* (Dresden n.d., ca. 1900).

Meyer, Rudolf. *Politische Gründer und die Corruption in Deutschland* (Leipzig 1877).

Most, Johann. *Der Kleinburger und die Sozialdemokratie. Ein Mahnwort an die Kleingewerbetreibenden* (Augsberg 1876).

Müffelmann, Leo. *Die moderne Mittelstandsbewegung* (Berlin 1913).

Naumann, Friedrich. *Die politischen Parteien* (Berlin 1910).

Nientimp. Hans. *Kolonialwarenhändler wehrt euch! Eine Standespredigt für die Detailhändler der Lebensmittelbranche und deren Lieferanten* (Düsseldorf 1913).

Oertzen, Dietrich von. *Adolf Stöcker, Lebensbild und Zeitgeschichte* (2 Bde.

2 Aufl. Berlin 1911).

Oldenberg, Karl. "Die heutige Lage der Commis nach neuerer Literatur" *Jahrbuch für Gesetzgebung, Verwaltung und Volkswirtschaft im Deutschen Reich* (1892), pp.749-812.

——————— . "Statistik der socialen Lage der deutschen Handlungsgehülfen" *Jahrbuch für Gesetzgebung, Verwaltung und Volkswirtschaft im Deutschen Reich* (1893), pp.1231-1250.

Ortloff, Hermann. *Die Mittelstandsbewegung und Konsumvereine* (Gautzsch b. Leipzig 1908).

Parisius, Ludoff. *Kreditgenossenschaften nach Schulze-Delitzsch* (Berlin 1895).

Pfeiffer, Eduard. *Über Genossenschaftswesen* (Leipzig 1863).

Pieper, A. *Das Zentrum und die wachsende gewerbstätige Bevölkerung nach den Reichstagswahlen 1912* (Mönchengladbach 1912).

Pierstorff, Julius. "Der moderne Mittelstand" *Vorträge der Gehe-Stiftung* Bd.3 (1911).

Pohle, Ludwig, "Die neuere Entwicklung des Kleinhandels" *Jahrbuch der Gehe-Stiftung zu Dresden* VI (1901)

Praeger, Max. "Die Mittelstandsfrage" *Volkswirtschaftliche Zeitfragen* Heft 201-202 (1904)

Pudor, Heinrich. "Zur Sozialpolitik des Mittelstandes I-IV" *Kultur und Fortschritt*, Heft 319-320, Heft 351-354; Heft 413-415; Heft 438-440 (Leipzig 1910-1912)

Rathgen, Karl. "Handelspolitik" *Wörterbuch der Volkswirtschaft* (Bd.2, 2 Aufl. Jena 1906-1907), pp.169 ff.

Reemtsen, Carl. "Der moderne Detailhandel" *Volkswirtschaftliche Zeitfragen* Heft 272 (1913)

Richter, Eugen. *Sozialdemokratische Zukunftsbilder: frei nach Bebel* (Berlin 1898)

Riesenfeld, Conrad Ernst. "Kaufmännische Schiedsgerichte" *Volkswirtschaftliche Zeitfragen* Heft 150 (1897)

Sauer, Eduard. *Die Schäden im Auktionswesen und ihre Bekämpfung* (Düsseldorf 1909)

Schaefer, Heinz. *Der Ausverkauf im Lichte des neuen Gesetzes gegen den unlauteren Wettbewerb* (Tübingen 1910)

Schär, Johann F. *Allgemeine Handelsbetriebslehre* (Leipzig 1911)

Schmitz, Peter. *Die Lage des Lebensmitteldetailhandels in Cöln.* Inaugural-Dissertation-Heidelberg (Cöln 1906)

Schmoller, Gustav. *Die Lebensfähigkeit des deutschen Handwerks* (Rostock 1897)

——————— . *Über einige Grundfragen der Sozialpolitik und Volkswirtschaftslehre* (Leipzig 1898)

——————— . "Was verstehen wir unter Mittelstand?" in *Die Verhandlungen des 8.Evangelisch-sozialen Kongresses, abgehalten zu Leipzig am 10. und 11. Juni 1897. Nach den stenographischen Protokollen* (Göttingen 1897)

——————— . *Zur Geschichte der deutschen Kleingewerbe im 19.Jahrhundert* (Halle 1870)

Schulze-Delitzsch, Franz Hermann. *Schriften und Reden,* Thorwart, H. (ed.) (5 Bde. Berlin 1909-1913)

Schuon, Hermann. *Der Deutschnationale Handlungsgehilfen-Verband zu Hamburg:*

Sein Werdegang und seine Arbeit (Jena 1914)

Schupp, Fr. and Wettstein, K.A. *Die Entstehungsgeschichte des ersten Allgemeinen Deutschen Handelstages 1861: Zum 50.jährigen Jubiläum des Handelstages* (Karlsruhe 1911)

Sittart, P.H.J. *Die Sozialpolitik des Zentrums* (Trier 1903)

Sombart, Werner. *Die deutsche Volkswirtschaft im 19.Jahrhundert* (Berlin 1903)

Statistisches Jahrbuch Deutscher Städte (Breslau 1891 ff.)

Staudinger, Franz. *Die Konsumgenossenschaft* (Leipzig 1908)

Steinberg, F. *Die Handwerkerbewegung in Deutschland, ihre Ursachen und Ziele* (Stuttgart 1897)

Steindamm, Johannes. *Beiträge zur Warenhausfrage* (Berlin 1904)

──────────. *Die Besteuerung der Warenhäuser* (Berlin 1903)

Stieda, Wilhelm. "Handwerk" in Conrad, J. et al. (eds.) *Handwörterbuch der Staatswissenschaften* (Bd. 5, 3 Aufl. Jena 1910), pp.377-393

──────────. *Die Lebensfähigkeit des deutschen Handwerks* (Leipzig 1897)

"Die Mittelstandsbewegung" *Jahrbücher für Nationalökonomie und Statistik* LXXXIV (Jan-Juni 1905), pp.1-20

Stillich, Oskar. *Die politischen Parteien,* Bd.1, *Die Konservativen* (Leipzig, 1908); Bd.2 *Der Liberalismus* (Leipzig 1911)

Stöcker, Adolf. *Christlich-Sozial. Reden und Aufsätze* (2 Aufl. Leipzig 1890)

Striemer, Alfred. *Zum Kampfe um die wirtschaftliche Selbständigkeit des Klein- und Mittelbetriebes* (München 1914)

Suchsland, Emil. *Die Klippen des sozialen Friedens* (6 Aufl. Halle 1904)

──────────. *Los von der Konsumvereine und Warenhäusern* (2 Aufl. Halle 1906)

Notwahrheiten über Konsumvereine. Eine Diskussions-Rede vom Kampfplatz mit der Sozialdemokratie (Halle 1904)

──────────. *Schutz- und Trutzwaffen für den gewerblichen Mittelstand in seiner Notwehr gegen die Konsumvereine und Warenhäuser* (Halle 1904)

Tille, Alexander. *Die Berufsstandspolitik des Gewerbe- und Handelsstandes* (4 Bde. Berlin 1910 ff.)

──────────. *Die gemeinsamen Interessen der selbständigen Gewerbetreibenden* (Leipzig 1912)

Troeltsch, Walter. "Über die neuesten Veränderungen im deutschen Wirtschaftsleben" *Vortragsexkurs in Stuttgart vom 21.Nov. bis 19.Dez. 1898* (Stuttgart 1899)

Verband für das Kaufmännische Unterrichtswesen, *Handbuch der Wirtschaftskunde Deutschlands* (4 Bde. Leipzig. 1901-1904)

Waentig, Heinrich. *Gewerbliche Mittelstandspolitik* (2 Aufl. Leipzig 1898)

Wagener, Hermann. *Erlebtes. Meine Memorien aus der Zeit von 1848 bis 1866 und von 1873 bis jetzt* (Berlin 1884)

Wahrmund, Adolf. *Das Gesetz des Nomadentums und die heutige Judenherrschaft* (München 1887)

Wegener, Friedrich. *Der Freiheitskampf des Mittelstandes* (Berlin 1906)

Weigert, Max. "Die Krisis des Zwischenhandels" *Volkswirtschaftliche Zeitfragen* Heft 53 (1885)

Wernicke, Johannes. "Ist die Mittelstandsbewegung eine Kulturbewegung? " *Deutsche Wirtschafts-Zeitung* (1909), pp.102-108

_____ . *Der Kampf um den wirtschaftlichen Fortschritt* (Jena 1910)
_____ *Kapitalismus und Mittelstandspolitik* (Jena 1907 2 Aufl. 1922)

_____ . *Der Mittelstand und seine wirtschaftliche Lage* (Leipzig 1909)

_____ . "Der Mittelstandskongress des Hansa-Bundes" *Deutsche Wirtschafts-Zeitung* (1911), pp.641-644

_____ . *Wandlungen und neue Interessen-Organisationen im Detailhandel* (Berlin 1908)

_____ . *Warenhaus, Industrie und Mittelstand* (Berlin 1911)

_____ . *Die wirtschaftliche und soziale Bedeutung der Warenhäuser* (Berlin 1904)

Whitman, Sidney, *German Memories* (New York 1912)

Wiedermann, Heinrich. *Der Reichsdeutsche Mittelstands-Verband! Ein Beitrag zur Lösung der Organisationsfrage des Deutschen Mittelstandes* (Münster i.W. 1913)

Wilbrant, R. *Die Bedeutung der Konsumgenossenschaften. Vortrag auf dem Evangelisch-sozialen Kongress zu Hamburg Pfingsten 1913 gehalten* (Göttingen 1914)

Wilden, J. *Handwerk und Industrie* (Berlin 1912)

Wilhelms, Robert. *Die Warenhäuser und ihre Bekämpfung* (Strassburg 1898)

Wilmanns, C. *Die "goldene" Internationale und die Notwendigkeit einer sozialen Reformpartei* (Berlin 1876)

Wirminghaus, A. "Wirtschaftliche Verhältnisse und Entwicklungstendenzen im Kleinhandel" *Preussische Jahrbücher* 141 (1910), pp.32-60

Wittenberg, Max. "Ein Blick auf den wirtschaftlichen Aufschwung am Ende des 19.Jahrhunderts" *Volkswirtschaftliche Zeitfragen* Heft 172-173 (1900)

6.   Assorted Sources and Literature (after 1918)

Ahrens, Werner. "Das sozialistische Genossenschaftswesen in Hamburg 1890-1914" Dissertation-Hamburg 1970

Alexander, David. *Retailing in England during the Industrial Revolution* (London 1971)

Allen, William Sheridan. *The Nazi Seizure of Power. The Experience of a Single German Town 1930-1935* (Chicago 1965)

Altrock, W. von. "Landwirtschaftskammern" in Elster, L. et al. (eds.) *Handwörterbuch der Staatswissenschaften* (Bd.6 4 Aufl. Jena 1923), pp.220-229

Anderson, Malcolm. *Conservative Politics in France* (London 1973)

Arendt, Hannah, *Elemente und Ursprünge totaler Herrschaft* (Frankfurt a.M. 1955)

Aron, Raymond. "Social Structure and the Ruling Class" *British Journal of Sociology 1* (1950), pp.1-16

Baasch, Ernst. *Geschichte Hamburgs 1814-1918* (2 Bde. Gotha-Stuttgart, 1924-1925)

Bachem, Karl. *Vorgeschichte, Geschichte und Politik der deutschen Zentrumspartei* (Bd.9 Köln 1932)

Banks, J.A. *The Sociology of Social Movements* (London 1972)

Barkin, Kenneth D. *The Controversy over German Industrialization 1890-1902* (Chicago 1970)

Baron, Salo W. "The Jewish Question in the Nineteenth Century" *Journal of Modern History* X (1938), pp.51-65

Barsky, Steven L. "Economic Backwardness and the Characteristics of Development" *Journal of Economic History*, XXIX, No.3 (1969), pp.449-472

Baumann, Friedrich. *Die Bevölkerung Hamburgs: Berufstätigkeit, Handel, Industrie, Einkommen, Vermögen, Wohnungs- und Lebensmittelbedarf* (Hamburg 1919)

Bechtel, Heinrich. *Wirtschaftsgeschichte Deutschlands im 19. und 20.Jahrhundert* (3 Bde. München 1956)

Bein, Alex. "Modern Anti-Semitism and its Place in the History of the Jewish Question" in Altman, A. (ed.) *Between East and West* (London 1958), pp.164-168

Bell, Daniel (ed.) *The Radical Right* (Garden City Anchor ed. 1964)

Berghahn, Volker R. "Das Kaiserreich in der Sackgasse" *Neue Politische Literatur* XVI (1971), pp.494-506

——————— . *Der Tirpitz-Plan. Genesis und Verfall einer innenpolitischen Krisenstrategie unter Wilhelm II* (Düsseldorf 1971)

Bergstrasser, Ludwig, *Geschichte der politischen Parteien in Deutschland* (München 1960)

Beutin, Ludwig. *Geschichte der südwestfälischen Industrie- und Handelskammer zu Hagen und ihrer Wirtschaftslandschaft* (Hagen 1956)

Birnie, Arthur. *An Economic History of Europe 1760-1939* (London 1930, reprint, 1966)

Böhme, Helmut. *Deutschlands Weg zur Grossmacht. Studien zum Verhältnis von Wirtschaft und Staat während der Reichsgründungszeit 1848-1881* (Köln-Berlin 1966)

——————— . *Prolegomena zu einer Sozial- und Wirtschaftsgeschichte Deutschlands im 19. und 20.Jahrhundert* (Frankfurt a.M. 1968)

Boese, Franz. *Geschichte des Vereins für Sozialpolitik 1872-1932* (Berlin 1939)

Bolland, Jürgen. *Die hamburgische Bürgerschaft in alter und neuer Zeit* (Hamburg 1959)

Boogis, F.D. "The European Economic Community" in Yamey, B.S. (ed.) *Resale Price Maintenance* (London 1966), pp.179-216.

Booms, Hans. *Die Deutschkonservative Partei* (Düsseldorf 1954)

Boree, Karl Friedrich. *Semiten und Antisemiten. Begegnungen und Erfahrungen* (Frankfurt a.M. 1960)

Born, Karl Erich. "Der soziale und wirtschaftliche Strukturwandel Deutschlands am Ende des 19.Jahrhunderts" (1963) in Wehler, Hans-Ulrich (ed.) *Moderne deutsche Sozialgeschichte* (Köln-Berlin 1966), pp.171-184.

——————— . *Staat und Sozialpolitik seit Bismarcks Sturz* (Wiesbaden 1957)

——————— . "Von der Reichsgründung bis zum ersten Weltkrieg" in Gebhardt, Bruno. *Handbuch der deutschen Geschichte* (Bd.3 Stuttgart 1960), pp.194-255

——————— . et al. (eds.) *Quellensammlung zur Geschichte der deutschen*

Sozialpolitik 1867 bis 1914 (Wiesbaden 1966)

Boorstin, Daniel J. *The Americans. The Democratic Experience* (New York 1973)

Bowen, Ralph H. *German Theories of the Corporative State with Special Reference to the Period 1870-1919* (New York 1947)

Bracher, Karl Dietrich. *Die Auflösung der Weimarer Republik* (Stuttgart-Düsseldorf 1957)

——————. *Die deutsche Diktatur. Entstehung, Struktur, Folgen des Nationalsozialismus* (Köln-Berlin 1969)

——————. Sauer, Wolfgang and Schulz, Gerhard. *Die nationalsozialistische Machtergreifung* (Köln-Opladen 1960)

Bramsted, Ernest K. *Aristocracy and the Middle Classes in Germany. Social Types in German Literature 1830-1900* (Chicago revised ed., 1964)

Brauer, Theodor. "Mittelstandspolitik" *G.d.S.* Abt.IX.T.2 (Tübingen 1927), pp.369-410

Bredek, Heinz. "Die Entwicklungstendenzen in den genossenschaftlichen Selbsthilfebestrebungen des mittelständischen Lebensmitteleinzelhandels von ihrem Beginn bis zur Gegenwart" Dissertation-Köln 1960

Bruck, W.F. *Social and Economic History of Germany from William II to Hitler 1888-1938. A Comparative Study* (Oxford 1938)

Bry, Gerhard. *Wages in Germany 1871-1945* (Princeton 1960)

Bucheim, Karl. *Geschichte der christlichen Parteien in Deutschland* (München 1953)

Buchner, H. *Warenhauspolitik und Nationalsozialismus. Nationalsozialistische Bibliothek. Heft 13* (München 1930).

Bücher, Karl. *Die Entstehung der Volkswirtschaft* (2 Bde. 16 Aufl. Tübingen 1922)

Büchner, Richard. "Warenhaussteuer" in Elster, L. et al. (eds.) *Handwörterbuch der Staatswissenschaften* (Bd.8, 4 Aufl. Jena 1928), pp.888-896

Die Bürgerlichen Parteien in Deutschland (2 Bde. Leipzig 1968-1970)

Bullock, Alan. *Hitler. A Study in Tyranny* (London rev. ed. 1965)

Bussmann, Walter. "Zur Geschichte des deutschen Liberalismus im 19. Jahrhundert" *Historische Zeitschrift* 186 (1959), pp.527-558

Campbell, Peter. "Le mouvement Poujade" *P.A.* 10 (1957),pp.362-367

Carsten, F.L. *The Rise of Fascism* (London 1970)

Cecil, Leman. *Albert Ballin: Business and Politics in Imperial Germany 1888-1918* (Princeton 1967)

Class, Heinrich. *Wider den Strom. Vom Werden und Wachsen der nationalen Opposition im alten Reich* (Leipzig 1932)

Cohen, Percy S. *Modern Social Theory* (London 1968)

Crüger, Hans. *Grundriss des deutschen Genossenschaftswesens* (2 Aufl. Leipzig 1922)

——————. "Konsumvereine" in Elster, L. et al. (eds.) *Handwörterbuch der Staatswissenschaften* (Bd.5, 4 Aufl. Jena 1923), pp.875-879

Dahrendorf, Ralf. *Gesellschaft und Demokratie in Deutschland* (München 1965)

Desai, Ashok V. *Real Wages in Germany 1871-1913* (Oxford 1968)

Deutsche Auslands-Arbeitsgemeinschaft Hamburg (ed.) *Hamburg in seiner politischen, wirtschaftlichen und kulturellen Bedeutung* (Hamburg 1931)

Duverger, Maurice. *Sociologie Politique* (Paris 1968)

——————— . et al. (eds.) *Les Elections du 2 Janvier 1956* (Paris 1957)

Engelmann, Bernt. *Die goldenen Jahre. Die Sage von Deutschlands glücklicher Kaiserzeit* (München 1968)

Engelsing, Rolf. "Lebenshaltungen und Lebenshaltungskosten im 18. und 19. Jahrhundert in den Hansestädten Bremen und Hamburg" *IRSH* XI (1966), 1, pp.73-107

Eschenburg, Theodor. *Das Kaiserreich am Scheideweg. Bassermann, Bülow und der Block* (Berlin 1929)

Eyck, Erich. *Das persönliche Regiment Wilhelms II. Politische Geschichte des deutschen Kaiserreichs von 1890 bis 1914* (Erlenbach-Zürich 1949)

Feldman, Gerald D. *Army, Industry and Labor in Germany 1914-1918* (Princeton 1966)

Festschrift 1870-1970. Einhundert Jahre Berufsorganisation des Lebensmittel-Einzelhandels (Bremen 1970)

Fischer, Fritz. *Krieg der Illusionen. Die deutsche Politik von 1911 bis 1914* (Düsseldorf 1969)

Fischer, Wolfram and Czada, Peter. "Wandlungen in der deutschen Industriestruktur im 20.Jahrhundert. Ein statistischdeskriptiver Ansatz" in Ritter, Gerhard A. (ed.) *Entstehung und Wandel der modernen Gesellschaft. Festschrift für Hans Rosenberg zum 65. Geburtstag* (Berlin 1970), pp.116-165

Frank, Walter. *Hofprediger Adolf Stoecker und die christlichsoziale Bewegung* (2 Aufl. Hamburg 1935)

Freedman, Maurice. *A Minority in Britain* (London 1955)

Freudental, Herbert. *Vereine in Hamburg: ein Beitrag zur Geschichte und Volkskunde der Geselligkeit* (Hamburg 1968)

Gay, Peter. *The Dilemma of Democratic Socialism. Eduard Bernstein's Challenge to Marx* (London-New York Collier ed. 1970)

Geiger, Theodor. *Die soziale Schichtung des deutschen Volkes* (Stuttgart 1932)

Gellately, Robert. "The Emergence of Political Anti-Semitism in Germany in the Last Third of the Nineteenth Century" M.A. Thesis Memorial University of Newfoundland 1970

Gerlach, Helmut von. *Von Rechts nach Links* (Zürich 1937)

Gerschenkron, Alexander. *Bread and Democracy in Germany* (New York reprinted 1965)

——————— . *Economic Backwardness in Historical Perspective* (Cambridge Mass. 1962)

Groh, Dieter. *Negative Integration und revolutionärer Attentismus. Die deutsche Sozialdemokratie am Vorabend des Ersten Weltkrieges* (Frankfurt a.M. – Berlin-Wien 1973)

Grünberg, Emil. *Der Mittelstand in der kapitalistischen Gesellschaft* (Leipzig 1932)

Guyot, Yves. *Le Commerce et les Commerçants* (Paris 1909)

Hakenstein, Fritz et al. *Der Weg zum industriellen Spitzenverband* (Frankfurt a.M. 1956)

Hallgarten, George W. *Imperialismus vor 1914* (2 Bde. München 1963)

Hamburg. Statistisches Landesamt. *Statistisches Handbuch für den Hamburgischen Staat* (Hamburg 1920)

Hamel, Iris. *Völkischer Verband und Nationale Gewerkschaft. Der Deutsch-nationale Handlungsgehilfen-Verband 1893-1933* (Frankfurt a.M. 1967)

Hamerow, Theodor S. *Restoration, Revolution, Reaction* (Princeton 1958, reprinted 1967)

——————. *The Social Foundations of German Unification 1858-1871 Ideas and Institutions* (Princeton 1969)

Hardach, Karl W. *Die Bedeutung wirtschaftlicher Faktoren bei der Wieder-einführung der Eisen- und Getreidezölle in Deutschland 1879* (Berlin 1967)

Hays, Samuel P. *The Response to Industrialism 1885-1914* (Chicago 1957)

——————. "The Social Analysis of American Political History 1880-1920" *Political Science Quarterly* LXXX, No.3 (1965), pp.373-394

Heberle, Rudolf. *Landbevölkerung und Nationalsozialismus. Eine soziologische Untersuchung der politischen Willensbildung in Schleswig-Holstein 1918 bis 1932* (Stuttgart 1963)

——————. *Social Movements: An Introduction to Political Sociology* (New York 1951)

——————. "Social Movements, 1: Types and Functions of Social Movements" in Sill, David L. (ed.) *International Encyclopedia of the Social Sciences* (vol.14 New York 1968), pp.438-444

Heberler, Lieselotte. *Der Deutsche Verband für das kaufmännische Bildungswesen 1895-1935* (Braunschweig 1936)

Heuss, Theodor, *Friedrich Naumann. Der Mann, das Werk, die Zeit* (3 Aufl. Stuttgart 1968)

Hirsch, Julius. "Der moderne Handel, seine Organisation und Formen und die staatliche Binnenhandelspolitik" *G.d.S.* Abt. V, T.11 (2 Aufl. Tübingen 1925)

Hobsbawm, E.J. *Industry and Empire* (London 1969)

Labouring Men (London 1968)

Hoebel, Heinrich. "Das organisierte Arbeitgebertum in Hamburg-Altona" Dissertation-Hamburg 1923

Höfele, Karl Heinrich. (ed.) *Geist und Gesellschaft der Bismarckzeit 1870-1890* (Göttingen 1967)

Hoffmann, Stanley. *Le Mouvement Poujade* (Paris 1956)

Hoffmann, Walther G. "The Take-Off in Germany" in Rostow, W.W. (ed.) *The Economics of Take-Off into Sustained Growth* (New York 1963), pp.95-118

——————. Grumbach, Franz and Hesse, Helmut. *Das Wachstum der Deutschen Wirtschaft seit der Mitte des 19.Jahrhunderts* (Berlin-Heidelberg-New York 1965)

——————. and Müller, J.H. *Das deutsche Volkseinkommen 1851-1957* (Tübingen 1959)

Hofstadter, Richard. *The Age of Reform* (New York 1956)

——————. "The Pseudo-Conservative Revolt (1955)" in Bell, Daniel (ed.) *The Radical Right* (Garden City Anchor Ed. 1964), pp.75-95.

Hohenlohe-Schillingsfürst, Fürst Chlodwig zu. *Denkwürdigkeiten der Reichs-kanzlerzeit.* Müller, K.A. von (ed.) (Stuttgart 1931)

Hood, J. and Yamey, B.S. "Middle-Class Cooperative Retailing Societies in London, 1864-1900" in Tucker, K.A. and Yamey, B.S. (eds.) *Economics of Retailing* (London 1973)

Hughes,, H.Stuart. *History as Art and as Science* (New York-London, 1964)

Hugo, Otto. *Der Mittelstand und die Deutsche Volkspartei* (2 Aufl. Berlin 1919)

Jaeger, Hans. *Unternehmer in der deutschen Politik* (Bonn 1967)

Jefferys, James B. *Retail Trading in Britain 1850-1950* (Cambridge 1954)

Joll, James. "Walter Rathenau: Prophet without a Cause" *Three Intellectuals in Politics* (London 1960), pp.59-129

Jones, Gareth Stedman. "History: The Poverty of Empiricism" in Blackburn Robin (ed.) *Ideology in Social Science* (London 1972), pp.96-118

Kaelble, Hartmut. *Industrielle Interessenpolitik in der wilhelminischen Gesellschaft. (Centralverband Deutscher Industrieller 1895-1914)* (Berlin 1967)

Kaufmann, Heinrich. *Kurzer Abriss der Geschichte des Zentralverbandes deutscher Konsumvereine* (Hamburg 1928)

Kehr, Eckart. *Der Primat der Innenpolitik. Gesammelte Aufsätze zur preussisch-deutschen Sozialgeschichte im 19.und 20.Jahrhundert.* Wehler, Hans-Ulrich (ed.) (Berlin 1965)

——————————. *Schlachtflottenbau und Parteipolitik 1894-1901. Heft 197 Historische Studien* (Berlin 1930)

Kellenbenz, Hermann. "Von den wirtschaftsstufentheorien zu den Wachstumsstadien Rostows" *Zeitschrift für die gesamte Staatswissenschaft* 120, 3 (1964)

Klemperer, Klemens von. *Germany's New Conservatism* (Princeton 1957)

Kocka, Jürgen. "The First World War and the 'Mittelstand': German Artisans and White-Collar Workers" *Journal of Contemporary History* vol.8 No.1 (Jan. 1973), pp.101-123

——————————. *Unternehmensverwaltung und Angestelltenschaft am Beispiel Siemens, 1847-1914: Zum Verhältnis von Kapitalismus und Bürokratie in der Deutschen Industrialisierung* (Stuttgart 1969)

——————————. "Vorindustrielle Faktoren in der deutschen Industrialisierung. Industriebürokratie und 'neuer Mittelstand'" in Stürmer, Michael. (ed.) *Das kaiserliche Deutschland. Politik und Gesellschaft 1870-1918* (Düsseldorf 1970), pp.265-286

Köllmann, Wolfgang. *Bevölkerung und Raum in Neuerer und Neuester Zeit* (Würzburg 1965)

——————————. "Industrialisierung, Binnenwanderung und 'Soziale Frage': Zur Entstehungsgeschichte der deutschen Industriegrossstadt im 19.Jahrhundert" *Vierteljahrsschrift für Sozial- und Wirtschaftsgeschichte* XLVI (1959), pp.45-70

——————————. *Sozialgeschichte der Stadt Barmen im 19.Jahrhundert* (Tübingen 1960)

Korsch, Karl. *Marxismus und Philosophie* (Leipzig 1923)

Krausnick, Helmut. et al. *Anatomie des SS-Staates* (Olten und Freiburg i.B. 1965)

Kremer, Willy. *Der soziale Aufbau der Parteien des deutschen Reichstages 1871-1918* (Emsdetten 1934)

Kublank, F. "Die Interessenvertretung des deutschen Einzelhandels" Dissertation-Jena 1930

Kuczynski, Jürgen. *Die Geschichte der Lage der Arbeiter in Deutschland von 1800 bis in die Gegenwart* (Bd.1, 3 Aufl. Berlin 1947).

——————————. *Die Geschichte der Lage der Arbeiter unter dem Kapitalismus* (Bd.4 Berlin 1967)

Kühnl, Reinhard. *Formen bürgerlicher Herrschaft. Liberalismus-Faschismus*

(Reinbek bei Hamburg 1971)

──────────── . Rilling, Rainer and Sager, Christine. *Die NPD. Struktur, Ideologie und Funktion einer neofaschistischen Partei* (2 Aufl. Frankfurt a.M. 1969)

Kulemann, W. *Die Genossenschaftsbewegung. Erster Bd.: Geschichtlicher Teil* (Berlin 1922)

Lambi, Ivo N. *Free Trade and Protection in Germany 1868-1879* (Wiesbaden 1963)

Lampert, K.H. "Strukturwandlungen des deutschen Einzelhandels" Dissertation-Erlangen 1956

Landes David S. (ed.) *The Rise of Capitalism* (London-New York 1966)

──────────── . *The Unbound Prometheus* (Cambridge 1969)

Laqueur, Walter Z. *A History of Zionism* (London 1972)

──────────── . *Young Germany* (London 1962)

Laufenberg, Heinrich. *Geschichte der Arbeiterbewegung Hamburgs* (Hamburg 1931)

──────────── . *Die Hamburger Revolution* (Hamburg 1919)

Lebovics, Hermann. "'Agrarians' versus 'Industrializers'. Social Conservative Resistance to Industrialism and Capitalism in late Nineteenth Century Germany" *IRSH* XII (1967), 1, pp.31-65

──────────── . *Social Conservatism and the Middle Classes in Germany, 1914-1933* (Princeton 1969)

Lecordier, Gaston. *Les Classes Moyennes en marche* (Paris 1950)

Lederer, Emil and Marschak, Jacob. "Der neue Mittelstand" *G.d.S.* Abt. **IX,T.1** (Tübingen 1926), pp.120-141

Lehe, Erich von. *Die Märkte Hamburgs von den Anfängen bis in die Neuzeit* (1911) (Wiesbaden 1966)

Lehmann, Hans Georg. *Die Agrarfrage in der Theorie und Praxis der deutschen und internationalen Sozialdemokratie* (Tübingen 1971)

Lemmel, John, *50 Jahre Geschichte des Vereins der Kolonialwarenhändler von 1872 in Hamburg* (Hamburg 1922)

Levy, Hermann. *Retail Trade Associations* (London 1942)

Lidtke, Vernon L. *The Outlawed Party. Social Democracy in Germany 1878-1890* (Princeton 1965)

Lindenlaub, Dieter. *Richtungskampf im Vereine für Sozialpolitik* (Wiesbaden 1967)

Lipset, Seymour Martin. *Political Man* (New York Anchor ed. 1963)

──────────── . and Raab, Earl. *The Politics of Unreason. Right-Wing Extremism in America, 1790-1970* (New York 1970)

Lütge, Friedrich. *Deutsche Sozial- und Wirtschaftsgeschichte* (3 Aufl. Berlin 1966)

Mackenzie, W.J.M. *Politics and the Social Sciences* (London 1967)

Mandel, Ernest. *Marxistische Wirtschaftstheorie* (Frankfurt a.M. 1968)

Mann, Golo. *Deutsche Geschichte des 19.und 20.Jahrhunderts* (Frankfurt a.M. 1958)

Mannheim, Karl. *Ideologie und Utopie* (Bonn 1929)

Marbach, Fritz. *Theorie des Mittelstandes* (Bern 1942)

Marcuse, Herbert. *Der eindimensionale Mensch* (Neuwied 1967)

Maschke, Erich. *Grundzüge der deutschen Kartellgeschichte* (Dortmund 1964)

Mason, T.W. "The primacy of politics — Politics and economics in National Socialist Germany" in Woolf, S.J. (ed.) *The Nature of Fascism* (New York

1969), pp.165-195.

Massing, Paul. *Rehearsal for Destruction* (New York 1949 reprint 1967)

Mauersberg, Hans. *Wirtschafts- und Sozialgeschichte zentraleuropäischer Städte in neuerer Zeit. Dargestellt an den Beispielen von Basel, Frankfurt a.M., Hamburg, Hannover und München* (Göttingen 1960)

Meerwarth, Rudolf et al. *Die Einwirkung des Krieges auf Bevölkerungsbewegung, Einkommen und Lebenshaltung in Deutschland* (Stuttgart-Berlin-Leipzig 1932)

Michels, Robert. *Zur Soziologie des Parteiwesens in der modernen Demokratie* (Leipzig 1925)

Miliband, Ralph. *The State in Capitalist Society. Analysis of the Western System of Power* (London Quartet Books 1972)

Mills, C. Wright : *Power, Politics and People. The Collected Essays of C. Wright Mills.* Horowitz, I.L. (ed.) (New York 1967)

—————— . *The Sociological Imagination* (New York 1959)

—————— . *White Collar. The American Middle Classes* (New York 1951-1956)

Mohler, Armin. *Die konservative Revolution in Deutschland 1918-1932* (Stuttgart 1950)

Mosse, George L. *The Crisis of German Ideology* (New York 1964)

—————— . *Germans and Jews* (London 1971)

Mottek, Hans. *Wirtschaftsgeschichte Deutschlands. Ein Grundriss* (Bd. 1 Berlin 1959, Bd.2, 1964)

Müssiggang, Albert. *Die soziale Frage in der historischen Schule der deutschen Nationalökonomie* (Tübingen 1968)

Nettl, J.P. *Political Mobilization. A Sociological Analysis of Methods and Concepts* (London 1967)

—————— . and Robertson, Roland. *International Systems and the Modernization of Societies* (London 1968)

Neuhaus, Georg. "Die berufliche und soziale Gliederung der Bevölkerung im Zeitalter des Kapitalismus" *G.d.S.* Abt. IX, T.1, (Tübingen 1926)

Neumann, Sigmund. *Die deutschen Parteien* (Berlin 1932)

Nichols, J.A. *Germany After Bismarck. The Caprivi Era, 1890-1894* (Cambridge, Mass. 1958)

Nieschlag, Robert. "Die Versandgeschäfte in Deutschland: Ihre volkswirtschaftlichen Funktionen und betriebswirtschaftlichen Gestaltungen" *Sonderhefte des Instituts für Konjunkturforschung* (Berlin 1936)

Nipperday, Thomas. "Interessenverbände und Parteien in Deutschland vor dem Ersten Weltkrieg" (1961) in Wehler, Hans-Ulrich (ed.) *Moderne deutsche Sozialgeschichte* (Köln-Berlin 1966), pp.369-388

—————— . *Die Organisation der deutschen Parteien vor 1918* (Düsseldorf 1961)

Noakes, Jeremy. *The Nazi Party in Lower Saxony 1921-1933* (Oxford 1971)

Nossiter, T.J. "Shopkeeper Radicalism in the 19th Century" in Nossiter, T.J. et al. (eds.) *Essays in Memory of Peter Nettl* (London 1972), pp.407-438.

Noyes, P.H. *Organization and Revolution* (Princeton 1966)

O'Lessker, Karl. "Who Voted for Hitler? A New Look at the Class Basis of Nazism" *American Journal of Sociology*, 74 (1968-69), pp.63-69

Parsons, Talcott. "Democracy and Social Structure in Pre-Nazi Germany" in

Essays in Sociological Theory (New York, Free Press 1954), pp.104-123

————————— . *The Social System* (London 1952)

————————— . "The Sociology of Modern Anti-Semitism" in Graeber I. and Britt, S.H. (eds.) *Jews in a Gentile World* (New York 1942), pp.101-122

Pesl, L.D. "Mittelstandsfragen. Der Gewerbliche und kaufmännische Mittelstand" *G.d.S.* Abt. IX, T.1, (Tübingen 1926), pp.70-119

Phelps, Reginald H. "Theodor Fritsch und der Antisemitismus" *Deutsche Rundschau* 87 (1961), pp.442-449

Phelps Brown, E.H. and Hopkins, S.V. "The Course of Wage Rates in Five Countries, 1860-1937" *Oxford Economic Papers* (1950), pp.226-296

Pieper, August. *Berufsgedanke und Berufsstand im Wirtschaftsleben* (2 Aufl. Mönchengladbach 1925)

Plessner, Helmut. *Die verspätete Nation* (3 Aufl. Stuttgart 1962)

Pohle, Ludwig and Muss, Max. *Das deutsche Wirtschaftsleben seit Beginn des neunzehnten Jahrhunderts* (6 Aufl. Leipzig-Berlin 1930)

Pridham, Geoffrey. *Hitler's Rise to Power. The Nazi Movement in Bavaria 1923-1933* (London 1973)

Probleme des Warenhauses. Beiträge zur Geschichte und Erkenntnis der Entwicklung des Warenhauses in Deutschland. Hrsg. vom Verband Deutscher Waren- und Kaufhäuser e.V. (Berlin 1928)

Puderbach, Klaus. "Die Entwicklung des selbständigen Mittelstandes seit Beginn der Industrialisierung" Dissertation-Bonn 1967

Pühle, Hans-Jürgen. *Agrarische Interessenpolitik und preussischer Konservatismus im wilhelminischen Reich (1893-1914)* (Hannover 1966)

————————— . "Parlament, Parteien und Interessenverbände 1890-1914" in Stürmer, Michael. (ed.) *Das kaiserliche Deutschland. Politik und Gesellschaft 1870-1914* (Düsseldorf 1970), pp.340-377

Pulzer, P.G.J. *The Rise of Political Anti-Semitism in Germany and Austria* (New York 1964)

Reichmann, Eva G. *Flucht in den Hass. Die Ursachen der deutschen Judenkatastrophie* (5 Aufl. Frankfurt a.M. 1968)

Reincke, Heinrich. *Hamburg, ein kurzer Abriss der Stadtgeschichte von den Anfängen bis zur Gegenwart* (2 Aufl. Bremen 1926)

Retzlaw, Karl, *Spartakus. Aufstieg und Niedergang. Erinnerungen eines Parteiarbeiters* (2 Aufl. Frankfurt a.M. 1972)

Rex, John. *Key Problems of Sociological Theory* (London 1961)

————————— . *Race Relations in Sociological Theory* (London 1970)

Rieger, Josef; Mendel, Max; and Postelt, Walter. *Die Hamburger Konsumgenossenschaft "Produktion"* (Hamburg 1949)

Rimlinger, Gaston V. "The Legitimation of Protest: a Comparative Study in Labor History" *Comparative Studies in Society and History* 2 (1959-60), pp.329-343

Ritter, Emil. *Die katholisch-soziale Bewegung Deutschlands im 19. Jahrhundert und der Volksverein* (Köln 1954)

Ritter, Gerhard A. *Die Arbeiterbewegung im Wilhelminischen Reich* (Berlin 1959)

Röhl, J.C.G. *Germany without Bismarck* (London 1967)

Rosenberg, Arthur, *Die Entstehung der Deutschen Republik 1871-1918* (Berlin 1930)

——————— . "Der Faschismus als Massenbewegung. Sein Aufstieg und seine Zersetzung" in Abendroth, Wolfgang. (ed.) *Faschismus und Kapitalismus. Theorien über die sozialen Ursprünge und die Funktion des Faschismus* (3 Aufl. Frankfurt a.M. 1968), pp.75-141

Rosenberg, Hans. *Grosse Depression und Bismarckzeit. Wirtschaftsablauf, Gesellschaft und Politik in Mitteleuropa* (Berlin 1967)

——————— . *Probleme der deutschen Sozialgeschichte* (Frankfurt a.M. 1969)

——————— . "Political and Social Consequences of the Great Depression of 1873-1896 in Central Europe" *Economic History Review* vol.13 (1943) pp.58-73

Roth, Günther. "Die kulturellen Bestrebungen der Sozialdemokratie im kaiserlichen Deutschland" (1963) in Wehler, Hans-Ulrich. (ed.) *Moderne deutsche Sozialgeschichte* (Köln-Berlin 1966), pp.342-365

Rubens, W. "Der Kampf des Spezialgeschäftes gegen das Warenhaus (mit besonderer Berücksichtigung der Zeit von 1918 bis 1929)" Dissertation-Köln 1929

Ruppin, Arthur. *Die Soziologie der Juden* (2 Bde. Berlin 1930)

Saile, Wolfgang. *Hermann Wagener und sein Verhältnis zu Bismarck. Ein Beitrag zur Geschichte des konservativen Sozialismus* (Tübingen 1958)

Sartorious von Waltershausen, A. *Deutsche Wirtschaftsgeschichte 1815-1914* (Jena 1920)

Sauer, Wolfgang. "Das Problem des deutschen Nationalstaates" (1962) in Wehler, Hans-Ulrich. (ed.) *Moderne deutsche Sozialgeschichte* (Köln-Berlin 1966), pp.407-436

Scheideler, Gert Udo. "Parlament, Parteien und Regierung 1890-1914" *Aus Politik und Zeitgeschichte* B12/71 (20.3. 1971), pp.16-24

Schieder, Th. *Das deutsche Kaiserreich von 1871 als Nationalstaat* (Köln 1961)

Schmidt, Gustav. "Innenpolitischen Blockbildung am Vorabend des Ersten Weltkrieges" *Aus Politik und Zeitgeschichte* B20/72 (13.5.1972), pp.3-32

Schmoller, Gustav. *Grundriss der Allgemeinen Volkswirtschaftslehre* (2 Bde. München 1923)

Schoenbaum, David. *Hitler's Social Revolution* (London 1967)

Schoeps, Joachim Hans. (ed.) *Zeitgeist im Wandel. Das Wilhelminische Zeitalter* (Stuttgart 1967)

Schorsch, Ismar. *Jewish Reactions to German Anti-Semitism 1870-1914* (London-New York 1972)

Schorske, Carl E. *German Social Democracy 1905-1917* ((New York, Torchbook ed. 1972)

Schramm, Percy Ernst. *Hamburg – ein Sonderfall in der Geschichte Deutschlands* (Hamburg 1964)

Schröder, Carl August. *Aus Hamburgs Blütezeit. Lebenserinnerungen* (Hamburg 1921)

Schüddekopf, Otto-Ernst. *Die deutsche Innenpolitik im letzten Jahrhundert und der konservative Gedanke* (Braunschweig 1951)

Schürholz, Franz. *Entwicklungstendenzen im deutschen Wirtschaftsleben zu berufsständischer Organisation und ihrer sozialen Bedeutung* (Mönchengladbach 1922)

Schult, Johannes. *Geschichte der Hamburger Arbeiter 1890-1914* (Hannover 1967)

Schulz, Gerhard. "Über Entstehung und Formen von Interessengruppen in Deutschland seit Beginn der Industrialisierung" *Politische Vierteljahrsschrift* 2 (1961), pp.124-154

Schumacher, Martin. *Mittelstandsfront und Republik. Die Wirtschaftspartei – Reichspartei des deutschen Mittelstandes 1919-1933* (Düsseldorf 1972)

Schumpeter, Joseph A. *Business Cycles: A Theoretical, Historical and Statistical Analysis of the Capitalist Process* (2 vols. New York 1939)

—————————. *Kapitalismus, Sozialismus und Demokratie* (2 Aufl. Bern 1950)

Schweitzer, Arthur. *Big Business in the Third Reich* (London 1964)

Sheehan, James J. "The Primacy of Domestic Politics: Eckart Kehr's Essays on Modern German History" *Central European History* vol.1. No.2 (1968), pp.166-174

Siegfried, André. *Tableau Politique de la France de l'Ouest sous la Troisieme République* (Paris 1913).

Silberner, Edmund. *Sozialisten zur Judenfrage* (Berlin 1962)

Sombart, Werner. *Die deutsche Volkswirtschaft im 19.Jahrhundert und im Anfang des 20.Jahrhunderts* (6 Aufl. Berlin 1923)

—————————. *Der moderne Kapitalismus* (Bd.2, 6 Aufl. München-Leipzig 1924)

Smelser, Neil J. *Essays in Sociological Explanation* (Englewood Cliffs 1968)
The Sociology of Economic Life (Englewood Cliffs 1963)

Spiethoff, Arthur. *Die wirtschaftlichen Wechsellagen. Aufschwung, Krise, Stockung* (2 Bde. Tübingen 1955)

Stearns, Peter N. *European Society in Upheaval. Social History since 1800* (London-New York 1967)

Sternberger, Dolf. "Der Staat der Gegenwart und die wirtschaftlichen und ausserwirtschaftlichen Interessengruppen, Rundtafelgespräch auf dem 11. Deutschen Soziologentag" in *Kölner Zeitschrift für Soziologie* (1952/1953), pp.204 ff.

Stegmann, Dirk. *Die Erben Bismarcks. Parteien und Verbände in der Spätphase des wilhelminischen Deutschlands. Sammlungspolitik 1897-1918* (Köln-Berlin 1970)

—————————. "Wirtschaft und Politik nach Bismarcks Sturz. Zur Genesis der Miquelschen Sammlungspolitik 1890-1897" in Geiss, Imanuel and Wendt, Bernd Jürgen. *Deutschland in der Weltpolitik des 19.und 20.Jahrhunderts. Fritz Fischer zum 65.Geburtstag* (1973), pp.161-184

—————————. "Zwischen Repression und Manipulation: Konservative Machteliten und Arbeiter- und Angestelltenbewegung 1910-1918. Ein Beitrag zur Vorgeschichte der DAP/NSDAP" *Archiv für Sozialgeschichte* XII (1972), pp.351-432

Stein, Hans. "Pauperismus und Assoziation. Soziale Tatsachen und Ideen auf dem westeuropäischen Kontinent von Ende des 18.bis zur Mitte des 19.Jahrhunderts, unter besonderer Berücksichtigung des Rheingebiets" *IRSH* (1936), pp.1-105

Sterling, Elenore. *Judenhass: Die Anfänge des politischen Antisemitismus in Deutschland 1815-1850* (Frankfurt a.M. 1969)

Stern, Fritz. *The Politics of Cultural Despair* (New York 1961)

Stolper, Gustav. *The German Economy 1870 to the Present*, trans. Stolper, Toni (London 1967)

Stürmer, Michael, "Konservatismus und Revolution in Bismarcks Politik" in Stürmer, Michael. (ed.) *Das kaiserliche Deutschland. Politik und Gesellschaft 1870-1918* (Düsseldorf 1970), pp.143-167

Thieme, Karl. (ed.) *Judenfeindschaft. Darstellung und Analysen* (Hamburg-Frankfurt a.M. 1963)

Tilly, Richard. "Soll und Haben: Recent German Economic History and the Problem of Economic Development" *Journal of Economic History* XXIX No.2 (1969), pp.298-319

Tirrell, Sarah R. *German Agrarian Politics after Bismarck's Fall* (New York 1951)

Tönnies, Ferdinand. *Gemeinschaft und Gesellschaft* (Leipzig 1887)

—————————. "Stände und Klassen" in Vierkandt, Alfred. (ed.) *Handwörterbuch der Soziologie* (Stuttgart 1931), pp.617-628

Treue, Wilhelm. "Wirtschafts- und Sozialgeschichte Deutschlands" in Gebhardt, Bruno. *Handbuch der deutschen Geschichte* (Bd.3 Stuttgart 1960), pp.315-413

—————————. et al. (eds.) *Quellen zur Geschichte der Industriellen Revolution* (Göttingen 1961)

Uhlig, Heinrich. *Die Warenhäuser im Dritten Reich* (Köln-Opladen 1956)

Wagenführ, Rolf. *Die Industriewirtschaft. Entwicklungstendenzen der deutschen und internationalen Industrieproduktion 1860 bis 1932. Vierteljahrshefte zur Konjunkturforschung, Sonderheft* 31 (Berlin 1933)

Wawrzinek, Kurt. *Die Entstehung der deutschen Antisemitenparteien 1873-1890* (Berlin 1927)

Weber, Max, *Gesammelte politische Schriften*, Winkelmann, Johannes. (ed.) (2 Aufl. Tübingen 1958)

—————————. *Wirtschaft und Gesellschaft* in G.d.S. Abt. III, T.1 (3 Aufl. Tübingen 1927)

Wehler, Hans-Ulrich, *Bismarck und der Imperialismus* (Köln-Berlin 1969)

—————————. *Krisenherde des Kaiserreichs 1871-1918. Studien zur deutschen Sozial- und Verfassungsgeschichte* (Göttingen 1970)

Wein, Josef. *Die Verbandsbildung im Einzelhandel. Mittelstandsbewegung, Organisation der Grossbetriebe, Fachverbände, Genossenschaften und Spitzenverband* (Berlin 1968)

Westrap, K. Graf. *Rede über Mittelstand, Handwerk und Kleinhandel* (Berlin 1920)

Wiedenfeld, Kurt. "Transportswesen" *G.d.S.* Abt. V, T.III (Tübingen 1930)

Wilson, John. *Introduction to Social Movements* (New York 1973)

Winkler, Heinrich August. "Extremismus der Mitte? Sozialgeschichtliche Aspekte der nationalsozialistischen Machtergreifung" *V.f.Z.* 2 Heft (April 1972), pp.175-191

—————————. *Mittelstand, Demokratie und Nationalsozialismus. Die politische Entwicklung von Handwerk und Kleinhandel in der Weimarer Republik* (Köln 1972)

—————————. "Der rückversicherte Mittelstand: Die Interessenverbände von Handwerk und Kleinhandel im deutschen Kaiserreich" in Rüegg, Walter und Neuloh, Otto. (eds.) *Zur soziologischen Theorie und Analyse des 19.*

Jahrhunderts (Göttingen 1971), pp.163-179

Wirminghaus, A. "Handelskammern" in Elster, L. et al. (eds.) *Handwörterbuch der Staatswissenschaften* (Bd.5, 4 Aufl. Jena 1923), pp.69-82.

Witt, Peter-Christian. *Die Finanzpolitik des deutschen Reiches von 1903-1913* (Lübeck-Hamburg 1970)

Wurm, Franz F. *Wirtschaft und Gesellschaft in Deutschland 1848-1948* (Opladen 1969)

Yamey, B.S. "United Kingdom" in Yamey, B.S. (ed.) *Resale Price Maintenance* (London 1966) pp.251-298

GLOSSARY

Bewegung	movement
Bund	federation
Detaillistenkammer	chamber for independent retailers
Einkaufsgenossenschaften . .	retailer purchasing co-operatives
Grossindustrie	big industry
Grosskapital	large-scale capital
Grosskapitalisten	big capitalists
Handelskammer	Chamber of Commerce
Handelstag	national organization of the Chambers of Commerce
Handel und Gewerbe	trade and industry
Handwerkskammer	artisans' chamber
Interessengemeinschaft . . .	community of interests
Kammer für Kleinhandel . . .	chamber for retail (small) trade
Kartell der schaffenden Stände	cartel of the producing classes
Mittelstand	lower middle class
Mittelstandsideologie	ideology of the *Mittelstand*
Rabattsparvereine	discount savings unions
Schutzverbände	protective organizations
Verband	organization
Verein	association
Vereinigung	association
Zentralverband	central organization

INDEX